MEMOIR

LIFE OF HENRY WARE, Jr.

BY HIS BROTHER,

JOHN WARE, M. D.

IN TWO VOLUMES.

VOL. I.

NEW EDITION.

BOSTON:
AMERICAN UNITARIAN ASSOCIATION.
1874.

Stereotyped by
GEORGE A. CURTIS;
NEW ENGLAND TYPE AND STEREOTYPE FOUNDERY.

MEMOIR

OF THE

LIFE OF HENRY WARE, Jr.

TO THE MEMORY

OF THE FATHER,

WHOSE EXAMPLE AND INSTRUCTIONS GUIDED THE LIFE AND FORMED THE CHARACTER

OF THE SON,

THIS BOOK

IS REVERENTLY INSCRIBED.

PREFACE.

This work was undertaken at the suggestion of some of the friends of my late brother, who were of opinion that it would be acceptable to the public and useful. They thought, also, that I was a suitable person to prepare it. In some respects, so far, especially, as a knowledge of, and ready access to, the requisite materials, and an intimate personal knowledge, are concerned, I perceived that this was so. As I proceeded, however, I was sensible, on the other hand, of some disadvantages arising from the same circumstances. Moreover I have found, that the exclusive character of my own occupations, for many years, has kept me from possessing that familiar knowledge of his external, which I have had of his personal history. On some subjects, therefore, there is reason to fear, that the book will be found often deficient and sometimes inaccurate. For such faults, I have only to plead in palliation the constant pressure of other duties, which has made it impossible to command the leisure for so deliberate an inquiry into these subjects as such a work demands.

The purpose had in view, and the plan followed, in this Memoir, will be obvious on its perusal; but the reader will enter upon it to greater advantage, if they are suggested to him in advance. The *purpose* has been to exhibit its subject, at all times of his life, in all the varieties of his character;—not merely as a minister, a professor, a man of the public; but also as a son, a brother, a husband, a father, and a friend;—not merely as a man of serious thoughts, of solemn occupations, of weighty purposes; but in all his other moods, cheerful, lively, gay, jocose, and, if it so seem to any, even trivial. The *plan* has been to tell the story of his life, and illustrate the formation and developement of his character, by the introduction of materials which will do it indirectly. I have endeavored to say nothing in my own words, which could be said in those of another, or which could be inferred from any thing said by himself. A very free use has therefore been made of the letters and papers of himself and others, though the amount selected bears but a small proportion to the whole mass from which the selection has been made.

I am aware, that there have been, of late, several

strong expressions of opinion, from sources entitled to consideration, against such a use of materials of this description. The feeling, which dictated these expressions, does not seem to be founded in justice. As the lives and characters of the dead furnish us some of the most efficient means for the instruction of the living, mankind have a sort of right to the use of whatever will contribute to so important an end,—so far, at least, as it can be without violating the feelings or rights of the living. A due regard for this consideration has, it is hoped, been had in the preparation of the present work.

J. W.

BOSTON, *December 14th*, 1845.

The first edition of this work seemed to many persons to be printed on too small a type for comfortable reading. In the present, a larger type has, for this reason, been adopted. There is no other change except the correction of a few verbal inaccuracies, and the addition of two or three letters or other papers.

March, 1846

CONTENTS

OF THE FIRST VOLUME.

LIFE OF HENRY WARE, Jr.

CHAPTER I.

HIS DESCENT—BIRTH—EARLY RELIGIOUS IMPRESSIONS, AND PREDILECTION FOR HIS PROFESSION—EARLY HABIT OF COMPOSITION—ANECDOTE—REMOVAL OF THE FAMILY TO CAMBRIDGE—DEATH OF HIS MOTHER—HER CHARACTER.

1794—1805. ÆT. 1—11.

Henry Ware, Jr., was born at Hingham, in Massachusetts, April 21st, 1794. He was a descendant, in the fifth generation, of Robert Ware, who came over from England among the earlier settlers of the colony, and fixed himself at Dedham, about the year 1644. Near the beginning of the next century, Joseph Ware, a grandson of Robert, removed to the neighboring town of Sherburne, and there became the father of a large family, many of whose descendants are still among the inhabitants of the place. One of his sons, John Ware, married into a family at Cambridge of the name of Prentiss, and Henry, the father of the subject of this memoir, was the youngest but one of his ten children. John Ware was a plain country farmer, probably not of the highest class, of small means, whose elder sons were all brought up to his own or some other laborious occupation. Three of them served in the Revolutionary war. Two were in the battle of Bunker's Hill, one of them a lad only fourteen years of age. A third, Joseph, the oldest of the number, lost an arm at the battle of White Plains.

He was father of the Hon. Ashur Ware, District Judge of the United States for the State of Maine. He lived always on the old family place at Sherburne, and, notwithstanding his mutilation, continued to lead the active life of a farmer. He was highly respected in the community in which he resided, for his strict integrity, strong good sense, and excellent judgment.

Henry was born April 1st, 1764. It happened that an eclipse of the sun took place on the day of his birth. The believers in signs among his friends prognosticated, from this coincidence and from his being born on All-Fools day, that he would be deficient in intellect. Notwithstanding this prophecy, however, he became fond of books very early; and, as he was of too slender a constitution when young to labor much on the farm with the other boys, this propensity was indulged. His proficiency was such as to excite the notice of the minister of the town, the Rev. Mr. Brown, who suggested, or at least encouraged, the idea of sending him to college. His father died in middle life, leaving behind him but slender means for the education or even maintenance of his family; but Henry, having a strong desire to procure a public education, persevered in his purpose, and under the direction of his pastor and friend, for whose kindness he always felt the deepest gratitude, he prepared himself for college in a very short time, and was entered at Cambridge in 1781, in his eighteenth year. His elder brothers, who were settled in life, contributed something to his support, and his very narrow means were eked out by the emoluments derived from keeping school during the winter months. He graduated with the first honors of his class in 1785. He was immediately engaged in teaching the Public Grammar

School of the town of Cambridge, at the same time occupying himself in the study of Divinity; and in October, 1787, he was ordained at Hingham, as successor to the Rev. Dr. Gay, one of the distinguished clergymen of his time.

He married, in 1789, Mary, daughter of the Rev. Jonas Clarke, minister of Lexington, whose wife was the granddaughter of the Rev. Thomas Hancock, her husband's predecessor in the parish. Mr. Hancock was undoubtedly quite a remarkable man, and was long and extensively remembered. He was distinguished for shrewdness and good sense; and, being withal a person of a very imposing presence, acquired great ascendency, and exercised much influence, over his brethren of the clergy. He was resorted to, from the confidence reposed in his judgment, for counsel on important occasions in the church, and his opinion always had great weight. He was commonly known by the title of *Bishop* Hancock; and this appellation is, even at the present day, familiar to some of the survivors of the last generation, who can recollect its use in their early years among those who were contemporaries with the old patriarch. One son of the Bishop, Ebenezer, a young man of great excellence and promise, was ordained as his colleague in the ministry, but died soon after, at the early age of twenty-eight, in 1740; another, John, was the minister of Braintree, and the father of John Hancock, President of Congress during the Revolution, and Governor of Massachusetts; a third, Thomas, was an eminent and wealthy Boston merchant, and a liberal benefactor of Harvard College, who, dying a bachelor, left the bulk of his great fortune to his nephew, John, whom he had adopted during his lifetime. A daughter, Lucy, was married to the Rev. Nicholas Bowes, of Bedford; and her daughter, Lucy Bowes, became the wife of Mr. Clarke, her grandfather's successor in his parish. The elder Hancock died in 1752, aged eighty-two, after a ministry of more than fifty years.

Mr. Clarke was a man of popular manners, of a kind and sociable disposition, and much beloved. His house was the seat of a very extensive hospitality, and was especially a place of resort for young clergymen. Four of his daughters married clergymen, but none of his sons were educated at college, or adopted their father's profession. Mr. Clarke was an earnest Whig, and took, as far as his calling would permit, an active part in the politics of the day. When the inhabitants of Boston were suffering so many hardships from the operation of the Boston Port Bill, and contributions for their relief were sent in from the neighboring country, he directed that his annual allowance of twenty cords of wood should be sent as his donation. Gov. Hancock, being a cousin of his wife, was a frequent visitor at the parsonage, and was on intimate terms with the family. There he spent the night before the battle of Lexington, in company with his partner in proscription, Samuel Adams, the house being guarded by a small party of militia. At three o'clock on the morning of the nineteenth of April, an alarm was given, and information received that the British troops were on their march from Boston. Mr. Clarke immediately took precautions for the safety of his guests, and had them conveyed in Mr. Hancock's carriage, under the charge of his second son, Jonas, (afterwards Judge Clarke, of Kennebunk,) to the house of the Rev. Mr. Jones, the minister of a settlement then called Woburn Precinct, now the town of Burlington. They went with great reluctance. When the troops approached the meeting-house, which was but a short distance from Mr. Clarke's, he sent his wife, and all his children but one, to a remote part of the town, where they remained through the day. But just as they were going from the yard, the firing of that morning—by which the first blood of the war of the Revolution was shed—took place; and they were startled by the whistling of a bullet somewhere near them, passing, as was supposed, between Mrs. Clarke and her daughter Mary, afterward Mrs. Ware, then a girl of thirteen. One of them had in her arms an infant child. Mr. Clarke, with his daughter Eliza, of between eleven and twelve years of age, remained at the house, which was thronged through the day with the American soldiers, whom they served with cider, bacon, and brown bread, many of them having left their homes before breakfast and travelled several miles without refreshment. For want of sufficient accommodations for so many, their guests were seated on the floor, and helped themselves with their fingers. About four o'clock in the afternoon, having exhausted his supply of provisions, Mr. Clarke left his house and joined his family. He died in 1805, aged seventy-five years, having brought up to adult age six sons and six daughters, on a salary of eighty pounds in money and twenty cords of wood. His ministry, like that of his predecessor, had extended over more than half a century.

Of ten children who were born of the marriage of Henry Ware, senior, and Mary Clarke, four daughters died in infancy; three sons and three daughters surviving to the middle period of life. HENRY WARE, JR., was the fifth child, and the oldest son. In beginning an account of his life, we may observe, that the interest which attaches to the early years of the subject of a biography does not depend upon the events and incidents of those years themselves, but upon the comparison which we may be enabled to institute between the circumstances under which the boy grows up, and the character which the man afterwards exhibits. The events of childhood and youth are in themselves comparatively unimportant; they may, indeed, vary but little in different persons. But the impressions left by them on the mind may be of the most opposite sort, according to the nature of the influences under which this period of life has been passed. Nor can we venture to predict with anything like certainty, from a knowledge of the boy, what the man is likely to be. A marvellous change often takes place in the transition from youth to manhood, which could never have been anticipated from any of the obvious indications of early life. Still this change may have been, and, perhaps, very generally is, the consequence of impressions, which were then made, but which at the time appeared to be entirely unheeded and unfelt. The seed was then sown, as it seemed, in vain; but, though it did not germinate, it did not die; and at some future period it quickens and comes into life and activity under new influences. There are some men, in whom the character of the child passes gradually into, and blends with, that of the man; the same tendencies are followed out, the same qualities are ripened,—the man is a continuation of the boy. There are others, in whom a great alteration takes place; the character undergoes a great apparent change, and one for which it seems difficult to account; new qualities spring up, and it almost appears as if new faculties had been developed;—the boy and the man are opposite. Yet, in both cases, it may be equally true, that the influences and impressions of early life have decided the ultimate features of the character, though their result has been brought about so slowly, and shown itself after so long an interval, that it is extremely difficult to trace the connexion. The man may be like the boy or unlike the boy; but, in either case, it is the influences acting on the boy, that have made the man what he is.

But, in the subject of this memoir, there was no such want of correspondence between the promises of childhood and youth, and the actual character of mature life. The seed did not lie dormant, but quickened as it fell; the summer and autumn only fulfilled, or more than fulfilled, the promise of the spring. It is seldom that we see so distinctly, in the man, the fruits of the influences which have acted on the boy. His character seems to have been in a regular course of formation from the very first; and we trace in him, in his earliest years, the same general traits which distinguished him in his after life. Hence the history of these years constitutes, perhaps, the most important part of his biography. Then impressions were made, a tendency was given, and habits of thought, feeling, study, and action were formed, which appear to have decided his whole future course. Above all, at this period he seems to have had steadily in contemplation a distinct purpose in life; a circumstance, which not only contributed to give a certain direction to the cultivation of his mind at the time, but had an important agency in the formation of those essential qualities, to which the success of his subsequent course is to be attributed. I shall endeavor, therefore, as far as my own recollection, or the materials which I have been able to collect, give me the means, to enter into a somewhat minute account of his early years, the circumstances under which he was educated, and under which his character was formed.

As a boy, he presented very much the same aspect as that which belonged to him when a man. He was then, as he was always afterwards, very pale, though not of an unhealthy look. He was tender, and suffered from several attacks of severe illness; but generally his health was good, and he was not regarded as a sickly child. He was sober and thoughtful both in countenance and disposition; peaceable and quiet in his amusements, but not withdrawing himself from the plays or the companions proper to his age. Yet there was then, as there was through life, something of bodily inactivity, an indolence of disposition, a want of physical vigor and sprightliness. He was docile and obedient, faithful in his studies and other duties, but still not forward, ncr of rapid progress, as a student.

It is impossible to designate the period at which religious impressions were first made upon his mind. It would be difficult, indeed, to look back upon any moment at which he was destitute of them. He had the happiness to be brought up under the guidance of parents, with whom religion was not so much a thing of times and seasons, as it was an element of their daily life and conversation. It was, therefore, presented to his mind in its most attractive form, constantly kept in view, held up as the most important concern in life, but divested of that air of formality and sadness, which so often makes it repulsive to children. Instruction on this topic was constant, but not burdensome. Family worship and the reading of the Scriptures were made an indispensable part of the duty of the day, but not protracted so as to be tedious to the young; whilst private devotion was so inculcated, as to make its omission felt as an act of ingratitude to the Creator. Every occasion of trial, sickness, or death, afforded an opportunity for gentle, but distinct admonitions, intended to impress on the young mind the uncertainty and dangers of life, the certainty of death, and the reality of eternity and judgment. The Sabbath was to be regarded as holy time, a day by itself, essentially different from the other days of the week in its object and employments; not as a day on which man was to be more religious than on other days, but on which religion was to become more peculiarly the subject of meditation and study. Still it was not made gloomy by tasks or restraints so severe, as to associate it with the idea of privation and austerity. It was suffered to be a day of cheerfulness, but yet of moderate restraint upon the buoyancy and playfulness of childhood.

When still very young, Henry manifested a predilection for the profession which he afterwards chose. This became the permanent bias of his mind at a much earlier period than is usual among children. It is, indeed, not at all remarkable, that the son of a clergyman should entertain a fancy for the calling of his father. The same thing happens with regard to every occupation. It existed in other members of the family, as well as in him. With all of them it was a favorite amusement to imitate the services of the Sabbath, even to their father's gestures, tone, and manner; and the different children officiated in turn, as each could collect an audience. There was nothing peculiar in this, for probably the children of most preachers do the same thing. But with Henry there was something more than this. What with others is a transient amusement, in him indicated, or at least contributed to give, a permanent tendency to his mind. The office of a clergyman became that on which his eyes were turned from boyhood. It might have been, at first, a childish fancy, but it grew into a settled purpose. The play was forgotten, but the preference with which it was connected, or which it had produced, grew with his growth and strengthened with his strength. From that time forward he kept it before his mind as a distinct object of pursuit, far more constantly than any serious purpose is commonly entertained in childhood. Whenever the subject of their future employment was matter of discussion in the family circle of which he formed one, as it usually is in such little communities, he was always of the same mind; his purpose always was to be a minister; and, as far as children are capable of entertaining distinct views concerning anything of which they know so little, his sisters and brothers also regarded this as his peculiar and appropriate destination. I doubt, indeed, whether the idea of a different one ever presented itself seriously or for any length of time, from the days when he preached a juvenile sermon of his own composition from a cradle turned on end as a pulpit, to that in which he actually assumed the office of a minister of the Gospel, and made his appearance in the sacred desk.

There is another circumstance in his childhood which is worthy of being recorded, as having probably had much influence in training his mind, and qualifying him for the place which he afterward filled. By some accident he was led very early to attempt, and gradually to form, the habit of composition. Many children make trials of this sort, but there are few who persevere so as to render it easy to them, or who continue it after the first impulse is over and it ceases to have the charm of novelty. But with him it was not so; he continued to derive pleasure from the exercise; he became more and more engaged in it, till it grew at length to be a fixed habit. He began as early as the year 1802, when he wrote some reflections on the death of a sister, expressive of the feelings excited in his mind by that event. This was followed at intervals by other efforts, and, after the age of nine or ten, these became more and more frequent. They were of various kinds. Sermons, history, biography, epics, and other poems, were all projected or begun, though seldom finished; but the predominating tendency undoubtedly was to the writing of verses; and, with the exception of a few pieces, those which remain of his earlier compositions are poetical.

To this early practice of expressing his thoughts on paper, and especially to the habit thus acquired of overcoming the difficulties of metrical composition, may be attributed very much that readiness in the use of the pen, both in prose and verse, for which he was certainly remarkable. Few persons write with so great facility. Writing, which to most men is a task, and to some even a painful one, was to him a positive pleasure. In the same way, also, he acquired a power of arranging and methodizing his thoughts on any subject with great quickness, as well as of clothing them rapidly with words. The influence which early efforts at versification may have in enabling a writer to acquire ease and readiness of expression, and perhaps still more in imparting something of attractiveness and beauty to his style, does not seem to be always sufficiently appreciated. It is not difficult to see how the discipline, which is necessary in order to make the language which carries our thoughts move gracefully to the music of poetical measure, will so cultivate the ear and the powers of expression, as to give ease, beauty, and harmony to the style of the same writer, when freed from the regular movement of verse. Neither can it be of less advantage to clearness of thinking, and consequently to perspicuity in expressing thoughts, that a writer should have been accustomed to commit them to paper. The surest preventive of a habit of vague and indefinite thinking, is the practice in early life of writing out our thoughts as soon as we begin to have them. We thus learn to think methodically and clearly from the beginning.

This habit continued with him through life. He thought, read, and almost lived with the pen in his hand, ready to fix and give form and feature to the ideas which arose in his mind, or were suggested by the books he read; or to note such passages in his reading as might serve him afterward for contemplation or other use. The amount which he thus committed to paper was very great. It is to be lamented that most of it was done in that desultory, irregular manner in which he was apt to indulge, on loose pieces of paper, on the backs of notes, etc., and not in regular volumes. Hence this practice was of far less value to him, except as an exercise and a discipline, than it might otherwise have been; and what he thus reduced to writing is of comparatively little value to others.

His early compositions cannot be considered as remarkable for anything except as giving evidence of the strong feelings which he entertained on religious subjects; though there may be somewhat more command of language than is usual at his age. The motive for inserting from time to time some of these juvenile exercises is sufficiently obvious. They are not presented as specimens of a precocious or even a particularly promising youth; they are mere elements of the history of his progress. If it be worth while to trace the formation of his mind and character at all, it is worth while to examine it in its earliest developments, whatever they may have been. I have alluded to the following production, as the first which he is known to have written. It still exists in his own boyish handwriting, as it was copied by him a few years afterward. It was composed when he was eight years and a half old.

"HENRY WARE ON THE DEATH OF MARTHA.

"Oh Martha! you have gone through your short pilgrimage, your life of troubles and afflictions. You have got to the tomb before us. You have gone through what we upon earth have got to go through. Your life was precious, and your character was pleasing. We all mourn for you, but we need not mourn, for you are going to a better world.

"Oh Martha! thou lovely child! you are now gone from this world, never to return."

There remain also, carefully copied into a little book, birth-day reflections for the years 1805–6–7, when he was respectively eleven, twelve, and thirteen years of age. They exhibit the strong and continued religious feelings which had been excited in him.

"BIRTH-DAY REFLECTIONS FOR THE YEARS 1805, 1806, 1807.

"April 21, 1805.

"As it has pleased the Lord God Almighty to spare my life another year, I would now make some observation upon it.

"May I the following year be impressed with serious thoughts and resolutions. Remembering my Creator in the days of my youth,—considering the goodness of the Lord in preserving me the past year from danger, and preserving me to the present time. It is owing to the goodness of the Lord that I am not consumed; blessed be his name for all his goodness toward me.

"By the late melancholy event* that has happened in the family, may I be led to make serious reflections considering that *Life is short!* That I must shortly (the Lord only knows when) quit this world of trouble and affliction, for a world where there is no weeping, where saints live together in peace, and enjoy everlasting life, and that if I wish to live in heaven above, I must live a righteous and holy life here below; but that if I live in sin, not believing in the word of God, I shall be cast into hell where none but devils dwell.

"May I obey my father and mother, according to the fifth commandment: 'Honor thy Father and Mother,' &c.; may I be kind to my brothers and sisters, and obliging to my playmates; and increase in all useful knowledge.

"And may the Lord God Almighty strengthen me in all my resolutions."

"April 21, 1806.

"Blessed be the name of the Lord God Almighty for all his goodness towards me; he has brought me in perfect health and safety to the twelfth anniversary of my birth; has carried me through all the dangers to which I have been exposed; has kept me in the land of the living, while multitudes are numbered with the dead; and has preserved me in perfect

* Death of my sister Martha Ann.

health, when some of my friends and companions have been languishing on beds of sickness. I have had sufficient meat and drink while others have had none.

> "'While some poor wretches scarce can tell
> Where they may lay their head,
> I have a home wherein to dwell,
> And rest upon my bed.'

"How shall I repay this kindness of the Lord? What shall I render to the Lord for all his goodness toward me? 'Words are too feeble to express the feelings which ought to take possession of my heart.' 'Bless God! O my soul, and forget not all his benefits.'

"While I am thus thankful for myself, I should not be unmindful of my friends. My father has been continued to see my twelfth birth-day, and his forty-third year. God grant that he may live to see my next. My mother—alas! she has been snatched away by the relentless jaws of death! But why should I lament her loss? She is doubtless happier than she could be in this world. A year ago to-day she pronounced a blessing on me for the last time! My brothers and sisters have all been continued alive another year, and I humbly pray God to spare them another year." . . . .

"This was left unfinished."

"April 21, 1807.

"The all-protecting power of God has been exercised towards me the past year. I have been preserved in life and health, and from all dangers to which I have been exposed. I am now brought to the thirteenth anniversary of my birth. I am still continued in the land of the living, while multitudes have been dying around me.

> "'Not more than others I deserve,
> Yet God hath given me more;
> For I have food, while others starve,
> Or beg from door to door.'

"How can I express my gratitude to the Lord for all his goodnesses towards me? How shall I reward them? They are more in number than I can count. I should thank the Lord that I was born and educated in a Christian land; that I have the holy Scriptures in a language that I can understand, 'which are able to make me wise unto salvation.'

"'Lord, I ascribe it to thy grace,
And not to chance as others do,
That I was born of Christian race,
And not a heathen or a Jew.'

"'The praises of my tongue,
I'll offer to the Lord,
That I was taught and learnt so young
To read his holy word.'"

There would seem to have been something in his character, even when very young, which inspired confidence and gave ground for reliance both on his discretion and on his courage. When not yet six years old, as his father recollected, he was entrusted with the important office of riding a horse to mill. The distance was about half a mile; the corn was thrown over the horse's back in a long bag, upon which the boy sat; and, after he had waited till it was ground, the meal was brought home in the same way. On these errands he never met with any accident; but on another occasion he was less fortunate. Being sent with several commissions to a considerable distance in the town, the horse which he rode became frightened and unmanageable, and finally ran away with him. His race home through the streets was not unlike that of John Gilpin; for, being burdened with several parcels, he distributed them one by one along the road, being obliged to part company with them in order to keep his seat, and at length lost his hat. The horse and his rider finally reached home together, at full speed, and in safety; but just before turning into the yard, they passed underneath a ladder which rested against a tree, and Henry, in order to avoid striking his head against it, slipped off to the ground unhurt. This adventure, I am quite confident, he attempted to commemorate in verse after the manner of Cowper. No remains of such a composition, however, exist, and it is probable he found the subject somewhat too difficult to grapple with.

When he was eleven years old, a change occurred in the situation of the family, which had a most important influence upon his prospects in life. In the winter of 1805, his father was chosen to succeed Dr. Tappan as Professor of Divinity in Harvard College; and, having accepted the office, he removed to Cambridge in the spring of the same year. This election very much divided the community, and was sharply contested in the board of Overseers, on account of the theological opinions of the candidate. It was, however, at last confirmed by them. This was a prominent event in the religious history of the day; and it was, if I am not mistaken, one of the earliest occasions, if not the earliest, on which the disposition was manifested to draw a line of division between those portions of the religious community, which have since become so widely separated from each other.

My father had been settled at Hingham originally on a salary of only four hundred and fifty dollars, which was gradually raised to seven hundred. But even this he had found to be far from adequate to the support of a very large family, and he had therefore increased his income by the common expedient of taking boys into his house to board and instruct. By his appointment at

Cambridge he was at once removed from very straitened circumstances to a condition of comparative comfort, and was enabled to provide for his children a much better education than they could otherwise have hoped to obtain.

This change in the condition of the family was followed speedily by one of those bereavements, which are so common that they leave but little impression beyond the immediate circle in which they take place, and which are yet there of so overwhelming an importance. Mrs. Ware, the mother of the subject of this memoir, had for many years suffered from very feeble health. She had been ill for some months, yet not so as to excite great apprehension; but soon after her removal to Cambridge she became rapidly worse, and died July 13th, 1805, in the forty-fourth year of her age. No human being could owe more to a parent, than Henry, as well as all the other children of his family, owed to that father who still survived. I trust that it will be made to appear in the course of these pages, imperfectly no doubt, how a part at least of this debt of gratitude was incurred. But of that other parent, upon whom so much of the early education of a family depends, her children, unhappily, can recollect nothing, except those kind and tender offices which maternal love knows so well how to perform during the helpless days of infancy and childhood. The influence which a mother is capable of having upon the character of children, is duly estimated. Many men, eminent for their piety and usefulness, have attributed their religious character and course of life to the impressions received from a mother's teachings or a mother's prayers, which were sooner or later effectual. But of the character of her who had the charge of

Henry's early years, and communicated the first impulses to religion and virtue, there are few who can now speak. Her contemporaries are all gone, and indeed none are left who knew her, except such as were of an age too immature to appreciate her character. The only remaining memorials are a few letters and other papers, chiefly written during sickness and affliction. They exhibit, above all things else, a well-regulated mind, feeling deeply, but enduring with cheerfulness and tranquillity; a pervading religious spirit, a constant reference to the love of God and to the kindness of his providence, and a high sense of the duty of submitting with patience and fortitude, and without repining, to the divine will. They exhibit precisely such a character as seems fitted to reproduce, by its direct and indirect maternal influence, the same qualities in a child of a docile and gentle nature; to sow the seeds which in *her* child actually grew and ripened into so abundant a harvest.

At the time when her sickness became alarming, Henry, with one of his brothers, was at school in Duxbury. A month before her death, she wrote to them as follows:

"MENOTOMY,* *Sunday, June* 9, 1805.

"MY DEAR BOYS,

"You will see by the date that I am at your uncle Fisk's, and it rains so hard I cannot have the pleasure of going to meeting with your sisters. I think I cannot now better employ my time than in saying a few words to my dear, my very dear, absent boys. You undoubtedly wish to know how I have been since we parted, and I have the comfort of telling you I am better. I hope you will have been writing to me to-day, as I desired when you left me, unless it should interfere with

* Now West Cambridge.

the employments Mr. Allyn assigns you for Sundays. I wish you to tell him that I wish each of you to write me a few lines every Sunday, if agreeable to him. I trust, dear Henry and John, that you will continue to behave well, and perform *all* your duties constantly and with pleasure, particularly your *religious duties.* As I hope you will recollect what I have often said to you on the subject, so I shall only now say, that you must not suffer this separation from your parents, your brother and sisters, to divert your thoughts from the greatest and first duty of your life,—your duty to God. Remember that he is everywhere present, and that his eye always beholds your steps, and keeps you from falling into dangers." . . . . .

A few days afterward, my father finished the sheet with the following words:

"Your mother is not so well since she wrote this letter, and is indeed much more unwell than when you left Cambridge. I beg you to keep this letter carefully, when you have read it, and not only read it, but attend most faithfully to the wishes and directions of a mother to whom you are more indebted than it is possible for you now to understand."

This direction seems to have been dictated by apprehensions which were only too soon realized. We were shortly summoned home to receive her dying blessing. I add to this brief account an extract from another of her letters, written to one of her sisters in the spring preceding her death, on the loss of an infant, a few months old, the fourth child with which she had been called to part. I insert it simply because it indicates very strongly in her, a state of feeling with regard to the divine government, which was always a predominant one in the mind of her son,—a feeling of perfect and unquestioning reliance on the wisdom, justice, and benevolence of God, and of submission without murmur, and even with cheerfulness, to the doings of his providence.

"I know these light afflictions do not produce in me those fruits, which we are told afflictions and trials are intended to produce on the hearts and lives of those visited with them. I think it is our undoubted duty to yield our souls to the stroke with perfect submission, and look up with the most reverential awe to the hand which inflicts it, yet with the most affectionate and perfect belief, that we are smitten in kindness and with the views and feelings of a parent who never fails to remember mercy, and that, in order to our being ready for a place assigned us hereafter, we must be trained and disciplined by methods best adapted to produce the effect. And who is to be the judge of the best means but He who holds all hearts in his hand, sees all their secret movements, and knows what will reform the heart and life, and bring us to a proper sense of his government and of our dependence on his sovereign disposal for every blessing we enjoy, and every evil (as we say) we suffer; though, so far from being *real* evils, they may be the truest blessings we receive from the hand of our Maker. If indulgence and kind and gentle treatment of *our* children do not form their manners and habits to what we mark out as suitable for them, we are obliged to adopt severity, we feel it necessary to inflict punishments and withhold rewards, and withdraw for a while those caresses and smiles, which constitute so great a part of the enjoyment and happiness of children. And never do we feel our affections so strong, or our anxiety for them so great, as whilst we see them suffering under this kind of correction, which we intend shall bring about a reformation, and make them more ready to submit themselves without obstinacy or reluctance to our authority,—knowing it to be the only means to establish that harmony between us, which is to produce their happiness and secure to ourselves proper regard and respect."

This letter was left unfinished, and the train of reflection never carried out; but who can doubt how much a daily life and teaching in this spirit, in the mother, must have done towards laying the foundation for a similar temper of mind in the child?

On the day of her funeral, our father gathered his children together into the room where she lay, and when they were by themselves, surrounding her coffin, himself calm and tranquil, spoke to them of the mother they had lost; of what she had done and suffered for them; of her example and her instructions; the influence this event should have upon their lives, and above all in making them feel the uncertainty of this life, and the duty of preparing for another. The impression made by this scene was of the most solemn and permanent kind; for, at the distance of forty years, it comes back to the mind with much of the distinctness of a recent event. We find in many of Henry's productions, at different periods of his life, passages evidently suggested by his recollections of his mother and of the circumstances of her death. He made it the subject of a distinct poem of considerable length, first written the same year, but enlarged and corrected afterwards; and he alludes to it also in a later one, in which many of the events of his own life are introduced. I subjoin a few of the passages here referred to, as illustrations of the state of his feelings and of the progress and formation of his character.

FROM "LINES ON THE DEATH OF MY MOTHER," WRITTEN IN THE AUTUMN OF 1805.

. . . .

"Yet many years I thought I should have trod
This stage with her, she pointing to my God,

Directing all my steps in virtue's ways,
And tuning my young heart to sing his praise.
She would have cheered my younger days of life,
And led me harmless on from worldly strife.
And when her years a numerous train had run,
And she declined with life's declining sun,
When trembling, furrowed age came tottering on,
I should repay her kindness as a son,
Support her arm, her sorrowing toils assuage,
And lead her down the hill of feeble age.

. . . .

" O may I live like her, and like her die;
Living, to God's commands my soul apply;
Blameless and virtuous be in all men's sight,
And try to prove myself to God aright;
Dying, to his just will my soul resign,
And count the triumphs of the righteous mine.
Mother, the last commands from thee received,
(When almost at the goal of life arrived,)
And all which when alive thou didst impart,
Be ever written on my faithful heart.
Those precepts ever be my guide, my friend,
My comforter, till life's drear journey end.
If ever from my heart those words be lost,
As sand upon the foaming ocean tossed;
If e'er from virtue's path, the perfect way,
In which thou taught'st me, I shall go astray
O! may thy sainted shade my ways reprove,
With all the kindness of thy former love."

FROM "MY DREAM OF LIFE," AN UNFINISHED

" How dear is every room beneath that roof!
There we assembled at the cheerful meal,
And asked Heaven's blessing on a band of love.
There the gay circle on a winter's eve
Gathered about the lavish blaze, and pressed
Within the chimney's ample range, to hear
The tales of wonder childhood loves to hear,

And age delights to tell. There stood my bed;
There I lay waiting for a mother's kiss,
And soft good-night; then breathless sought to catch
Her last faint footstep as she slow retired;
Then drew the blanket on my face and slept.
Time in its lengthened flight has wrought such change,
That hardly could I recognize those walls;
But that sweet evening kiss, I feel it now,
I hear that soft good-night, that parting step
Still faintly fall upon my waiting ear.
The past comes thick around me; faded shapes,
But beautiful, of all that once have been,
And are no more. I sit beside the hearth,
And weep at scenes that once were only joy.

"O! what is tender like a mother's love,
And what can pay its loss? To her I looked
To cheer and guide me in the fearful way
That leads through toil and peril into life;
And trusted then, when strength and wealth were mine,
To rock the cradle of her fading age,
As she had soothed the infancy of mine.
But Heaven refused the boon. There is a grief
Severe with double anguish; when the heart
Sinks burdened with a present woe, and waits
For darker evils hastening in its train;—
Such grief was ours." . . . .

"What darkness followed then!
It settled down upon the present scene
In thick dismay, and on the future cast
An ominous shade, involving earth and life
And hope. The sacred light of home was dimmed:
The tender smile, the voice of patient love,
The anxious counsel, the directing eye,
Cheered the sad pathway of my youth no more.
The shadow settled on my heart. The world
Had other lights, but none to fill that void;
And friends, but none that wore a mother's heart."

In "*Jotham Anderson*" are many passages relating to the early life of this imaginary personage, evidently suggested by his own recollections and experience. In this work he speaks of his mother thus:

"Were all mothers like mine, how greatly would the obedience of the young Christian's pilgrimage be facilitated and its peace ensured! I love to dwell on the memory of that honored woman. My earliest recollection of her is in the act of teaching me to pray, when she every evening took me on her knees, and, clasping my little hands, made me repeat after her my childish petitions. Methinks I still see the beautiful expression of her maternal eye, and feel the kiss, full of affection and piety, with which she closed the service. At such times she would explain to me the purposes of prayer, and teach me to love the good Being, who gave me father and mother, and made me happy. It was her practice, also, to seize the moments when my young heart was overflowing with cheerfulness and good-will, to remind me of the Father above, and direct my gratitude to him."

CHAPTER II.

HIS EARLY EDUCATION, AT DUXBURY, CAMBRIDGE, AND ANDOVER—ENTRANCE INTO COLLEGE AND COLLEGE LIFE—WINTER AT BEVERLY IN KEEPING SCHOOL.

1805–1812. ÆT. 11–18.

Of his early education I recollect but little. He was taught partly at home, and partly in the private and public schools of his native town. In the course of the years 1804 and 1805, he spent considerable time in the family, and under the tuition, of the late Rev. Dr. Allyn, of Duxbury. Dr. Allyn was a classmate and intimate friend of his father, and was held by him in very high regard. He was a man remarkable, among the clergymen of the day, for his many eccentricities of manners and habits, but not less so for his strong good sense, a quaint and original humor, and unalloyed benevolence and kindness of heart. Here, it is believed, Henry began his preparation for college.

After the College Commencement of 1805, Henry, with his brothers, was placed under the tuition of their cousin, Mr. Ashur Ware, a graduate of the preceding year, who became at the same time a member of his father's family. He remained under his care till the spring of 1807, when, on the election of Mr. Ware to a Tutorship, Mr. Samuel Merrill, of the class of 1807, took his place. In September of the same year, he was sent to Phillips Academy, in Andover, of which Mr. Mark Newman was then Preceptor; and here he continued till his admission into the Freshman class at Cambridge, in September, 1808.

At Andover, he boarded in the family of Mr. Isaac Chandler, a very respectable and pious farmer, at the distance of about a quarter of a mile from the Academy, in company with a number of other boys of the same age. This was his first initiation into promiscuous society of those of his own age, at a public school, away from the influences of parents and home; and here, probably, he was exposed for the first time to the temptations to impurity of thought, language, and conduct, from which so very few escape in those perilous days of our life. In him, happily, any such taint was slight and transient. It seemed barely to have tarnished for the moment the fair surface of his mind, and to have left no stain behind it. He was much aided in his escape from the dangers of his age and situation by the continuance, in some degree, of the same parental guidance which had already done so much to give him a right tendency. It was the custom of his father to keep up as frequent a communication with his children, when they were absent from home, as the pressure of other duties would permit; and his letters, though not consisting of labored and regular admonitions, seldom failed to contain some hints or short expositions with regard to modes and objects of study, the cultivation of good habits, or attention to moral and religious duties, which probably had the more effect from their incidental character, and this very absence of formality. The following are extracts from his letters to Henry while at Andover; those which called them forth, or which were written in reply to them, having been lost.

"Sept. 26, 1807.

"I hope you are laying up knowledge now as fast as you can. Let me advise you, particularly, to make great use of your memory, and make great exertion to strengthen it. No faculty we have is more improvable; and no one is more apt to be neglected. It will be well to copy the choicest passages of the classics into your blank book; but it will be still better to imprint them indelibly in your memory.

"Your handwriting I wish you to improve in. I am glad you have the opportunity of instruction, and hope you will be most diligent in the hours assigned to it, to acquire at least a decent, if not an elegant use of the pen. You are now at the best age for attaining that accomplishment. I hope you will not undervalue it, and that you will give me specimens of your improvement in your letters."

One of the subjects touched upon in this letter, the improvableness of the memory, with the great importance of attention to it as a part of education, was a point upon which his father frequently insisted in his letters and on other occasions. He was led to do this by what he regarded as a mistake which he had made in his own case, from an erroneous early impression, that this faculty is not to be improved by cultivation, but is a gift bestowed by nature on some, and denied to others.

"March 8, 1808.

"I was gratified with your letter, as a mark of your attention, as an evidence of your improvement, as an assurance of your happiness, and as giving me a pleasant account of your progress the preceding week. I this moment hear of an opportunity of sending your Huntingford, and shall hope to receive as good an account of succeeding weeks, as you gave me of the first. . . . . I am very glad to have you send for Huntingford. I hope you will exercise yourself in it as much as you can, besides what you have occasion to do as an exercise in the Academy. Not that I wish to press your studies beyond your ability and health. You must allow yourself a proper proportion of exercise, but be careful to make some good use of all your fragments of time, which are not devoted to your exercises, nor necessary for relaxation. It is your use of *fragments of time* which are usually lost, that is to make you a scholar. I hope, by the end of the term, you will have a good account to give me of other gains, beside those of your Greek Testament on the Sabbath."

"JUNE 23, 1808.

. . . . . "Let not your plan of coming home distract your attention from the exercises of the Academy. Give your whole attention to your studies till the hour of relaxation, and then *relax entirely*. Habituate yourself to undivided attention when you do attend, and when you unbend, do it *entirely*. Never let the thought of amusement break in upon your studies, nor the thought of your studies mar your enjoyment."

The four years of Henry's college life were passed in his father's family, who then lived in the old Sewall house, lately taken down, which stood nearly opposite the head of Holyoke Street. Of this period, I find few memorials. Living at home, and having but little taste for promiscuous company, he did not mix much with college society, and probably made fewer college intimacies than most young men who receive their education within the walls of a University. He was scrupulously attentive to his duties and exercises; a faithful but not a very hard student, and maintained a respectable rank in his class. He did not appear to aim at a very high standing as a scholar, and this principally, as I appre-

3*

hend, because he had no conception that his abilities were such as to place it within his reach. I doubt if it ever entered his mind, that, even if he were disposed, he could have contended successfully for the higher honors of his class; he did not dream that such success was in his power, even had it been an object of desire. Had he believed it to be so, he would probably have both desired and sought it, and thus have been a much harder student. But he acquired knowledge easily. A moderate amount of labor enabled him to appear as well in his recitations as he wished, as well as he supposed it possible that he could, and he consequently devoted much leisure time to reading and to studies of a general character.

At this period of his life, inded, eminence, high reputation, or great distinction in any way, does not seem to have entered into his anticipations. No one probably, who knew him at this time, would have supposed him capable of a career so successful as that which awaited him; no one would have been more surprised than himself, could it have been predicted. This trait was strikingly characteristic of him through life; the success he attained was always greater than he expected, or even dared to hope; it came upon him by surprise. I do not mean that he was without ambition; that he did not seek and value reputation; that he did not enjoy applause. The love of praise, of popularity, was in him a strong natural feeling, as he was fully sensible, and one against whose undue influence he felt it his duty carefully to guard. But he did not very highly estimate his power of doing that which would enable him to gratify this feeling. His ambition was not up to his ability. He would have been perfectly satisfied and contented with a much lower rank, both in College and in life, than that to which he attained.

His rank as a scholar will be indicated in some degree to those who are acquainted with the principles on which they were at that time distributed, by the College honors which he received. In his Junior year, he took part in a Latin Dialogue, at one of the usual public exhibitions. In his Senior year he gave a Latin Oration at Exhibition, and at the Commencement in 1812, when he graduated, he delivered a poem, the subject of which was "The Pursuit of Fame." This was received with a good deal of applause. He was a member of all the College Societies, for admission into which scholarship was a necessary condition; and in their literary exercises, as he did also in his College themes, he frequently indulged himself in his propensity for writing in verse. He delivered a poem before one of these societies, and the annual discourse before an association which existed among the undergraduates for mutual religious improvement.

Beside thus stating my own recollections of my brother's College life and character, I have the satisfaction of being able to introduce the following extracts of letters to me from two of his classmates, Charles G. Loring and Peleg Sprague, relating to the same subject. Mr. Loring writes thus:

"We were not, properly speaking, intimate in College; for we were both diligent students, and he resided, as you know, at home, and very seldom mingled in our amusements, excepting as a member of societies devoted to mental improvement. I felt towards him, however, very early, a profound respect, and a constantly growing personal attachment. His excellent sense, perfect purity and benevolence, always shining clearly through his quiet, retiring, and somewhat exclusive, though never unkind, manners, produced in me a gratifying consciousness of elevation in companionship with him, and led me to seek his society as a privilege.

"His recitations, though not brilliant, were always accurate and entirely unambitious. I do not remember ever being impressed with the thought that he aimed to excel others; while his industry and devotion to study, and punctual attendance upon all College exercises, showed forcibly his high sense of duty to himself, and of the privileges with which we were favored; and, although they procured for him rank, never seemed directed to that end.

"I cannot recall any one whose career at Cambridge was so perfectly typical of his future life. The same gravity, gentleness, firmness, and kindness of demeanor; the same elevated sense of duty; the same earnest, unpretending piety; the same entire self-devotion, which so eminently distinguished him among the best and greatest of men in his mature years, were characteristic of him there."

Judge Sprague says:

"While at College, as he was the son of a professor, and did not live within the walls, his classmates had not the gratification of seeing him so much as they wished. He rarely joined in their amusements, never in those of the gayer kind. His conduct and demeanor were always irreproachable, and such even then, as would have adorned the profession for which he was destined; and yet so free from austerity and reserve, so full of kindness and sympathy, that he was esteemed and beloved by all. I verily believe, that not one of his classmates, at any time during his whole college life, felt towards him other than emotions of friendship."

In the winter of 1810–11, he availed himself of the permission, which was frequently given to undergraduates, to teach a school in the country during the winter months. The vacation then extended to seven weeks, occupying the greater part of the cold season; and several weeks of the term were allowed by the Government, in order to make out the amount of time required for an engagement of this sort. This privilege was of great advantage to the poorer class of students, in enabling them to procure the means of education; but it was resorted to in my brother's case, as much for the benefit which might be derived from this kind of discipline. A school was engaged for him in the town of Beverly, and thither he went in the latter part of December. The following letter will convey the best idea of his experience in this new situation,—one certainly of no small responsibility, and of considerable trial to a lad of his age; for it is to be observed, that at this time he wanted four months of having completed his seventeenth year. This letter, besides its connexion with him, may serve to illustrate some of the customs and the state of the schools at that time.

TO HIS FATHER

"BEVERLY, DEC. 28, 1810.

"MY DEAR FATHER,

"I believe that I promised to write to you as soon as I arrived here, but I have been so engaged that I have not had time. Whether this letter will reach you before Tuesday or not, I cannot tell; but I hope you will receive it to-morrow. That I am very much engaged you can easily conceive, when I tell you that I have in my school sixty-five children, men and women together. There are four boys older and larger than myself, and, from what I can hear, there are yet to be more of the same *genus*. Girls there are many, as much as 15, 17, or 18 years of age; but it luckily happens that they are disposed to be peaceable and orderly. Only six study Arithmetic;—three of these are just entering on *multiplication*,—two are in *reduction*,—and one in the *rule of three*. Almost all the girls (of whom are about one third of the whole) study English Grammar, and only one boy; and one intends studying Latin next week. And now, having heard of my situation here, you will probably be glad to know how I came into it. And I assure you that I have a very amusing account to give you of my journey to this place. To begin, then:—I was so afraid of being left by the stage, that I left Uncle Clarke's with scarce half a dinner, and, to complete this grievous misfortune, I had to lounge about the market for half an hour before the *vehicle* was ready. This therefore I entered with eight more; and a shabbier set than we, I believe, never entered stage-coach. Thus we travelled to a tavern about half way to Salem (but in what town I know not); and till we got into a bar-room there, where one man was pretty talkative about *flip*, and the stage-driver about his pay,—till then, I say, I heard not a word spoken, save and except that one sailor cursed the driver, and another asked what was the matter.

"After this we had company a little more talkative, and so arrived at Salem just about candle-light. The driver refused to carry me to Beverly; so I left my trunk at the tavern, to be carried over in the Newburyport baggage-wagon. I did not like the plan very well, but I did not see as I could do better; but, when I got to Mr. Eliot's, I hired his horse and his neighbor's chaise, and so went and brought it home,—sixty-six cents, and twenty-five cents toll! But to return from this digression;—I went as far as Beverly Bridge in the stage, and walked from there. With much difficulty I found the house of Andrew Eliot, who was to board the school-master. There awaited my arrival two of the school committee, who gave me much sage advice, and administered many admirable admonitions, and instructions, and directions; particularly with regard to Mr. Pilsbury, who kept this school last year, whom they affirmed to be the very best master they ever knew. 'He had a most curious way of punishing his scholars; he used to talk to 'em, and fairly shame 'em out on't,—and he used to pinch their ears, and everybody but *two* was very well satisfied with him,' &c. In such conversation, we passed about half an hour, and then I took leave, and went over to Salem, as aforesaid. But I must not forget that they inquired about my recommendations, whether I had any from my *minister*, &c., and said it would be best to get one, as it was usual. So the next morning, down went I to Mr. Abbot's, to be examined, and, after reading, ciphering, &c., I was permitted to become school-master. Indeed, *Mr. Abbot* said that Mr. Hedge's letter to him, and my College standing, were recommendations sufficient. But it was thought best that I should be examined, in order to satisfy the District. I drank tea at Mr. Abbot's, and thence went with him to his evening lecture, where he spoke extempore, for about an hour, on the excellence of the Christian religion.

"I keep seven hours a day;—from half-past eight to twelve, and from one to half-past five. I shall soon keep eight hours, as the committee say it is usual. There have been considerable objections made to my taking Saturdays, in order to make out the time; and I have agreed partly, till I hear from you, not to keep them.

"Tell Lucy and Mary, that they have taught me to be so *polite* to ladies, that I have got laughed at for it in my school; for, when one of these young ladies, my pupils, the other day came to me with her pen, I gallantly rose from my chair, and made my very best bow,—at which the boys laughed. However, I have learned here to think a little better of girls than I used to; for, after they have been out, the boys never come till they are called, but the girls always return of their own accord before their time is out.

"I believe that I am very well situated here. My living,

as far as I can see, will be pretty much in the same style that it was at Andover, but vastly more clean. Mr. Eliot is a sociable, jolly, facetious fellow, and altogether very pleasant. I live about a mile from the meeting-house, and the post-office where I have got to carry this letter to-night (it is now half-past seven); and so, if this be not writing fit for a school-master, or a letter fit for one that has read Cowper, the time, circumstances, &c., of the case will plead in excuse. I wish that I had time and paper now to relate many conversations which I have heard here, but I must leave it for some future occasion. I am well, and hope the same is the case with all at home. Having nothing better to send, I send this hope, and my love to all,—and therewith subscribe myself

H. Ware, Jr.

"N. B. I feel myself more like a man, in company and in school, than I expected. I really believe that there is some magic in the mighty word *Sir*, which has a potent influence in these things. But, by the way, I must say a word in blame of my school-house. Such a little, dirty hole for seventy children, I never saw; we are as crowded as can be, —no comfort at all. Some of the boys have to stand out on the floor while the others write."

During this residence in Beverly, he boarded in a family entertaining opinions of religious doctrine differing entirely from those in which he had been educated, and which were held by the friends with whom he had always been associated. He was consequently in the way of hearing a good deal of conversation and discussion on the subject of religion, of a different character from that to which he had been accustomed. His mind was thus freshly excited concerning it, and he became much interested and somewhat anxious and disturbed. He wrote a letter to his father, in the course of the winter, exhibiting this state of mind, and asking his opinion and advice upon several points, with regard to which he felt doubts and difficulties. This letter, which would have been of interest in showing the progress of his mind on religious subjects, has unfortunately been lost; the answer to it, however, which I insert, serves very well to indicate what were the topics to which it related.

FROM HIS FATHER.

"JAN. 17, 1811.

"I received yours of Tuesday, this evening. I had begun to apprehend that you had neglected writing, because you were unable to give so good an account of yourself as you would wish. I am in some measure relieved from that apprehension, though I am sorry to have you think you shall not give satisfaction. Allow no such fear to discourage you from the very best exertions of which you are capable. Let the largeness of your school stimulate your ambition, and call forth energies adequate to the occasion. I shall be very glad to have you keep an evening school, if you find yourself adequate to the task. Any exertion, not beyond your strength, will be useful to you.

"In your account of the religious state of the place, and prevalent opinions, I think it possible you may not have acquired a perfectly accurate knowledge of it. The consequences, which we think irresistibly follow from men's opinions, are often such as they totally disavow. At any rate, the religious opinions of serious and conscientious persons are entitled to respect, even from him who believes them to be most absurd and contradictory. It may be very useful to you to hear conversation on religious subjects, and to converse yourself, even on controversial subjects. Two things you will learn by it, if you exercise that good sense, which I hope you do;—one is, to bear contradiction with patience, and treat persons with deference who hold opinions to which you cannot subscribe; the other, not to think it necessary to give up an opinion, and immediately think it wrong, because you don't find yourself able to defend it. Many truths are liable to *insuperable objections*,—I mean objections, which no finite mind is capable of removing in a perfectly satisfactory manner. Such, I will venture to say, are the doctrines to which you allude in your letter, which side of the argument soever you take up. Yet one side or the other, notwithstanding such objections, must contain the truth.

"I hope you will learn to hear whatever is said with candor;—to treat all persons and opinions on religious subjects with great delicacy,—and be deliberate, cautious, and conscientious in forming your own.

"I know not how I shall send your flute; still I may possibly either send or bring it to you. I do not however see what use you will make of it. You say nothing of society—acquaintance—visiting. I trust therefore that your time is not much taken up in that way; and am not sorry that it is not."

There is no doubt that the experience of this winter was of much value to him, partly by giving him confidence in himself, preparing him for a similar occupation after leaving college; and partly by renewing, and fixing more deeply in his mind, his interest in religion, as a system of doctrines, as well as a rule of life. His intercourse, it should be remarked, was not exclusively with those of different religious opinions, beyond the family in which he boarded; he attended, in part at least, the preaching of the Rev. Abiel Abbot, and formed some personal acquaintance with him.

CHAPTER III.

BECOMES ASSISTANT IN THE ACADEMY AT EXETER, N. H.—HIS CHOICE OF A PROFESSION—CORRESPONDENCE WITH HIS FATHER—JOURNAL.

1812-13. ÆT. 18-19.

At the time of his leaving College, in August, 1812, Henry was four months past his eighteenth year. He immediately engaged himself as an assistant in the Academy at Exeter. This institution, which has always held so high a rank among preparatory schools, was then under the care of that very distinguished instructor, Dr. Benjamin Abbot. It was with no little solicitude, that he undertook a task so responsible in itself, and to him quite formidable, when he considered his youth, his very youthful appearance, and the great reputation of the school and its head-master. The strong feeling of diffidence, which he very naturally experienced, with regard to his success, did not interfere with those exertions which were necessary to secure it; and there is reason to believe that he soon manifested a competency for the office, which secured the respect of the students, and the confidence of the Principal. In a letter to his wife, written since his death, Dr. Abbot says:

"It gave me great pleasure to receive a note with your signature attached to it. It revived the recollection of a past happy period of my life, when associated with your beloved husband in the instruction of youth. I well remember my impressions, when he first made his appearance in Exeter, and my fears, from his youthful appearance and inexperience in teaching and government, that he might be found inadequate to his station. These fears, however, were soon dissipated. The sweetness of his disposition, his open frankness of manner, and acknowledged scholarship, soon gained him the love and confidence of his pupils, the respect and affection of his brother instructors. His two years' residence in this place left an impression on all who had the happiness to know him, and is still fondly cherished in the recollections of all who survive him."

Of the time spent in Exeter, he used always to speak with the most unalloyed satisfaction. He frequently reverted to it in after life, and seldom without some expression of pleasure. All his recollections of, and associations with, the place, the people, and his residence there, were of the most happy kind. He was then thrown for the first time, for any considerable period, on himself and his own resources. He found himself at once in the midst of an agreeable and cultivated society; among persons, to whom he could give, and from whom he could receive pleasure. Before this he had mixed but little, and always with some reluctance, in general company. He was, constitutionally and hereditarily, shy and bashful. The effort to go among people, especially those older than himself, was almost painful. He had consequently associated but little with persons out of the circle of his immediate relatives; for even at College, as has been already said, he was far from mingling much in the society of his classmates. On first going to Exeter, therefore, he felt but little confidence in his power of rendering himself acceptable, and hardly supposed it possible that he should be expected to meet, on terms of equality, the kind of society into which he found himself immediately and most cordially invited. "I well recollect," says Dr. Abbot, in the letter just quoted, "the extreme diffidence, or rather, I should say, humble opinion of himself, so uncommon in young men fresh from the University, which made it difficult to persuade him to accept invitations to dine, or mix with the more elderly and learned of our society." This reluctance, however, was not of long duration. The very familiar and unceremonious habits of the place; the kindness with which he was welcomed; the pleasure which he received and which he presently found himself capable of imparting, speedily removed all constraint, and he was soon established as one of a delightful circle, with whom his intercourse was constant, and of a very improving character. In no part of his life, probably, did he ever enjoy society so much, for its own sake, as at Exeter. Some of his warmest personal attachments were formed there, and he made many friends, including the venerable Principal, by whom he was always held in strong regard, and whom he never ceased to love to the end of his life.

But his residence there was not merely a fortunate and happy one as it afforded him an opportunity for the gratification and the improvement to be derived from intercourse with cultivated society; it contributed in various ways to fit him for his subsequent duties and responsibilities. It afforded a kind of discipline, which his previous retired habits and home education, as well as his temperament, rendered absolutely necessary in order to prepare him for his entrance into the world. In other respects, the years spent at Exeter were a very important portion of his life, in their bearing on those which followed. It was while here, that he finally fixed on his profession, and began the study of it. We find also, that here he chiefly formed those habits and modes of study, matured in his mind those views of the nature, objects, and duties of the ministry, and began that collection and preparation of materials for future use, which aided him so much in his subsequent progress, and contributed so largely to his ultimate success. I doubt if there were any equal portion of his life, in which so distinct a progress and development of character were to be noticed. This would have been true to some extent, perhaps, of the same years, wherever spent; but much of their favorable influence seems to have been connected with the circumstances in which he was placed.

His first letter, giving an account of his arrival, introduction to his duties, and first acquaintance with the society of the place, is wanting. The following is a part of the answer to it.

FROM HIS FATHER.

"CAMBRIDGE, SEPT. 14, 1812.

. . . . . . "The first thing that strikes me in your letter, is your handwriting. I advise you to adopt a larger letter, and to persevere in the use of it, at least as large as that in which I am now writing. You will hereafter enjoy the benefit of it.

"I am glad to find you are so well pleased with your lodgings; you can hardly be too solicitous to make yourself agreeable in return, by habits of sociability, civil attentions, and a constant regard to those personal and domestic habits which form so considerable a part of the character of a young man.

But you are in no small danger, on the other hand, of being drawn away too much by the love of pleasant society. I hope you will be on your guard, and early prescribe to yourself such rules and limits, as will consist with your duty, your improvement, and the expectations of the place.

"Your first care must be to secure the character of competent ability and unfailing fidelity, as an instructor in the Academy; your next, to gain all that you can, consistently with this, for your own improvement. Though I feel an entire confidence in your present correctness of mind, it is impossible for me not to feel some solicitude upon your first going into the world to act for yourself at so early a period. It is for you to show whether my confidence or my solicitude have the best foundation.

"I wish you would write to me soon, and largely, respecting every circumstance in your situation. I wish you to tell me whether you have fixed on a profession; if you are still not fully resolved, let me know the state of your mind, its balancings, and what, and in what degree, are its preponderances."

TO HIS FATHER.

"EXETER, SEPT. 23, 1812.

"I received your letter last evening; had I seen it sooner, I should have written very differently by Folsom. I said nothing then which I intended, and shall be able to say but little now; for I have been engaged all to-day and this evening, and must send early to-morrow. You wish to know of my situation. I can hardly describe it by writing, and must leave it for my return. I am, however, perfectly contented and pleased, am treated like one of the family, and consider myself as entirely at home, and a pleasant home it is. I have formed but few acquaintances; but I foresee that I shall have a good deal of visiting to do. If I may judge from what I have seen, it will be very agreeable. I hope, however, that there will be no reason to complain that I neglect my duty for company, or that I am not faithful to the extent of my abilities, though they should be found not competent to the task. The expression of your confidence in my present intentions gave me great pleasure, and it shall be my constant study to prove it well-grounded, and to dispel all solicitude with respect to my adherence to the habits in which I have been educated. I hope my connexion with Dr. Abbot and the other gentlemen in this place, will keep me right. Though he is a very pleasant and easy man, my respect for him is so *awful* that I cannot learn to consider him as a companion. I believe there is no boy in school feels worse to be detected by him in a fault than I do, when I think he is listening to my recitations. The duties of the Academy are less arduous than I expected. The language department is not so full now as usual; the difficulties of the times occasion that more should study English.

"I know nothing of what is going on in the world; I should be glad if in your letters you would let me know what the great and the good are doing."

FROM HIS FATHER.

"SEPT. 25, 1812.

"You wish to know what the wise and the good are doing. If I were disposed to be gloomy and cynical, I should say they were sitting still, and waiting to see how the foolish and bad will come out. It is not, however, exactly so, but it is too nearly. Folly and wickedness are more active, and wisdom and virtue less so, than would be for the peace, improvement, and happiness of the world. In the two great interests that engage the chief attention of men, and produce most of the excitement that we either rejoice or mourn to see,—religion and politics,—the greatest zeal, activity and influence are not always to be considered as certain marks of the greatest wisdom, or the purest sincerity; it is well if they happen not in company with both intellectual and moral qualities of an opposite character."

TO HIS FATHER.

"Oct. 3, 1812.

. . . . . . "With respect to a profession, &c., it is a long business, and one which I cannot enter upon at present. Such thoughts as shall at any time occur to me, I shall transmit to you, hoping to receive your advice and direction. The first thing, I believe, to be done, is to consider which will make me the best and the happiest man, and in which I can do most good. This is as far as I have got yet; and, though I have always been of opinion that a clergyman's life is the most respectable and happy, and most useful, or at least capable of being the most useful to society; yet a thousand difficulties and dangers present themselves at the very outset, which have deterred me from choosing it. Until these are in some degree removed, as I hope they may be by your assistance, I shall be totally undecided; and at present I see but little prospect of my beginning any study so early as next year, and perhaps it is best I should not. The more I think on the subject, the more unsettled I become. However, there is no knowing what a day will bring forth, and I believe that present anxiety will do but little good."

The following passage is extracted from a letter written at this time to a brother who had just entered college. A young man of eighteen will not often be allowed to assume the office of a Mentor, nor be listened to with respect; in this case, however, the undeviating propriety of his own conduct and his strict adherence to duty, as it gave him some right to advise, established also a claim to the confidence of those whom he addressed.

TO HIS BROTHER WILLIAM.

"Oct. 24, 1812.

"But I wish to speak seriously with you, for you are entering on four years, that may be happy or miserable, that will bring you good or evil, as you choose. And, as I have lately passed over the ground before you, and know its dangerous places, and how it should be travelled, I am particularly anxious that you should start right, so as to get through well. For, though I know you will scarcely believe it, a great deal, indeed almost all, depends upon the first setting out. Only begin rightly. Of a bad beginning it is hard to correct the evils, and the greatest danger of commencing ill lies in the company you keep. I wished to have written to you earlier, to urge you earnestly to form no intimacies, till you have found out who are your likeliest fellows. For if you make acquaintances early, you do it without a knowledge of their characters, and it may be a permanent injury to you; for you are more likely to fall into the company of the bad than of the good, because the latter are cautious and reserved, while the former drag into their train all they can seize. Late as this warning comes to you, I hope it will not be too late for you to profit by it. The path of your duty is plain, and I know you are inclined to pursue it. Let your resolution not flag, but walk straight forwards, and justify the hopes of your father and friends. There will be more pleasure in hearing them say, 'Well done,' when you have finished, than in all the scenes of irregular pleasure which college affords."

The following extract relates to "The General Repository and Review," a quarterly periodical publication, projected and edited by Professor Norton. This was a work of high character, and took the lead in the theological discussions of the day. There were too few at that period, who could suitably appreciate such a work, and it continued in existence but a few years.

TO HIS FATHER.

"Nov. 23, 1812.

"I received your subscription-paper on Saturday. I have showed it to Dr. Abbot, but he gives me slight hopes of obtaining subscribers here. For, though there are a number of literary men here, their thoughts and business are very distant from anything of this kind. Show them a political magazine, and they might patronize it; or a light work of polite literature, which might serve for recreation after the bustle of a busy day; but they feel no interest in theological controversy, or literary discussions, which must be studied in order to be relished. Of the work itself, he spoke in high terms, and said, very clearly, such a thing ought to be supported, but its tone is a grade too high for our country yet; it ought to have more entertainment and less abstruseness; and, till this is the case, till its plan is very essentially altered, it cannot flourish. Mr. Hildreth said, it was too heretical; make a 'Panoplist' of it; give long, and wondrous, and dolorous accounts of conversions, revivals, &c., and it would do well enough. I cannot determine with certainty as yet, but from what I know of the place, and from Dr. A.'s conversation, little or no increase of subscription can be expected from this quarter. I am very sorry to find this is the case; for, the more I see of the book, the more I admire it."

It will be seen from the following letter of his father, written in March, 1813, that notwithstanding the expressions of doubt as to his choice of a profession, contained in the letter of October 3d, the prevailing bent of his mind was to the study of divinity. Indeed, I do not imagine, that he had really so considerable a hesitancy upon the subject as he himself supposed. What his predominant inclination had always been, I am confident from my own recollection; still, when it became absolutely necessary to decide the point, he felt doubts and misgivings which he had never experienced when looking at the subject from a distance. The office of a minister he had always regarded with a species of awe, as one of peculiar sacredness, and as requiring a special sanctity in those who assumed it. It was natural, therefore, that he should hesitate for a moment, when called on to determine, and should distrust somewhat his own fitness for the task. No one, indeed, who enters this profession without something of these feelings, can be regarded as fit to enter it. In his case, whatever may have been the state of his mind while he had the subject under consideration, no one who had known him could have entertained the least doubt how the deliberation would end. The letter itself sufficiently indicates the topics of that which suggested it. It was written soon after he had spent one of his vacations at home.

FROM HIS FATHER.

"MARCH 4, 1813.

"I expected to have received one or two letters from you before this time; but I presume your reason for not having written is that which prevented Father Wibird from getting up before sunrise,—mere respect, a sense of decorum,—you had too much respect for your father to write before him. That restraint will be taken off now, and you need no longer be prevented by any scruples of delicacy, and I hope you will not by want of leisure or want of inclination.

"Your letter to Lucy was calculated to give me some alarm. I consider there is always danger that persons naturally bashful and taciturn, when they once break through the restraints of nature and constitution, will also break over those of decorum and modesty, and go into the opposite extreme of impudence. The very effort it costs to overcome the reluctance of nature has a tendency to hurry you to an extreme; as the violent push required to open a sticking door endangers your tumbling on your nose when it opens. I trust, however, you will have care enough to keep your centre of gravity, and good sense enough to apply to moral and practical purposes that law in physics, by which a body is disposed to move with an irregular and dangerous force, which has had a resisting power suddenly removed.

"I am sorry you find so little time for study. I should exceedingly regret your own improvement being retarded by your business, and the time greatly protracted of your qualifying yourself for your profession. From your observations the evening before you left Cambridge, I inferred that your tendency was prevalently toward the study of divinity. If that be the case, you will of course bend your reading in that direction. As you teach the Testament, you will give it a more critical view than you would otherwise do. I would advise you also to write constantly on subjects connected with your studies, and on which you are reading. Remember Lord Bacon on reading, writing, conversation,—'the *full*, *exact*, and *ready* man.' I should think, that, in the intervals of school, books connected with biblical and ecclesiastical history, being lighter than strictly theological books, might be preferable. And there is, perhaps, no better introduction to the study of divinity, than a thorough acquaintance with the history of the Jewish and Christian churches."

I may add, that a journal which he kept, though somewhat irregularly, at this period of his residence in Exeter, bears marks of the prevailing tendency of his mind. His thoughts, his mode of viewing every subject of which he speaks, and of remarking on the books which he is reading, all show clearly where his heart was. In this journal are several analyses of sermons, which he heard, and remarks upon the style and manner of the preachers; especially a full account of the preaching of Dr. Parker of Portsmouth, showing a very just appreciation of the peculiar excellences of that eminent divine, and corresponding in a remarkable manner with the estimate he formed of him at a more mature period of life, when he became his biographer. I quote from this journal, as an evidence of this tendency of his thoughts, and also as an example of his mode of thinking at this period, the following passage, which forms the conclusion of some remarks suggested by the reading of "Solomon's Song."

"I cannot bear to hear that same language held to the incomprehensible Jehovah, which is used in expressing a worldly passion to the beauty of a day; it is shocking to me. A person of an ardent disposition may thus imagine to be the expressions of a fervent piety, what are only the overflowings of the natural temperament. Indeed, I object altogether to the publishing of very ardent and fervent devotional exercises. They come into the hands of simple people, whose mind is naturally less warm and enthusiastic, but who intend and endeavor to live a Christian life; but, when they see this extravagance of feeling in others and compare it with their own more quiet and placid state, they begin to think that all is not right in themselves, and they are afflicted and in despair at what is perhaps no more than the result of the natural constitution of their minds. Or it may lead others, who are quite as warm, and do not regulate their minds by reason, to create in themselves a factitious spirit of devotion, and to construe enthusiasm of feeling into real piety. Such, too, will be the natural effect of flaming accounts of conversions and revivals upon weak but warm spirits; they will readily fancy in themselves what they admire in others and wish to experience; and thus we shall have a sickly, high-wrought state of feeling supplant the milder but more steady flame of pure and rational religion;—rational, not in the sense of those who would exalt reason as infallible, and set up its decisions in opposition to those of revelation, but only so far as it guides and directs our faith and practice, going hand in hand with the heart, the faithful servant of God."

The following is Henry's answer to the letter from his father last quoted. It should be stated in explanation of the concluding remark in it, that he was at this time teaching the Greek Testament in the course of his duty as an instructor, and took the opportunity to give to it a more critical attention than was required in the mere preparation for his exercises, using the Cambridge reprint of Griesbach's text.

TO HIS FATHER.

"March 14, 1813.

"How far the course I desire would be practicable, I know not; as far as it would, I am determined to pursue it. At present, my chief concern is to become a religious man; to regulate my conduct, and form my habits, so that I may conscientiously exercise the office of a minister. And I find it no easy matter to become what I wish; the more I look into myself, the more evil propensities and secret faults I find which need correction; and then, if I make a virtuous resolution in the morning, it is ten to one that I break it before night. Till I can make myself the character I think I ought to be, I shall not think of coming forward to teach others. I believe I might learn to my satisfaction the speculative and theoretical parts of religion. I might learn to criticize and comment, and give good advice, &c., very well; but unless I felt and lived according to what I taught, constantly and directly, it is plain I should only be enhancing my own guilt and danger. I find I have been very prolix, and I am afraid tedious; but I wish to write to you as I feel and think, for I wish your remarks and advice.

"I have found two small errors in Griesbach, which perhaps you have not;—2 Peter i. 3, and in James ii. 14, ἔργα is written with an aspirate ἕργα; which last, however, is rather of *curious* than *real* importance. With respect to γενήματα, I doubted whether it were not a various reading, and therefore did not note it in my margin."

Whilst at home, during his next vacation in May, the question of his profession was definitively settled; he commenced his studies in earnest and with more system. His correspondence with his father now assumed more distinctly a professional character, and the remainder of his residence at Exeter will require little more than extracts from this correspondence and from his journal, to convey a pretty just idea of the gradual manner in which his character was forming, and of the earnestness with which he was preparing himself for the great work of life.

TO HIS FATHER.

"May 30, 1813.

"I have been reading a few sermons, but none, indeed none that I ever read, struck me so much as Mr. Channing's at the ordination of Mr. Codman. It seems to me powerful and impressive beyond example. It must be a treasure to young ministers, and ought to stop effectually the cold sermonizing of your rationalists, who maintain the strange contradiction, of religion without feeling. If such a thing were possible, it would be scarcely worth having, I think. It seems to me Mr. Channing has exactly drawn his own character, as far as I know it. There are the same traits of unaffectedness, earnestness, and solemnity in himself and in the portrait he has drawn. Is it not strange that I should have heard no more of this Sermon?

"I find myself greatly perplexed and doubtful in respect to many of the controverted points of doctrine, i. e. of some of them I think scarcely at all, but concerning some I am anxious; they haunt me perpetually, and, while many think them of such vast moment, I am sometimes afraid it is wrong to keep myself wavering. But yet, is it best to dabble in controversy at present, or let light come in by degrees as I pursue the study of the Scriptures? With respect to one thing, however, the Lord's Supper, I think I ought to be immediately determined. I had by some means, perhaps naturally enough, been led to look on this institution with a superstitious awe, bordering on horror. I thought it was a mystery which it would be criminal to look at familiarly, and to partake of the bread and wine required a degree of sanctity and an indescribable, mysterious something, which only a few favored spirits, not 'touched but rapt,' could attain to. These notions, with a long train of appendages, I got at Beverly, I believe. But, from my own study of the Bible, I have been led to think them erroneous, and that nothing should prevent me, but that I am in duty bound to become a partaker. Will you write me your opinion, and advise me what treatises to read, that will give me most correct views of the subject, its nature, design, and history, and the obligations of those who partake it? Are Clarke's Sermons on this subject to be trusted?

"In this letter I have talked very freely, probably like a novice; but I have two objects in view, (a little distinct from absolute want of information,) which I am unwilling to give up. First, to draw from you all the assistance I can; for what I obtain in this way, I shall prize more than if I obtained it otherwise. Second, to habituate myself to writing seriously, that you may see my manner, and tell me wherein it is faulty and how I may correct it. Not that you are to consider my letters as elaborate essays, for I never write more than one copy; but yet the general character of my style will be visible, and may perhaps afford fair subject of criticism. I know that I am asking what will give you much trouble; but I have been so accustomed to apply to you, and have found you so ready always to assist me, that I have learned to believe you consider it rather a pleasure than a task."

FROM HIS FATHER.

"JUNE 5, 1813.

"I will take up your letter by paragraphs; so that, if you complain of it as desultory, I may be able to throw back the charge of it upon yourself.

"I am glad, then, that you have read Mr. Channing's Sermon. Its impression is such as I should have expected, for I think it one of the happiest efforts of pulpit eloquence. But I do not know exactly what you mean by the cold rationalists, who maintain religion without feeling. Never, perhaps, was a charge more unjustly applied than that usually is. In no sermonizers will you find higher degrees of true warmth, more glowing zeal for truth and virtue, or more ardent piety and benevolence breathed forth, (free, to be sure, from the wildfire of fanaticism, and the consuming flames of bigotry and sectarianism,) than in those whom modern cant stigmatizes as rationalists. The gentleman with whose Sermon you are so justly enraptured, is a striking example. The thing itself which you mean to censure, I most heartily join with you in censuring; but you will find that coldness is not exclusively the attribute of the rational. You will find that the irrational may also be cold and heartless.

"With respect to points of controversy with which you are haunted, it is very natural and very proper that you should wish, and seek, to have your doubts and perplexities removed. But you have very properly expressed the precise course which you now ought to take; 'let light come in by degrees, as you pursue the study of the Scriptures.' A sudden flash may give you what you think to be a distinct view of objects for the moment, but the darkness will be the deeper and more perceptible as soon as it is over. The only light that will be a safe guide to you, will be the slow, gradual, but sure opening of the day.

"I am very glad you have turned your thoughts to the Lord's Supper. I have been hoping, that both you and your sisters would propose the subject to me before this time. I wish you would write to them upon it. I am gratified, too, that by recurring to the best guide on the subject,—the Bible, —the mystery in which you saw the ordinance enveloped, is dissipated. Nothing surely can be more astonishing, or humiliating, than that an institution so perfectly plain and simple, should have been susceptible of such corruption and perversion.

"The best treatises you can read on the subject, are the simple account of its institution by the Evangelists, and Paul's account of it in his Epistle to the Corinthians.

"Dr. Clarke's (I suppose you mean Dr. John, of Boston.) 'History' and 'Design of the Lord's Supper,' I think are perfectly correct, and ought to be highly satisfactory to the inquirer.

"It is a subject on which I think very little light is needed, and long treatises are tedious and useless; what is wanted, is, not more true, but less false light.

"If, when we go to the Bible, we leave behind us our prejudices, false views, the 'mystery we got at Beverly,'—and take our notions from the simple account we there find, we shall be terrified with no spectres, and need no light on the subject. Nor will the ordinance lose any of its interest by becoming more intelligible, and less mysterious and awful.

"You are right in feeling a confidence in my readiness to give you any aid in my power, and in believing that I shall be very far from thinking it a trouble. I am glad to have you write to me on serious subjects, and it gives me pleasure that you treat them seriously. Except the affectation of unnatural and disproportioned seriousness in trifles, nothing can be more offensive than levity on subjects really serious and important. I trust you will carefully avoid, alike from feeling and from principle, both the one and the other.

TO HIS FATHER.

"JUNE 13, 1813.

"In speaking of rationalists, I did not mean to say there were any to whom the censure would apply in its full extent, much less to give all the name, to whom I suppose many would apply it. But I think there is a tendency to that extreme, especially in persons just entering the ministry. They are so afraid of the opposite enthusiasm and superstition, that, in their attempts to avoid it, they fall into an error equally great. While they assert the rights of reason, is there not danger that they will urge them too far, and refuse altogether the exercise of feeling? that they will regard religion too much as a study, something to be thought upon and reasoned about, and in which all feeling should be repressed as leading to deception and error? From trying revelation at the bar of reason, is there not danger of coming at last to make it sole arbiter, and exalting it above the former? And may not a man become at length so completely rational, as to hesitate upon any emotion of gratitude and love, and to inquire, 'Do I not feel too much?' and instead of asking himself, 'Have I sufficient humility and penitence?' to ask, 'Have I not more than I need? Would not less answer the purpose?'. I would not have men give up their reason and become fanatics; but neither do I wish them, on the other hand, to give up feeling. I would let both have their influence, and each act as a check on the other; for I think it is in the proper mixture and regulation of these that the perfection and beauty of religion consists. I do not think our opinions here at all different; but I fancy I can see a danger where you see none. And the reason is, I am at a greater distance from the centre, and hear many observations which never reach you.

"Since writing to you last, I have read Campbell's 'Lectures on Systematic Theology and Pulpit Eloquence.' I do not remember ever to have heard of the book before. I was delighted with it; it has perfectly removed all haste to be satisfied on controversial points, and has completely convinced me in regard to the right way of study, though in truth I had few doubts before. Indeed, it would require all the sound judgment and discretion of Campbell himself to follow his plan perfectly, so as to reap all the advantages of which it is capable; but let every one do it in his measure, and there can be no question of its benefits.

"I have dipped a little into ecclesiastical history, and find it exactly like all others, but a melancholy account of the weakness, folly and contentions of mankind, whose blessings seem only to be exceeded by the abuse of them, and who make themselves miserable in proportion to their means of happiness. Christianity never was purer than at present, since the days of its first professors. I have been taught to believe that the pride of human reason was opposed to its progress, and could not receive its doctrines without corrupting them. But ignorance is as proud as learning, quite as unyielding in support of its opinions, and as great a corrupter of the truth."

In his journal, he enters into the following more extended course of remark, suggested by the perusal of the work of Campbell alluded to in the last letter. It indicates the existence of a state of opinion and feeling on the subject of religion, which was strongly characteristic of him through life.

"Campbell's 'Lectures on Systematic Theology, and Pulpit Eloquence,' I have accidentally met with; and though I do not recollect having heard of them before, I have borrowed them, trusting I should find nothing of this author but what is valuable. Nor have I been disappointed. I have been highly interested and instructed by their perusal, particularly those in which he speaks of the manner in which young men should study, and the course they ought to pursue. Upon which points I was not before perfectly satisfied, but am now. He seems to have marked out with great precision the province of reason, and to have defined with much accuracy its limitations; he neither allows it too much scope, nor too little; he does not exalt it above revelation, but asserts its freedom to declare for itself what revelation is; he sets it above the control of men, but still requires its submission to God. Upon this point I have been not a little jealous. I have been afraid lest men were urging the point unwarrantably far, freeing reason from all restraint and maintaining its all-sufficiency. Now it would require al. the sound judgment and discrimination of Campbell himself, to follow with exactness the path he has recommended, and therefore only few can arrive at the degree of excellence it seems to promise. Still it is apparent that if all would follow it to the utmost of their abilities, with proper seriousness, humility, discretion and perseverance, they might attain much nearer the correct standard than in any other way. But the misfortune is, few have discretion to know and stop at the right point; the ardor of youth urges everything to extremes; and, if freed from all restraint of man, they are apt to become conceited and cold rationalists. Such, I am afraid, is the tendency of our Cambridge students; they study religion too much as a science, too much as a business of mere grammar and lexicon; they seem to regard it as a subject to be reasoned upon, to exercise their ingenuity; and appear almost to forget that it is something to be felt; while they sharpen the wits and inform the head, they are not careful to polish the heart, and rectify the affections. I hope that I say too much, that I express myself too strongly, and charity obliges me to think I do. Yet, I have such a jealousy and dread of this thing, I feel so strongly the danger of this tendency, and believe I have seen so plain indications of what I have mentioned, that I cannot persuade myself I am altogether wrong."

CHAPTER IV.

SECOND YEAR AT EXETER—CONTINUATION OF CORRESPONDENCE WITH HIS FATHER—PROPOSES TO RELINQUISH HIS OFFICE—FIRST APPEARANCE IN THE PULPIT.

1813-14. ÆT. 19-20.

A LONG and severe illness in the family at Cambridge put a stop at this period to all correspondence, except that which related to it; and the following extracts from letters to one of his brothers contain the only accounts of his occupation in the interval.

"JULY 29, 1813.

"I believe I have read and studied a good deal this summer; but, I don't know how it is, I do not feel so much more learned, as I thought I should. What a misfortune it is that the knowledge which appears so vast at a distance, should so dwindle away as you approach it, and shrink to so small a thing as you make it your own. You think, if you could stand on *that* pinnacle of the mountain, you should feel vastly above your present height, and be almost contented with your elevation; but, alas! when you get there, you do not perceive that you are raised, so much still remains above and so little below you."

"OCT. 9, 1813.

"And now allow me to speak of myself. I am studying pretty diligently, but with very little satisfaction; for I find my memory grows weaker every day, and I cannot call to mind, at the end of the week, the contents of the book I read at the beginning. This, however, may be partly fancy; I hope it is, though it is certainly partly true. Let me say at least, (though I suppose I have said it before,) the more I read, the more I discover my own ignorance. The letting knowledge into the mind is like carrying a candle into some vast unexplored cavern; while you stand at the entrance, you do not imagine its depths to be very great, but, as you go forward, it opens, and expands on every side, seeming to increase its dimensions as you proceed, and you are astonished at every step to find yourself still far from the end. And the resemblance holds in yet another respect; as the candle leaves not light in the spots it has passed over, but darkness closes upon them, so the traces of knowledge are erased, and leave no monuments to show that they have been, except, as it were, a few dim candles, stuck here and there upon the sides of the cave."

His original engagement at Exeter expired with the close of the academic year in August, but the mutual satisfaction which existed between him and the government of the institution, rendered his continuance in his office desirable to both parties; and he accordingly decided to remain in it for another year. This year, like the last, furnishes little matter of record, and our account of it must be confined chiefly to selections from his correspondence.

TO HIS FATHER.

"OCT. 16, 1813.

"But a truce with trifling, which perhaps is not very intelligible. I have read the third volume of Michaelis,—not being able to get the first, and not being willing to read the second. I opened the book with great expectations, and was disappointed. I was interested in what he has written concerning a Harmony; but, for the rest, I expected something of more importance and interest than the discussion of dates, and the balancing of probabilities. I was disappointed with Lardner in the same way; and I must freely confess, that I find the reading of this kind of investigation a perfect task. It has already occasioned me several evenings of labor, from which I have only learnt how ingeniously trifling great men may sometimes be; how diligently and artfully they will toil to maintain the certainty of a point, which, common sense at once shows, must always remain doubtful; how they will twist and turn, and even run counter to their own rules, for the sake of establishing one out of fifty suppositions, no one of which can bring more than probability in its support. Beausobre and L'Enfant delighted me; there seems to be nothing unimportant, nothing superfluous or unnecessary, either in matter or words; and everything is so neat, that it engages the attention closely, and may be read without weariness. I have read besides Taylor's 'Scheme,' and Allix, from both which I believe I have learned considerable. Dr. Prideaux is too diffuse, and tells his story most tediously. I have spent some time in composition, and have had one or two fits, more or less severe, of the poetic mania,—from which, however, I have since recovered, and am now perfectly well."

FROM HIS FATHER.

"Oct. 20, 1813.

"You will find the first volume of Michaelis more interesting; but you must not expect entertainment, in the common sense of the word, in dry criticism. The second volume, it seems, was too forbidding for you to look into;—well, it is not a book to be read, but consulted, and at the proper time you will look even into that volume with no small interest.

"Taylor and Allix were well worth your reading. Taylor must also be *studied;* but, if you have learnt *much* from Allix, you have probably something to unlearn. He has some pleasant whims,—but they are whims. Some of his opinions, had he lived at the present day, he would not have held. It may be said of him, as Robinson said of Calvin; 'He knew not all things, and had he lived later, would have been as ready to receive further improvements, as he was to adopt those of the day in which he did live.' Prideaux is diffuse,—'tedious,' if you please,—but I hardly know where you find more rare and useful information within the same compass, than in his volumes.

"I am glad you have got well of the poetic mania; and that you have exercised yourself some in sober prose. By all means practise yourself in writing. If you reluct, bring yourself down to it by resolute self-command.

"You seem not to have heard of *the book* * which engages all the attention here at present;—Mr. English's apology for leaving his profession. You will have heard of it, however, before you receive this,—for it will pass like wildfire through the country; and like that too it will flash, and crackle, and sparkle, and dazzle, and amaze for a moment, and then go out, or be put out, and all will be as quiet as before; and, as soon as the first meteoric effect is over, our eyes will recover themselves, and we shall see things as clearly, and in the same light, as if nothing had taken place.

"I shall be anxious to hear how the book strikes you and others, before its *natural history* is made known. *This* will occasion you as much surprise at least as the book itself."

* The *book* here alluded to was, "The Grounds of Christianity examined by comparing the New Testament with the Old; by George B. English." Mr. English had studied divinity at Cambridge, and had been for a short time a preacher. The materials, and much of the detail of his work, were drawn from English deistical writers of the last century. It excited much attention for a time, but was speedily forgotten. It was answered briefly by Mr. Cary, colleague pastor with Dr. Freeman, of the Stone Chapel, and more fully by Mr. Everett, at that time minister of the Church in Brattle Square.

TO HIS FATHER.

"Oct. 26, 1813.

"I see you are not altogether pleased with the remarks I made on my reading. They were too short to be perfectly correct, and written in too much haste to give exactly the impression I intended. They conveyed the idea that I am squeamish, difficult in my reading, and so fond of what is light and entertaining, as to be disgusted with whatever is not of this character. You did not say so much, but I fancied I could see it implied. I hope it is not exactly true; certainly I am not such a simpleton as to expect entertainment merely in the study I am pursuing; I know that much diligent and painful application must be my lot. When I say that Michaelis is dry, and Prideaux diffuse, I do not subtract one particle from the excellency of either, nor do I refuse to benefit myself by the information they contain. I only mention one of the most obvious qualities of each; and, though I characterize them by their faults rather than by their merits, it is so common a fault with young critics, that I hope it may be forgiven.

"I saw that Allix was whimsical, but I should not have supposed that his book contained any very great errors to be guarded against. I thought his whims very innocent; but, if they contain any hidden poison, I wish it might be pointed out to me.

"I don't know what to think of the subject of the typical application of the Old Testament. It seems there must be such a thing, but I do not understand what is meant by it. Ought we to say that the tabernacle was built in order to prefigure the church, or is it only referred to as an apt comparison? Was Jonah three days and nights in the whale's belly *because* the Messiah was to be so long in the earth, or did Christ, finding the fact to be so, only allude to it by way of similitude? And so of other instances. There seems to be a difficulty of the same kind here, as in the question of the divine prescience, where we may either say, This event happened *because* God foreknew it, or God foreknew it *because* it was to happen. If we admit any actions in the Jewish commonwealth to be pre-significant, there seems to be no reason why *all* should not be; for something must have happened under the Christian dispensation, to which they may all be compared."

FROM HIS FATHER.

"Nov. 5, 1813.

"I must have expressed myself differently from what I intended, for you to infer any dissatisfaction with your remarks on your reading. But I think you will find that your imagination, or perhaps conscience, had more to do, than your logic, in drawing the inference."

FROM HIS FATHER.

"Jan. 21, 1814.

"It is a pretty important part of your preparation for your profession, to learn to write sermons easily and well. I will suggest for your consideration, and recommend to your trial, what occurs to me as the *best* course to be pursued for that purpose; at least, a good one. I would begin by reading some of the best sermons, and making abstracts of them into a book kept for that purpose. This I would do once or twice a week, or oftener, with great care. After practising this for some time, and on several authors, I would choose subjects, and form original plans of discourses upon the several models of those of which I had taken abstracts.

"By comparing abstracts thus faithfully made with your own original schemes, you would be able to make a pretty just estimate of their value, and at the same time be learning the best method of arranging and disposing the materials of a sermon; what formal divisions to make, and what implied ones. Another advantage you would gain also; that of diversifying your manner of treating subjects, which would be the consequence of practising on different authors. Besides, these abstracts would always be valuable, as indexes to bring to your recollection important thoughts and views on interesting subjects; and your own original plans would be a valuable resource to repair to whenever you should have occasion to complete a discourse on any of the subjects of them.

"I think the following a good plan of an abstract:

"1. Take down the general heads of the discourse, by marking the numbers in the middle of the page.

"2. The particular heads, by marking them in the side margin.

"3. As many particular thoughts under each as you choose, marking and numbering them half an inch forward in the line, or against the head to which they belong, inclosed by a brace.

"*Specimen.*

"Rom. xiv. 29.—'Let us, therefore, follow after the things which make for peace.'

I.

"Consider what is due from us to the *church* in order to peace.

"1. Every member of the church is bound to external communion with it.

"2. Every member is bound to join in communion with the church *established* where he lives, if the terms of communion be lawful.

"3. Every member is obliged to submit to all the laws and constitutions of the church.

{ "1. As to the orderly performance of worship.
{ "2. As to the maintaining of peace and unity.

"4. Nothing but unlawful terms of communion can justify a separation.

"5. Hence, neither *unscriptural impositions*,—nor *errors*, nor *corruptions* in doctrine or practice, while *suffered* only, not *imposed*,—nor, lastly, the pretence of *better edification*, can justify separation.

II.

"Consider what is due from us to *particular Christians* in order to peace.

"1. In matters of opinion to give every man leave to judge for himself.

"2. To lay aside all prejudice in the search after truth.

"3. Not to quarrel about words.

"4. Not to charge men with all the *consequences* deducible from their opinions.

"5. To abstract men's persons from their opinions.

"6. That we vigorously pursue holiness.

III.

"Motives to the duty laid down.

"1. From the nature of our religion.

"2. From the precepts of Scripture.

"3. From the unreasonableness of our differences.

"4. From their ill consequences.
- 1. To virtue.
- 2. To the civil state.
- 3. Christianity.
- 4. The Protestant religion.

"You may thus have in a very small compass, to be seen at a single glance, what will bring to your recollection all you wish to remember of a sermon.

"I have given this example, not for the sentiment,—which, perhaps, is not exactly correct in every respect, though it is in the main,—but because I had the analysis ready prepared, and it is a good example of the manner."

The occasion of the last letter, or what suggested it, does not appear. The plan here laid down was that which my brother adopted and essentially followed through life. Probably at this period it had considerable influence in directing his attention to the advantages of a clear method in the writing of sermons, and of acquiring a habit of systematically arranging his thoughts when composing them. This mode of procedure became also his usual practice with regard to everything he wrote. He seldom began a composition of any importance with a merely general idea of what he meant to say, and of the order in which he was to say it. He endeavored to see his way through his subject before he began to write, and sketched out very distinctly the larger divisions, and frequently the subdivisions, and even hints of particular thoughts and illustrations. It was his habit, also, whenever his attention was directed to a subject with especial interest, to give a body and form to his thoughts by laying them out in an orderly manner, as if he were about to write upon it at length. This contributed, unquestionably, very much to give clearness, unity, and due proportion of parts to his writings, although their actual divisions were not always apparent; as the skeleton gives stability and symmetry to the fabric of the body, but does not deform it by thrusting its rough and ungainly projections above the surface.

TO HIS FATHER.

"Jan. 29, 1814.

"I like the plan you sent me very much, and I think I shall undoubtedly make it useful. From reading a sermon of Blair's to-day, I find, however, it will require more attention and judgment than I at first anticipated. Although he has regularly divided his discourse into its parts, a much more complete and careful division would be necessary to a proper sketch of its matter and design; and it is a business of no small nicety to separate the leading ideas, and state them in language so accurate and comprehensive as to place the full scope in a clear view before you. Much doubtless will be learnt by practice;

and I hope to acquire a facility of analysis, which will be of no small service to me, and of some advantage in all my reading and studies; as it will give a habit of reading with a particular attention to the main design, and to the manner in which all the parts are made subservient to it. There are many sermons, however, and probably not a few of the best, which were written without any preconcerted plan, and which it would be next to impossible to divide into parts as you recommend. They are rather general and random, though fine, remarks on some given subject, (like Miss H. More's 'Practical Piety,') of which, as they seem to aim at no given end, so we cannot discover the method or order, or discern on what principle their succession depends. But you would probably say, these are no models; and, if so, I need not ask what I intended, how I should manage to make a sketch of them.

"You make the *plan* of a discourse of more consequence than I thought was done by any one; and, from the manner in which you speak, one would be apt to imagine that the effect of a sermon depends more upon the arrangement of its parts, than the care and force with which those parts are written. In giving rules for a composition which is required to be critically perfect, this is certainly of the highest importance; but is a sermon such? Does not more of its effect depend on the skill with which any topic is wrought up, on striking passages, than on the general connexion of the whole? True, even allowing this, a fine passage will fail of its effect, if its connexion and dependence on the main subject be not discernible. But I mean, if we lay out the plan, and arrange the ideas so thoroughly before we write the parts, shall we not leave too little room for that free play and range of thought and imagination, which give a glow and fascination that nothing else can give? Do we not cramp and confine the mind too much by determining its course and limiting its excursions so exactly? and, especially, will not that warmth and animation be wanting, which we always find greatest when we write on a subject fresh and newly started in the mind? I suppose, however, that here you would give, and I should certainly take, a discretionary power of making alterations in the given plan, whenever, in the warmth of composition, the course of thought took an unexpected turn, and led to pertinent discussions which had not been foreseen. Surely, however good the original plan, a part of it should be sacrificed in such a case; and the sacrifice would be abundantly compensated by the chance of giving something new and interesting, instead of what would probably be written in a dry and lifeless manner, because written by force, and by opposing the natural current of ideas.

"Upon looking over what I have written, I find I have tried to make some small objection to your scheme, or to point out some imperfection in it, but without success; and, if I have made myself intelligible, I believe I have said nothing which you will not immediately admit, or indeed which is not a truism, necessarily implied in what you wrote."

TO HIS BROTHER JOHN.

"FEB. 6, 1814.

"Dr. Spring preached here last Sunday; and, as I may not have an opportunity again, I will give you a specimen of his discourse. Perhaps, said he, the men of the world cannot conceive of a parent's feeling perfectly satisfied (that was the expression) at the sight of his son suspended from the gallows as a punishment for his crimes,—but so the Christian is; and he intimated, that he was not only so, but highly pleased. He added, that the sight of sinners in torment was unquestionably to be one source of the happiness of good men in another life. This, one of his hearers said, was making you very amiable saints."

TO THE SAME.

"FEB. 12, 1814.

"I believe I wrote you a shabby letter last week; I hope never to do so again. I wish I could have received an answer before now; but, as you have not seen fit to gratify me, I sit down to scrawl a little against time of need. One never feels so much the need of a friend's letters, or so much feels a disposition to write to a friend, as when one is in a serious mood, bordering a little perhaps on the melancholy,—or, at least, more than usually troubled with thought and reflection. I have been just so for a few days, and have longed if possible to pour myself out to you. I have been thinking of my profession, musing upon its vast importance and tremendous responsibility, and, above all, its difficulties, which seem to increase in number and magnitude the nearer I survey it. Not that I have ever been thoughtless or indifferent to these things; but you know there are seasons, when the mind acts with more than wonted vigor, and the feelings are impressed with unusual force; when the soul seems to turn back into itself, and become the object of its own contemplations. O! there is a happiness in such periods, which no words can express; and, though a mind that should be constantly, unceasingly in such a frame, would unfit the man for the active exertions which life requires, yet such a season occasionally returning is invaluable; the soul seems to come from it cleansed and purified, with all its worldly contamination removed, and with spirits fresh and wholesome.

"I have been led into this frame by reading a beautiful biography of Spencer, an English clergyman; the effect of which was probably heightened at this time by the interest I have been taking in Everett's ordination. It would be impossible to contemplate two such men, of my own age, entering the ministry, without feeling deeply affected, and having the mind filled with an awful enthusiasm. Spencer was one of the wonders of the age. From his very childhood he had had a strong attachment for the ministry, and loved nothing so much as preachers and preaching. He preached first at the age of seventeen, and was settled at Liverpool at twenty; he died suddenly about three months after his ordination. He was an enthusiast of the first and purest order. His whole soul, all his powers of intellect and feeling, were devoted entirely to his profession; these gave him a wonderful success and unbounded popularity; perhaps not even Whitefield was more eagerly sought after. He preached without notes, and his discourses were usually upwards of an hour in length. But you must get the book and read for yourself; and, though I cannot expect you to feel as I have done, I think your sober judgment must concur with me in my admiration, if not in its degree. So pure, so interesting a character, of such strict propriety and correctness, and so humble with all its greatness, I never heard of; and my first wish is, that I may be like him, as far as is possible, in everything that is pure, lovely, and of good report. Some things there are, indeed, which I would not wish to follow; still, not to long for his eminent excellences would betray a want of feeling and goodness. The secret of his eloquence undoubtedly lay in his enthusiasm, understanding the word in a good sense; and that none can hope to rival, who have not a heart as finely framed as his,—the same warmth, ardor, and sensibility. Much, too, of his animation and effect must be attributed to his extempore speaking, which gives a liveliness, an energy, a glow to eloquence, that is not otherwise attained.

"I have really begun to consider seriously, whether I shall not attempt learning the art. I do not mean for constant practice; but some subjects may be much better treated by extempore discourse than by written; and much of the illustration and exhortation of every sermon might be left for the management of the moment. It is unquestionable, that there is a life, a soul, as it were, transfused into unpremeditated expressions, which appeals with far greater force to the sympathy of hearers, than anything which can be written. There is a *je ne sais quoi* in the countenance, the tones of voice, the gesture, which goes directly to the heart, and which you in vain try to give to a written production. Animated declamation, even if it be rather flat sense, will be more effectual, than the most elaborate composition read in the usual way; and accordingly we find, that the sermons of celebrated extempore preachers are scarcely worth reading. Dugald Stewart, in his 'Essays,' intimates, you may remember, that the art may be acquired by any one; and, if I could obtain it, what a saving of time there would be!

"I have been engaged for a few evenings in writing a discourse on Profanity, to read in the Academy to-morrow. Wish me success."

FROM HIS FATHER.

"Feb. 28, 1814.

"I read your letter to John, which he received last week; and, though neither enthusiasm, nor the love of enthusiasm, is a very distinguishing trait in my character, I am not displeased to see some of it in you. It is of use to have such an example presented to excite emulation, as that which you meet with in the life of Spencer; still, however, they are to be contemplated and followed with caution. Every real excellence is not to be attempted by every person; and it is neither a reproach, nor ought it to be a discouragement, to any one, that in some very peculiar and exalted character there are traits to which he cannot aspire. One, who has quickness of mind and self-possession enough for the purpose, may doubtless become a more popular speaker without writing than with; but I much doubt, whether any man could become so useful a minister. And you are totally mistaken in the imagination, that time would be saved except by the *loss* of that which were more than an equivalent. He who aspires to a respectable kind of popularity by extempore preaching, must not be sparing in labor to prepare himself for it. Not only must his *general* cultivation and *particular* preparation be great; he must also be always wrought up at the time of appearing in public to a high degree of excitement. Besides, the best of what are pressed upon the world for extempore effusions, are in a great degree, if not wholly, *memoriter* productions.

"I would not discourage, by any means, the cultivation of the talent for extempore speaking; it is of great importance to exalt it to as high perfection as you are capable of; and it is doubtless too much neglected. But, as far as my observation has extended, I should think that the attainment of any considerable degree of excellence or usefulness in it could not be general or very common.

"Looking over the first part of this letter, I find it to be not exactly what I intended. It is too general, vague, indefinite. It may, however, do for hints; and you will discriminate, where I have not. Continue to indulge and cherish the glow of virtuous feeling; there is no danger from it where the intellect is also cultivated *pari passu*. If your understanding is enlightened, there is no danger of feeling too much."

The person of whom the following letter contains a notice, was a son of Dr. Abbot, the Principal of the Academy, a young man of rare qualifications for his profession, and one who filled, whilst he lived, a large place in the hopes of the religious community. Of my brother's subsequent intimacy with him, and the very high regard in which he always held him, there will be occasion to speak hereafter.

TO HIS FATHER.

"FEB. 28, 1814.

"I expect to send this letter by Mr. J. E. Abbot. He preached here on Sunday, and gave, I believe, universal pleasure. His sermons glowed with the amiableness of his disposition, and all the pure feelings of his heart. They rather produced a general tranquillity of feeling than any distinct impression; they soothed and calmed the mind into a placid, serene temper; there was nothing to excite or exhilarate. He appears to have studied simplicity, and carefully avoids all ambitious display. He delights to speak of the meek, peaceable character of the gospel; he dwells much upon the characters of God and the Saviour; he returns to them often, and seems loath to quit them. To such discourses his manner is not ill-fitted; the tones of his voice are interesting, and keep the attention alive, and they do not require much *energy* in the delivery. Lamson has suggested a reason why they did not give more an impression of talents; they speak so much of what is amiable and lovely, that the mind of the hearer is tranquillized, and so totally dissolved in the gentle feelings he excites, that everything exterior is forgotten, and he does not remember to criticise or admire. This, I think, is a true account of the matter; and it gives a pleasing specimen of Mr. L.'s talent of criticism and philosophical investigation.

"I am engaged now, as I suppose you know, in Ecclesiastical History. I have read and pretty carefully studied two volumes of Mosheim, and all Gregory. But I find, that, after all the labor I have spent, upon what has certainly no very great charms of interest, I must expect to retain but very little of it; it slips from the memory almost as soon as it enters, and I find myself as unknowing as before. I am somewhat comforted for this, from hearing J. Abbot make the same remark with respect to himself. It is said somewhere, that things enter and are retained in the memory by means of the imagination. If this be true, it will account for the slippery nature of church history. There is nothing to *stick* to the fancy, —no entertainment,—no interest. Some strange notions and practices, indeed, excite our *curiosity;* but, when that is gratified, they pass through the mind and are forgotten. Most of the other matters excite only *disgust*, which the memory is not willing to nourish and keep alive. Or, if some few interest the feelings, the train of events is so short, that we have but little aid from association, and the impression is only weak and transient. All I hope, is to have a faint, glimmering view of the outline of events, and here and there an isolated fact. Of the first four centuries I have endeavored to treasure up the history of opinions, and eminent men, and the progress of corruption; but the following ages, as they passed in darkness, I am willing should remain so. It is too late to change their complexion; and the little light we can throw upon them from this distance, serves only to make their darkness visible.

"Besides this, my reading has been, some in the Old Testament; some in the Greek New, (of which I never condescended to peruse the translation, for it passes through my mind with less impression, and in it I do not so readily and clearly discover the force of reasoning, &c.); two volumes, 12mo.; besides other miscellaneous. I have copied sketches of sermons, as you recommended, and written one. Thus you have the amount of my labor."

FROM HIS FATHER.

"FEB. 1814.

"I have not yet heard Mr. John E. Abbot preach, but have heard highly favorable reports from those who have. He is spoken of as I should expect, as very interesting and impressive. You will have the advantage of entering into life with a set of young men of your own standing, in the same profession which you have chosen, who will carry with them as much talents, learning, piety, study, respectability of character, and resolution to do good in the world,—I will venture to say,—as ever came on the stage in this country at one time. The present prevailing taste in students for the critical study of the Scriptures will constitute an era in the theological character of our ministers; it will continue and gradually produce great changes,—I hope, more just views, and at the same time more of the Christian temper. I hope, that what constitutes true liberality will be better understood and better practised, that the style of preaching will be more scriptural, serious, practical, and that, the true nature and design of the gospel being better understood, they will be kept more constantly in view. You have great excitements to exertion, and your mind I trust is taking a right direction."

TO HIS SISTER.

"FEB. 23, 1814.

"DEAR HARRIET,

"I had a letter from John last week, in which he told me that he had been to Hingham, and had had a very pleasant visit. He told me, too, how pleasantly you were situated, and how happy you seemed to be. You may be sure I was very glad to hear this; for I take a deep interest in your welfare, and in whatever is preparing you to be a useful, amiable woman. No doubt, you feel thankful, as you ought, for the blessings which surround you, and are sensible of your obligations to improve your great privileges. Your advantages for improvement are very great; and, as they are made easy and pleasant to you, you ought to use the utmost diligence and exertion to make the most of the golden opportunity; the season of youth will not last forever; and middle life and old age can neither be happy nor respectable, unless youth is improved. When you grow older, you will have less time to devote to the cultivation of your mind; but you will have a good deal of time for thought and reflection, in which the ideas and knowledge you acquired in youth will be vastly important to you; and, if you have not a good deal laid up beforehand, how barren will be your mind, how unprofitable your meditations! Besides, as you will feel the want of information, both to supply you with matter for thought, and for conversation, you will look back with exceeding remorse and sorrow on the valuable moments you wasted in youth; and you will wish that you could live them over again, that you might spend them better. Improve, then, every privilege you enjoy; collect now a fund of useful knowledge and innocent amusement, which may remain in your memory, and entertain you in future times. But above all, my dear girl, remember how valuable and necessary is a good, pleasant, amiable temper. Be careful to form good habits, and so obtain a good character. You have excellent models around you;—imitate them in everything that is pure and lovely. If you see anything in any of your companions particularly agreeable and lovely, try to copy it. And, if you find anything disagreeable, examine whether there be not something like it in yourself, and correct and avoid it for the future. In this way, you will become as amiable and lovely as any one could desire. And especially never forget your Bible and your God; you know your business is as much to prepare yourself for another world, as to become useful in this."

Toward the close of the second term of this year, he became strongly desirous of relinquishing his connexion with the Academy and returning to Cambridge.

TO HIS FATHER.

"April 1, 1814.

"I believe I have hinted to you, that I begin to be weary of Exeter. I wish now to let you know exactly how matters stand; for it is my settled determination, if possible, to throw up my connexions at the end of this term, to retire from my elevated station to the *sober tranquillity of private life.* I must have very much mistaken my talents, if ever I imagined myself fit for an instructor. I have expressed my doubts to you before, particularly once, I recollect, during the last vacation. I have taken particular pains to examine myself this term; to compare what I do with what I think I ought to do; to compare the progress of my classes with those taught by the Preceptor, and my discipline with his; the result is little to my honor, and still less to my satisfaction. I am convinced I have but little, scarcely any, faculty of teaching; that I am a real injury to the Academy, as I occupy the place of another, whose endeavors would be more successful and useful, if not more faithful and constant. I do not accuse myself of want of fidelity; I believe the deficiency is in the original cast of my character; which I have endeavored in vain to remedy. I have not energy or uniformity enough for my station, and I have been unable to obtain them. Can I then conscientiously keep a place, the duties of which I am unable to perform? Ought I not immediately to leave a situation in which I believe myself to be doing hurt rather than good? Ought I to encumber an office which perhaps many a deserving young man is ready to fill, who needs its profits, and is competent to its duties? I expected to improve, or I would not have engaged myself for another year. Of improvement, I have given up even the most distant hope; and I feel ashamed to meet Dr. Abbot, and live so kindly and familiarly with him, while I am conscious how ill I am serving him.

"But, besides this, I feel anxious to progress in my profession, and I feel that I am losing time here. To be sure, I am young enough to delay yet for some time; and were I satisfied with my doings here, I should think nothing of this; because I know the inconvenience you must suffer from my being with you, and dependent on you for support. But it is natural that I should wish to commence that which is to be my pursuit through life. It is plain that little time can be given to my studies here. Seven hours in the Academy are seven hours of severe mental toil, and require a proportionate relaxation. This leaves not much to myself. If I apply myself two evenings successively without interruption, I become harassed and debilitated, unfit to labor either at home or in school. Hence, I *must* pass part of every evening abroad, and accidental circumstances will not unfrequently make a whole evening necessary. This makes my mind giddy, unsettles it, deranges its ideas; and so, much of the profit of study is lost. Deduct all this, and how much will remain for steady application?

"I think, too, my habits of study have been injured from another cause. In the daily routine of business, one object follows another in quick succession. I am now reading of the sack of Troy, now a chapter of the New Testament, and now one of Esop's Fables; and besides this constant change of the attention from one object to another, it is momentarily called off to the persons and things around me; thus it is in a perpetual state of fluctuation, and cannot fix for any length of time upon any one thing. In this way I find a habit of mind has been formed; for I cannot without the greatest effort confine my attention, when I am studying, to any single subject. I soon grow weary, and am compelled to change my occupation frequently; and, even during the little time I am able to devote to the same subject, I am perpetually called away by trifles, and have my train of ideas broken and scattered by the most unimportant accident. This, to a student, is a great evil; for that man only can make progress and rise to eminence who has his mind perfectly under his control, and can at any time muster its scattered powers, and direct its efforts without interruption or weariness to whatever subject he pleases. Without this command of the thoughts, this power of continued attention, his mind must bear a trifling character, and be incapable of extraordinary exertion, or of producing great effects.

"E—— has preached here, and left those feelings behind him which might have been expected. His eloquence completely entranced his audience; in the forenoon he drew tears from many an eye, and in the afternoon he led us as one man on a crusade. Still they think he is too rich for common use, and would prefer A——. Miss E—— gives as a reason for this preference: 'One seems more like a dying man speaking to dying men; the other, like some superior intelligence, discoursing to mortals of what they ought to feel and know, but as if himself were too far exalted to require such feelings or such knowledge.'

"One copy of Buckminster's 'Sermons' has been received in town. Dr. Abbot expressed the most unbounded admiration. They were read aloud to a number of persons, who were almost silent in their praise, because they could find no words to express themselves."

FROM HIS FATHER.

"April 9, 1814.

"Your letter, my dear Henry, which I have just now received from the office, is written with so much attention, care, and apparent deliberation, that I am precluded from asking you, whether it was not the dictate of some momentary feeling, and the effect of something incidental. It seems to express a deliberate determination, and I must so consider it. Nor will it probably be to any purpose, as I am entirely unacquainted with the *particulars* which have given the impressions under which you have come to your present decision, to say anything on the probability, that you may have allowed your feelings too much to influence your judgment, and a morbid irritability to give you more sombre views and gloomy feelings than are just and reasonable.

"But, previous to any arrangements on the subject, it will be proper for you, if you have not already done it,—not *proper* merely, but *indispensable*,—to consult Dr. Abbot; to know his wishes; to open your mind as freely and fully to him on the subject as you have done to me; to be kept back from it by no feelings of reserve, or timidity, or false shame. But you will recollect, that you have no right to take into the account the consideration of your own studies. If you find that Dr. Abbot is satisfied with your services, is not willing to have you leave the Academy till the expiration of your engagement, or is not able to procure a supply for your place with which he is satisfied; you have no right to wish to relinquish your engagement.

"But, if you find that it is perfectly agreeable to Dr. Abbot, that a supply can be procured entirely to his satisfaction, and that no injury or disappointment accrue, I shall not say a word to prevent your taking the course you wish. You are a better judge than it is possible for me to be, what the exigencies of the case require, or will justify. If it is your deliberate opinion, that you have not succeeded well as an instructor, and that your services are not useful, and you find that better can be rendered by some other person, you must be extremely careful not to add to the chagrin you naturally feel in not equalling your wishes, and satisfying your own expectations, by exposing yourself to the charge of anything dishonorable in your manner of leaving your employment.

"I will further suggest to you to consider, how far your impatience to be engaged in the study of your profession may be the foundation of your self-dissatisfaction,—or serve to increase it, and to make you restless in performing your duty, impatient to get away from it, and dissatisfied with your success to an unreasonable degree. I hope you will carefully probe your motives to the very bottom; and, by all means take no step that will be unhandsome as respects Dr. Abbot, to whom you owe and feel so much respect, attachment and gratitude."

TO HIS FATHER.

"APRIL 14, 1814.

"The general purport of your letter is exactly what I had anticipated, that is, so much as relates to the propriety of my leaving Exeter, if circumstances are as I stated them. I was pleased to find, too, that the course you say I ought to have taken is that precisely which I have taken. I conversed with

Dr. Abbot some weeks ago. He said I must not be discouraged,—I succeeded as well as young men in general. He had hoped I should stay another year; it would be difficult to supply my place at this season, and I certainly would not leave him destitute. When I urged the subject, he said 'We will talk of it some other time;' and here the matter has rested. Some particular expressions he used were flattering to me; but it was evident from the general course of his remarks, that he was no less disappointed than myself with the result of this second year's experiment. I shall speak to him again to-morrow, and will let you know the issue.

"The resolution I have taken is nothing sudden; it has been some time forming, and I have considered it on every side. A man does not readily fall into a belief of his own incompetency; it must have been forced strongly on my notice, or I should not have seen it. I have examined my motives, I trust, faithfully; and though I have perhaps a little impatience to answer for, yet I am convinced they are substantially such as I have stated them. I regret very much that there is nobody in or near Cambridge who could take my place; for, without a successor, I should be compelled to remain, let who would object and be dissatisfied.

"April 15. I have seen Dr. Abbot again; he seems unwilling to have the subject mentioned, and is decidedly against my leaving him. He seemed glad when I told him that nobody could be procured at Cambridge, though, if there could be, he would have exchanged me for him. So that, if nobody springs up from some other quarter, I am inevitably fixed here for the summer,—doomed to perpetual anxiety, and disappointment and chagrin. However, I must make it an occasion of moral discipline; and instead of brooding upon it with gloom and sullenness, to the injury of my temper, I must try to make myself better by it; and if I can succeed in subduing all impatience, and becoming quite content, I shall think I may be so in almost any state. I shall not probably write again, as the term is near its close. In the vacation, I will tell you what I have done, and what I have left undone; how much time I have spent profitably, and how much idled and trifled away. And I shall idle away the vacation, except what time I spend talking with you,—for I am jaded out; three weeks' romping will be hardly enough to make me a man again.

"I believe I have nothing to say more, except to give my love to all. Mr. Buckminster's 'Sermons' are read here with enthusiasm. For my own part, I prefer them much to any others I have read. In the first place they contain a vast deal of matter; the compression is astonishing; there is not a word which has not its weight, nor a sentence which does not bear directly on the subject. Everything is to the purpose, and everything is said exactly as you want it. And, withal, they have all the impressiveness and animation that will not allow the attention to flag, which arise from true eloquence."

Here the matter rested. No further attempt was made to procure any one in his place. He spent the vacation in relaxation at home and in visiting some relations in the District of Maine, and returned to his duties in an improved state of mind and body. There is little doubt that indisposition, induced by the exhausting nature of his occupations, something of the same state of health, as that from which he afterwards suffered so much under the operation of similar causes, had induced that morbid view of his situation which seems to have so strongly possessed him. The manner in which he writes after returning to Exeter, at the beginning of the next term, shows plainly enough that no other explanation is needed.

TO HIS BROTHER JOHN.

"JUNE 4, 1814.

"The exercise I took in the vacation has done me a vast deal of good. It has recruited my strength and spirits, restored the tone and vigor of my mind, expelled the blue devils, and given to nymph Cheerfulness her rightful authority. Everything around me is smiling and propitious. The fair month of May, indeed, as you observe, has been in a wayward humor, and treated us most foully, but our academic term has commenced with most propitious smiles. The Preceptor's first act was to dismiss one of the irregulars, and protest most solemnly against the smallest disorder, the slightest infringement of the strictest discipline. We have enjoyed a perfect calm ever since, which promises to be lasting; and there seems, besides, to be an unusual disposition to studiousness, as well as regularity. My own studies, I believe, go on as well as can be expected. I have accomplished a good deal, as I always can at the beginning of a term, but I grow capable of less and less as it draws to a close. Mr. Hildreth is to supply for a few Sabbaths at Portsmouth, and I have engaged to read in his place during his absence. I don't know whether this is a perfectly regular and proper step, but I was earnestly requested to do it. Mr. Whitman had done it before, and I thought it would be of service to me, as undoubtedly it will be in many important respects."

He accordingly officiated for several Sundays in the place of Mr. Hildreth, who was one of his fellow-instructors in the Academy. The following letters furnish a sufficient account of the circumstances under which he thus, for the first time, appeared in the pulpit, of the degree of success which attended the attempt, and of the feelings which he experienced in connexion with it.

TO HIS FATHER.

"JUNE 29, 1814.

"I do not know what you will say to my entering the pulpit in this way; I was in hope to have had a word from you about it before this. For my own part, I confess, however, that I had no hesitation on the subject, whether right or wrong I cannot tell; but in truth I have always had a strong inclination, it might very well be called an innate propensity, to preach, for I do not know whence it arose; and I seized this opportunity, more, perhaps, from a desire to gratify my favorite wish, than from any very distinct reasons of any kind. I have made the experiment, and I think some good will result from it. That which regards my preparation for a public speaker, is very obvious, and I am glad to find, that I can speak so loud with so little fatigue. Its inward effects on my own mind and heart are more important and more doubtful. I am sorry I cannot perceive all I wished and hoped. One valuable piece of self-knowledge, however, I have had abundantly and mournfully confirmed, that my ruling passion is the love of praise, and that it will require the utmost vigilance and most constant exertions to prevent my being made the slave of vanity, and doing all things to be seen of men. It would be melancholy, indeed, if I should go through life preaching Christ for my own sake, and quite as attentive to my reputation as to that of the gospel, turning the pulpit into a stage from which to display myself to the world. I try to speak with as much openness as possible to you, as, if it is a case which admits of it, I wish your advice.

"I have read one sermon from Sherlock, four from Porteus, and one of his lectures (from the pulpit, I mean.) I had never seen Porteus before; I admire them very much; they are sensible, and pious, and eloquent, in everything exactly to my taste, except that there is a want of distinctness in the divisions of his discourses. Sherlock's are very fine. I think they contain a great deal of valuable good sense, and might many of them be studied to great advantage. They are, indeed, much better suited to the closet than the desk; not half of what is valuable can be carried away from a single reading; and I think, or it may be the fault of my own dulness, that he has some obscurity in his arrangement and way of treating a subject, though he pretends to be very methodical; and he takes frequently so little pains to show us the connexion between the commencement of one paragraph and the close of the preceding, or sometimes how a whole paragraph has *any* bearing on the subject, that the reader is often obliged to stop, and ponder, and make from his own reflections a link, which the writer was too proud to furnish. Dr. Butler would have admired this, if we may judge by his preface; but it does not at all please us smaller heads of modern growth.

"I must confess, Tillotson disappointed me; not but that he has a great deal of piety and good sense, but there is a smaller fund of the latter than I expected; he is quaint, and he strings his good remarks together so loosely and carelessly that they lose half their beauty and attraction from the awkward position in which he places them. I believe I have heard him praised for a simple style, but he wants compactness and neatness exceedingly.

"Perhaps you will say my remarks are not very important, and are too much employed on the externals, the mere dress of thought. I have not, however, passed lightly over the matter, but have endeavored to appreciate it as I ought. But the more I read, the more I am convinced of the necessity of arranging thoughts properly, if we would have them attractive and forcible; and, as L—— has taught me that a man's manner of writing may be generally considered as a pattern of his manner of thinking, and that whatever looseness, incorrectness, &c., we find in the former, has its origin in the latter, I attend to this subject principally with a view to learn how thoughts should be managed and arranged, to learn what faults are to be avoided, and what excellences imitated, in marshalling and stationing ideas. Am I intelligible? It is with this intention of improving myself in what I now consider a very important point, that I make criticisms of this kind. I could wish to divide and arrange a discourse as neatly as Blair or Buckminster; I think here they excel. Then, if I were a city preacher, I should wish to write it like Porteus; if a country preacher, like the sermons in 'The Christian Observer,' with one more degree of animation. Blair's style would not do, for he is too moderate, and has too much sameness; nor Buckminster's, for it is too finished.

"However, after all, if a man has a clear head and a good heart, he will do well enough without troubling himself about models, much better than he can ever do by the latter alone, if he wants the former, or either of the former. Indeed, it is nothing but the lamentable fastidiousness of taste produced by learning and refinement, which makes this study and artifice at all necessary. A sermon in a barn extempore, from a man who never read anything but his Bible and Psalm Book, but who speaks in earnest, and because he feels, will have more effect on more persons, will give rise to more good and pious feelings and actions, than the most eloquent and finished harangue that was ever penned. Still I would not have all preachers made on this model; the learned and refined must have preachers suited to them, as well as the more rude and simple; they cannot, both classes, drink religion from the same vessels, though they may draw it from the same fountain; and, perhaps, as he is the more excellent artist who makes glass tumblers for the rich, than he who makes wooden bowls for the poor, so he is the more commendable and praiseworthy, who can recommend religion to the higher classes in such a way as to influence their consciences and lives."

FROM HIS FATHER.

"JULY 1, 1814.

"I received, yesterday, your letter of no date, and received, as I always do from your letters, a great deal of satisfaction from its contents. As you are capable of perceiving the foible by which you are endangered, and of feeling the necessity of guarding against it, I have reason to hope, that you will so keep before your mind the higher and better motives of action, as to leave that in question only its proper degree of influence. The opposite fault, that of indifference to public opinion, you will not forget, is also to be guarded against. Indeed, I know not where, in the moral any more than in the natural world, there is a Scylla without its Charybdis on the other side. I hope you will be under a safe pilotage of sound sense and upright intentions, which will steer you safely between them.

"If you find yourself competent to the task, I am not sorry that you have the opportunity of reading and performing worship in public. It may be made a very useful discipline to you in many respects. You will learn the compass and strength of your voice, and its modulation, and something of your power of engaging the attention of an assembly by your manner, and may receive hints by which to correct any faults of attitude, enunciation, or gesture. What is more important, it will give an intellectual stimulus, teach you to read and judge of sermons with different and better discrimination, help you to form a good taste in writing, and probably more *practical* than you would otherwise do. Most of all, it will produce a moral excitement, bring into exercise your religious affections, enable you to understand more of your own heart, and thus give you means and motives, which you had not before, of self-correction, and religious and moral improvement.

"The notices you have taken on these subjects are a pledge to me, that you will lay yourself open to improvement in all these respects. *One* effect of this anticipation of study and preparation, I hope you will guard against,—that of impatience and precipitation. I shall wish you to go through a considerable course of preparatory study before you commence preaching, though I shall have no wish for you to defer it beyond a reasonable length of time. *Another* hope I have is, that, in gaining confidence and the power of self-possession, you will lose no part of that modesty which becomes a young man."

His services were so acceptable to the Society, that he was engaged to read to them as long as he remained in Exeter. Dr. Abbot, in a letter before quoted, alludes to the same subject. "About this time it occurred in our little Society, where most of our respectable and educated gentlemen attended worship, that the desk was to be left vacant for a few Sabbaths, and Mr. Ware was applied to to supply it by performing the devotional exercises, and reading from printed discourses. I was at first astonished at his accepting the invitation, and went to church with much anxiety for my young friend; but I was soon relieved, and delighted with his self-possession, the propriety and ardor of his devotional exercises, the skill and judgment of his selections of discourses, and his very interesting manner of delivering them. We were all delighted with him; so much so, that, at the close of the engagement, Judge Smith* exclaimed to me, as we left church; 'I have often attended church in Boston, New York, and Philadelphia; and I do not recollect ever to have been better satisfied with exercises and services of four Sabbaths, than with this young man of yours. He will be eminent in his profession.'"

* Hon. Jeremiah Smith, at different times Governor and Chief Justice of New Hampshire.

CHAPTER V.

STUDIES DIVINITY AT CAMBRIDGE—STATE OF EDUCATION THERE—HE IS APPROBATED—RESULTS OF SELF-EXAMINATION—FIRST PREACHING—ORDAINED PASTOR OVER THE SECOND CHURCH IN BOSTON.

1814-17. ÆT. 20—23.

In August, 1814, he left Exeter, and returned to Cambridge, to finish his theological studies as a resident graduate at the University. He now lived in his father's house, in habits of constant daily intercourse with him, and studying under his personal direction. All the members of the family were also at this time at home; and this period, therefore, furnishes none of those materials for biography, which are afforded by the familiar interchange of letters. The stated provisions for theological education at Cambridge were, at this time, very scanty. The studies were pursued under the general superintendence of the Professor of Divinity, who laid out a regular course of reading; but this course was merely advisory. There were no exercises, except a single one every week in the criticism of the New Testament; no examinations, no instruction in parochial duty. There were no opportunities for practice in public speaking, except at the weekly meetings of a society of the students, of which Mr. Norton was at this time president. At these meetings there were devotional exercises and a sermon, followed by observations and critical remarks. No examinations being held, no authority or license to preach was derived from a connexion with the institution; but, at the close of a suitable period of study, which was, however, by no means of uniform length, the student presented himself to some Association of ministers, by whom, after they had made such inquiry respecting his qualifications as were judged necessary, and heard a sermon of his composition, he was, to use the phrase of the day, *approbated.* This body claimed no authority in this matter, and did not regard themselves as having power to require any particular amount of qualification, any regular course of study, or any definite period of time spent in preparation; nor did they profess to confer any rights. Their certificate was merely one of recommendation.

On his first return to Cambridge, my brother had been invited by Mr. Norton, then librarian of the College, to take the office of sub-librarian. This was a place of small emolument, but occupied very little time, and occasioned no considerable interruption to the regular prosecution of his studies. He held it for one year. During the period of his professional preparation, his attention was by no means exclusively confined to this object. He continued to keep up his interest in general reading, and frequently indulged in poetical composition. In the winter of 1815, on the conclusion of the Treaty of Peace with Great Britain, he delivered a poem at a public celebration of the event, in Cambridge, and, in August, 1816, the annual poem before the Phi Beta Kappa Society. Both of these performances were received with a good deal of favor on their delivery, and the former was printed.

He received his certificate of approbation on the 31st of July, 1815. Of the state of feeling in regard to his own character, and in regard also to his profession, with which he entered upon the duties of that profession, many parts of this volume will, I trust, present sufficient evidence. But there is none more satisfactory than that which is contained in the following paper, written on his twenty-first birth-day, April 21st, 1815, only a few months before he began to preach. It was probably seen by no one during his lifetime. On the envelope was written,—"*To be opened and read for improvement, once a month.*"

"April 21, 1815. It has pleased my heavenly Father to prolong my life to the close of its twenty-first year. Threescore years and ten is a long date for the life of a man: how few reach it, and yet nearly one third of this longest period is already past. And, if we calculate the length of life from the majority of instances, probably not less than half of mine is now spent. In a world of so much uncertainty, how can I hope to live yet another period of twenty years; for how many are continually falling around me in the interval between twenty and forty. How has this large portion of my allotted existence been improved? Have I fulfilled the designs of my being? Have I been diligent and useful? Have my privileges and opportunities been so employed as to give bright prospects to the future, whether I continue in the world or quit it? With gratitude to God I would acknowledge his past goodness. It has been very great and very undeserved. Few young men come forward to the world under so favorable auspices.

"From my very childhood I have been allowed the leisure and the means of cultivating my mind, and preparing to move in the higher walks of usefulness and respectability. My parents were pious, virtuous, and faithful; they early instilled into me the good principles of religion and virtue, the fear and love of God, and set themselves an example of all that is good and excellent. It pleased God, indeed, early to remove my beloved mother, and I have no distinct knowledge, but a general and pleasant impression of her virtues. The love I then bore her has left a savor in my heart. My father has been kindly spared until I am able to appreciate his worth, and derive the highest advantage from his experience, and example, and instruction. Under his eye, influenced by all the motives which the presence of a loved parent can inspire, I have passed the term of collegiate education, and learned that God has intrusted me with talents, which may make me respectable and useful, and which I am not to suffer to lie inactive and unoccupied. I bless him for them; and pray that I may feel the obligation they impose of greater vigilance and virtue, than belongs to those who have been less favored. I have also had given me two years of happiness and improvement in the fine circle of Exeter. I had there much to be thankful for, and have only to regret my impatience for a change of scene; for I was in a most favorable situation for the improvement of social and benevolent feeling, and the cultivation of my moral and religious affections. I look back upon this time as a period of great progress in my Christian course. But the warmth and zeal of those days have faded away into colder and more indifferent feelings since my return to Cambridge, although I have great cause for gratitude in my opportunities of study and improvement.

"Here, then, in this short retrospect, are crowded how many reasons of praise to Almighty goodness! How many invaluable opportunities and privileges! What precious blessings in the past, what high and sublime hopes for the future! But how poorly have I improved them! My exertions in duty have been wavering and unequal, my resolutions of virtue have been feeble and soon broken; I have suffered my conscience to be hardened, to be sluggish and slow to give warning, and have allowed my passions or a momentary interest to make me deaf to its suggestions. Hence I have in some great degree lost that quick perception and high sense of duty, which all ought to cherish, and without which a man can neither be eminent nor virtuous. This, I think, is my great failing, indifference, indolence, apathy, insensibility to motives ; hence a decay of religious affection, of piety and thoughtfulness. I do not forget God, but I allow myself to neglect him ; I do not shun duties, but I perform them sluggishly. Hence I suffer time to be wasted, and opportunities to pass unimproved. This indolence also has extended to my body. I have dreaded exercise and indulged in sloth till my health suffers, and this renders me unable, as well as indisposed, to study. The same indecision and love of ease have led me to an indulgence of appetite ; I practise no self-denial ; temperance, although I frequently resolve it, is not one of my virtues. This indulgence again acts on my mind, increases sloth, and weakens the motives to vigorous and careful living. I have learnt to muse of virtue instead of practising it, to be satisfied with loving goodness, and looking forward to the time when I *shall be* good, without being so, i. e. without being so to the degree and extent that I conceive a Christian minister should be. For I will not, from false or pretended humility, say that I am the vilest of sinners; I know I am not, though a very great one, one who has hope only in the mercy of God. But, instead of that progress and continual improvement, that reaching forward to great things, that aspiring to perfection, which Christianity requires, and St. Paul so vehemently urges, I lament before God that I feel myself depreciating. O Father, most gracious and merciful, pity and forgive me ! Help me to reform, and to live a life acceptable to thee through Jesus Christ thy Son ! I would have more ardor, and vigor, and perseverance, and approve myself worthy of my high vocation; more readiness to hear the call of duty, and more alacrity in obeying it. I would feel more constantly and sensibly the obligations my situation imposes on me; the motives which should urge me; I desire to waste less time, and become more faithful and studious. I have undertaken the gospel ministry. I feel it to be a station of labor and responsibility; no common exertions will enable me so to qualify myself, that I can discharge its duties with perfect satisfaction, or answer the demands of my conscience, my friends, or my God.

"I am sensible that my father and friends look upon me with anxiety and much hope; and shall I indulge my indolent habits and disappoint them? Shall my great opportunities and privileges be wasted, and all that God and men have done for me come to nought? O! I feel that I have grown hardened; I am not easily moved as I once was; I am asleep to strong motives, sunk in a lethargic calm; I pray that I may be awakened. I will endeavor, I will make an effort, and, strong in the Lord and in the power of his might, regain those feelings and habits I once possessed; that feeling of piety; that lively sense of duty; that self-government and those studious habits, which I have lost, and which must be recovered or I fall. My situation has peculiar temptations to distract my attention and break fixed habits; to these I have yielded instead of resisting them. Now they must be overcome.

"Since the winter vacation I have accomplished scarcely anything of study; the time has almost been wasted, and, instead of improving, I am afraid I have grown worse in both my religious and literary character. Indeed, my health has been bad; perhaps my complaints are the beginnings of a disease which may end fatally. I pray that I may be prepared for any event, and equally glorify God in my life or my death. If God please, I would that my days might be prolonged; for I earnestly desire to be better prepared, and to be the instrument of some good in the world ere I leave it. I wish I might not merely pass over a few years of time, and leave no trace of good; but I would do something for the cause of virtue and the happiness of man; so that, when I shall be called to another state, I may meet with some who shall greet me with love and gratitude, and may receive the approbation of my Saviour and my God.

"But, great God, thy will be done. I am in thy hands; may I acquiesce in thine appointments. Whatever time thou shalt allot me, may I well improve it, and cultivate the powers thou hast given me. May I ever fix my eye upon thee and upon duty, and, through thy grace in Jesus Christ, my Lord, become such as thou wilt delight to own and to bless. O, forgive my past follies; help me in time to come; delight to bless me; and finally grant me to see thy presence and glory in peace, through Jesus Christ, the Son of thy love, the Saviour of men."

But with all such sober views, there was still nothing gloomy or distrustful in his habitual state of mind. He was constitutionally cheerful, even when laboring under considerable indisposition, and looked on life with much of hope for the future, as well as of gratitude for the past. In a letter written about this time he says:

"I am not one of those who look only at the dark side. I think the world has a great deal more happiness than misery in it; and that, upon the whole, life is a very good thing. For my own part, at least, I have infinitely more reason to rejoice with gratitude, than to complain; and I cannot help sometimes thinking, that some of those who so bitterly complain of the evils and burdens of this world, will have reason to think it a very tolerable one when they have seen another. I think that with a contented disposition, if a man will resolve to be cheerful, he may always be pretty happy; this is one of the first requisites."

The two following extracts from other letters of this period serve also to illustrate the nature of his views and the condition of his mind. The first was written to a friend, in relation to some criticisms upon the preaching of a young clergyman; the second to a brother, who was about beginning the study of divinity.

"APRIL, 1815.

"I am sorry to find you speak as you do of his preaching. You may be correct; but I cannot help thinking, that he *must* yet make considerable progress. His mind certainly has not reached its full maturity; and, while its powers ripen, I see no reason why his skill in using them should not improve. I am sorry if his manner is so uniformly delicate and polished. I like some roughness; I should learn to sleep, if my minister were never venturesome, and never hazarded a bold idea or expression. I like to be roused and interested in different ways at different times. But I think you claim too much, when you demand from a preacher great talents and scholarship, and fertility and originality, at once; we should not thus have more than two in a century. A very moderate degree of each is sufficient. I set a less value on his public duties as orator and instructor than most people do, and more on his private duties. It is in the last, that he has most real religious influence; and it is from his performance of them, that most of his people will form their opinion, and learn to love or despise him. So that a man of good feelings, amiable disposition, &c., may have great influence and be an excellent pastor, though his sermons display very little erudition or talent. It is necessary, indeed, that there should be some great men to preserve the grandeur and respectability of the Christian institution; but these may be few, and I think are comparatively of little importance."

"Above all things, do not be led into our profession by the idea that your success in life will be easiest. I think this motive ought not to have influence in choosing it. The motives ought to be religious ones; and I should esteem it a profanation to preach heavenly truths merely for the sake of *this world's* goods. For my own part, I never would have entered it, unless I had preferred it altogether beyond all others. Conscience ought to have more concern than anything else, in embracing it."

The following passage from a letter of a somewhat later date, to the same brother, shows how much he was awake to the dangers of his office, as well as to its duties and difficulties.

"Dear W., while we preach of time and eternity to others, do not let us become hardened to the impression ourselves. No men are in greater danger than we, of being without religious sentiment. Here lies our danger, and here must our guard be placed."

Some time elapsed, it does not appear why, between his receiving a certificate of approbation and his beginning to preach. He did not appear in public till the 8th of October, 1815, more than two months from the date of his examination. He made his first essay at West Cambridge, in the pulpit of the Rev. Thaddeus Fisk, a classmate, friend, and brother-in-law of his father. On the 22d of October he preached, for the second time, at Cambridgeport, and afterward, with but one exception, on every Sabbath, till he was ordained. In the next February he was employed four Sabbaths at the Second Church in Boston, left vacant the preceding year by the death of the Rev. Dr. Lathrop; in April, four at Lexington; in May, four at the Church in Brattle Square, Boston; and, in September, three at Charlestown. These were the only vacant parishes in which he preached as a candidate for settlement.

His preaching attracted at first no particular attention, and made no strong impression. Expectation had not been excited with regard to him, either on the part of his friends, or of the public. To the public, indeed, he was almost wholly unknown; for, although he had always been respected as a scholar, writer, and speaker, and though the excellence of his character, and the soundness of his views of his profession, led those who knew him to expect an acceptable and useful teacher of religion, yet there had been nothing brilliant in his previous course to make him the object of particular regard. There had been nothing to point him out as a man destined to popularity or eminence. He did not himself look for great success; and his reputation as a preacher was so slow in its growth, and stole upon him in so gradual a manner, that it came to him at last as a sort of discovery, to his own surprise, and, as to the degree of it, indeed, to the surprise of many of his friends.

There is no doubt an advantage in beginning with such moderate success. A young person can hardly enter upon life with any circumstance so unfavorable to his ultimate reputation and usefulness, as highly raised expectations. Many a worthy man has broken down under the burden of a reputation in advance. He must have more than ordinary qualities, who can survive it. It is better the world should wonder that it has not heard of a new candidate for its attention before, than that it should wonder why it has heard so much.

Mr. Amos Lawrence, a warm friend to him through life, in a letter written to Mrs. Ware since the death of her husband, gives the following account of his first appearance in a Boston pulpit, on the 5th of January, 1816, and of the impression which he then made.

"The first time I ever saw your husband, was at a Friday Lecture, in Brattle Square Church, and the first time he ever preached in Boston. He was so agitated as to make me feel deep sympathy and pity for him, in the commencement of his services; but very soon he seemed to have forgotten himself, and to be thinking only of his Master and the work he was to perform. The unction and spirit, in which the services were continued and closed, led me to ask, with many others, 'Who is this young man?' and from that time forward, I cherished his acquaintance, honored his character, the more I became acquainted with him, and loved him as a friend."

The comparatively slight impression, which his early efforts made upon the public, is strikingly shown by the fact, that a long interval elapsed between his first and second engagements to preach in the church of which he afterwards became the pastor. As already mentioned, he preached at the Second Church in Boston as early as February, 1816. This Society afterwards heard a number of other candidates, and he was not invited a second time till the following October. An invitation to become their minister followed immediately upon the conclusion of the second engagement; but the vote to give this invitation, though a decided, was far from a unanimous one. Of forty-six votes he received but thirty-six; the rest being given for his friend, Mr. Thomas Prentiss, afterwards ordained at Charlestown. Still, the opponents of his election, though preferring another, were not unfriendly to him; and many of them became subsequently the warmest of his supporters.

This invitation was given on the 17th of November, 1816, and was answered in the affirmative on the 30th of the same month. The ordination took place on the first day of the ensuing year. The council on this occasion was composed of the following ministers; Messrs. Holley, Channing, Frothingham, Lowell, and Parkman, of Boston, with delegates from the New South and Brattle Square Churches, which were destitute of pastors; Drs. Kirkland and Ware, of the University Church, Dr. Holmes of Cambridge, Dr. Fisk of West Cambridge, Dr. Allyn of Duxbury, Mr. Tuckerman of Chelsea, and Mr. Colman of Hingham. The sermon was preached by the father of the candidate; the prayer of ordination offered by Dr. Fisk; the charge given by Dr. Allyn, and the right hand of fellowship by Mr. Parkman. The day of his ordination was one which could never be forgotten by any of those, whose interest in the occasion, or in the person, was such as to lead them to associate the aspect of the season with the services in which they were engaged. The sun was bright, the sky clear and brilliant; and, although in the very midst of winter, the air was so soft and mild as to remind one of the finest weather of our early summer. It almost seemed to many, who were most deeply interested in the event, as if, through the smiling face of nature, Providence were indeed bestowing its blessing upon a connexion destined to be so happy in its results to all parties. Very often have those who sat under his ministry referred in after times to the remarkable character of the day, as if there had been something in it prophetical of the many prosperous years which were to follow.

The Society, over which Mr. Ware was ordained, was at this time the smallest in point of numbers, and probably the least opulent, of the Unitarian congregations in Boston.*

* This was indicated by the small amount of salary which was at first paid, viz., twenty-five dollars a week, and wood, not exceeding thirty cords a year.

To use the words of his successor in the ministry,—

"The day of the consecration of this sacred tie will ever be a memorable era in the history of this ancient church. For several previous years, owing, amongst other unfavorable circumstances, in part to the age and infirmities of Dr. Lathrop, this Society had suffered a material diminution of numbers and vitality. But God had henceforth in store for it better things than even the glowing anticipations of the new preacher's most sanguine friends ventured to predict. Entering upon his arduous work with no startling exhibitions of eloquence or zeal, with no straining for sudden effect, but with a devoted purpose to be laborious and faithful, and a single eye to the sacred objects of the ministry, the first fruits of his well-sustained efforts gradually and steadily ripened around him. The spiritual and external interests of the parish advanced with a regular and healthy growth. Another golden age, like that which it had enjoyed under the first of the Mathers, dawned upon the prospects of the church. The throng of worshippers swelled from Sabbath to Sabbath. The influence of the pulpit became more powerful and deep. Its invitations to holiness became more persuasive; its calls to duty more stirring; its appeals to the conscience more pungent; its discourses to the understanding more convincing; its addresses to the affections more constraining." "There were more splendid edifices than these old walls. There were more wealthy and fashionable and highly cultivated congregations, than that which gathered around him with attentive faces and captivated hearts. There were more graceful rhetoricians and more learned theologians occupying the sacred desk. But where was there a temple more fragrant with the breath of devotion, more beautiful with the spiritual adornings of holiness and peace? Where was there a Society more harmonious or more engaged? And

This was afterwards increased to $1800 per annum; and, from time to time, several grants were made to him by distinct votes of the Society.

where was the preacher, whose whole air, and action, and tones, were more suited to the messages of Heaven, whose discourses and whose prayers had more power of moral and spiritual effect?" *

There were many circumstances in his new situation which made it a peculiarly desirable and happy one for him. Boston has always been distinguished, at once for the high character of its clergymen, and for the great respect in which they have been held by the community in which they lived. A place here has therefore been always looked upon as a most fortunate allotment. Here also he was surrounded, both in the town and in its immediate neighborhood, by a large number of his brethren of the same religious sentiments with himself, with whom he could take counsel, and on whose support he could depend. Then he was to reside in the immediate vicinity of the places of his birth and education, and in constant connexion with all the members of his family. Besides all these advantages, he found in the character of the parish itself a source of satisfaction. It was composed chiefly of individuals of the middle portion of society; neither the very poor, nor the very rich; neither the very ignorant, nor the highly cultivated; the kind of people whom he supposed to be most likely to listen readily and with profit to his preaching. He was not ambitious of being the minister of a Society composed of persons of what are called the higher classes,—the rich, the fashionable, the refined, the intellectual. He was diffident of his ability to come up to their standard of preaching, or of adapting himself to their spiritual wants. His subsequent progress

* "Sermon on the Death of the Rev. Henry Ware, Jr. By the Rev Chandler Robbins."

shows, that he undervalued his capacity, and that he was capable of producing right religious impressions upon one class as well as upon another. But this feeling of distrust, before he had made trial of his powers, was not unnatural. The following letters to several persons, though somewhat various in their subjects, display very well the state of mind, on this and many other points, with which he entered on his new duties.

TO THE REV. J. E. ABBOT.

"JAN. 1817.

"DEAR ABBOT,

"I was glad to receive your note proposing an alteration of our arrangement, for I shall very much prefer making the exchange on the third Sabbath of February. I depend upon seeing you, if possible, when in town next week. I take this opportunity to tell you how perfectly happy I have the prospect of being, here. The situation seems exactly suited to my wishes and habits. I say this, because you may recollect I was rather backward in answering your remark the other day, that this was to be preferred to any other parish in town. I really think it is; but I have been sometimes a little mortified to be spoken to about it, as if I was disappointed at not being invited to ———. People have very kindly made comparisons to me, demonstrating that that was not a very desirable place. Now I can say *to you*, though I could not to every one, that I am, and have been, of the same opinion; yet, when folks talk in this way to me, I must hold my peace; for, if I say what I think, I shall be thought to be crying, 'Sour grapes.' I feel myself now among my equals; there is no restraint on my feelings and my intercourse with my people; indeed, I have every reason for gratitude that my lot is so pleasantly cast, and have only to pray that I may be faithful; and may you and I, my dear Abbot, go pleasantly through a longer ministry than was permitted some of our brethren, and yet not be so happy, as to receive the greater part of our reward in this world."

"FEB. 2, 1817.

"As for my situation, it appears to be everything I could wish. I have every prospect of being happy and useful. My people are all in the middling class, many families exceedingly pleasant, all united and very cordial towards me. Indeed, I am afraid only of being too happy. 'We should suspect some danger near, when we possess delight;' so singeth Watts, and with some truth. It is of no use, to be sure, to be looking out for storms when the sky is clear; yet, I confess, I look with trembling sometimes on the perfect freedom I enjoy from everything unpleasant or trying. It is dangerous to have every wish gratified, and more than gratified."

"1817.

"Don't take these hints hardly; you know I mean well. I have been led to think of such things by my late visits in my parish, where, seeing so many in quick succession, I have an opportunity of comparing the manners of different people, and of noticing their effects on myself. For the most part, I have been welcomed with an ease and cordiality most gratifying; cheerful, smiling faces, and an extended, eager hand, have greeted me at my entrance. In such cases the impression is always favorable. In others, however, I have been accosted as we accost strangers and others at our house,—no advancing, no welcome in loud words, no smile, no outstretched hand. I have been chilled, and yet I have had no reason to believe there was not as much warmth and cordiality at bottom. I have in this way learnt to behave myself better, and have no doubt my demeanor is very much better than it was a month ago.

"I am so used to writing sermons, that I have prosed away here most unconscionably. Let me now talk, if I can; and, first of all, let me tell you how happy I am; too happy, I am afraid. I seem to have come into exactly the spot for which I am suited, and among exactly the people with whom I can be happy. And from all I can learn, directly and indirectly, they are inclined to an affection toward me greater than I could hope. I have only to pray for strength to do my duty."

"1817.

"The duty of commemorating our Lord in the Supper, I think we are not enough apt to consider in the simple and abstract light of a duty which we must perform, and for the neglect of which there can be no more reasonable excuse, than for the neglect of prayer, or of the duties of social life. We always think more of it than we ought, in connexion with other circumstances and events, so as to be influenced by these quite as much as by the sense of duty; this often occasions embarrassment, when, by attending merely to the latter circumstance, our path would be very easy. This, to be sure, is too much the case in everything; but I have found it particularly so here, and am myself very prone so to speak of it in my conversation. I feel that this is wrong. We ought to remember it is a requirement of us as Christians, a simple testimonial of our faith in the greatest thing the Deity has done for man, and a token of regard and gratitude, and pledge of love, to the best friend of our race. If Jesus has indeed done all that we believe, we cannot easily excuse ourselves for neglecting to acknowledge it; we shall almost feel a spontaneous desire to do it; and, as he has prescribed a method in which it should be done, it is nothing more than obedience to the human feeling of gratitude, and the command of our Sovereign at the same time, to come to his table in his name. We have already in our own bosoms felt and acknowledged the claims and obligations of the Gospel; these claims and obligations cannot be greater after our professing them, than they are before. This, I think, is the proper way of considering the subject; nothing can be more simple, and nothing approves itself more readily to a rational mind, even if it were not a prescribed duty.

"Then, again, if we consider the ordinance in the light of an exercise of our pious feelings; and consider how naturally this contemplating the life, instructions, death and promises of Jesus Christ, has a tendency to strengthen these feelings, and increase our faith in his gospel, and make it dearer to us, by calling up to our thoughts his character, and the imitation of it he requires in us,—to lead us to a resemblance of him in his meekness, purity, benevolence, amiableness, and other traits, which make him the most delightful of all characters we can contemplate;—I say, if we consider its operation as a means to effect all this, we shall see its value more clearly, and be more desirous of putting ourselves within its influence. It undoubtedly has a great effect in cherishing piety and benevolence, not necessarily and miraculously, but by its natural influence over those who seriously attend it. These are my views on the subject; I believe you will fall in with them, and, if you do, you will, I doubt not, (and that you may, you have my earnest prayers,) experience a good deal of satisfaction in the performance of the duty. Many laugh at it, and at us, because they imagine we attribute to it some mysterious, supernatural, sanctifying efficacy. We attribute to it no such thing; we believe nothing concerning it,—Jesus Christ and the Apostles have taught us to believe nothing concerning it,—but what is perfectly reasonable and agreeable to all we know of the operation of things and events upon our feelings and characters in the usual administration of the government of Providence. Those who sneer at us, as practising an unmeaning and superstitious form, know nothing of what we do, and have mistaken the ravings of some half-crazy enthusiasts for the doctrine of the New Testament."

CHAPTER VI.

HIS VIEWS OF PASTORAL DUTY—VARIOUS LABORS—HIS MARRIAGE AND PLACE OF RESIDENCE—DEATH OF MR. THOMAS PRENTISS—SICKNESS AND DEATH OF MR. JOHN E. ABBOT.

1817–1818. ÆT. 23–24.

HE began his ministry full of plans for usefulness, and eager in the search of means for improving the religious character of those who were placed under his charge. Among his earliest duties, as he conceived, was to form a personal acquaintance with all the members of his parish and their families; to learn their condition, to interest himself in their affairs, and especially in their children. He considered it as very important not only to form, but to keep up this acquaintance by an intimate and sufficiently frequent intercourse. He had a decided opinion of the value of this relation of a clergyman to his people. He felt that it gave him a hold on their minds, which imparted double force to the instructions of the pulpit. He thought that he ought to be so familiar with them, and with their characters and concerns, that he should be regarded by them as a friend, who rejoiced with them when they rejoiced, and mourned with them when they mourned. He well knew that the same teaching on the Sabbath, which would fall powerless from the lips of a stranger, would enter deeply into hearts that were warmed and opened to the speaker by the holy sympathies of a personal Christian intercourse. No doubt the constant pressure of other occupations, the great variety of calls which were made on his time and attention, both in and out of his parish, and the very uncertain and languid state of his health, which so often made the requisite bodily exertion a great effort, prevented him from acting up to his intentions in this particular, and from accomplishing what he regarded as the full measure of his duty. He often felt and expressed something like self-reproach at what he feared had been his remissness in this respect. Still, even in the degree in which he was able to follow out his convictions, he found reason to believe that his personal intercourse contributed very much to his usefulness as a minister, and to the efficacy of his preaching.

He was especially attentive in times of sickness and affliction; judging that at such seasons right impressions are most likely to be made, good influences received, and an interest excited in religion. But he was not forward, in his parochial visits, (I speak from the statements of a highly esteemed member of his parish,) to introduce religion as a subject of conversation at any rate and as a matter of course, without regard to the proprieties of the occasion. "He never was in the habit of *forcing* the conversation to take a religious turn; but he was ever ready to *allow* it to do so." Religious impressions were the indirect, and not the direct, purpose of his familiar visits. He had no air of formality in the houses of his parishioners, or in their sick chambers. He did not talk much, or harangue, on subjects of consolation. A few words of interest or of comfort, a few suggestions, in a mild manner and a gentle tone of voice, were all that he usually indulged in. Indeed, he felt great reluctance at the expression of feelings of any intensity; and so great was the difficulty in bringing himself to it, that he was sometimes deterred from visiting, in cases of very deep distress, from the feeling of utter incapacity to express in words anything of that sympathy which he felt. The following passage from a letter, written at this period to a very dear friend, laboring under severe affliction, shows how clearly he had detected the existence of this peculiarity.

. . . . . . "I want to give you consolation; yet, when I am with you, I have found my lips sealed. I know not, indeed, whether this is not best. If the case were my own, I think I should want no sympathy but that of silence. 'The heart knoweth its own bitterness,' and I feel confidence that you, acquainted as you are with sorrow, will go to the effectual sources of consolation. .

"My father's dislike of ostentation in religion has, I fear, had upon me an injurious effect. It has made me silent on the subject, backward to introduce it; has made it difficult for me to speak of it with warmth, much as I love it; so I often am, and shall be, placed in unpleasant situations on this account. It is, however, dislike of *cant*, as well as of ostentation; there is a common-place chit-chat on the subject which is offensive, and from a dread of that I am apt to say nothing. Yet certainly the providence of God, and a future state, are themes too elevated and glorious to be ashamed of. But we feel as if we could not speak of them without debasing them.

"It is not wrong for you to mourn and feel desolate. I am always indignant at one who *chides* a mourner. Neither is it wrong to cherish so dearly the memory of your departed friends. If the objects of our affection are worthy, then I think it right to love them warmly. It would not be if death separated us forever; but, as virtuous friendships commenced here shall be continued and perfected hereafter, why should we be forbidden to form them? I think I cannot love a good person too fervently, provided I love him *for* his good qualities, and can feel willing that he, like everything else, should be disposed of according to the pleasure of Heaven. It is true we must part; but I believe, as God is good, no virtuous affection or feeling can be lost; and I am sure nothing would tempt me to love my father less, so long as I look forward to the time when he shall be an heir of glory, and I shall be incited to strive to be fit to meet him in heaven."

He very well knew, that it is upon the young of his congregation, that the minister is to expect to produce the most decided impression,—especially when he is himself young. Among the first objects of his attention, therefore, were services intended for their special improvement. Very early in his ministry he became interested in the establishment of a Sunday School in the northern section of the town, and in various other ways engaged himself in the religious instruction of the children of his own flock. One of his exercises was introduced to those for whom it was intended by the following sketch.

"Plan for a Society among the Young Ladies of the Second Church.

"There are advantages to be derived from familiar conversation on religious subjects which cannot be derived from public preaching. Much information may be imparted respecting the Christian religion, and much explanation of the sacred Scriptures, in private meetings, which cannot well be given from the pulpit. Devotional feelings may be excited and cherished; ardor in religious things promoted; and we may do much to quicken one another in the discipline of life, and improve one another in the Christian graces. We can provoke one another to good works.

"In order to do this, I wish to propose that some of the young ladies of the Society should unite themselves to hold regular meetings for this purpose. What is most to be desired is such a knowledge of the New Testament as shall teach its meaning and spirit, lead us to love to read it, to understand it, and to live by it. Let the object of the Society be, therefore, to study the New Testament. We will commence with one book. Let the ladies make themselves familiar with a certain portion, reading such books in connexion with it as they can obtain. We will then read it together. I will make such observations as may tend to explain difficult passages. We will converse upon them, any one asking questions, and making remarks, with the utmost freedom; and I will read from books observations on such subjects as may be naturally started in the course of conversation.

"In some such way as this, I doubt not we may spend an hour once a fortnight very pleasantly, and very properly; and I shall be happy to be thus able to acquaint myself more intimately with the young people of my flock, and assist them in becoming Christians."

He carried into effect a plan for a regular meeting on some evening of each week, among the male members of his congregation, chiefly the younger part of them, for social conversation and discussion on religious subjects. This began by small gatherings at his own house, where there was little formality, and the interchange of opinions was carried on in a very familiar way. Afterwards, as these meetings attracted more notice, and the interest in them increased, they were held in a room in the upper story of the tower of the old church, capable of containing one hundred and fifty or two hundred persons. This had been usually occupied as a place for the rehearsals of the singing choir, but was now made to answer the purposes of a vestry. It was often crowded, and on some occasions the assembly adjourned to the church. These exercises were especially attractive to young persons; and many, of both sexes, who were in the habit of attending them, became in this way the subjects of permanent religious impressions. After a time, a weekly lecture in the same room took the place of these meetings. This, in like manner, proved peculiarly attractive to young persons, and was especially attended by a larger proportion of young men than are commonly present on such occasions. It was the case throughout his ministry, that not only these lectures, but the services of the Sabbath, were found to draw together an unusual number of this class of hearers, who, from time to time, as they settled in life, became permanent members of the congregation.

Such private services were, if it be proper to use such a term, more decidedly a source of *enjoyment* to my brother, than those of a more formal character. On these occasions he felt greater freedom in communicating himself. He seemed to feel nearer to his audience, and opened his heart to them with a fulness and earnestness which made their way more directly to the hearts of his hearers. The following passage, from the Sermon I have already quoted, refers to his recollections of these exercises, and displays also the warmth of feeling with which he looked back, even near the close of his life, to the scenes and incidents of his early ministry.

"In one of the last conversations which I held with Mr. Ware, his thoughts, as was always the case when we were together, reverted to his old parish; but on that occasion with more than usual interest. I had never heard him express his affection for it so warmly. There was an unwonted tenderness in his tones. The pent-up feelings of years seemed to pour forth in a few glowing words. The habitual reserve which covered the strong emotions, whose existence in his bosom no one could doubt, was for the time forgotten. The veil, that spread before the sacred treasures of his soul, was for a moment lifted up. He told me of those persons and scenes whose images were nearest to his heart. He told me of those hours and occasions of his ministry which were of dearest remembrance. And amongst them all, and, as he said, most beautiful and precious of all, were the friends who had stood near him in that humble room, and the evenings that were there spent in social devotion. I shall never forget the emphasis with which he said, 'The two happiest evenings of my life,' and repeated, 'yes, the two happiest of my life were, one of them, when we had met to converse upon the Lord's Supper, and the vestry was so full that we were obliged to adjourn to the church; and the other, when, after an interesting discussion, we sang together at parting, as if every soul present felt the grandeur and joyousness of the sentiment, the hymn which concludes with this glorious verse,' which he then repeated:

"'Then let our songs abound,
And every tear be dry;
We 're marching through Immanuel's ground
To fairer worlds on high.'"

At the time of his ordination, and till his marriage, my brother boarded in the family of Mrs. Burditt, a highly respectable member of his church, who resided in Back Street, now Salem Street, directly opposite

Stillman Street. In the October after his ordination, he was married to Miss Elizabeth Watson Waterhouse, the daughter of Dr. Benjamin Waterhouse, of Cambridge, a lady with whom he had been intimately acquainted from childhood, and for whom he had many years entertained a very warm regard.* On his marriage, he moved into a house in Bennet Street, often called North School Street, at a very short distance from his church. This part of the city was then far less eligible as a residence, than it has since become; and many of his friends urged his selection of a more agreeable place of abode. But he decidedly preferred to live in the midst of his people. "His," as he said, "was a North-End parish, and he must be a North-End man." Nor could he be afterwards persuaded to remove to a different part of the town, even when, by the changes in and accessions to his parish, a very large portion of it came at length, as it continues now, to be composed of inhabitants of other sections.

In the course of the same year other events occurred, which in different ways were deeply interesting to him, and produced powerful and permanent impressions on his mind. Very soon after his own ordination he was called to take a part in that of the Rev. Thomas Prentiss, over a church in Charlestown. Mr. Prentiss had been his contemporary and fellow-student at Cambridge, both before and after graduation. They had pursued their studies in divinity together; they had entered the profession very nearly at the same time, and entertained a strong mutual regard. The settlement of Mr. Prentiss, as so near a neighbor, was a most grateful circum-

* The children by this marriage were two sons and a daughter. One son died in infancy.

stance to both of them; and they had naturally looked forward to many years of ministerial intercourse and of friendly coöperation in their plans of usefulness. These hopes were not to be fulfilled. In September, Mr. Prentiss was seized with fever, and died after a very short sickness, whilst his friend, who had so recently welcomed him to the fellowship of the churches, was called upon to pay the customary tribute to his memory at his funeral. The sermon preached on this occasion was the first publication of Mr. Ware after his ordination, and indeed was the only occasion of his appearing in print during the first two years of his ministry. He writes thus to an absent sister concerning this event, which occurred about the time of the prevalence of a very fatal epidemic in Cambridge.

"Sept. 1817.

"As you seem anxious about Cambridge, I will say, the sickness has abated, and neither of the children has been sick since Charles. That our large family should have escaped is a subject of great gratitude, and I hope you do not forget it in your daily prayers. You have doubtless seen, by the paper, that Mr. Prentiss, of Charlestown, is dead. It was a most severe and sudden affliction; he was sick of the typhus fever but eleven days, and most of the time delirious, so that when I called I could not see him. He died at twelve o'clock on Saturday night; and on Sunday morning before breakfast I went over to his lodgings, and saw his mother, weeping but in the attitude of resignation, Miss B—— in the utmost distress, and many friends in lamentation. He was a worthy man and good Christian; he had done his duty, and has left few behind who will be more active and faithful in doing good, or would be more affectionately remembered. Warnings are multiplied on warnings, and we must be ready, my dear Harriet, to meet whatever may befall us or our friends. Three young men, about to be connected with Cambridge ladies, have been within a few weeks snatched away; there may be a fourth. I am not superstitious, but I do not expect at most to live many years, and may live many years fewer than I expect. I can only pray that I may be spared till I am fit to go, and that I may never cease to make my friends happy."

In the same year, also, began the fatal disease of another very near friend and brother in the profession, John Emery Abbot, to whom allusion has already been made, and who was now pastor of a church in Salem. Mr. Abbot was to my brother an object of peculiar affection, and the prospect of his loss was a very sad and melancholy one. He thus speaks of him in letters written at the commencement of this sickness to his brother-in-law, the Rev. Joseph Allen, of Northborough.

"Dec. 1, 1817.

"I spent the Sabbath preceding yesterday with brother Abbot in Salem. His situation is truly most alarming. A violent cough which yields to nothing, profuse night sweats, and extreme weakness are his symptoms. The physicians give very little encouragement, and those friends, who know most of his situation, think his case almost hopeless. I saw him but a few minutes; he was not permitted to speak, but insisted on talking to me, and therefore I left the room. He sat on a sofa, upheld by pillows, met me with a smile, and, I am told, maintains an unbroken serenity and cheerfulness. I could have said it would be so with Abbot; he is as much a real and perfect Christian as I know. Sickness and death will not dismay him. God grant we may not lose his example, for I do think it is much to us."

"MARCH, 1818.

"Brother Parkman was at Salem last Sunday, and tells me, respecting Abbot, that his friends are considerably encouraged. He gains strength, and, though danger is not all past, because his fever continues, yet they are planning for him a removal to Exeter. I know not an event for which I could be more sincerely grateful. . . . . .

"I wrote the above some days ago, and now have to add, with a heavy heart, the tidings that brother Abbot has relapsed; his unfavorable symptoms have returned, and with them have vanished all the hopes of his friends. God's will be done. This loss, however, will be long felt; but it must teach us (I hope the application is not irreverent) 'to purify ourselves even as he is pure.' We hear, also, from Exeter, that Mr. Hurd is attacked with complaints threatening to terminate in consumption; it is thought, indeed, that he is already past hope. Add to this, we are in daily expectation of hearing of the death of Dr. McKean, who, by the last account, was just wavering on the brink of the grave. And you have seen by the papers, that Mr. Thacher has already departed; a man never to be spoken of without love and admiration; whose loss to the cause of simple Christianity and practical religion is greater than that of almost any man that could be named; who has not left behind him a man exhibiting in his character so rare a union of many qualities, any one of which would be sufficient to ensure respect. When I think of the early departure of such men, I feel more and more *the reality* of that future state, in which they may finish the labors they could only commence here. It is the only thing which, to human eyes, can 'vindicate the ways of God.'"

This attack, however, did not produce so immediate a termination of Mr. Abbot's life as there seemed then reason to anticipate. He rallied sufficiently to excite in his friends those flattering hopes of ultimate recovery, with which the disease that had prostrated him is so apt to delude; and he became well enough to bear a removal to his father's house, where he passed the ensuing summer.

TO THE REV. J. E. ABBOT.

"Aug. 1818.

"My dear Friend,

"It is many, many weeks since I saw you; but I often think of you, and rejoice in every hope of your restoration to health. There was a time when we thought it was commanded you speedily to join the company of those who had entered on their reward, and we offered our prayers for you, fearing that they would come back empty. But we thank God for the hope, that you may yet labor with us upon earth, and that the large company of your friends shall not yet be called to mourning. Thacher is gone, and others stand feebly in their places; so that we are doubly grateful for every one who is threatened, and yet spared. I dare say that you have felt as much thankfulness on account of the sickness itself as on account of its removal, because you must have found it a most salutary discipline; and, if *you* are a gainer, *we* will be satisfied. I do not know exactly how you are at present. When I heard last, you were still gaining, but slowly. I am hoping, that ere long you will be able to show yourself to your friends here; all will give you a hearty welcome, and none more hearty than myself. I long to show you my dearest friend; and, if it be not best that I should be disappointed, I shall at the same time show you the beginning of a little family, that is to increase my joys and my privileges greatly.

"Greenwood is soon to fill Mr. Thacher's place; he is really a delightful preacher, and has excited very uncommon attention."

In the fall of this year there seemed sufficient improvement to justify the experiment of a removal to a warmer climate, and Mr. Abbot accordingly spent the winter in Havana. While there his complaints again increased, and he returned home only to linger through the summer, and die in the following October.

The friendship between these two young men, which, though of so short a continuance, was of so strong a character, is the more interesting from the uncommon similarity that existed between them in their persons, their manners, and their characters. Of their personal resemblance, there were some very striking evidences. When Mr. Ware first went to Exeter to reside, on going to Dr. Abbot's house, he was, to his great surprise and almost consternation, familiarly seized upon, and most cordially welcomed, by some of the family, who had mistaken him for Mr. Abbot. The mistake here was only amusing; but, after Mr. Abbot's death, a similar one occurred under circumstances, which, at the time, produced a more serious impression.

TO MR. ALLEN.

"JULY 17, 1820.

"Walking in the Mall a few days ago, a young man came up and shook me eagerly by the hand, saying, '*How do you do, Mr. Abbot?*' I looked at him a moment, still holding his hand, and he said, 'My name is ——— ; I suppose you don't remember me, I saw you when you were sick at Havana.' I was exceedingly struck. He was surprised to hear of Abbot's death, and could scarcely believe I was not he." *

* The strong resemblance in *character* is noticed in a striking manner, by the Rev. Dr. Brazer, the successor of Mr. Abbot, in a sermon preached by him on the Sunday after the funeral of Mr. Ware. "I cannot," he says, "in the conclusion of these remarks, offer anything approaching to a just idea of the character of this distinguished and devoted servant of God in Jesus. Perhaps I may best give a glimpse of it to you, my friends, by adverting to the striking

He wrote a biographical sketch of his friend, which was published in one of the early numbers of "The Christian Disciple," and was also prefixed to a volume of Mr. Abbot's Sermons, which he collected and printed a few years afterward. While engaged in the preparation of this Memoir, he expresses himself thus in a letter to one of his sisters:

coincidence it bears with that of his early friend, your yet loved pastor, my immediate predecessor in office here, whose biography he wrote. Those who best knew both, will at once perceive, in reading this just and beautiful tribute,* that the delineation of its author was warmed into a life-like truthfulness by his sympathies with its subject, and that, in describing the character of the sainted Abbot, he is depicting many of the leading traits of his own. The same singleness of aim; the same devoutness of spirit; the same absorbing devotion to that Master whose name they had named; the same high estimate of their sacred office; the same diligence and fidelity in their appropriate duties; the same modesty, mildness, and gentleness of manner, united with an all-pervading earnestness of purpose; the same preference of the religious *character*, before merely professional gifts and acquirements; the same reverential culture of the affections, as the sources of the truest inspiration; the same study of their own hearts as indices to the hearts of others; the same tenderness of conscience, united with the highest possible standard of duty, which enabled them to search and move the consciences of others; the same practical aims in the best of causes, and the same untiring perseverance in carrying them into effect; the same independence in the formation of their own opinions, united with the same catholic spirit in according the same right to others; the same skill and diligence in finding, and in making, opportunities of religious improvement; the same appreciation of practical goodness as the highest human greatness, and the same desire of being useful to others as the best earthly distinction; the same absence of all selfish ambition and undue reference to the opinion of others, which freed them from much ceaseless, barren, and crippling misery;—all these traits of character were common to both. The same integrity, sincerity, simplicity, and consecrate repose of manner marked their private walk; and a similar placid zeal, chastened fervor, simple earnestness, and subdued yet subduing pathos, pervaded their public ministrations. In a word, both endeavored, as ministers and in their personal relations, to form themselves on the example of their Lord; and to them both may be applied more truly, than belongs commonly to even good and holy men, the comprehensive eulogy, which, in the Biography above alluded to, Ware applied to Abbot, they were '*men of the Beatitudes.*'"

* First published in "The Christian Disciple," Vol. II., for the year 1821.

"FEB. 8, 1820.

"I have received aid from several of Abbot's friends in the compilation of a Memoir of his life and character, into which I have entered at considerable length, and hope I have not attempted it in vain. To me he seemed the purest and most faultless exemplification of the Christian character which I have ever known; and it has afforded me the greatest pleasure to look over the various testimonials and records of his worth which were sent me, and to form from them something for the improvement of the world and for my own."

CHAPTER VII.

STATE OF THE RELIGIOUS WORLD AT THE COMMENCEMENT OF MR. WARE'S MINISTRY—VISIT TO THE SOUTH—ORIGIN OF "THE CHRISTIAN DISCIPLE" AND "THE CHRISTIAN EXAMINER"—HE BECOMES ITS EDITOR—FORMATION OF A CONGREGATIONAL CHURCH IN NEW YORK—LETTER OF DR. CHANNING—LETTERS TO DR. M'LEOD—FAILURE OF HIS HEALTH—CONVENTION OF 1820—HIS IMPRESSIONS OF MR. WEBSTER'S ORATORY.

1818-20. ÆT. 24-26.

Beside entering earnestly into the appropriate duties of his profession, Mr. Ware soon became engaged in most of the benevolent and religious plans of the day, and with a heartiness which at once made him a welcome coadjutor. He came into life at the time when the dividing lines had just become distinctly drawn between that portion of the Congregational clergy who held Unitarian, or, as they had usually been called, Liberal opinions in theology, and those who were denominated the Orthodox, or Evangelical. It was a period of much religious excitement, and of some acrimony of feeling; and a controversy relating to the different points in dispute was carried on between distinguished members of the opposite parties with much zeal, vigor, and ability, partly in the periodical publications of the day, and partly in separate pamphlets. This controversy extended over a period of several years. My brother, as will have appeared from many expressions made use of in his letters, was disinclined, both from feeling and principle, to the discussion of mere doctrinal points; yet his opinions with regard to the subjects in dispute were of the most decided character, and this disinclination was the result, not of any doubt as to where the truth lay, but of a conviction that a Christian minister would be better employed in promoting holiness of life, than in preaching the doctrines of a sect. Hence, for the most part, he avoided sectarian discussion in the pulpit, though not at all backward to assert or defend his opinions, when occasion demanded; and, although not taking the field precisely as a combatant, his zeal and earnestness in all religious movements soon made him indirectly one of the most active members in promoting the interests of the body with which he was connected.

In December, 1818, he made an excursion to the South, as far as Washington, partly with the view of improving his health, but quite as much for the purpose of preaching for a new Unitarian Society, which had been recently established in Baltimore, being the first of the kind, it is believed, which had ever existed beyond Philadelphia. On his way thither he preached on one Sabbath in New York, where, however, there was then no regularly organized Society, and once in Philadelphia. In Baltimore, he remained three weeks.

In the beginning of the year 1819, a plan was proposed for the publication of a periodical work, which should be, in some degree, the organ of the Unitarian body. In carrying this into execution, my brother took an active part. It proved eminently successful, and, in its results, has had no inconsiderable influence in promoting the dissemination of the religious opinions for the defence of which it was intended. In the year 1813,

"The Christian Disciple," a monthly journal, had been established in Boston, at the suggestion of Drs. Channing, Lowell, and Tuckerman, and the Rev. Samuel C. Thacher. The Rev. Noah Worcester, who had recently distinguished himself by "the union of talent in writing, and skill in reasoning, with Christian gentleness of manner and a catholic largeness of spirit," which his productions displayed, was induced to become its editor. He removed to Brighton in May of this year, for the purpose of taking charge of it. The original design of this work may be best expressed in the words of those who proposed it to the editor. "We need," they say, "a periodical publication, which shall be adapted to the great mass of Christians, and the object of which shall be to increase their zeal and seriousness, to direct their attention to the Scriptures, to furnish them with that degree of Biblical criticism which they are capable of receiving and applying, to illustrate obscure and perverted passages, and, though last, not least, to teach them their Christian rights, to awaken a jealous attachment to Christian liberty, to show them the ground of Congregationalism, and to guard them against every enemy, who would bring them into bondage. Our conviction of the importance of this work has been strengthened by the appearance of a publication in 'The Panoplist,' recommending the immediate erection of Ecclesiastical tribunals." "We have no desire to diffuse any religious peculiarities. Our great desire is to preserve our fellow-Christians from the systematic and unwearied efforts which are making to impose on them a human creed, and to infuse into them angry and bitter feelings towards those who differ from them. Our great desire is to direct men to the word of God, and to awaken in those Christians who receive this as their only standard, a more devout, serious, earnest, and affectionate piety, than they often discover."* "The Christian Disciple" had continued in existence from this period to that of which we are speaking, but, for the last few years, had somewhat languished. It had become, in fact, an object of but secondary interest to its editor, who had engaged himself with all his soul in that remarkable enterprise, to which his efforts were chiefly directed, and with so much success, during the remainder of his life, the Abolition of the Custom of War. At the close of 1818, it was his desire to give up his editorial charge, that he might concentrate all his powers on this great work. The first notice which I find of the interest taken by my brother in the plan for remodelling the "Disciple" is contained in the following letter.

TO MR. ALLEN.

"JAN. 1819.

"I take up pen at this moment, only for the purpose of giving you a little item of information respecting 'The Christian Disciple.' Mr. Worcester has resigned all connexion with it, and the Boston ministers, with Mr. Norton, have taken it into their own hands, and pledged themselves to support it. It is agreed to change the plan; to make it a standard work of Liberal Christianity, to enlarge it, and to publish it once in two months. It is designed to hold about the rank of 'The Christian Observer,' and to draw together all the strength of the party from every part of the country. It will embrace a Miscellany and a Review. I know you will be rejoiced to hear of this. It is a noble design, and is entered into with a

* A more full account of this matter is given in Ware's "Memoirs of the Rev. Noah Worcester, D. D.," pp. 51 et seq.

warmth and sense of its importance, which insure success. It cannot but do good. Each Number is to contain eighty-eight pages, and ten of us are pledged to afford at the rate of eight pages for each Number, either writing it ourselves, or procuring it from our friends."

In a letter, with which I have been favored, from the Rev. Dr. Willard of Deerfield, since the death of my brother, is contained some notice of this matter.

"Prior to his settlement in the ministry, my acquaintance with your brother was very slight; but, in the winter of 1818-19, I was invited to meet with a number of clergymen in Boston, who had undertaken for a time to superintend the publication of 'The Christian Disciple.' Mr. Ware was one of them; and I was peculiarly struck with the rare combination of candor and decision, with which he expressed his opinions on various subjects. The impressions I then received were confirmed by the whole of my subsequent intercourse with him. He was frank and unreserved in the expression of his own views; but, as he had no fondness for skepticism or contradiction, his mind was open to any substantial arguments, by which his previous opinions might be either matured or changed; and he was equally prompt in acknowledging the force of such arguments."

The first Number of the work in its new form was published in March, 1819, and met with far greater success than had been anticipated. It had been superintended by Mr. Ware, and he gives an account of its reception by the public in the following letter, which also contains an allusion to another enterprise in which he took an active part.

TO MR. ALLEN.

"MARCH, 1819.

"Tell me what you think of our new 'Disciple.' It is quite welcomed in this town. A considerable increase of the subscription has taken place, I myself having procured forty-seven, five of them in New York. Did I tell you that we had organized a Christian Tract Society, and are even now beginning to print? Each of the Boston ministers subscribes twenty dollars, expecting the necessary sum to be partly made up by the rich of the several Societies, and the money's worth to be received in Tracts. Three hundred dollars are already subscribed, and more is expected. Mr. Colman is publisher, under the direction of the Christian Disciple Society. 'Our spirits are stirred within us, seeing the whole city given to idolatry,' as is said of Paul. We are beginning to work, and, I hope, shall work to some purpose. I am to superintend the second Number of 'The Christian Disciple.' It will probably be quite as good as the first; I only fear, not sufficiently popular."

He became ultimately the permanent conductor of the work, and continued its management to the close of 1822. The interest taken in it on its first appearance was very considerable. The list of subscribers immediately and rapidly increased, and it has since continued to be one of the most uniformly well supported journals of the country. Its character, and the principles on which it has been conducted, have been essentially the same to the present day, when it has reached the thirty-second year of its existence. Several changes have taken place in its form and size, and, in the year 1824, when it came under the editorial charge of Mr. Palfrey, its name was changed to "The Christian Examiner." Its first editor not only superintended the publication, but had the task, no easy one, as every editor of a journal well knows, of securing from different individuals the respective contributions they had engaged to furnish. He was also one of the most prolific of its supporters, and probably the amount of his composition considerably exceeded that of any other single person. In July, he thus writes concerning this work and the Tract Society; and in the last paragraph refers to his preaching to a new Society which had been formed in the city of New York, where he had spent three Sundays in the month of June.

TO MR. ALLEN.

"JULY, 1819.

"With this goes 'Disciple,' No. 3, which, I think, is a good Number in itself, but, I fear, rather heavy to many readers on account of the length of the pieces, and not sufficiently popular.

"Communications from the country will, as you say, be valuable to many readers. Variety, to suit various classes of readers, must come from various classes of writers. I am happy to say, that two Tracts are in the press, and one, Mr. Channing's Sermon, (two thousand copies,) will be out in a day or two. Part of my subscription I intend sending to you. Part of it, I shall sell to my people, having drawn up a paper saying, that any one for seventy-five cents per annum shall have all that are published. I think thus I shall obtain thirty dollars, and then I can increase my subscription to forty.

"Now, then, for New York. On my first arrival there, I was a little disappointed at the small number of those who attended worship, the first Sabbath (three services) only about two hundred persons. But, on farther consideration, I found it quite as many as could be expected; and on the two following Sundays there were many more, and on the last the chapel was quite full. It is calculated to hold three hundred and over. The number of proprietors is about thirty, and more than half of them have families. Their interest is of a very enlightened sort, calm and yet fervent; they understand the merits of the case, and are perfectly decided without any partizanship, and really liberal without bigotry or latitudinarianism. I think them in an admirable state, and some of them very serious, religious men. There can be no doubt of their final, though very gradual, success. They are unable to build a church at present, but have the promise of several rich men to join them whenever they shall undertake it."

The formation of this Society was an important event in the religious history of the day. In the spring of 1819, several gentlemen in New York, principally from Massachusetts, associated themselves for the purpose of procuring such preaching as was in conformity with their ideas of religious truth. There was at this time in the city no church in which there was manifested the slightest tolerance for the opinions in which most of them had been educated. In April, Dr. Channing preached to a small assembly of hearers in a private house. The Society afterward procured a hall in the Medical College, in Barclay Street, where public worship was held; and Dr. Channing was followed successively by Mr. Palfrey and Mr. Greenwood, and, in June, by Mr. Ware. During this visit it happened to him (what was indeed very rarely the case) to fall into a state of great despondency with regard to the prospects of the cause. He usually entertained the most cheering and hopeful views of the ultimate success of Christian truth; but he seems at this time to have been in a manner oppressed by a consideration of the apparent inadequacy of the means to the accomplishment of the proposed end. He found himself almost a stranger and unknown, in the midst of a large city, whose whole population, so far as they had any religious feeling at all, entertained a thorough hostility to the views which he had undertaken to advocate, looking upon the little handful with whom he was associated, as a crew of heretics and infidels; and he shrunk from the overwhelming odds which seemed to be staked against him. While in this frame of mind, he wrote to Dr. Channing, from whom he received an answer that gave him fresh hope; and the clouds, which for a time had hung about the prospect, seem soon to have been dissipated.

FROM THE REV. DR. CHANNING.

"BOSTON, JUNE 16, 1819.

"MY DEAR SIR,

"Your letter has been strangely delayed. I have just received it, and therefore may have seemed negligent of your request of advice and encouragement. You remember the language of the Psalmist, 'Why art thou cast down, O my soul? *Hope in God.*' I regret that you have not more to animate you; but the true use of difficulties is at once to confirm our devout submission, and to call forth conscientious exertion. There is a satisfaction in adhering to a good cause, when it droops, as well as when it prospers. We have but one question to settle; Are we preaching God's truth? are we holding forth a purer system of Christianity than that which prevails? are we inculcating doctrines, which, if believed, will make men better, and fit them more surely for future happiness? If we believe this, we must not sink; for, if our convictions be true, our cause is God's, and will prevail; and, if we err, our sincere aim to serve him will be accepted, and will be over ruled to good.

"Your letter discourages the hope of the speedy erection of an independent church in New York; and I perceive you expect little from ministrations in an obscure chapel. On this last point I cannot agree with you. If our friends have zeal enough to withstand neglect; if they love Christianity as much in an unostentatious building, (by the way, a much better one than the upper room in which Paul preached,) as in a splendid church; if they have *made up their minds* to worship God according to their best understanding of his word, I have no fear of the result. If they have Scripture, and its Author, on their side, Providence will send them friends. My only fear is, that they are not prepared to 'take up the cross;' that the Gospel, without its worldly accompaniments, may not be enough for them; that the struggle may be an exhausting one, not being sustained by a deep feeling of the importance of their principles; and I fear this, not because I think them inferior to most men, but because the union of unconquerable zeal with calmness and charitableness of mind is so uncommon. As to their best course, I agree with you, that they should call attention to the subject of their peculiarities. Good books and tracts, exposing the error of Calvinism, would be very useful.

" As to the style of preaching, it should be *distinctive* and *earnest*. We should mark plainly, openly, in direct language, and by strong contrast, the difference of our views from those which prevail, letting this difference appear in our discourses, on ordinary as well as disputed subjects; *but* we should *always* let men see that we hold our distinguishing views to be important, only because they tend to vital and practical godliness. We should give them to men as means and motives to a Christian life; teaching them how to use them as helps to virtue;—and we should always assail the opposite sentiments as unfriendly to the highest virtue, and earnestly and affectionately warn men against them, as injuring their highest interests. I have but one more remark. Christ preached to the poor; and, I think, that no system bears the stamp of his religion, or can prevail, which is not addressed to the great majority of men.

"I do not wish to see a Unitarian Society in New York, made up of rich, fashionable, thoughtless people. I wish friends and adherents, who will be hearty and earnest; and I believe these qualities may be found mainly in the middling classes. Can no inquiry be instituted among these to learn whether they are favorably disposed to your object?

"My sincere regards and best wishes to all our friends. I wish to hear often.

"Your affectionate brother,

"Wm. E. Channing."

In the subsequent progress of this Society Mr. Ware took a constant and deep interest; this being known, frequent recourse was had to him for assistance and advice during the early years of its existence. There can hardly be a stronger testimony to the practical and useful cast of his mind, than the frequency with which he was called upon, even at this early age, and after so short a period passed in the active duties of life, for that sort of counsel, in the management of affairs, which is usually sought only from the lips of age and experience.

Though a little out of the order of time, some further circumstances, growing out of his interest in this Society, will be best stated now. In the autumn of this year, they felt themselves sufficiently encouraged to undertake the building of a house for worship; and, with this view, were incorporated as a distinct body, under the name of "The First Congregational Church of New York." In the spring of 1820, they proceeded to the erection of their church; and my brother, being present in the city for the purpose, made an address on the laying of the corner-stone, which took place on Saturday, the 29th of April. On the evening of the succeeding day, he attended a service at the Reformed Presbyterian

Church, and heard there a sermon from its pastor, the Rev. Dr. M^c^Leod, the text of which was the disputed verse, 1 John, v. 7, of the three heavenly witnesses. This was claimed by the preacher as genuine, and was made the occasion of severe animadversion upon the Unitarian belief. On the evening of the next Sabbath, Mr. Ware was naturally led to attend again at the same church, and Dr. M^c^Leod took then for his text a passage of Scripture, which had been inscribed on the plate deposited under the corner-stone of the new church,—"This is life eternal, to know thee, the true God, and Jesus Christ, whom thou hast sent;" and proceeded to remark again on the opinions held by Unitarians, with especial reference to the ceremony of the preceding week. The attack in these sermons was so direct, and seemed so likely to increase the unjust prejudices already existing against this class of Christians, that my brother felt himself called upon to make some reply. Accordingly, on the spur of the moment, and without any full opportunity of consulting books, or weighing the subject deliberately, he wrote and published two Letters, addressed to the preacher; the first containing a general sketch of the argument in relation to the disputed text, and the second, some remarks in reply to the statements in the second sermon. This pamphlet was published on the 11th of May, only four days after the delivery of the second sermon, and a copy of it was sent, accompanied by a respectful note, to Dr. M^c^Leod, who returned the following answer.

TO THE REV. HENRY WARE, JR.

"Sir,

"I have received your polite note of the 11th, and have attentively perused your two printed Letters, a copy of which you had the goodness to present to me. I have no right to complain of the liberty you have taken in addressing me from the press, on a subject of which I treated in the pulpit; and I have no reason to complain of the style of your correspondence. That you should have misunderstood, and of course misrepresented, some of my remarks, was to have been expected, without a supposition of intentional misrepresentation. Your religious principles are as different from mine, as are those of Zoroaster from the faith of Abraham.

"I hope you will have the goodness to accept a copy of my '*Sermons on True Godliness*,' in which my views of Christianity are contained. They differ essentially from your views. Be assured, Sir, that you have an interest in my humble prayers to the only true God, that you may be accepted of him through the righteousness of Jehovah Jesus.

"Your humble servant in the glorious gospel,

"ALEX. McLEOD.

"*New York*, 13*th May*, 1820."

On the succeeding Sabbath, Dr. McLeod preached a third discourse, of the same tendency with those which had preceded, containing personal allusions to some of the most distinguished professors of Unitarian opinions, and some reply to the pamphlet. The attention, which was in this way called to the important subject in controversy, proved in the end, probably, beneficial to the prospects of the new Society.

The interest, which Mr. Ware felt in the prosperity of his New York friends, was of course increased by the circumstance, that in the winter of the succeeding year, 1821, his brother William became their pastor. This interest was a permanent one, originating, perhaps, in personal and accidental associations; but was strengthened by the view which he afterward took of the importance of the city of New York, as a wide field for implanting and cultivating Unitarian sentiments. It continued to the end of his life, and frequently manifests itself in his correspondence with his brother, and in letters to the Rev. Dr. Dewey, afterward pastor of the Second Congregational Society, which was formed in that city.

Previously to his ordination his health had been very good; but, within no very long period, he became afflicted with some of those bodily infirmities, from which he was seldom afterward entirely exempt, though not the subject of any actual disease. He suffered frequently from severe headaches, which for the time prostrated him entirely; from pains in the sides and chest; and from some dyspeptic difficulties. Even in the intervals of such attacks, he was rarely free from a sense of languor and indisposition to bodily exertion. Still, he often forced himself to no inconsiderable exertions, both of body and mind; but these were unequal and irregular; and a tendency to the procrastination of duty, especially that of writing sermons, the result partly of constitution, and partly of indisposition, made it occasionally necessary for him to crowd much labor into a small space. Hence, he was sometimes obliged to make great and unusually continued efforts. He frequently sat up very late at night, and indulged in other irregularities of the same kind; habits well suited to undermine the health of any student, especially one of so frail a fabric as his. He said to me, within a few months of his death, that he had through life felt the greatest repugnance to regard his health as an obstacle to any exertion, or to offer indisposition as an excuse for omitting a duty, or even for declining to engage in any extraordinary task. He could not bear to be petted or to pet himself. He was reluctant to think, when he saw anything which required to be done, that he was not well enough to undertake it. His disregard of the common dictates of prudence, in everything that concerned his health, was such as often to grieve, and sometimes to irritate, his best friends. The following is an example of the mode in which he was willing to deal with himself. On one occasion, when he was to give a lecture in the evening, he was so ill in the afternoon as to require the administration of an emetic. It had produced no effect when the hour arrived. Feeling well enough at the time, he entered church, happening then to live directly opposite, went through with the service, and then hurried home in season to experience the proper effects of his medicine.

But perhaps we are not always patient enough with those who, like him, are struggling with physical infirmity. Those who join a slow and unenterprising temperament with a sound and healthy body,—who are moderate in their purposes, and indisposed to active exertion,—can have little tolerance for one who, with an earnest and eager spirit, always full of new designs, always pressing forward in some new purpose, is chained to a frail and feeble frame, which he is obliged to drag after him at every step. In such a man, it is not so much a disregard of the laws of bodily health, as an entire forgetfulness that he has a body to take care of at all. When reduced by sickness, he would lament his imprudences and resolve on reformation; but, the moment he became well enough to begin again his usual occupations, he would plunge into them with the same recklessness as before. The following extracts from letters, written within the first few years of his residence in Boston, are somewhat miscellaneous in their character, but contain, among other matters, allusions to his health.

TO MR. ALLEN.

"JULY, 1818.

"The Books of Mr. Thacher's Library sold at a pretty good price; the Polyglot at nineteen dollars per volume, and Wetstein at fifteen. The best books sold rapidly and high. I bought Locke's Works at five dollars per volume, a very fine copy. I have been induced to look into his Defences of his 'Reasonableness;' and, although, as in all controversies, there is much of personality, yet there is, what you do not always find in the second or third reply on the same subject, something new in each. Some passages may be selected quite equal to any in the original work. In looking over his works, I am more than ever sensible of his real greatness. He was an original thinker, and thought on a great many subjects. His treatise on 'Education' appears to have been the very commencement of the modern improvement in the discipline and instruction of young children. His 'Essay on Human Understanding' laid the foundation of modern metaphysics, the metaphysics of common sense. His 'Reasonableness of Christianity,' his Preface and 'Paraphrases,' with his 'Letters on Toleration,' commenced, and have been successful in building up in the world, the Christian liberality of the present day. So that he did, what perhaps no man else has ever done, *altered the habits of thinking* among men, upon *three very important subjects*, and thus gave a cast to the character of society, which must affect it forever.

"I am not wholly free from pain in my side, which forbids my applying myself closely to study, and I am therefore pretty indolent. I do nothing more than write my sermons. I have been engaged a good deal in assisting the establishment of new town schools, visiting every family in my neighborhood, about two hundred, to know the names and ages of their children. Schools are to be established for children between four and seven years old.

"*Sunday Evening*, *July* 12.—I have passed a happy day. For eight days past, I have been uniformly better in health and feelings, than for more than six months previous. I preached this morning *on Family Worship;* this afternoon, *on the Use to be made of the Old Testament Characters.* This last sermon I commenced writing last night, at half past nine, and finished at nine this morning, which is my greatest feat in writing. The case was this; a sermon, which I had commenced and intended finishing for to-day, I had mislaid, so that it could not be found; and, rather than preach an old sermon, I wrote this, which was not very bad."

TO THE SAME.

"SEPT. 13, 1819.

"You perceive by the papers, that Mr. Huntington is dead. Thus we pay an annual tribute to the grave; who shall go next? He has been so little with us, that we shall not feel his loss like that of Thacher, or like that of any man who had associated more with us; but we cannot help being affected by it. The age of a Boston minister is thirty-two years; it is sad to think, that we may none of us pass that period; for myself, it is the very limit of my expectations."

In the course of the summer of 1820, he became so seriously indisposed as to occasion much anxiety in his friends and people. To an aggravated degree of the symptoms before enumerated, from which he frequently suffered, was added a constant and harassing cough. It was judged necessary, in the month of July, that he should suspend his labors for a while. He accordingly left home in the latter part of that month, and took a journey on horseback into the interior of the State. He was absent about a fortnight, visiting and preaching at Princeton and Deerfield on his way, and returned with health and strength much improved. His cough, as he informed us, subsided almost entirely after only two or three days' ride, of twenty or thirty miles, and, by the time of his return, was quite gone. It may be stated, for the benefit of any of his professional brethren, who may suffer in a similar manner, that, at no time of his life, did any remedy produce so distinct and well-marked benefit, as exercise on horseback in this way, namely, riding through the country from town to town, at a moderate pace, and living in a very simple manner, chiefly on bread, milk, and eggs. He seldom, however, added to these means entire rest from his usual labors; since he was not willing to go unprepared to preach, and in fact usually preached more frequently than he did at home, as will be seen in the account he gives, in one of his letters, of a short tour for recreation, which he took in the succeeding summer with his friend, Mr. Greenwood.

TO MR. ALLEN.

"1821.

"Preached on Wednesday the ordination sermon at Bridgewater, from Rom. xii. 11, '*Not slothful in business, fervent in spirit, serving the Lord*,' which I called the *minister's motto*; and went to Plymouth, &c., calling on all the ministers as we went on. Preached for Haven, at Dennis, on Friday evening, who holds two meetings on every week, his people being in a state of excitement, and he being not a little Orthodox. Spent Sunday at Brewster, preaching three times. On Tuesday evening, preached at Provincetown; Wednesday morning, at Truro; Thursday evening, at Sandwich. Thus it was quite a missionary tour. The Methodists began an excitement, which has spread throughout the Cape, and made preaching a very frequent affair. It would do a great deal of good for us to go down there oftener. It would be the most useful journey you could take, and one of the pleasantest. All are hospitable, and everything new and strange. I want to describe it to you."

Some years afterwards he says, speaking of his frequent absence from home,

"I go many journeys, but none for pleasure, and no long ones; and, in the present state of the churches, I should think it wrong to go where I could do no good to anybody."

On the separation of the District of Maine, as it was formerly called, from the old Commonwealth of Massachusetts, and its erection into a distinct State, in 1820, a convention was called for the purpose of considering whether, in consequence of this event, any amendment of the Constitution was necessary. My brother was chosen a delegate to the convention, from the town of Boston. With a single exception, he took no part in the business of this body, but was an attentive listener to its debates. He was particularly interested in that which took place on the subject of constitutional provisions for the support of religion. This subject, as will be recollected by those conversant with the history of the time, excited a great deal of attention, and called out much talent, as well as much feeling, in those who were engaged in it. A letter to Mr. Allen contains his recollections of the close of this debate, and some account of the impression made upon him, at that time, by the efforts of the distinguished statesman, who has since filled so large a space in the parliamentary history of the country.

TO MR. ALLEN.

"SATURDAY, P. M., DEC. 30, 1820.

"DEAR BROTHER,

"You will have learned from the papers, which I have sent you, the progress and conclusion of the business before the Convention, when you left it on Wednesday evening. I was surprised that you went away so early, and regretted that you should lose the most animated part of one of the most able and animated debates which has occurred. It must have been after you went away, I think, that Mr. Saltonstall made a very powerful speech, (much finer than that which you heard, and finer, indeed, than almost any one from anybody,) and that Mr. Webster closed the debate with an overwhelming burst of roused and indignant eloquence. It was in the same tone with those which he had previously made, and the torrent was irresistible. He undoubtedly, by his strenuous and repeated exertions, turned the balance of opinion, and caused the rejection of Williams' resolution,—179 to 186. After the countenance which had been given to it by Judges Parker, Dawes, and Wilde, and the appearance of unanimity in the forenoon, when the question, if taken, would have been carried by an almost unanimous vote, it undoubtedly required all the vehemence and effort of Webster and his friends to obtain the decision which was given. Such vehemence and efforts I have never at any other time witnessed. There was as much talent in the debate on 'the Senate,' but it was not so roused, so excited to strong action; there was more cool argument, and less fervid eloquence. Every one, on Wednesday evening, was full of strong feeling, as well as of able reasoning. You may discern this in the tone of the debate, as reported; but, to understand it fully, you should have heard the tone of the voices also. Webster was excited almost to frenzy, and he spared neither person nor thing, to show the badness of the measure, and the inconsistency of those who advocated it. He said afterwards to Mr. Tuckerman, by way of apology as it were, that he felt that the cause was gone, and nothing but a desperate exertion could recover it. He made this, and recovered it.

"If the State is a gainer, all the credit is due to Webster. He is a wonderful man. I am more sensible of his superiority to other men, every day. No man so quickly and so thoroughly discerns a whole subject, and elucidates it in so clear, precise, and concise a manner. His mode of speaking is peculiar; altogether unfettered by any rule, and exceedingly various. He has three distinct styles. The first is his slow, unimpassioned, deliberate manner, when he is stating simple facts, or plain reasoning; which is very distinct and forcible, without being animated, like the manner of a very good reader. This, I think, exceeding beautiful. The second, is when he is interested in the discussion of some important topic, and has become warmed by the subject, or simply by the action of his own mind. This is slow, various, animated, and presents the finest specimen of elocution I have ever witnessed. This is his best and most powerful manner. The third is different from either of the former, as if it were that of a different man. It is when he is excited by other causes than the subject merely; when he is impatient and irritated at the conduct of others, or at something which has occurred in debate. He is then very rapid; a perfect torrent of words; his voice is loud, on a high key; his emphasis sharp, and almost screeching; his gesture perpetual and violent; his face alternately flushed and pale. This was his manner on Wednesday evening, carried to the extreme in his last speech. In this he is far less pleasant, though perhaps not less effective, than in his other style. He overpowers and oppresses, as well as convinces, you. This variety of manner, suited to every kind of subject, and every frame of mind, is one of his remarkable traits; it is one of the secrets of his power;—for, being altogther natural and never assumed, it leads you into the heart of the subject, and prevents your being wearied, as you would be, by the recurrence of monotonous tones"

CHAPTER VIII.

HIS OCCUPATIONS—SICKNESS IN HIS FAMILY—PREACHES AT AMHERST, N. H., AND UNDER WHAT CIRCUMSTANCES—FORMATION OF THE ASSOCIATION FOR MUTUAL RELIGIOUS IMPROVEMENT—ESTABLISHMENT OF SUNDAY EVENING SERVICES FOR THE POOR.

1821-22. ÆT. 27-28.

During the years which had elapsed since my brother's settlement, few events had occurred in his ministerial life which require particular notice. Though called away much to other duties, and interesting himself constantly in everything which he believed would promote the cause of religion, still his thoughts were principally engaged by the cares of his parish, and his people always occupied the chief share in his affections and his attentions. For them he labored constantly and zealously; and, notwithstanding the amount of his exertions abroad, he prepared himself faithfully for the pulpit, and found time for intimate personal intercourse with the members of his Society; and this, though suffering such frequent interruptions from ill health. Besides writing many articles, some of them of considerable length and requiring much thought, for "The Christian Disciple," he performed the wearisome and often vexatious duties of its editor. He added to the regular exercises of the Sabbath a weekly Lecture on Friday evening, and met the children of his parish, at stated times, for personal instruction. As a recompense for these exertions, he had the satisfaction of seeing the number of his hearers regularly increase, but especially, of witnessing a more devoted personal attention to religion in the families of those to whom he ministered.

In May, 1821, occurred the centennial anniversary of the erection of the church in which his Society worshipped. He availed himself of this occasion to enter into a minute investigation of its history; and his labors were rewarded by the accumulation of a good deal of curious and interesting matter, more than is usually found in the annals of parishes, which he presented to his Society in two discourses. These discourses were published.

Some things relating to this year have been anticipated; and there is nothing further to record except that he seems to have been more than usually busy with his pen. Besides contributing at least as much as usual to "The Christian Disciple," he became a frequent writer for "The Christian Register," a religious newspaper, which was established about this period.

The year 1822 was passed principally at home. There had been already considerable sickness in his family; but, in the course of this year, the health of Mrs. Ware, which had for a long time been very delicate, became more seriously impaired, and she exhibited symptoms of a gradual but certain decline. Their youngest child, also, a boy, became in the summer very ill, and the alarming condition of both induced them to try the effect of a change of air. Their house in town was accordingly given up, and they removed to one in the upper part of Cambridgeport, about a mile from the College. Here several months were spent, but with-little benefit to either of the invalids. They returned to Boston in the autumn.

In August, he visited Amherst, N. H., and spent a Sunday there, at the request of a number of persons, who were not satisfied with the preaching which they usually heard from their minister, and had consequently separated themselves from the Congregational Society of the place. They had not formed themselves into a regularly organized body, but proposed to have public worship in the Court-House, not anticipating any opposition. On my brother's arrival in the town, however, he was greeted with a formal protest, both from the clergyman in question and from a large number of the Society, who objected to his appearance, as a proceeding not conformable to established usage, as an unwarrantable interference with the rights of the minister and people, and as tending to disturb the harmony of the place. The circumstances of the case did not seem to him, on careful consideration, to authorize this interference. It appeared, that some of the persons at whose request he had come, had been denied the privileges of Christian fellowship by the church and its pastor, on account of their alleged heretical opinions, and that all of them had formally seceded from the parish. It appeared, also, that the clergyman, who had taken the lead in this affair and felt himself so much aggrieved, was only a colleague, and the junior pastor of the church; that the senior pastor, a man advanced in life and perfectly respectable in his character, was comparatively liberal in his views, and had no objection to the proposed services; but that, with a singular want of decorous regard for his age and station, he had not been once referred to, or consulted by, those who thus undertook to speak as if they alone had rights in the matter. Taking all these things into consideration, my brother found no sufficient reason for relinquishing the design which had brought him there, and accordingly, after a mild but firm reply to these remonstrances, he preached as he had been requested. Subsequently other services were held, and a Unitarian Society was finally established. But the number of worshippers was insufficient for its maintenance, and, after a few years, it ceased to exist.

In the autumn of this year, an Association for Mutual Religious Improvement was formed by some young men belonging to several of the Unitarian congregations in Boston. It was founded in an excellent spirit, and proved in the end a very important instrument, not only in aiding in the formation of a religious character among its members, but also in promoting a variety of benevolent and religious operations, especially Sunday schools, and meetings for social worship, among the poor. It is with a view to its connexion with the last-named object, that the existence of this Society is here referred to.

In November, 1822, a series of religious services, on Sunday evenings, was projected by my brother, intended for those of the poorer classes, who had no stated places of worship, who were very irregular in their attendance at church, or who neglected it altogether. It was found, that the number of such persons in the city was very considerable; and the plan was entered into with the hope, that lectures given in their immediate neighborhoods, in an informal way, might attract their attention, and excite an interest in religion.

This plan was carried into effect with the coöperation of the Rev. Messrs. Parkman and Palfrey, and with the assistance of the Society just alluded to. Its members entered heartily into the necessary measures. They procured suitable rooms and other conveniences, attended and assisted at the meetings, and encouraged the attendance of those for whose benefit they were held. On some occasions, when the minister who was to officiate was accidentally detained, his place was taken by a member of the Society, who conducted the devotional exercises, and read a printed discourse. These meetings were held at four different places, (though, I think, not regularly in all of them,) in the North and West parts of the town, namely, in Charter Street, Hatters' or Creek Square, Pitts Court, and Spring Street. The meeting in Charter Street was held at first in a Primary School room, and afterward in a small chapel, built by Mr. Henry J. Oliver, and intended by him partly for purposes of this sort and partly as a school-room. This chapel was dedicated in May of the next year, by a religious service, conducted by the Rev. Dr. Jenks and my brother, the latter of whom gave a discourse on "the Uses of Extraordinary Religious Meetings." The meeting in Pitts Court was also held in a school-room, occupied during the week by Mr. Badger, a member of the Society; and that in Hatters' Square, in a private room in an old, dilapidated, and very large house, which formerly stood there, inhabited by a great number of families of the poorer sort. This building, as I am told, was formerly the meeting-house of the Congregational Society of Watertown, which, more than a hundred years ago, when a new church was to be erected, was taken to pieces, removed to Boston, and converted into a dwelling-house. Here the accommodations, and probably the audience, were of a humbler character than elsewhere. Few families in the house or in the neighborhood occupied more than a single room each; and in one of these rooms, as I am informed by a friend who took at the time a lively interest in the lectures, these poor people would collect, part of them, for want of other accommodation, seating themselves on the sides of the bedstead, and listen to the instructions of the speaker, whose desk was a pine table, and whose only light, a single tallow candle. The singing was conducted by some of the young men of the Association, who were delegated for this purpose, and who always performed their part of the duty with the most exemplary fidelity. These meetings were fully attended, and were followed by the most satisfactory results; and, if they were blessed to that class of persons for whom they were especially designed, they were not less so to those who benevolently engaged in their management.

I add a letter which gives some account of one of the earliest of these meetings. It is from the pen of the gentleman already referred to. He adds to this account many useful suggestions with regard to missionary operations among the poor, which were afterward carried out successfully in practice by "the Ministry at Large."

FROM HENRY J. OLIVER.

"Dec. 30, 1822.

"Our meeting in Hatters' Square, last evening, was encouraging. A pretty general notice was given; in one house I went into, there were eleven families, and the little which was seen of them brought to mind, what a mingled condition is ours! In one room was a man who was sitting by the fire, who had been confined to the house (room?) over two years. In two other rooms was sickness also; and last week a woman of forty-five years was buried, and, as one of the neighbors said, 'like a dog;' no prayer, and hardly any one in the house knew she was dead, till the town hearse came to the gate. Only one of these families attend meeting, it is believed. A neighbor said, 'Much is done for the heathen abroad, while we have them at our own doors.'

"Three or four persons out of this house were got into the meeting, and, with about twenty others, constituted those who were the *subjects* of the lecture. The others, about the same number more, were of those who always will be found, from parishes out of the pale of which they do not go on the Sabbath, but, at an evening meeting, feel under less restraint to their minister or church, and indulge themselves in hearing those they have seldom or never had an opportunity of hearing before. Text, 'What shall I do to be saved?'—discourse, half an hour in length. Sang Portugal, Wells, Mear; and, from expressions after meeting from one and another, a general satisfaction appeared to exist."

These meetings were followed, and ultimately superseded, by the establishment of the Ministry at Large, under the care of Dr. Tuckerman, who removed from Chelsea for this purpose in 1826. How far the plan of operations, just described, was the occasion of, or served to suggest, the more extended and systematic enterprise to which it gave place, I am not able to judge. The same Association, however, which had most earnestly supported the former, continued to lend efficient assistance in the promotion of the latter. The chapel in Friend Street was built, in 1830, chiefly by the exertions of its members; and this, as is well known, has been followed by the erection of the chapels in Pitts, in Suffolk, and in Warren Streets, as part of the same system of operations.

My brother's immediate connexion with this ministry did not extend beyond the spring of 1823. At that period the state of his own health, and more especially the failing health of his wife, and the consequent interruptions and absence from home, interfered with this as well as many other engagements. But his interest in it never diminished; and he had the happiness to live to see the Ministry at Large recognized as an integral part of the organization of the religious community, and established in many other places both at home and abroad.

On the last evening of the year 1822, he preached a sermon in his church from the text, "So teach us to number our days, that we may apply our hearts unto wisdom." The audience was large, and the service impressive. He found that he had judged rightly in supposing that the season was a favorable one for an earnest appeal to the hearts and consciences of men on the subject of religion, and he continued the service every year during his ministry. The practice has been adhered to by his successors, and has become a custom rendered almost hallowed in the Second Church by time and sacred associations. Some of his most effective efforts in the pulpit were on these occasions, and Mr. Robbins speaks of them and of the custom which they originated in the following words:

"I allude to the Lecture at the Close of the Year; a sacred and affecting occasion; which has always been associated with his image, and will be so, henceforth, still more intimately;—an occasion which I hope may be solemnly kept by our children, when we, like him, shall be safe from the wear and injury of years;—an occasion which I pray may never become obsolete in the Second Church, so long as it has a name amongst the members of Christ. Mr. Ware was peculiarly qualified to do justice to a service like this. His feelings were alive to all the solemn and elevating influences of the hour. His spirit easily sympathized with its deep religious influence. He interpreted its solemn lessons, as a prophet would interpret the symbols of momentous truths. His preaching was never more impressive than on these occasions. The most powerful of his published sermons was delivered at the close of the year 1826. The memory of that discourse and that night will go with many of us to our graves. My own impressions of Mr. Ware, as a preacher, were stamped at that time,—once for all, and forever. The fame of his preaching, mingled, perhaps, with some chastened feelings, and some desires reaching after the Eternal, had drawn a little company of my classmates from Cambridge to this church. We stood in the crowded gallery. The preacher's subject was 'the Duty of Improvement,'—a theme most applicable to the characters and feelings of the young. Every word, and tone, and gesture was calculated powerfully to impress the youthful mind. But the closing sentences, especially, came home to the heart with a thrilling effect. Their sounds lingered on the ears of hundreds throughout that night. Their distant echoes come back to me now. No words from mortal lips ever affected me like those. I can see his very look,—I can hear his very tone, as, with the unction of a Paul, he uttered the solemn charge, with which that discourse concludes. 'I charge you, as in the presence of God, who sees and will judge you,—in the name of Jesus Christ, who beseeches you to come to him and live,—by all your hopes of happiness and life,—I charge you let not this year die, and leave you impenitent. Do not dare to utter defiance in its decaying hours. But, in the stillness of its awful midnight, prostrate yourselves penitently before your Maker; and let the morning sun rise upon you, thoughtful and serious men.' "

CHAPTER IX.

RELIGIOUS REVIVAL IN BOSTON—LETTERS—SICKNESS AND DEATH OF HIS CHILD AND WIFE—DISPOSAL OF HIS FAMILY.

1822-24. ÆT. 28-30.

THE winter of the year 1822–3 was the period of a vigorous revival of religion among the Orthodox churches of Boston and the vicinity. The excitement was extensive, and the zeal of those engaged in it, which was very great, did not appear, to persons of different sentiments, to be always sufficiently moderated by Christian discretion, or kept within the bounds of Christian charity. There was some secession from Unitarian societies of persons who were led, under the excitement of the times, to believe that their faith had not been well founded; numerous additions were made to the churches of the Orthodox, and the result was probably an increase in the relative numbers and influence of that sect. Mr. Ware felt that this matter was regarded with somewhat too much of indifference by his brother ministers. He did not look upon it as a light affair, or as one in which it became them to be passive and uninterested spectators. He thought himself and them to be called upon for exertions, not to prevent that attention to the subject of religion, which had been excited, but to turn it to good account. He thought that they should avail themselves of the open state of the public mind, and of the disposition which manifested itself among all people of all sects to think and talk on religious matters, to produce serious impressions, and establish a permanent interest in the minds of the community.

At this period, while his mind was interested in the subject, he addressed a letter to the Rev. Dr. Parker of Portsmouth, asking his opinion and advice in relation to it. The topics of his letter are sufficiently indicated in the answer which he received.

FROM THE REV. DR. PARKER.

"PORTSMOUTH, FEB. 24, 1823.

. . . . . . "What then is to be done by Christians who find themselves thus rudely assailed, and their characters most cruelly aspersed? They are to place themselves on their religious principles, and to find their support in them. They are to go to their work animated by a warm, rational, and benevolent zeal, and to confide in God for success. Though reproached, they must meekly endure the trials, and guard themselves against being poisoned by the spirit which they lament in others. Though they witness much that is irrational and even ludicrous in the efforts of those, who are adopting every species of management to promote a work which they ascribe *wholly* to God; yet the rational Christian is not to hope that good will result from the unsparing use of ridicule. This is a weapon which cannot be used without danger in defence of the sacred cause of religion. It will not be felt alone by those who *lead*, but it will be felt most deeply by those who *follow;* it will wound and alienate them, and many of this class are really honest, and by persevering kindness may be brought to consistent goodness.

"Nor can any good be effected by a systematical opposition to what is usually called a revival of religion. Such opposition will appear to many,—and among these will be found many really pious people,—to be made to religion itself. Should such a state of things exist among you, as you apprehend, I doubt not but that it may be turned to good account. You will find your people more constantly turning their thoughts to religious subjects. You will have opportunity to address them with pungency upon the truth, which many of them, no doubt, have suffered to lie rather indolently upon their minds. You will feel it to be your duty more frequently to converse with them affectionately in *private*, as you perceive that they eagerly and feelingly enter upon religious conversation. In discharging this duty, you will strengthen and gratify the best feelings of your heart. If need be, you will not refuse, as you may be able, to hold extra meetings for religious purposes, always preserving that decorum, that affectionate, rational and yet moving form of address, which distinguishes enlightened Christians from dogmatists, enthusiasts, and fanatics.

"You see how dangerous it is to ask me questions. I have tried your patience, and perhaps, too, manifested a disposition to dictate on a subject on which I need instruction. I will say no more, but merely express my persuasion, that, though you may be called to a severe trial of some of the Christian's graces, you will have ultimately occasion to rejoice; and my earnest wish is for your success in every effort to do good.

"Your friend and brother,

"NATHAN PARKER."

The following extracts from other letters, written during the period we have just gone over, serve further to illustrate some of the subjects which have been already alluded to, and to show what was the course of his thoughts on several other topics.

TO A YOUNG CLERGYMAN IN DOUBT ABOUT ACCEPTING AN INVITATION TO BE SETTLED.

"JULY 2, 1821.

. . . . . . "For myself, however, I feel much less decided. I have always been an advocate for a man's going wherever there was a clear call, and have always wished that there was more of that sense of duty, which would lead to making some sacrifices for the general good of the church. Now, B—— is a place of importance, where a man may be very useful,—yes, and very happy; and how is it, that one should not make such a sacrifice, as would be required to go and do so important service? Other men are giving up friends, country, and home for life; and cannot we go two hundred miles, not into the desert, not among pagans, but among civilized Christians, and within three days' journey of all that we love? I confess that such considerations influence me a little, and not a little.

"I have thought, from many things in your letters, that you had a considerable liking to the place, and it is more than confirmed by the contents of this. I have no doubt you would be happy and useful, probably as much so as in any place; for truly, from what I can observe, *place* is of little consequence."

TO HIS BROTHER WILLIAM.

"JAN. 28, 1822.

. . . . . . "I preached a sermon yesterday on 'Heresy,' which my people, some of them, want to have printed, but I shall not do it.

"1. 'What is Heresy?' answered by an examination, *seriatim*, of all the texts in which the word αἵρεσις is used. 2. Wherein consists its sinfulness. 3. Wherein its danger. 4. The history of the church, showing that heresy is always the *minority*. 5. Be not fond of giving the name to others. 6. Be not concerned if others give it to you.

"I preached my extempore lecture on Friday evening to a great crowd, on the question, 'Why are you not a Trinitarian?' I. (negatively) 1. Not because the doctrine is a mystery. 2. Not because I elevate reason above revelation,—but, II. (positively) 1. Because the favorite phraseology of the doctrine is not Scripture language, but human (copious examples.) 2. Because the doctrine is not once written in express terms in the New Testament. Only three texts pretended; one of them a forgery; the other two say nothing of *personality* or *unity*, therefore do not prove it. 3. Because there are four strong and explicit denials of the doctrine, which have never been shown to be consistent with it, and cannot be so shown, viz., John xvii. 3; 1 Tim. ii. 5; 1 Cor. viii. 6; Mark xiii. 32. In examining this last text, I spoke of the two natures. This is only half of the subject, which I am to finish next week."

TO THE SAME.

"MARCH 9, 1822.

"What you say of your preaching is encouraging, but I want to hear more minutely. I think the opinion of Demosthenes should be amended so as to read, '*Courage* is the first, second, and third thing for the orator.'

"Your plan for a course of sermons I think excellent; but I really cannot at once direct to books which may help you. The best aid you will derive from reading over and over, with a view to the subject, the books of the New Testament. You must keep in mind the principles of Locke's Preface and some of Campbell's 'Dissertations,' and Taylor's 'Key.'

"As to Controversial Preaching, to be sure, it is less pleasant, and, for the main purpose, less profitable; but, in your situation, absolutely necessary, with more or less directness, for nearly half the time. And, under this necessity, it is a real comfort, that it is the easiest preaching possible. One may write two good doctrinal sermons, while he would be laying out the heads of a decent spiritual or moral one. Because,

First, the train of thought is old, familiar, and beaten; you have nothing to do but to talk on, and catch up such illustrations as suggest themselves. Secondly, a good doctrinal sermon is made up of scriptural quotations, and illustrations, and arguments from them; all which is easier than invention on a subject of duty which is not at the moment particularly interesting, and gives life to you by the necessity of turning over dictionaries and commentaries; an exercise in itself profitable to both mind and body. So that you may regard doctrinal preaching as the very best thing one half the time for the parish, for the adversary, and for yourself. Only never forget to be scrupulously good-natured and squeamishly fair. The most detestable thing on earth is bad passion and unfairness in the pulpit; and I would a thousand times rather that you were blind and dumb too, than hear that you are guilty of such an offence.

"I have been intending to write to you an Epistolary Treatise on Expository Preaching and on Extempore Speaking, and on one other topic which I now forget. On all subjects I shall throw in a word as occasion may offer, and wish you would let me know what you think of my suggestions. As to Expository Preaching, you know my opinion. I advise you to read carefully Mr. Tuckerman's articles in the first volume of 'The Disciple.' I plead for it strongly, as, First, most useful to the people. Secondly, to the cause of truth, especially in your situation. Thirdly, most pleasant and interesting, also, to hearers, who really are vastly more pleased to hear even a common-place explanation of an important or curious passage of Holy Writ, than a very logical, philosophical, and elegant discussion of a topic in morals or metaphysical divinity, the use of which they cannot fathom, and of whose beauties of arrangement, allusion, and diction, very few have any perception. Fourthly, it is easiest also to yourself.

"Everything that Dr. Mason said on this subject in his farewell sermon, I hold to be perfectly true and well founded

14*

and worth attending to, except his assertion of its difficulty; for a man, who has been well grounded in theology, and the principles of Biblical knowledge and interpretation, will find the labor comparatively easy, and rather a recreation. He may, to be sure, so far dig, and search, and inquire, and examine such minute questions of profound and far learning, as to make it exceedingly laborious. But this is not necessary in order to useful exposition. Not many books need be consulted, for the most part, nor any extraordinary learning be brought into requisition. Most passages cannot need them for elucidation; and, as to the main object, doctrinal and practical inferences, they come upon you in crowds without being sought. Take the Book of Acts. What more profitable or interesting, than to remark on and exhibit, *seriatim*, the evidences it contains of the truth of Christianity, of the doctrines preached at that time, of the characters of the Apostles and others, and all the ten thousand moral lessons that are implied and inculcated? And how can it be anything but a pleasant and easy task to do this, adding to your knowledge at every step, and making a dozen sermons without being conscious of one hour's *labor?* I do not know any book to be preferred to this for this purpose."

TO THE SAME.

"March 29, 1822.

"I suppose you would account it a small objection, that a man always grows tired of writing a series of sermons before he has got through; and, as to a settled order of controversial discourses why you must be guided entirely by views of expediency in your situation. I suppose, for my own part, it is necessary, and therefore you are right. But, as to your plan, I fear you will find some serious difficulties. First, it is impossible that it should be *fully* executed; for such an introduction of texts, as would produce satisfactory results, could not be brought forward except in a long series of sermons, which would stand a chance of being dry, from the inevitable accumulations of Scripture quotations. Secondly, you would be obliged to examine every text which is accounted strong on the other side—a delicate business, in doing which you never would satisfy yourself or others. It is the hardest of tasks to make the explanations in any measure intelligible to a mixed audience, who will be confounded with your talk about various readings, translations, grammar, &c. &c.; and yet most of those texts absolutely require such critical discussion. You cannot, however, omit any of them in an examination of witnesses.

"This is a great difficulty. Another arises from the very nature of cross-examinations. It is too great a piece of courtesy into which we have fallen, in suffering our adversaries to choose the witnesses, and being ourselves contented to show our ingenuity in proving that their testimony is not to be listened to. It is very impolitic. Everybody knows that any one may find witnesses to come into court, and some evidence, pretty plausible too, may be adduced on any side of any question; and he would be a fool that would rest his cause on the contradiction which he might detect in the witnesses of the other side. The justest cause would be lost in this way. Yet this is the mode which we have too much followed. And I venture to say, that those texts are too *crusty* ever to be set aside, except by diligently, repeatedly, constantly, arraying our texts on the other side, and preöccupying the ground with them. *You* are not a Unitarian because those difficulties were removed first, and the way so cleared; but because you got so settled on the opposite texts, that no counter texts could move you, whether explicable or inexplicable. And this must be the true course; when the mind is filled with the arguments for the Unitarian doctrine, they are so strong, that the difficulties and obscurities on the other side vanish of themselves.

They have no weight, even if they cannot be cleared up. In this view I consider it more necessary to be repeating continually four or five texts and simple considerations on our side, than anything else.

"This leads to another remark; you like your plan because it forbids repetition. I dislike it for that very reason. Repetition is very necessary. There are some texts which ought not to be kept out of sight a moment; some arguments also. But enough of this, and perhaps I do not precisely enter into your plan. At any rate, through the Historical books you can pursue it without much difficulty, and with great probable good.

"As to the matter of preëxistence, it were best to leave it alone. It is of small consequence, and I am not sure, for one, that it is not the truth. There is a good deal of the language of our Lord and the Apostles, which I cannot find satisfactorily explained on any other supposition. But this is a subject on which I acknowledge myself profoundly ignorant, and willing to remain ignorant, till I reach a world where I shall be more sure of knowing the truth."

TO THE SAME.

"December 2, 1822.

. . . . . "In regard to the matter of catechizing, I think it should be continued, without interruption, through the whole year, unless circumstances forbid; otherwise the children may lose, during the intermission, what they have learned. Perhaps an occasional intermission may be well, but not at regular times. As to the mode, I conceive that the learning and repeating of answers is the smallest part of the business. It amounts to nothing, unless you explain, and be sure they understand, and fix *ideas* in their *minds*, rather than *words* in their *memories*. For example; let the answer, which the child gives, be the basis of a new question; and follow it up with question after question, and illustration upon illustration, as long as you can go, and until you are sure that every important word is understood, and every important truth felt. In doing this, appeal as much as possible to their own experience, and ask *personal* questions relating to their own conduct and habits. This is the mode which I have practised, and which I conceive to be the true mode. Others pursue the same. A great interest is sometimes excited among the children in this way. They become very earnest; they ask explanations of their parents at home, and thus do *them* good also. You sometimes, too, may found an address or exhortation to them on some sentiment which comes up; and this may aid you in forming the habit of extemporaneous speaking.

"Your former letter, by mail, I received, and proceed to answer it. I rejoice at the spirit in which you seem to begin your winter's work. I never yet have doubted you, and doubt you less and less daily. I am glad that Greenwood encouraged you; it was just and kind. I am glad you printed in 'The Unitarian Miscellany.' It will do good to others, and credit to yourself; and everything will be good for you, which helps to increase a just and rational confidence in your own powers.

"I am concerned at the account you give of your eyes. Bear up as you can, and make the best of it. If there were no other reason, their situation is an imperious one for ridding yourself of your troublesome anxiety respecting your devotional service, of which you complain. Whenever you cannot study, *get up and talk aloud on some subject.* Do this an hour a day; make it a settled habit. Do no talk at random, but on a given topic, and as if you addressed an audience. Recite, in this way, the last chapter in morals, or the last novel, or sermon, which you have read. In one year after pursuing this plan, you will have gained a facility of expression, and command and fluency of language, which will enable you to preach with collectedness and confidence.

"Depend upon it, I do not exaggerate. I, myself, never practised half so much as this in private; and yet I speak once a week, and sometimes oftener, without anxiety or failure; though sometimes I get mortified. Do but consider, what a saving of eyesight and anxiety this would be, and how much time you may, in the mean while, redeem by this mode of study; how many fine chapters of fine authors you may lay up in your mind by thus repeating them aloud in your own words, and with your own emendations, &c. &c. Do try it. Especially, as regards your prayers, let your seasons of private personal devotion be more frequent and longer continued, and consist not merely of a mental exercise, but of the audible utterence of your sentiments and petitions.

"You complain of difficulty in manner, and you suggest the only cure,—familiarity with your sermons. No man can do his best, if he be a stranger to his manuscript. Men have, in spite of your skepticism, finished sermons on Wednesday. Some always do it. For myself, I never write well till Saturday; but it is very much habit. And, from what you say of yourself, I conceive that you have no duty more important than that of writing early in the week, at least a great proportion of your sermons, that you may have time to read them over. I feel your difficulty; but, unless you can find some other way of becoming familiar with your discourses, you ought, at any sacrifice, to take this mode, and write on Monday.

"As to Sunday schools, we begin to think them important, and shall establish some soon. I hope you will do the same. There are signs of a better spirit and growing zeal amongst us. We are opening private Sunday evening lectures among the poor in different parts of the town, and intend to introduce the Cambridge students to the good work. Other matters, also, too numerous to tell.

"My dear wife is better, and, I trust, gaining. The babe is declining, and probably will be taken from us. But it could not go at a better age, and we ought to be content, that

God should disappoint us. I never have known trouble, and it may be good for me.

"Write when you can, and let us exchange a list of subjects.

"Χάρις καὶ εἰρήνη.

"Your brother HENRY."

In the autumn of 1822 he writes

TO MR. ALLEN.

. . . . "I have made up my mind to resign my editorship. Four years is long enough; and I do not feel it right to throw away so much time in such drudgery. The income is no compensation, and nothing but my zeal for the cause would be stimulus enough. I can now do more good in some other way.

"I have commenced my Friday evening service, and think of a Sunday lecture besides; to be preached on a series of connected subjects, by such gentlemen as may be willing to help me. What do you think of the plan?"

This respite from editorial labor did not continue a very long time; for, in the course of the next year, or next year but one, we find him engaged in the management of "The Christian Register," in connexion with Messrs. Gannett, Lewis Tappan, and Barrett, each of them taking charge of one page. The paper was changed in form and appearance, and Mr. Ware had the general superintendence and the charge of all the original matter. This arrangement, however, was only temporary.

Through this winter, he was laboring constantly under great anxiety with regard to the health of both his wife and his youngest child. On the 2d of December, 1822, he speaks of them thus:

TO MR. ALLEN.

"I am glad to be able to say, that there is a gradual and decided improvement in Elizabeth's health and appearance, though I dare not flatter myself. As to little Henry, we have every reason to apprehend that he will not be spared long. He wastes rapidly, but suffers little. Yet we are not despondent; for we remember your boy, and build hopes upon his recovery.

"The anxiety and apprehension I am undergoing in relation to my family are something new to me. I have never yet known adversity, nor anything but the accomplishment of every wish of my heart. No man has been more blessed. But I have always *thought* of the afflictions which are inevitable in human life, and trust I have, in some measure, prepared myself to meet them. That I need them, I am very sensible; that they would do me good, I cannot doubt; yet how earnestly could I pray that the cup might pass from me. But then life would not answer its end, and there are some duties of the ministry, which no man seems capable fully of performing till he has met them. See 2 Cor. i."

The child, with occasional promise of amendment, continued to linger till the middle of March, 1823, when its death is thus noticed:

"He remained much in the state in which you saw him, growing, indeed, a little weaker, and, toward the last, suffering more. He passed through a severe agony at about five o'clock on Thursday morning; after which he seemed to go to sleep quietly, and in that state breathed away his life. We were as much prepared for the event as parents probably ever are; and our first feeling, I think, was one of relief, that he was at length quit of his sufferings, and would never know pain more."

The health of Mrs. Ware fluctuated for a year longer. In the summer, in company with her husband, she made a short journey through Pennsylvania and New York; but, though her condition occasionally improved for short periods, she regularly declined; and, after her return in the autumn, hardly again left her chamber. She died on the 9th of February, 1824, at the age of thirty.

These were the first severe afflictions which my brother had ever experienced since arriving at mature life. His letters contain many intimations of his sensibility to this exemption from all great calamities; and the almost trembling solicitude with which he looked forward to the trial of his faith and hope, to which they would subject him, when they should occur, as he knew they must. On the present occasion, as on the loss of his child, the long sickness and the protracted and unusually severe sufferings of the deceased, as they had prepared him for the separation, had, in a certain degree, reconciled him to it. He writes to a sister thus:

"FEBRUARY 23, 1824.

. . . . . "You may more easily imagine, than I could say, what is the state of my feelings, and how desolate I am as I look forward. I have not only lost a most devoted and exemplary wife, but the event sets me adrift in the world, breaks up my plans, and changes my whole lot. Yet I, perhaps, have as many alleviations as fall to any one's share in an affliction of this nature; and, considering the protracted sufferings to which she has been subject, and which she would have continued to endure, I look on it as a release for her, and pray that it may be a salutary trial for myself. But there are moments when I hardly know how to bear it. Yet I have been looking forward to it for two years constantly, and had become so familiar with the expectation, that I almost feared I had grown indifferent to it, and shuddered at my own insensibility.

"The children are uncommonly hearty and very happy. They feel nothing of their loss, and appear to regard it but as a visit which mother is making to little Henry. I am only middlingly well myself, but, by air and exercise, hope to be soon strong."

The following is a letter to the sister of his wife, Mrs. William Ware.

"SUNDAY, APRIL 1, 1824.

. . . . . . "As to talking, I have no heart for it, and am glad to be silent. I believe it is far better to be thus, than at board, both on my own account and the children's. I do not know that I could be more situated to my mind. I am too much occupied to have many hours for thinking on my situation, though there are some, of a bitterness you may well imagine. Sometimes I think I have no heart, and wonder at my insensibility. At others, I know not how to support myself. I was at Mrs. May's the other evening, and Mrs. Greele sung the whole of Sir J. E. Smith's Hymn, with such expression, that I was completely overcome, and could bid nobody good night. I never felt the beauty of that hymn before. I was called to a wedding last Sunday. It had not occurred to me what a scene I was to witness; and, being therefore off my guard, when I found myself in the middle of the service, I was quite overcome, and with difficulty could command myself so as to go through. Such are some of the trials of feeling I am constantly meeting; who is there that can enter into them as you can?

"I often think I could almost complain, that you must be away from me. There is none other that has been with me as you have, or whose presence could now give me that indescribable sort of soothing and support, which is just what I want, and all that I want. But I must not indulge this. To all the world I seem as I have always done. Nobody knows what my loss is, or what I feel in secret. There is nobody but you, to whom I can tell it; and, if I thought I should add to your unhappiness, I would hold my tongue. But I cannot deny myself the satisfaction of giving vent to some of my feelings. It was at the close of Sunday, and days like this, that, after the service of the day, I used to taste the full and peculiar enjoyment of domestic happiness; and, at the return of this time, I cannot tell you how I feel it. What could I do without the children? They take up my time and beguile my feelings; and yet it is thinking of them, that serves to aggravate the sadness of my situation.

"Dear Mary, I am not repining, or murmuring against Providence; but I shall be the easier for giving way to these expressions, and shall be the more composed to find comfort in my prayers."

Of the sources of consolation to which he turned, we have sufficient indication, by referring to those which he was in the habit of pointing out to others, when laboring under similar afflictions. What these were, and in what manner he was accustomed to exhibit them, can in no mode be so well displayed, as by introducing the two following letters, not written, indeed, at this period, or with reference to his own state of mind, but still most suitable to be read in connexion with this, the greatest trial of the kind which he was called on to encounter. It should be observed concerning the second letter, that it was written at the request of a friend, who desired his aid in removing certain painful associations in her mind with regard to death.

"My dear Sir,

"I have been more concerned than I can express, to hear of your affliction, and take the earliest moment to assure you of my sincere and deep sympathy. Your boy appeared to me a child of promise as great as parents are ever blessed with. You had a right, as far as, in the uncertainty of earthly things, we can ever have a right, to place your hopes upon him, and calculate upon deriving happiness from what he should be and do. I believe I can imagine, in some measure, what must be the feelings of a parent at the removal of such an object of affection and hope. I have often looked upon my own boy with the apprehension that he might be taken from me when I was cherishing him most dearly; and I have known that the grief of a parent must be most bitter indeed. But, then, we have been accustomed, in the cultivation of our religious spirit, to reflect on the appointments of Providence, and to feel that all blessings are merely lent by God's favor, and are to be recalled at his pleasure. We have enjoyed them as temporary possessions only, and we yield them up to Him who gave them, not without sorrow at the parting, but yet as an event by no means unexpected.

"It is now that we find the value of our religion, and can rejoice that we are Christians. If it were not for the firm persuasion that this is true, and for the confidence and trust which it may inspire, it seems to me the hour of sorrow would be utter darkness. Without the knowledge of a just and fatherly Providence, which we obtain here,—without the glorious truths, promises, and hopes, which we find here,—what is there that could give any tranquillity, could reconcile us at all to adversity, or save us from absolute dismay of heart and despair? If I did not feel any of the trust which religion gives, I should leave my mourning friends to themselves; I could not speak to you. I should regard it as an empty mockery of their sufferings. For the amount of consolation then would be; 'You cannot help it,—you cannot help it. And what comfort is there in that? How I rejoice, then, that we are Christians. For, if men will open their hearts, a balm may be poured in, which shall soothe the most troubled soul. Now we can say, not only, 'You cannot help it,' but, 'It is well that you cannot.'"

"MY DEAR MRS. T——,

"I have this moment received your letter of the day before yesterday, and hasten to reply. I was overcome with surprise at hearing of Mr. A.'s death; for I had hoped, from your report, that he was recovering. I can fully sympathize with your feelings at his removal,—valued friend that he was, and full of promise as his character and talents were. But your first feeling, of course, must be, that, the more fit he was to live, the more fit to die; the greater reason there may be for mourning, the greater reason for being comforted; and the thought of what he was, the pleasant recollections that are associated with his name, will give a sort of melancholy pleasure amid grief; while the thought of what he *is*, and the expectation of meeting him again in a higher state, will give at times even a joyfulness to your mind.

"I say, the thought of what he *is*. You have seen his body resting in its dark house, and have come away, you say, impressed with that unpleasant image. But is that *he?* Is that body the friend that you loved? Certainly not; he is farther from that tomb than you are, and does not waste a thought upon it. Why then should you? When I think of what he *is*, I am thinking of the spirit,—I forget the body; I almost forget that he ever had a body; I fancy him to myself living, rejoicing among the spirits of heaven; and, while I think of him thus, I feel quite as much delight as sadness. This is what I think you should make an effort to do. Why should you be turning your thoughts at all to the poor clay he has left behind, when you have it in your power to turn them to those pure and happy scenes where he is now enjoying, as we may reasonably trust, such felicity as earth cannot give ?

"Let me tell you a word of my own experience. I have lost many very near and dear friends; but I declare to you, that, by following this rule which I advise you to follow, I have always found more than consolation, even a high and singular pleasure in the midst of grief. I have forced my mind away from the body, the tomb, the decay, and have allowed it to think only of the immortal soul, freed from earth and happy in heaven. I have buried my dead,—that is, their bodies,—not only out of sight, but out of mind. I have not suffered myself to feel that my friends are dead, but only that they have gone home, are living in another place, a better place,—still thinking, active, loving, and happy; thus, in fact, they are not dead to me; as our Saviour teaches, they all are alive unto God. So unto my heart they are alive; and I scarcely am conscious that they ever had bodies that could decay. They, themselves, are imperishable.

"I lately removed to Mount Auburn the remains of two, dearly beloved, and long since gone. I opened the coffins, and saw that nothing remained but dust. There was nothing in this at all unpleasant to my feelings; quite otherwise; for it made me feel a sort of triumph in the faith, that Death had done his worst, and yet that he had not touched my friends. They were not here. I had been thinking of them, and almost speaking to them, for years, as the happy and glorified creatures of heaven. I could not fancy them as having anything to do with that poor dust before me; and the sight of it only served to awaken gratitude to my Saviour, and strengthen my feeling of nearness to heaven.

"Excuse me for dwelling thus on my own case. I have done it because I felt I could thus more easily explain what I mean, when I beg you to think no more of the perishing body. Why should you not come from the tomb of your friend, as I came from that of mine, lifted to heaven, rather than troubled by earth's darkness and decay? Why should you not come away repeating to yourself the words of the angel, 'He is not there; he is risen.'

"You will gather, from what I have expressed, my views on the two points about which you particularly ask me. The truth is, my dear friend, that I have the fullest and most undoubting conviction, that the soul, immediately on the death of the body, passes to its final state; that consciousness is not for a moment interrupted; and that death is, in fact, to the spirit, nothing more than going from one mansion of the Great Father's house to another. I do not feel, therefore, as if my friends were dead; my feeling is, that they do not die; 'He that believeth in me shall never die.' Do you remember Newton's beautiful hymn?

"'In vain the fancy strives to paint
The moment after death,
The glories that surround the saints,
On yielding up their breath.

"'One gentle sigh their fetters breaks!
We scarce can say they 're gone,
Before the willing spirit takes
Her mansion near the throne.'

"This seems to me the true expression; and then, when we too quit the flesh and follow them, I think we shall as certainly know them there as we knew them here. I cannot conceive it should be otherwise. It cannot be, that they and we shall be worshipping together through eternity in heaven, perhaps, side by side, and not know each other. I am as confident that I shall know them, as that I shall know my Saviour; it would be absurd to suppose, that the twelve Apostles will not know each other, or that Paul and his converts will not, when he has called them his crown of joy, in the day of the Lord. Yet if they are to recognize each other and renew the friendship and intercourse of earth, so must it be with all the faithful; and it is a most beautiful and comforting thought.

"If I have at all met your wishes, I shall be grateful; and, if I can clear up anything further, say so, and let me write again. I feel that it is not always easy to enter into another's feelings, and I may have failed to do so now. Indeed, I always feel the insufficiency of human aid, and the appropriateness of the Psalmist's prayer, 'Give *Thou* help from trouble, for vain is the help of man.' May He bless you and yours.

"Very sincerely, your friend,

"H. WARE, JR."

By the death of his wife, my brother was left in charge of two children, at an age peculiarly requiring a mother's care. He was not well adapted, by his natural temperament, or by his acquired habits, to be charged with this responsibility alone. Though not at all insensible to the proper relation and duties of a parent, he naturally tended to an abstracted state of mind, to a complete absorption in his own thoughts and his own occupations, which led to a species of neglect of those thousand little points, which are so necessary to domestic discipline, but which can only be properly attended to by a mother.

In his case, also, the confidence which he had felt, that the interest of his children, in this particular, would always be cared for, had made him easy in the indulgence of the desire to devote himself, perhaps too exclusively, to his studies, his parish, and the public. For some months after his wife's death he continued housekeeping, with the aid of his sister Harriet, afterwards Mrs. Edward B. Hall. This arrangement lasted till the autumn, when he gave up his house. His children, still under the charge of the same sister, were sent to Northborough, into the family of Mr. Allen, and he himself took lodgings at Mr. Heywood's, one of his parishioners, residing in Salem Street.

CHAPTER X.

STATE OF HIS CHURCH AND PARISH—POEM ON THE VISIT OF LAFAYETTE—EXTEMPORANEOUS PREACHING—VARIOUS PUBLICATIONS—COMMENTARY ON THE BIBLE—AMERICAN UNITARIAN ASSOCIATION FORMED—BUNKER-HILL MONUMENT CELEBRATION.

1824-25. ÆT. 30-31.

THE following letters relate to some of the subjects and events which interested him during the season subsequent to the occurrences recorded in the last chapter.

TO MRS. WILLIAM WARE.

"MAY 24, 1824.

"There is no time for writing like that when one has just received a letter; and therefore I begin this the moment I have read yours by Mr. Fox. It is Election week, and I shall probably not be able to finish till Saturday; but I will at once pour out my egotism, as you express yourself to have been concerned, from my silence, lest I was not well. It was only my eyes, and my driving about the parish. My eyes are better, and my health is greatly improved by my constant exercise abroad. Since March, I have made about three hundred parish visits, besides many others. I have about forty families yet to visit. I intend to persevere in the same course through the summer, as I find I do good, and may thus prevent the necessity of journeying. My seeing New York is out of the question, as I said in my last. I shall go to New Bedford and Nantucket, but probably not elsewhere.

"I talk of sending Harriet and the children to Northborough for a month, if Lucy can have them; and, as she wishes to make a visit home, I shall have a few weeks entirely alone. I shall not be sorry for this. I have not been enough alone, and I do not care how much time I have for the parish, now that I feel engaged in seeing it. We are organizing our church as a religious and charitable Society; to have quarterly meetings, to aid benevolent purposes, to help each other in temporal and religious things, and to promote a spirit of union and mutual acquaintance and interest. I think we shall also try a plan, which Mr. Walker has adopted. The members, in rotation, invite such as they are acquainted with tc spend Sunday evening at their houses in religious conversation, the minister with them. Thus, different circles meeting at different places, by and by all the members meet and become known to all others. Great good must come from it."

Of the ordination of Mr. Gannett, as colleague with Dr. Channing, he says, July 6th, 1824:

"We had a most delightful ordination on Wednesday. It is not possible for you to conceive the excitement produced by Dr. Channing. I never have seen the enthusiasm equalled. To hear such a sermon, is one of the memorable things in a man's life. It forms an epoch in his existence. You will soon see it, I trust. Gannett excites a strong interest in the parish, and he will doubtless be a great acquisition to the town."

The first of the above letters refers to a plan, which he had carried into effect, to increase the prosperity of the church, to promote its religious influence and its power of doing good, by giving it a more social aspect, and to use means for creating sympathy and securing coöperation among its members. His own words, however, will serve best to explain his views. They are contained in a report made to the church.

"The great principle, on which the prosperity and edification of the church must depend, appears to your committee to have been entirely overlooked in the general habits of all the churches with which we are connected. This is the *principle of association, union, sympathy, coöperation.* The church is, in its very essence, *an association.* Its very design and constitution is to effect the purposes of personal improvement, and to extend the influence of religion, by mutual counsel, aid, and coöperation. Hence, the Apostles emphatically call it *one body*, and its members, *members one of another.*

"If this be forgotten, and, instead of a constant union in worship and action, Christians only meet infrequently at the table of the Lord, this primary purpose is lost sight of, and it cannot, therefore, be expected that the greatest religious prosperity should be attained. When Jesus framed the model of his church, he in a manner set the example, the first example, of that union by systematic association, which has since extended so far, and has wrought such powerful effects in the world. Is it, then, consistent, that the church should be the first to relinquish this principle? And must it not be expected to become weak and inefficient by abandoning it, just in proportion as it first became strong by adhering to it? Let us, then, henceforth resolve to regard this church as an association, actually and actively united for the accomplishment of religious and benevolent purposes."

The result of this attempt was not only an increased activity, zeal, and religious interest in the church, but the gradual accumulation, by voluntary contributions, of a fund, which was at length sufficient for the erection of a spacious and commodious vestry.

The Society, in the mean time, had been constantly increasing. The meeting-house, which had remained unaltered from its original construction, was so arranged, in the old-fashioned manner, as to accommodate but few hearers in proportion to its size. Several slight alterations had been made from time to time, to increase its capacity; but, in the summer of 1823, it was determined to remodel it entirely. The interior was accordingly taken out, new galleries were made, the pews were reduced in size, and their number was increased. There was, as a consequence, a very considerable addition to the number of families in the congregation.

The summer of 1824 was rendered memorable by the visit of Lafayette to the United States. He visited Boston in the latter part of August, and attended the Commencement at Harvard College in the last week of that month. Mr. Ware participated deeply in the general enthusiasm excited by this event, and was accidentally led to take a part in the public services to which it gave occasion. Lafayette had accepted an invitation to attend the annual celebration of the Society of Phi Beta Kappa, on the day after Commencement. The selection of Mr. Edward Everett, as the orator of the year, rendered it certain that so far the literary entertainment of the day would be worthy of the occasion. But the person originally appointed to deliver a poem failed to make his appearance, and my brother came to supply his place under the circumstances described below.

"August 28, 1824.

. . . . . . "You may, perhaps, guess what an exhilarating week this has been. Nothing can exceed the splendor and happiness of the occasion. The scenes in the meeting house, and at the Phi Beta Kappa dinner, beggar description. You have seen, by the paper, that I presumed to manufacture a poem for the occasion. It happened thus. On Sunday evening, Father told me two remarkable dreams of Mr. Packard and Mrs. Fluker, about the year 1794. They struck my fancy, and, amid the strong excitement of the week, I versified them; and, Percival not appearing, I offered to declaim them. I hope I have escaped the charge of presumption, which I suppose I deserved, but, in the fervor of the season, had no time to think of. If any assail me with it, 'I 'll print it, and shame the fools.'

. . . . . "Everett's oration was very fine. The concluding address to Lafayette was one of the most affecting and overpowering efforts of eloquence I ever witnessed; it shook the whole audience, and bathed every face in tears. When he sat down, it was followed with nine cheers and an interminable clapping. Luckily I had spoken first. Two hundred dined with the Phi Beta Kappa, and there was a stream of wit and fine feeling flashing and flowing for two hours, with a brilliancy and rapidity that left no time to drink or speak, or to hear anything but cheerings, and clappings, and laughings. Lafayette enjoyed it highly, and cannot meet anything in America to surpass or equal what he has seen and enjoyed this week. What a favored man is he! enjoying 'a triumph,' as Everett very well said, 'such as consuls and monarchs never knew.' One toast of Lafayette, at the Phi Beta Kappa, has not found its way into the paper; it was a comparison of the political institutions of America with those of Europe, and ended with an application of these words of Cicero: 'Quæ est in hominibus tanta perversitas, ut, frugibus inventis, glande vescantur?'"

It is not intended to give an account of all Mr. Ware's literary productions in each year, as we pass over it. The more important ones will require some notice; but, for the remainder, the reader is referred to the complete list of his published writings, given at the close of the work.

In the course of the year 1824, he published an Essay, entitled "Hints on Extemporaneous Preaching." This subject had engaged a considerable share of his attention for some years, as is shown by several allusions in his letters from Exeter. He had a strong impression of the value of the ability to preach extemporaneously,—of the greater impression which is frequently thus produced,—of the absolute necessity, under some circumstances, of being able to improve particular occasions to the advantage of hearers, by remarks suggested by time, place, and events. He was not naturally fluent; he had not that ready current of words which flows from some persons without effort, and often without ideas. Besides this, a constitutional diffidence, or rather, it might be called, bashfulness, stood very much in the way of his efforts; and, although sufficiently self-possessed when speaking in public with common preparation, he was much less so when attempting to address an audience without a written discourse. Still, his strong conviction of the importance of this accomplishment induced him to persevere in acquiring it. His first attempts were made in the weekly evening meetings which he held with his people; and it was not till after long-continued discipline here, that he ventured to trust himself in the delivery of an unwritten discourse from the pulpit. He did this for the first time in August, 1819, on the subject of "the Pharisee and the Publican." From this time, to the end of his ministry, he continued the practice. About one in six or seven of the new discourses, which he prepared in every year afterwards, was extemporaneous. Of the labor and difficulty which attended him in this discipline,—of his frequent misgivings and imperfections, and sometimes, as he regarded them, failures, he frequently spoke in his letters.

TO HIS BROTHER WILLIAM.

"APRIL 6, 1827.

"Don't give up the ship for one unfortunate fire. Why, I have suffered worse than Indian torture fifty times; but then I had Indian perseverance; and it is only by not flinching, that we can gain the great end at last. You must expect, as a matter of course, sometimes to do ill. The state of mind, state of health, stomach and bowels, nature of the dinner you have just eaten, &c. &c., all these unaccountably affect the power of the mind. And, then, sometimes you will make too much preparation, that is, try to arrange *words*, and sometimes make too little, that is, arrange no *thoughts*, and in either case you will flounder. After beginning, it were wicked to be disheartened. *Up again, and take another;* that 's the mode in which children learn to walk, and by which you must learn to talk."

He persevered through all discouragements, and at length acquired a great readiness at extemporaneous speaking, especially on the occasions for which he chiefly valued it, viz., where some event or circumstance, as in public meetings, for instance, required immediate attention. Under such circumstances he spoke most easily and most happily without any preparation, uttering the thoughts which were suggested at the time. The extemporaneous discourses, which were delivered in the regular course of his duty, were prepared with considerable care, and probably very little time or study, if any, was saved by this method. Still, it proved a most valuable aid to him in after life, when, from disease of the eyes, he was unable to write out his sermons at length, or even to read those which were written.

The results of his reflection and experience on this subject were embodied in the work just mentioned. It met with much favor, and he received from persons of many denominations expressions of the satisfaction which had attended its perusal.

The habit which he had labored so faithfully to acquire himself, he labored to induce others to acquire; and one object of his exertions, when he was subsequently an instructor of young clergymen, was to induce them to aim at this accomplishment, and to assist them in attaining it. This book has passed through several editions, both in this country and in Europe.

He also published, in the same year, "The Recollections of Jotham Anderson," intended to illustrate the life of a New England country clergyman. It appeared originally in "The Christian Register," in separate numbers, afterwards collected into a volume, of which two or more editions have been printed. This book, though professedly fictitious, embodies many recollections of his own early life, and many of the experiences of his more mature years. There is probably very little of it which has not its foundation in reality, though no part in which the story is an exact picture of life. It was published anonymously, but the authorship was suspected some time before it was actually acknowledged. In a letter of March 9th, 1825, he thus speaks of it:

"I hear that it is reported at Martha's Vineyard, that I wrote 'Jotham Anderson.' Do you know anything about it? I see the old gentleman is at work again, and would be as glad to know if it is I, as Sosia was to know himself. My impartial judgment would lead me to decide it can't be I; for I don't see how in the world I could find time for it now, while I am writing tales for children, and carrying a volume of sermons through the press. My impression, therefore, is, that the folks at Edgarton Old-town must be a little mistaken."

The other productions referred to in this extract were, a little book, written for the amusement and instruction of his son, called "Robert Fowle," which he also published; and a volume of "Sermons on the Offices and Character of Jesus Christ," which he printed in the spring of 1825. These discourses were not prepared with any view to publication. They were written in the ordinary course of ministerial labor, at various times; but, constituting a tolerably connected series, and exhibiting what he thought important views of the subjects to which they related, he believed their publication would be useful. They were extensively circulated, and afterwards reprinted.

About the same period he projected, and began the preparation of, a "Commentary and Family Bible." He writes thus of it:

TO MR. ALLEN.

"I am seriously thinking of undertaking a Commentary and Family Bible. Who else will do it? With my feelings of its importance, is it not my duty? The task is enough to frighten one; but it must be done by somebody,—and he must remember the Discontented Pendulum. What do you advise me? Father rather urges it; he mentioned it of his own accord. Walker says, that it will be as well received from me as from any one, and that he knows no one else who is likely to grapple with it. Tell me what you think. I frankly confess it appalls me, and I think myself better suited to something else. I have not the learning, &c., and my habits of thinking and writing give me a predilection for some other work. But I must do something,—and is not a man bound to do what he knows will be most useful, if he has reason to think he can do it usefully? And, if people tell him so, must he not think so? I want to decide soon; for, unless I have something on hand, I waste time too abominably for man to bear, who has an account to give. Besides, in my solitary state, I cannot be happy without an object, which shall strongly interest and engross me. I only want to know what that object should be; a poem,—a romance,—a system of divinity,—a history,—or anything that I can do. Let me know what, and I 'll go to work."

June 16th, he says: "I have begun my Commentary in earnest, and have revised the translation as far as Matthew, xi."

To this attempt he had been rather urged by others than led by his own preference. Labor of this kind was somewhat distasteful to him. His studies and habits of thought had not led him in this direction. It was, besides, a task requiring too long attention to one object, for a person of his temperament, which disposed him to engage in enterprises to be completed by a few short, frequent, and vigorous efforts, rather than in such as required protracted and patient labor. Hence, although for many years he occasionally worked upon this Commentary, and made some progress, he never entered into it with that zeal and earnestness, which were, with him, essential to the accomplishment of his purposes.

In the "anniversary week" in May, of this year, 1825, was formed the American Unitarian Association; an event in which he took much interest, and which he did much to promote. "Have you heard," he wrote to his brother, June 9th, "of our great 'American Unitarian Association,' formed in Election week? I hope something from it. Burton is scouring the land for auxiliaries. You must have one in New York. The officers are, E. S. Gannett, Secretary, (and his whole soul in it,) Lewis Tappan, Treasurer, (and his soul the same,) A. Norton, J. Sparks, and J. Walker, Directors. The objects of it, cheap doctrinal tracts, missionary preachers, and a bond of union to all of the name throughout America. We have a Vice-President in every section of the country, all laymen." Of this Association he was always an active member, and, both as Foreign Secretary and as one of the Directors, took a constant interest in it, and contributed much to its successful operation.

In May, he writes thus

TO HIS SISTER HARRIET.

. . . . . . "I do not at all wonder that you are inclined sometimes to distrust yourself wholly; for there is no more difficult task. You are very inexperienced, and those who have had the most, and the most successful, experience, are very prone to be dissatisfied with themselves. It is a painful state of mind, to be sure; but salutary, I believe;—

for when one is quite self-satisfied, one ceases to take the necessary pains to do well. We need the feeling of deficiency to keep us awake and active. So, also, in regard to your own personal improvement, that sense of deficiency, which is sometimes almost desponding, operates to keep one humble, and to show the necessity of continued watchfulness and exertion. What person did you ever know to improve, who felt perfectly satisfied? Who ever became all that he ought to be, that fancied himself already such?

"I have felt all that you describe; I have been spell-bound and harassed by the same constitutional thoughtlessness and carelessness. It subjects me to constant mortifications and shame; and my great misfortune is, that my success in my calling, which I never can think of without amazement, serves to render me too insensible to a fault, which I am ready to think hidden by attainments in other particulars. I mention this only to show, that I fully enter into your case.

"'Where, then, is the remedy?' you ask. In the remedy for all habits, which grow up, as this has done, from natural tendencies and long neglect of counteraction; only in equally long struggles against it, long and patient effort, continued and unrelaxing perseverance. It must be made a *business*,—perhaps *the* business of life. This is *our* peculiar trial. In other respects we are more happily constituted, and, by the infinite blessings of education and situation, are saved from other moral temptations, and virtue is made easy. But, in all that, there is no credit,—I had almost said, no virtue; because no effort. We must make effort for something; and this is that something; here lies our probation. If we habitually regard it in this light, we shall not despair, but shall go on cheerfully.

"The great point is,—and in this we specially have to struggle against this constitutional evil,—to maintain a strong, active, and fervent spirit of devotion; to secure the constant and paramount action of the religious principle and religious motives. I fear, that it is here we especially fail, and that our carelessness in this must be cured, before a thorough remedy can pervade our characters. I judge of your case by my own. I do think you have probably erred in this particular,—that carelessness, I mean, of which you speak,—more than I did; I have been more favorably situated. But I have perceived in you, for a long time, a visible and growing improvement; and, with the desire you manifest to go on, I do not doubt, you will completely conquer at last. Do not, however, rely on the sufficiency of any but the highest motives.

"This is a long sermon; but I feel as if I were preaching to an eager listener, who will not throw it away. I hope it is to the purpose. If not, tell me; and tell me in what point, of any sort, I can say a word to help you. How can I be better or more interestingly employed?

"The management of Sunday is a hard problem. Who knows what is too much and too little? Perhaps the children might be separated part of the day. As to making it burdensome to them, it would never do; and I do not like that it should be the most laborious in the week to you. You ought to have some time for your own reading and improvement."

In June, he gives an account of the ceremonies attendant on laying the corner-stone of the Bunker-Hill Monument.

TO THE SAME.

"JUNE 16, 1825.

"Can you conceive the bustle and confusion we are in? Everybody and everything is crazy with preparation for to-morrow. The streets have been thronged, for two days, with people on foot and in carriages, going to Bunker-Hill. To-day it has been an uninterrupted procession, a clogging crowd. The hill is thick and black with visitors. Charlestown Bridge, at times, is so thronged as to be almost impassable. Strangers from everywhere fill the town. Every respectable tavern and boarding-house has been more than full for two nights; and last night, I am told, some were compelled to pass in the streets. Several companies of soldiers encamp on the Common to-night. Preparation is made, in a splendid tent, to dine about five thousand. Tables have been partially laid this three days; and the rain last night soaked the table-cloths, and filled the plates and dishes. The amphitheatre, on the side of Bunker-Hill, is calculated to seat nearly ten thousand people, two thousand seats being for the ladies. The preparations are truly magnificent, and the public excitement is great beyond description. I will write you to-morrow an account of what is done, as I dare say you will like to hear from me, as well as from the papers.

" *Saturday, June* 18. The great day is over; and, as I am sure the papers will not tell the truth, or, at least, *my* truth, about it, I will relate my experience. The day itself was as perfectly delightful as you ever have in June. The procession began to form at ten o'clock; consisted of probably from eight to ten thousand; reached my meeting-house at twenty minutes past eleven, and entered Charlestown Square at twenty minutes past twelve. We formed a large square around the site of the intended monument, and all was perfectly orderly till after the corner-stone was laid, of which ceremony I could neither see nor hear anything.

" After that, all was disorder. Nobody knew what was to be done,—even the marshals had not been informed,—and, therefore, instead of forming the procession again, and going quietly to the seats, the crowd made a tremendous and tumultuous rush down the hill, and seized all the best ones, at once. Then a long time was employed in clearing them, so as to give rightful persons their rightful places. But, alas! nobody knew where his rightful place was, and some were driven from several before they could find their own, and many found none at all. In a word, nothing could be worse done than this part of the affair. Before half of the procession had come down and were seated, old Mr. Thaxter began his prayer; but there were a thousand people talking as loud as he; a hymn was sung, but still no quiet. Webster rose; but now the rabble from behind burst through the guard, and came down through the alleys, and choked them up.

"I left my seat in despair, and went off. I walked round the outskirts, and tried various places; but in vain. I caught a sentence now and then; but the crowd was made up of boys and men, who cared nothing for the speech, but were talking and joking and walking about. So that, whereas it is perfectly certain, that all on the seats, that is, more than ten thousand, might have heard, if they had been properly and quietly arranged, it turned out that not more than a third of that number heard anything. Half of the ministers and others, who most cared to hear, were excluded. I made out to press my way at last, so as to hear the orator's conclusion, of fifteen minutes. He was about an hour or more.

"The same disorder reigned at dinner. Nobody knew where he was to go; nothing could be seen or heard in so great a crowd; and, when it came to the songs and toasts, guess, if you can, the intolerable hubbub. I soon grew tired and came away; got home, horribly fatigued, and went to bed with a sick headache. No doubt, above one hundred thousand people were out. Among other matters worth mentioning, there was a scarcity of water at dinner. After walking and sitting in the sun and dust for more than five hours, we found no pitchers holding more than a pint; and when we had replenished them twice, lo! there was no more to be had. So that some men actually could not eat because of their thirst."

The following letters, written in July, refer to the death, by drowning in Charles River, of a brother, about nine years old.

"JULY, 1825.

"I was in at the examination of the Senior Class. Father was called out; and I heard the distant whisper, which informed me of some catastrophe. I rushed out, also. For some time we could not find who sent for us, nor where we were to go; but, in the street, one and another told us, that it was Mr. Ware's child, at the old bath. You may guess with what feelings we hurried on together, not knowing whose child, and I, of course, dreading it was John. Our suspense was not relieved till we had been on the bank for some minutes. I found that John had not undressed. Who knows what a day may bring forth; and who can preach like Providence?"

"JULY 17, 1825.

"The funeral was on Thursday,—very private, but a few persons,—all in violent grief, as you may suppose. C——'s agony was particularly touching. Poor Edward was so timid, and so little venturesome, that it seems the more affecting that he should have been taken. But it is probable that he suffered nothing after the first fright. As he never lifted his head above the water, there is no doubt he died at once. It is a great satisfaction to believe, that the horrid feeling of such terror was not protracted. It was precisely twenty years that day since the death of our mother, as, perhaps, you observed. Is it not remarkable, that six of us have grown to maturity, as we have? And do you not sometimes look round with a sort of apprehension, as if a breach must soon be made, and as if you would ask where? I have felt so these six years; but I am more wedded to life than I was then."

CHAPTER XI.

FAILURE OF HIS HEALTH, AND A JOURNEY FOR ITS RESTORATION—VISITS THE INTERIOR OF NEW YORK—HIS ACCOUNT OF AN EXTRAORDINARY RELIGIOUS EXCITEMENT THERE—LETTERS—VISIT TO NIAGARA—RETURNS WITH IMPROVED HEALTH.

1826. ÆT. 32.

It is not possible to make particular mention of all the multifarious objects which had engaged his attention during the last few years we have gone over. He had been constantly occupied in very active duties in his parish, both as a preacher, in and out of season, and as a visiter; as a preacher on various other occasions away from home; as a writer in the "Christian Examiner" and "Christian Register," and for some time as a conductor of one or the other of them; in fine, as an active mover in all public enterprises for promoting benevolent and religious purposes. He had done all this with so little regard to his capability of physical endurance, that, in the beginning of 1826, he was completely exhausted, and his health so much impaired, as seriously to alarm his friends. But, nevertheless, as was usually the case with him, he continued hopeful and cheerful. In May, he writes thus to his friends in New York:

"If I had not bound myself to Boston, by positive engagements, I certainly should have taken you by surprise this week, for I am not only on an impatient tiptoe, but I have been rather troubled with pains and disturbances in my chest; so that, after plastering, blistering, and dieting, I was quite beat out on Sunday, and longed for the wings of a dove to fly away. But I am bound here fast till the first of June, and then I shall fly away, whether I have wings or not. Indeed, I am better; notwithstanding this cruel excess of heat, I am a good deal better, and shall soon cease to ail. I have a multitude of matters and plans to talk over with you. I hope your good New York hospitality will allow me some hours of undisturbed quiet with you. One plan is to fetch you home with me. Another is, to spend one week in going up the river, and to the western part of the State, to attend the annual Conference of the *Christians*, &c. More when I see you.

"I expect to bring with me, to New York, one of my young men, who is of an excellent spirit, and who will please you, Sampson,—of not great education, but one of nature's good men. I am very happy in a little knot of young coadjutors in my parish.

"I am just now listening to a delightful band playing at a distance; the music stealing through the still midnight air, windows open, a perfect calm, and a beautiful bright moon, half veiled by clouds, in mid-heaven. It comes sweetly along, 'like the memory of joys that are past, pleasant and mournful to the soul.' It is just midnight, and memory, as well as imagination, grows busy."

His condition was far from being so favorable as he represents it in this letter; but he engaged, with his usual zeal, in the meetings of the Anniversary week, especially in that of the American Unitarian Association, up to Wednesday, but left the city, quite exhausted, on that day for Northborough, whence he wrote the next morning to his friend, Mr. Gannett.

"JUNE 1, 1826.

MY DEAR GANNETT,

"Every mile that I rode, increased my regret at leaving the doings of the week, and confirmed me in the persuasion that I had done right in coming away; and I am sorry for nothing about it so much, as that I have left upon your hands an additional burden of care. I hope you will throw it off upon some one else. I intended to see Sewall, but my engagements on Tuesday rendered it impossible. I think that he will take one page, at least; the first or second, as you may prefer, though not ready to take the whole. I suppose some arrangement with him will take place at once. Pray let it be with an express stipulation, that the paper* shall not get a character of perpetual carping and fault-finding with 'the Recorder,' and other *Autodoxies*. We are always in danger of it, and it would be a great and offensive evil.

"If I had brought with me my notes of the speeches, I think I could have done something with them, though they are very slight. I fear you cannot use them, or any one else. Saltonstall will send a sketch of his remarks, and perhaps Judge Story and the others would do the same. You can judge if it would be best to ask them. I think, decidedly, that as full an account of the meeting, as possible, is desirable. Everything was admirable.

"Pray keep yourself well and strong. I shall rejoice to hear, that you are fully relieved from the drudgery of the paper, and spared to other duties. Meanwhile, my strong-hearted coadjutor,

"Yours, ever,

"H. WARE, Jr."

He preached at Springfield on Sunday, and, leaving there on Monday, reached New York in manner and form as follows:

* "The Christian Register," of which he was then one of the Editors.

"NEW YORK, JUNE 7, 1826.

"This is to inform you, and all concerned, that I had a hot ride to Springfield, and got there at seven o'clock; took a bowl of milk at the tavern, and a cup of coffee at Peabody's; having been smothered by heat all day. Left Springfield Monday morning, at five o'clock; rode ten miles to breakfast; calamitously cold,—thick clothes, and great coat,—yet no comfort. Reached Hartford at half past ten; spent till eleven in seeing fishermen draw their nets and take nothing. Started for New York; fine passage; so cold, obliged to keep below. 'Any library on board?' 'No, Sir.' 'Any books?' 'No, Sir.' A pleasant prospect, truly. Not a soul that I ever saw before; so I sauntered and slept, and read a few tracts, and a good many old newspapers, and slept again. Turned in at seven, P. M., and slept well till we landed at New York, at five, Tuesday morning, and at six went to William's. Have been dull and stupid; no life in me. I think of going to Niagara, or Lebanon Springs; anywhere, where I shan't have to see any one. I have been reading Mrs. Royall's 'Travels,' the most entertaining book I ever saw; full of information; a woman of very keen and perspicacious observation; saw seventy steeples in Boston; discovered that Ward Nicholas Boylston gave to College its whole library; is going to publish two volumes more of information equally accurate. When you get into the dumps, read it."

TO MR. GANNETT.

"NEW YORK, JUNE 12, 1826.

"One of the few things, which have disturbed me since I left home, has been, that I quitted you without putting a laborer in my place; and I fear that you may have been driven to inconvenience thereby. I long to hear how you have managed, and what arrangements the Executive Committee has been able to make with Sewall. I hope that by this time you are fairly rid of the drudgery.

"I hope you will give my people a word when you can; and if sometimes having an unengaged half day, you will bestow it on them, it will be particularly acceptable to them, as well as oblige me. I am desirous that you should preach to them an 'India' sermon. Mr. Samson means to go about the subscription, and the matter must be set before them in proper order, and with power. Will you let him know *when* you will do this, if in your power to do it at all?

"I hoped to have given you from here a few paragraphs for the paper; but it hurts me too much to make the effort to write. If I become able, as I proceed, you may depend on hearing. I feel, for the three last days, better symptoms. I start on horse-back for Niagara to-morrow or next day, and trust to grow fat and stout soon."

In New York he was delayed by various causes; he remained there about a fortnight, bought a horse, and on the 26th of June, began an equestrian journey to Niagara. The best account of this expedition will be his own, contained in his letters to various friends. Before setting out, he had already improved somewhat in strength, but still continued to suffer much from many of his ailments.

"WEDNESDAY, JUNE 28, 10 A. M.
(*written with pencil.*)

"Dear W. and M. I have ridden ever since five, without finding a tavern; so, being both hungry and tired, I sit on a rock beneath an *umbrageous shade*, ('sub tegmine fagi,)' and improve my time by writing. I had a fine ride the day I left you. I suspect you had a shower, but it did not touch me. I arrived at Kingsbridge, thirteen miles, about eight; got to the edge of Greenburg next morning, seven miles, to breakfast,—a fine, old, clean house, kept by fine, old, clean people, Van Wyck. I was quite delighted, though the same room served for parlor, bar-room, and bed-room; excellent milk, delicious bread and butter. By eleven, I got to Tarrytown, seven miles; and, being very tired, stayed till to-day. I might have breakfasted at Sing Sing; but, as I past there a little after six, I preferred to go on. I am now in the Highlands; but the Highlands have no taverns, and I hear and see nobody. This morning's ride has been most beautiful. The river is in view for miles, crowded with vessels, and many romantic spots on shore. I enjoy myself and my horse, who does well. Riding cheers me. I feel no better than when in New York; but, as I was dull there, being cheered is something. If I ever get to a tavern, I will write some more.

"Said tavern I found at half past ten; one room on a floor; folks washing; no hay, but exceeding good bread. Shall have to decamp soon. On my way, met two little Highland lasses, of whom I bought six cents' worth of raspberries. On asking, 'How far to a tavern?' they said, 'they had n't seen none go by to-day.' I had other conversations, equally pleasant and peculiar. For some miles I have lost sight of the river, and the road is very little frequented, and human habitations are scarce. About a mile from this little inn I fell in with Peekskill, passed through, and at four, P. M., am at the Phœnix Hotel! no other house within miles. Said Hotel one story high, not old and neat. Here I shall bivouac, fearing I may go farther and fare worse Thirty miles to-day, and not a little tired."

"REDHOOK, HERMANN'S INN,
"FRIDAY, JUNE 30, half past six, P. M.

"Dear W. & M. My mind misgives me that you did not get the letter which I sent from the *Pheönix* hotel. I left it for the stage-driver to put into the office at Peekskill, in order that you might surely have it by last night; but, as I forgot to leave a douceur, I take it for granted he forgot it. I therefore hurry to write again, to tell you I get on bravely. This makes a hundred and seven miles, as near as I can find, for no two persons agree touching any distances. I came from *Pokepsy* to-day, either twenty-six or thirty miles, nobody knows which. Rhinebeck is very pleasant. Poughkeepsie is very disagreeable. Redhook pleasant. This tavern is low, small, but tolerably comfortable; and, what is 'a sight for sair e'en,' possesses a handsome landlady, of genuine New England stamp, the first specimen I have met with; for, in truth, the greater part of the taverns are misery of the first water. Horse does exceedingly well. I reach Catskill to-morrow, and shall probably spend Sunday and part of Monday there. But where shall I keep 'Independence'? I must make an oration to the woods.* Doubtless they will murmur applause. I wish I had been weighed at New York; I have been very thin, but prognosticate a good fattening. If it were not for occasional soreness and pain, I should think I was fit to go home now."

"CANAL BOAT, CONNECTICUT, JULY 5, P. M.

"I remain just about so, except that for two days I have again had a little more uneasiness in my chest; no great, however. I took a boat on reaching the *canol* this morning, and shall arrive at Utica to-morrow noon. My last week's tour has been quite pleasant. I have seen the glorious Catskill, and written myself an ass in the album. I then crossed a very beautiful country, though rather by cross-roads, and got to the canal at six this morning. Thus far we have followed the banks of the Mohawk, which are pleasant and sometimes beautiful. The number of boats astonishes me; we certainly pass one at least every ten minutes. It is dull work on the whole.

* This allusion is explained by the circumstance, that he had been selected by the city authorities of Boston to deliver an oration before them, on the semi-centennial celebration of the Declaration of Independence. The state of his heal h had made it necessary, after having once made an engagement to accept the appointment, to ask to be relieved from fulfilling it.

No beauty of country can keep away ennui, in this indolent way of moving without motion, a whole day, at three miles an hour."

The interior of New York was at this time the seat of an extraordinary religious excitement; and, on arriving at Utica, July 6th, and proceeding thence to Trenton, he found himself in the midst of it. In a letter to Mr. Gannett, he gives some account of the state of feeling, especially with regard to the Unitarian Society at Trenton. This letter states things as they were seen and heard, under the immediate influence of the strong passions and prejudices of the period. That they were much colored and distorted, by the medium through which they reached my brother's mind, no one, looking back at this distance of time, will probably doubt. Some of the statements, particularly that which ascribes to Mr. Finney the assuming of a blasphemous title, were called in question at the time, and shown to be unsupported by any sufficient evidence. The general picture was found to be true; there was little exaggeration in the general impression given of the feverish and almost delirious state of the public mind; but some of the details had become magnified.

The expediency of bringing up, at this distant day, accounts like these, of so painful a character, may be thought doubtful. The religious body, concerned in movements of this kind, may regard themselves as misrepresented by them; to a certain extent they probably are so. But such events are a part of the history of the time; the misconceptions and misrepresentations of one party by another, are a part, also, of this history; and the history of the times is the only true back-ground of the picture of the individual. There is another reason for perpetuating these narratives, inserted as they are intended to be, not as certainly true in all their points, but as believed to be true at the time. The party referred to may feel that they are unfairly represented, and that false views are given of their motives, character, and intentions. Now, those impressions were made upon the mind of a man unusually kind in his feelings towards his opponents, disposed to a charitable construction, not inclined to a harsh estimate of other sects; yet they feel them to be erroneous. If they are so, should not the fact be a lesson to both of the parties? If, on the one hand, the extravagances of a few fanatical individuals, and the excesses of an excited community, at a particular time, are painted in somewhat too high colors, and regarded too much as the legitimate results of the opinions and policy of a particular sect,—may it not happen, on the other hand, that the apathy of the opposing party, their disapproval of the whole class of means of which these are a part, the cold regard in which they hold the whole matter of revivals, may be also exaggerated, and their motives be misconceived, and not be so attributable to religious indifference as has been supposed?

TO MR. GANNETT.

"UTICA, JULY 9, 1826.

"The great excitement which has existed for some time in this town and neighborhood, you have probably heard of. It has been attended with occurrences of outrageous and vulgar fanaticism, such as, I hope and believe, have never been paralleled; and, in its whole tone, has had a tendency to render religion disgusting to sober observers. To frighten by any means, the most unwarrantable, has been the great effort; and the indecorums, the breaches of good manners, the profanity and blasphemy, which have been committed, are almost incredible. The great leader is either a crazy man or an impostor. He calls himself 'the brigadier-general of Jesus Christ;' which is a characteristic specimen of his manner. In his manner he is copied by all the subalterns, most of whom are the young men from Auburn; who are let loose, during vacation, on the neighboring country, being boarded, it is said, at the expense of the institution; and who go round in bands, assailing passengers in the street, and prying into families, and, in the most impudent way, catechizing and threatening. The prayer for Colonel Mappa you have seen, I dare say; it ought to be published in the 'Register'; ought it not? It is a specimen of the style in which things are done.

"Let me give you a few other specimens. It is common for these young men to ask a passenger on the road, 'Where are you going?' He answers; and they say, 'No, you are not.' 'No! what do you mean?' 'Why, I say, you are going to hell!' This has become a by-word among the children, a lesson of profaneness to them, who are heard rehearsing the question and answer perpetually. Some one asked the great preacher (Finney) to lend him his horse. 'I have not any horse,' said he. 'No horse? Is not that your horse in the stable?' 'No, that's Jesus Christ's horse; if you are going on an errand for him, you can have him.' One of the preachers gave out that he could get his horse removed to any place he pleased, by prayer; could pray him out of one pasture into another. When displeased, the common phrase is, 'I will go and tell God of you,' &c. &c. You would hardly credit some of the stories It is proposed to write a history of the thing and publish it. Finney has at last been obliged to leave Utica, where he was for a long time; for the better part of the people became so disgusted, that they began to stir themselves, and then, perhaps, a Unitarian Society might have been collected; but things are hardly ripe yet.

"In this spirit and form a violent assault was made upon Trenton, and it was given out that the society should be crushed. 'Only pray, only keep praying, and we shall soon root them out,' said the brigadier-general. And they did pray, abusively, about persons, against persons, at all times, and in all places. Their emissaries were prowling about, sometimes eight, and even more, at a time. They left not a stone unturned. But, by the power of the truth and the blessing of God, the Society is firmer, more earnest, and more prosperous. It has gained accessions in number and in zeal. The minister has worked hard, perseveringly and successfully. Under such circumstances I could not resist the request to preach; and, as I am so much improved in strength, shall probably do it again. If a people ever deserved countenance, it is this people. For twenty years they have held up the banner through the burden and heat of the day, amid many discouragements and neglects; yet have they persevered with a spirit which does them great credit. They are much more numerous than I supposed. They are most intelligent, respectable and devoted, and, with their minister, should be held in constant remembrance by their more favored brethren."

TO THE REV. ISAAC B. PEIRCE OF TRENTON, N. Y.

"ALEXANDER, SUNDAY MORNING, JULY 23, 1826.

"I passed Wednesday night at Auburn. I intended to visit the Seminary in the evening, for the purpose of acquainting myself with its state, discipline, course of instruction, &c. But all the young men were at a prayer-meeting, and I went there too; and there arose to speak a man whom I soon settled in my thought to be the notorious Finney. He gave directions for the manner of praying, not so as to be accepted, but so as to produce *most effect* on the sinners present. Their prayers, he said, should be short, and they should particularly avoid all rehearsal of the divine attributes, in the introduction, as this tended greatly to let down the tone of feeling. A strange assertion! Some of his directions were exceedingly good. These young men prayed; their *only* object was to frighten. I do not believe they thought of anything else. And such unscriptural prayers I never heard. Violent, loud, full of gesture, full of denunciation, one half occupied in threatening sinners with hell, and the other half with hurling anathemas at those elders and other professors who do not join this work of revival.

"I have a poor memory for individual expressions, or I could repeat to you some most shocking language. One or two instances I remember;—'Thou knowest, Lord, that we would not thus plead with thee, if thy glory were not at stake; but thy glory is at stake; thou knowest, O God, that thy glory is at stake.' Sometimes they were strangely familiar, both in words and in tone of voice. 'Why, Lord, thou hast but just come here; don't go away again yet.' But, on the whole, it is not profitable to repeat such things. He made a long speech afterwards in the same strain; and I can now believe any stories I have heard of him. He has talents, unquestionable talents, but no heart. He feels no more than a mill-stone. There is proof, which no one who sees him can resist, that he is acting a cold, calculating part. This is a harsh charge, but I cannot avoid it. His tones of voice, his violent, coarse, unfeeling utterance, his affected groanings, his writhing of his body as if in agony, all testify that he is a hypocrite, and yet I try not to be uncharitable.

"Mr. Lansing, minister of Auburn, spoke and prayed in the same fashion, but with far more propriety of speech. But, in the whole evening, there was not one word, or look, or accent of tenderness, or one that indicated the slightest compassion for those poor wretches whom they were striving to deliver from damnation. This amazed me. If men are sincere, how can they help feeling and expressing pity above all things? What can we think of those who riot in damnation and torments, and seem to take delight in wrath and vengeance? I inferred from their language, that there is a strong opposition to their doings among the religious people of Auburn."

TO HIS BROTHER JOHN.

"JULY 10.

"I am now in Rome; not the Eternal City, mistress of the world, which, if you recollect, was situated in Italy; but Rome in that great State, which appropriates to itself great names, if not great things; and, but for a quarrel, it might have been, instead of Utica, the great city of the West. The authorities of the place thought the canal *must* go through the town, and therefore they stood out for exorbitant prices; and the State, rather than pay them, carried the canal through a hideous swamp, which everybody thought impassable. Now the Romans mourn, and all their great prospects are transferred to Utica. A pretty picture of wars.

"Your letter I got yesterday, and was rejoiced to see it. The parish have done a kind and handsome thing, and I am very grateful to them. [Referring to a vote to supply the pulpit during his absence without expense to him.] I continue to improve, as you may suppose. This horseback and change are wonderful. I am not all the time free from pains and some other troubles, but I make out to feel that I am gaining. I have hardly ridden more than twenty-three miles any day. I get excessively fatigued, and am obliged to lie down three or four hours at mid-day.

"Utica is beautifully situated, and beautifully built, and gives uncommon pleasure to the eye of a visitor. The passing of the canal through the centre is a circumstance that imparts a romantic charm, especially in the evening, when the multitude of boats, with their lights reflected from the water, gliding among the houses, the bridges thronged with persons looking on, the streets all alive with passengers, and the boat-bugles filling the air with music, constitute a sort of enchantment to one who is there for the first time. The weather for three days has been almost insupportably hot; I should think 98°. I could not ride yesterday after nine in the morning, and think I shall be unable to ride to-day."

He had been earnestly advised on this journey to avoid all professional exertions, and, fully intending it, had gone wholly unprepared, dressed in a light-gray thin frock and pantaloons, altogether in as unclerical a garb as could well be imagined. He felt, however, that the call at Trenton was so strong, as to justify the experiment of preaching under almost any circumstances.

TO HIS SISTER HARRIET.

"TRENTON, SUNDAY EVENING, JULY 16.

"I left all my sermons at New York, and took not a black rag of clothing with me, in order that I might not preach; and yet here have I stayed nine days *on purpose* to preach, in borrowed clothes too! a bottle-green coat!! Well,—there 's something new under the sun. I found the Society here just so situated, that I must have been less than a man to have refused to preach; and, finding that I did good, and excited attention, and strengthened weakness, I could not help staying a second Sunday. And I am so happy as to have got through perfectly without harm, I believe. I preached extemporaneously;—people from all the neighboring towns. There never were so many here together before, and the impulse given by a stranger from Boston is a great good to them. I have found excellent people here, and have highly enjoyed myself. I am greatly better than I was, and, having had this delay, conclude not to go to Quebec, but return directly from Niagara.

"My stay at Trenton has enabled me to learn something of the state of the country. It is full of Unitarians. Every village has them, and the time is coming, when societies will exist all around here. Trenton Falls are the most beautiful and splendid object of the kind which I have seen. Imagine a succession of hills, one above the other, of solid rock. Imagine an earthquake to cause a deep rent of two hundred feet in their centre, laying open a vast chasm, rocky and precipitous, its sides perpendicular, for two miles in extent. Then suppose a stream of water to rush through this chasm, a perpetual descent over rocks the whole distance, and sometimes leaping down ledges of ten, twenty, and thirty feet, so shattered as to be perfectly white, and the rocks so disposed as sometimes to throw one sheet directly against another. If you understand me, you have Trenton Falls. Nothing can exceed the variety of the scenery. The sides are all covered with green woods, and sometimes, in a narrow pass, where each side overhangs, there is a perfect smoothness of the waters, which are rendered by the situation black as ink. All travellers visit them now, —thousands; yet, four years ago, they were not known beyond the village. Mr. Sherman, formerly minister, once expelled from Connecticut for heresy, first made them known, and keeps a house for the entertainment of visitors,—the best house I have seen. He is a genius and a scholar. He has just written a new system of English Grammar, wholly original and highly ingenious."

TO THE SAME.

"Bloomfield, July 21.

"Remember, that in your person, or (to speak more exactly) in your appellation, are comprised all the folk at Northborough; and therefore this and other epistles are to them alike. With this proviso to quiet your and their jealousy, I proceed to say, that during this shower, I sit in the wide entry of this inn, master and mistress gone away, four children playing, and one crying, with a chequer-board in my lap and the inkstand on the chair, and send home my affectionate thoughts to friends and children, even as the sweet swan of Mantua saith :

'Dulces *repastus* reminiscitur Argos :'

In which line, by the way, I fancy there is a false quantity. But there is truth enough to make up for it; for, being interpreted, it signifies, 'Having dined on *sour* milk, he bethinks himself of his *sweet* friends.' I have not Dryden by me, or I would give you a more poetic version. At any rate, however, I hope it won't rain all the afternoon, for I had calculated it should read thus: 'After dinner he thought of going to see Elder Millard,' who lives only five miles off. But, instead of talking with him, I 'll while away an hour at Northborough. It 's so seldom that I feel any willingness to write, that it 's well to work while the fit is on me, or (seeing it rains) to make hay while the sun shines.

" I rode from Trenton, fourteen miles only, on Monday, and stayed at Whitesborough. Tuesday, I rode thirty-six miles, through Vernon, Oneida (the Indian village), Lenox, Sullivan, a small manufacturing town in a glen, to Manlius, an ugly, awkward village on a steep hill-side. Wednesday, thirty-three miles, through Orville, to Syracuse, a pretty large town, bran-new, right amongst the stumps of trees, which make a strange contrast with the fine houses, streets, and churches. The canal passes directly through, and makes a good deal of business. One mile distant is Salina, where is an immense salt spring, yielding one hundred and ninety thousand gallons an hour. It is pumped up by machinery, which is worked by water from the canal, and which distributes it to a multitude of salt-works that cover the face of the land. Salt is the staple article of Salina and Syracuse. Then I came to Camillus, Elbridge, and Auburn, sweet jumble of names. Auburn disappointed me. It is large, pretending, huddled, but not neat or beautiful. It stands on the top principally of one hill, and in the valley and on the side of another. Here I attended a prayer-meeting, whose horrors and blasphemy have not done ringing in my ears yet. Here is the State Prison and the Theological Seminary; or, as it has been appropriately styled, the *prison of the mind.*

"Thursday, thirty-three miles, to Cayuga, on the Lake of that name, which I crossed on a shabby bridge for twenty-five cents. The lake is very tame and unpicturesque, as are all the other lakes in this neighborhood, though pretty large. Then to Seneca Falls, and Waterloo, a pleasant village on the Seneca River, and Geneva, a large and beautiful town on the Seneca Lake. It is laid out principally in two fine, wide streets, overlooking the lake, one below the hill, and the other at its top; very compact and city-like, and with good taste and good effect. I put up for the night eight miles this side, and passed the night in company with a large party of bed-bugs, who feasted riotously, and disturbed my repose. There are a great many of this dissipated class in this part of the world. To-day I reached Canandaigua at nine o'clock. The country here is very beautiful and fertile, and laid out in rich, well-cultivated farms. It looks older than any I have seen. Canandaigua lies at the head of the lake, on a beautiful slope, built with great elegance and taste; trees, gardens, and front-yards much after the style of Worcester, Springfield, and Northampton, though naturally a finer site. It is by far the handsomest town I have seen. Bloomfield is a pleasantly situated town, standing on a hill much after the fashion of Lancaster. It has the reputation of being a rich agricultural town. The whole land is more fully peopled than I supposed; inhabitants are found everywhere on the road; no desert tracts; villages frequent and pleasant.

"All the papers are full of the death of Adams and Jefferson, as well they may be. Was ever anything so wonderful? I preached on the occasion at Trenton. I drew from their history, first, an encouragement to our country; secondly, an encouragement for Unitarianism."

TO THE SAME.

"ALEXANDER, JULY 23.

"In this eminent village (of thirteen houses) I have passed a quiet Sunday. I arrived here at half-past six this morning, having ridden from Batavia, eight miles, and being unwilling to ride further because of the Sabbath. But light clothes won't disguise a parson. He can be seen through them as easily as if they were only a robe of light. You remember Virgil sweetly singeth,

'Nimium ne crede colori;'

a most poetical verse, the sense and beauty of which I now for the first time fully comprehend. It means, literally rendered, (Dryden's version is more paraphrastic,) *The priest is a ninny* (the right reading being unquestionably *ninnium*) *who trusts to the color of his clothes to keep him incog.* And the poet goes on to say somewhat about blackberries, which I need not quote; but it amounts, if I remember, to this: 'You might as well make a blackberry pass for a currant by taking off its black coat, as turn a minister into a gentleman by the same process.' Now, I have been smelt out almost everywhere; people look at me and stop swearing;

'And, strut and swagger as I will,
I 'm nothing but a parson still.'

"When I was going quietly to meeting this afternoon, the minister accosted me in the street, and asked me to help him. I declined, saying, 'I am a Unitarian.' But the Presbyterian still wished it, and so I went and sat by him, or, as 'honest Will' more expressively phraseth it,

'Accoutred as I was, I plunged in;'

and, when he had done his sermon, I rose and exhorted on the same subject for ten or fifteen minutes. The people were very attentive, some of them shed tears, and none of them slept. Well, when I got back to the tavern, I learned from the landlady, who has held a long talk with me, that her husband and another gentleman said they knew I was a minister when I first arrived; but she had told them that she did n't believe it. So once more, as Virgil says, 'Never trust to a white coat to rub the black off a minister's back.' The minister invited me to go with him to attend another meeting four miles off. But I excused myself. Well, you say, what will happen next? Two Sundays in a bottle-green coat, and a third in a light-gray!

"After writing to you on Friday, I passed the evening with Dr. Millard, author of 'The True Messiah Exalted,' whom I found a sensible, interesting man, about thirty-three years of age. He received me with a most hearty welcome, seeming delighted to behold me, and tried to persuade me to spend Sunday and preach. I longed to do it, but had resolved to deny myself, and so I peremptorily denied him. I believe I was right; but, indeed, I regretted it, for I shall never be there again, and it would have been an opportunity to rivet one of the links of the great Unitarian chain of connexion, and a very important one too. If I should be unable to go home by the canal, (my present plan,) and should be obliged to ride, it is not impossible that I may give him a Sunday on my return.

"*Wednesday, P. M.* Here am I at Niagara Falls and in Canada. I arrived yesterday afternoon at four o'clock. At four miles' distance I first saw the cloud of vapor, which rises from them, and which may be seen twenty miles off. There also I first heard them, but their thunder is by no means so loud as I expected. I do not hear them in my room with door and window shut, though I am only a quarter of a mile distant. I have, yesterday and to-day, travelled over the whole ground, and seen them in every possible position. I expected to be disappointed in the first view, and therefore was not. After looking and studying them for hours, and in all points of view, in all directions of sunlight, I have got something like a sense of their magnitude, and a feeling of their sublimity. But it is a very difficult matter to persuade yourself of, or rather to comprehend, their vastness. I am not going to describe them, but will just say, that, as in every respect they answer the highest expectation, so in some they go beyond it. The Horse-shoe Fall is far more extensive than I supposed; the quantity of spray is vastly greater. The Rapids above are hardly less grand than the very cataracts; they would be visited as wonders, if there were no cataracts.

"The American Fall is not so far inferior to the British as is generally supposed. It is not so extensive, but has its own peculiar beauties; and one of the very finest points of view is at its base, a spot seldom visited because difficult of access. It is entirely white, while the British is a mixture of the most brilliant green and white. The rainbow is a very trifling decoration. These are the main points of remark from your present correspondent.

"I shall be able, when I see you, to tell you fifty things you never dreamt of. I wish you were with me, and a dozen others of us. How sad to go about looking at such things alone. Not a face here I ever saw, not a voice that I know, and not a soul that I can converse with."

TO THE SAME.

"Lake Ontario,
"The Good Steamship Frontenac, July 30.

"After last writing from the Falls, I matured my plans for a homeward jaunt; in doing which I found it necessary to skip Rochester, so that, if you have sent letters thither, all is, I shall never get them. I exchanged my poor, dear horse for another, and on Friday went to see the wonderful works at Lockport, where the canal, for a mile or two, is dug down through solid rocks, and where there are five locks in connexion, of most beautiful construction. The village itself is just budding amongst the burnt trees and broken stones, and consists of log houses, stone barns, stone fences, and stone grog-shops. But there was not a house there five years ago, and in five more it will be as large a town as Worcester.

"I returned to Canada yesterday afternoon, and came on board this boat, by which I design to enter the St. Lawrence as far as Ogdensburg, thence to Plattsburg, thence across Lake Champlain to Burlington, thence to Connecticut River, and down the river to Northborough. I cannot go to Quebec without greater expense of time and money than I can afford. My health is good, but the seed of my troubles is not killed, and uneasiness and cough still worry me a little."

Pursuing the route indicated in the last letter, he landed at Ogdensburg, and passing through the intervening portion of the State of New York, arrived on Saturday, August 5th, at Port Kent on Lake Champlain, in improved health and excellent spirits, but with his funds entirely exhausted; to which particulars the following epistle, which he despatched to his friend, the Rev. Mr. Ingersoll at Burlington, abundantly bears witness.

"Sunburnt and tired, a disconsolate traveller
Rests from his steed at the inn of Port Kent;
Neither a spendthrift, a drunkard, or reveller,
Yet emptied his purse to the very last cent.

Pity his case then, dear good Mr. Ingersoll;
Send him two dollars (the sum is but puny), or
Sad lack of help shall on Sabbath-day wring your soul
For leaving embargoed
Yours, Henry Ware, Junior."

Having received the aid thus solicited, he spent the Sunday at Burlington, and, afterward passing through Vermont and New Hampshire, reached home on Saturday evening, August 19th, having occupied in the excursion fifty-four days, ridden one thousand one hundred and sixty miles on horseback, and about five hundred in various conveyances. He did not seem at first to have made that improvement in health, which had been anticipated. A few days after his return he wrote to his brother in New York:

"AUGUST 27.

. . . . . . "It is true, I have improved less than I hoped, but I am still improving, and you need not fear but that I shall take care of myself. I have brought home with me my horse, and I propose to be on his back constantly. I plan to remain in Boston but three days in a week, including Sundays, and the other four to be travelling. I have several excursions in view, of two to four days each, which I shall take. By doing this, and studying none till November, I hope to do well."

In October he speaks thus of his health and other matters:

"OCTOBER 18.

"As to myself, you may depend on it that your accounts have deceived you as to my health. I am weekly gaining ground; everybody here says so. I preach little more than half the time, without great fatigue; I ride on horseback every day that is not foul, from five to twenty miles; eighteen miles to-day, twelve yesterday. I have a good appetite, and not much oppression from food; sleep pretty well, work very little, and I mean to live thus active in body and idle in thought all winter. I have given up some of my usual duties, and do not mean to be burdened by any extra cares. I say this to remove your anxieties. Many of my friends and parishioners have urged a voyage, but I could not think myself justified in such a step, while I felt all the benefits of it were gradually coming to me at home. I cannot perceive now, that I am not as well as ever; and, to convince you of it, I have half a mind to ride on horseback to New York, and catch you napping. I go in this style to Northampton the week after next.

"I wish I could tell you exactly what our condition is here, but in truth I do not know myself. Dr. B—— has drawn away some from our Societies, and I suspect that Orthodoxy rather gains ground. Many of our ministers and more of our laymen think no exertions should be made; and their sloth by the side of Orthodox zeal produces very unfavorable impressions. Some are awake and active, and will prevent the cause from sinking, if they do not promote it. Our greatest evil is want of ministers; openings appear everywhere, but we cannot make use of them. Our Theological School is so poor, that it almost languishes; three applicants went away because there was no support for them. We mean to create scholarships in our several parishes. But, in accomplishing our various designs, we are obliged to call so often and for so much money, that I am afraid we shall disgust our people. My parish raised last year more than five hundred dollars for the Theological School, and have now just raised four hundred and seventy dollars for India, besides about three hundred for other purposes of less magnitude. We have appointed Mr. Tuckerman Pastor of the Poor, and his support comes from the ladies of our several Societies."

In the course of the autumn, the good effects of his long absence continued to manifest themselves. He improved much, and by winter was in better health than usual, and was able through the whole season to accomplish more than he had perhaps ever done before.

In November, he wrote thus to one in the ministry,

who was laboring under much despondency as to his success in his calling.

"NOVEMBER 13.

"It distresses me to hear you speak so distrustfully of yourself. When I know your good purposes and principles, and your felicity of expression and real power of communicating thought, it grieves me, that, for want of a little of that confidence with which so many are overstocked, you should make yourself miserable. Why not acquire it? All my power of doing anything, which has led to the reputation I have got, (God knows how little I deserve it, and there are moments when I think of it with unspeakable wonder and shame, for I cannot take to myself any credit,) has been owing to a stern resolution and vow to throw off my diffidence, and substitute for it a certain nonchalance and affected indifference. This was hard to do, and I suffered enough; but gradually I did it, and now, after ten years' practice, I am pretty bold. I had my fears, my mortifications, my horrors of all kinds; but I determined to overcome them, or they would have overcome me.

"I do wish you would do the same. You would relieve yourself of a world of trouble; and it is all you want, in order to have your true worth rightly appreciated by yourself and others. You have a perfect right to assume boldness, and to feel as if speaking with authority. Who has the right, if not the minister of Christ? If he feels as he must do, on the great subject he treats, let him give way to his feelings; let them have full sweep; let him not repress them, subdue them, but cherish and express them. There is power enough in them to overcome and drive away the other feelings which weigh down a timid mind. Give them the mastery, and they will subdue those other feelings of a more selfish character, which really ought not to intrude on him who is speaking for God, nor be suffered to palsy his exertions.

"Do you not know that almost all the eminent men, whose

lives we are acquainted with, passed through similar trials; and, by struggling with them, became eminent? Do not give way to desponding feelings. If there be truth in man, believe me when I say, you have no cause. Your despondency makes the very evil you fear. Instead of dwelling on your own situation, and nursing the thoughts that dishearten you, shake them off, allow them no entrance; give yourself to your duties alone, and let your interest in them increase and increase, till it absorbs all your feelings, and till it drives these melancholy thoughts away. Do not reject this advice, for it is really wholesome, at least, well meant, and the result of experience. Make an effort, I beg of you, and God give you success."

CHAPTER XII.

FORMATION OF A NEW SOCIETY IN NEW YORK—SERMON AT THE DEDICATION OF ITS CHURCH BY DR. CHANNING—MR. WARE INVITED TO BECOME ITS PASTOR—HE DECLINES—HIS REASONS—HIS SECOND MARRIAGE—PLAN FOR A NEW THEOLOGICAL SCHOOL—ITS FAILURE—LECTURES ON PALESTINE—THEIR OBJECT AND SUCCESS.

1826-28. ÆT. 32-34.

A NEW Unitarian Society had been formed in New York, and their church was dedicated in the latter part of November of this year. The sermon, on the occasion, was preached by Dr. Channing. It was one of those great efforts by which he many times produced so remarkable an impression. His reputation, already so widely spread, drew together a very large audience, and one of a different description from that which usually attended in a Unitarian church. In a letter to my brother is contained an account of this performance. "Mr. Channing preached with wonderful animation and power, to an overflowing house, for an hour and a half, on the tendency of Unitarianism, beyond any other form of Christianity, to form characters of pure and exalted piety." "If I am not greatly mistaken, it is the most remarkable sermon he ever preached. B—— said he never was so excited in his life,—that, when he got home, he began jumping over the table and chairs like one crazy. The audience was such as probably no other preacher in this city ever had power to draw. So, also, in Chamber Street on Sunday morning; the house was filled full, and of the cream of the community. Of the dedication sermon what shall I say? It was altogether, and beyond all comparison, the greatest oral communication I ever listened to. The man was full of fire, and his body seemed, under some of his tremendous sentences, to expand out into a giant. He rose on his feet, thrust up both arms, and screamed, as one may say, at the top of his voice, and his face, say those who saw it, was, if anything, more meaning than his words."

In the course of a few weeks after the dedication of the new church, my brother Henry received an invitation to become its pastor. In their letter the committee say: "We beg leave to express our deep conviction, that the prosperity of this church, and of the great cause to which it is devoted, is intimately connected with your acceptance of this invitation." Some intimations that a movement of this kind was intended, had already been made to him, and, in answer to them, he had, some time before, thus expressed himself to his brother already settled in New York: "I wish you would think and say nothing about my removal. It is absolutely out of the question. I have looked at it, turned it over, longed for it; if there is anything I should prefer in this world to anything else, it is this. But it is impossible, and I will not deceive myself or you by any false hopes. I shall always come and see you when I can, and be with you as much as I can; but to live near you is not to be granted me this side heaven." After so decided an expression of his feelings on this subject, the invitation came upon him unexpectedly. There is no doubt, as the above passage implies, that, on many accounts, he felt a strong inclination to accept it.

Not that he had any reason for dissatisfaction with his situation in Boston. It was everything which he desired. His attachment to his people and to the community was very strong. But having taken a peculiar interest in the formation and prosperity of the church at New York, and regarding that city as a great and most important field for the planting and growth of liberal principles, he had an earnest hope, that, with a coadjutor, with whom he was so closely connected, and with whom he warmly sympathized, he could do something to further this object. There were also some strong feelings of a personal nature, both on his own and his children's account, which would have been gratified by a residence there. The step was urged upon him very earnestly from many quarters, and he gave it a serious consideration. The motives presented had undoubtedly much weight; he took ample time for deliberation, and looked at the matter from every point of view. Still, although it was almost painful to him to resist the solicitations of so many friends, he came at last very decidedly to that conclusion, to which his natural impulse tended from the first. The following extracts from his letters exhibit the conflict of his feelings on this subject.

TO HIS BROTHER WILLIAM.

"DECEMBER 21, 1826.

"I find to-day, that my advice to you, to get a minister at once, recoils on my own head. I have before me the communication of the committee, and a private letter from H. D. S——. I did not expect, after all the explicitness which I have used on the subject, that it would come to this. Do the gentlemen consider it possible for me to accept their offer? I have given to them no encouragement, nor to you. I have been plain, unequivocal, decided, allowing always that the situation itself would not be unpleasant, but not wavering a hair's breadth from the determined assertion, that I could not take it. After this, their letter embarrasses me, and must embarrass them,—*them*, for it will not now be so easy to make another selection, or induce another to come,—*me*, because I must either answer them without consulting my people, and thus perhaps not seem to treat them with all the respectful consideration, which is due under such circumstances, or I must consult my people, and thereby give rise to suspicions, and hard thoughts, and probably harsh words among them,—at any rate, turn their attention from the religious state in which they are growing, to a matter which will not favor their religious growth. For it cannot be concealed from them, that the affair has been before me some time, that I have been consulted before the church was built;—and then how can I persuade them that I never have in any way sought or encouraged the application? I feel greatly embarrassed. I would have been spared this crisis, and how to get over it in the best way I know not. If it were possible to keep it secret, I should get on, but I suppose no precautions on my part would effect this.

"I cannot say to you on this subject what I have not said before. If I were free to live and work with you, to be, with my children, near you and Mary, to labor in one of the finest fields which God has opened in our country would be of all things most pleasant and desirable to me. I could not ask, I could not fancy, a place more to my liking. This I have said, and still say. But, unless my views of duty are changed, I cannot, you know I cannot, leave this place for that. I will not go over all the ground; but there is one reason now operating, more powerful than ever. The Orthodox interest is full of energy, and an assault is making on us, which it will not be easy to repel. Every voice and every arm is needed here; and I can say to you, what I could not say elsewhere, that there are needful measures to be taken of essential and vital importance, which I think will not be taken unless I am here. Now, unless this state of things changes, I cannot quit my post; it would be treason."

TO THE SAME.

"DECEMBER 25, 1826.

"My last was written before reading your long letter, (of which I have to-day received the codicil or postscript.) I have perused it carefully, and have read it and talked about it to father and John. I acknowledge the power of some considerations;—you have stated them, as father expressed it, so as to make an exceedingly strong case. Some of them I had not seen in the same light before. You may rely on my giving them all fair weight. I am in for it, and will not decide till I have canvassed the matter thoroughly. If I know my own heart, I have no desire but to learn what is right and do it; not an easy matter, perhaps, and certain to be attended with unpleasant consequences, whichever way the balance may turn. Why then did you force me to it? What you say of my parish being no obstacle surprises me; the very circumstances you name render it a chief obstacle. I am bound to it in a peculiar way; and their uncommon kindness to me, instead of rendering easy, renders difficult a separation. If my parish were out of the way, there would be comparatively small room for hesitation. For, as you say, whatever I can do for the church at large, I can do as well in New York (and perhaps more of it) as in Boston. I have a thousand daily interruptions here, which there would not annoy me.

"Your cause will not suffer for want of advocates, you may rest assured. I have been already compelled to hear counsel on your side several times, and able counsel too. One thing I rejoice in, that the circumstances are of such a character, as will prevent, I think, all possible imputation of bad, and wrong, and selfish motives, whatever my decision may be; I may mistake, but I think it impossible. I am sure none such will govern me.

"I write because I cannot help thinking about it, not because I have anything worth saying. That I am perplexed and embarrassed, you may easily suppose. May I only be led right! If it were merely a personal question, how easy!—but it is a question of great complication and very extensive bearings.

"*Dec.* 26. I find, in reading this over, that I have probably given you the impression that everybody favors my removal. Not so. Some urge me as strongly against it, as others for it. I stated what I said, in order to convince you that I am determined to deliberate, and view the whole matter thoroughly on every side; and, although I am still persuaded that I cannot go, yet, for your sake, as well as from the importance and greatness of the question, I will look at it impartially. Depend upon it, you have a strong pleader in my heart; and, if there were no other voice, I should be at your side at once."

TO THE SAME.

"JANUARY 3, 1827.

"After much anxiety and painful suspense, I have sent a negative answer to the call. I found it was impossible to do differently, though I did my best to persuade myself that I might. And now it is over, and I will say no more about it. If it had pleased Providence to throw us together, it would have been delightful indeed; but as it is, we must be content to labor and live apart."

TO MRS. WILLIAM WARE.

"JANUARY 6, 1827.

"You will perceive that your two kind letters, with William's last, came after I had despatched my definitive. I can therefore give no heed to your arguments, which, indeed, seem to me to be without force. I could do nothing for my health in New York by working less, for I think no one should take that post who will not work more; and I certainly could not think myself justified in going into it, without spending far more labor than I undergo here. So that, so far as health is concerned, the Boston station would be the more favorable. You say, 'my *inclination* should have a *little* place.' I found at last, that it had a *great* place, and that without it the other reasons for removal would have weighed little indeed. If you and William had not been where you are, I doubt if I should have hesitated an hour."

His determination was made up at last very clearly and decidedly. It left no doubts or misgivings behind it, and at no subsequent period did he view it with regret. He was governed principally, as I think, by these considerations:

1. The general opinion which he had always maintained, that ministers should be slow to consent to a removal from one parish to another; never for the sake merely of bettering their worldly condition, nor without a probability of greater usefulness in a new situation.

2. The opinion, notwithstanding his view of the importance of the spread of liberal principles in New York, that still the great battle for them was to be fought in Boston, and in the surrounding community. He believed that their dissemination abroad depended on their condition here, and that whoever was capable of doing great good at any point out of the centre, could do as much or more at the centre itself.

It was on the same grounds that he had more than once opposed the removal of some of the leading clergymen from Boston and its neighborhood, for the doubtful purpose of building up new Societies even at important points.

In June, 1827, he was married to Miss Mary Lovell Pickard, daughter of Mark Pickard, Esq., formerly a merchant of Boston, and gathered his children again around his own hearth. Except occasional visits, he had now been separated from them about three years, during which they had been in the families of his sisters, Mrs. Allen, at Northborough, and Mrs. E. B. Hall, at Northampton. This, to one whose domestic affections were very strong, had been a great privation; and nothing but incessant occupation could have rendered the separation even tolerable. This re-union, under circumstances peculiarly favorable to his and their welfare, and also to the successful prosecution of his professional duties, was one of the happy events of his life; and the year which followed it, whilst it was one of the most active, was also to all human appearance one of the most successful of his ministry. He had, in the fullest manner, those testimonies to the efficiency of his labors, which were to be found in the increased attention paid to his preaching, the increasing fulness of his congregation, and multiplied proofs of the consideration in which he was held by the community.

His marriage was followed by a visit to the city of New York, where he preached three times on the 17th of June. From thence he took a short journey into the interior of that State, again visiting his friends at Trenton, and spending a Sunday with them. In the course of the year he made other excursions in various directions; but, agreeably to what he says in one of his letters, ("I make few journeys, and none for pleasure,") these were for some purpose, or were made to subserve some purpose, connected with his great objects. In August, he passed a short time in the Old Colony, going there for the purpose of preaching the annual Academy Sermon at Sandwich, on Thursday, August 23d, and, on his way there, having also preached the day before at Plymouth. In September, he gave the sermon at the dedication of a church in Saxonville, Framingham, built by the proprietors of the manufacturing establishments in that place. In October, he visited the State of Maine, and delivered an address before the Kennebunk Unitarian Association on, "the Trinity," which was published afterwards as a tract. In November, he went to Dover, N. H., in order to assist in the gathering of a society in that place, and in the same week he preached before the Female Humane Society of Marblehead. During the preceding summer he had also been engaged in selecting, preparing, and carrying through the press, a volume of the sermons, and extracts from the sermons, of his deceased friend, John E. Abbot, a labor in which he took peculiar delight. He had, in addition to all these extra-parochial engagements, a Bible class once a week on Monday, and on every Tuesday evening his house was open to his parish, who met there in an unceremonious manner for religious intercourse and conversation.

In the course of this season a plan was suggested, in which he became interested, for establishing a new theological school, on liberal principles, somewhere in the State of New York. It was proposed that this should be effected by a union with the sect of "*Christians*," who were numerous in the interior of New York and the Western States, and whose views of Christian doctrine assimilated very closely with those of the Unitarians of New England. This project seems to have been suggested by Mr. Clough, one of their prominent leaders, as appears from the following letters.

TO MR. ALLEN.

"JULY 23, 1827.

"We have had no little talk here within a few days, respecting a new theological school. Mr. Clough has proposed, that the Unitarians and 'Christians' should unite in one, on the Hudson River. Many of us think favorably of the plan, and are disposed to patronize it, if feasible, but are a little fearful that it is not. Others start strong objections to it *in toto.* Something must be done to gain us an increase of ministers. Has the matter ever been a subject at your Association? I wish it might be."

TO THE REV. I. B. PIERCE.

"AUGUST 1, 1827.

"I am sorry to say to you, that Mr. Gannett will not be able to leave here and visit you this summer. He has however been appointed delegate to the 'Christian' Conference at West Bloomfield, in September, and I hope will then be able to give you a call. Meantime I presume that you have learned from him all that may be necessary respecting your labors for the Association, in which I pray you may be successful and happy. Labors of this sort are most needful to be done, and nothing is more desirable than that our preachers should be so multiplied, and our means of support so increased, as to enable us to send messengers throughout the land. But at present the most that we can do is little. You will be glad to know that the Theological School at Cambridge is flourishing, and that our recent Exhibition was the most promising we have ever had. If, instead of six we had twenty such young men, we could speak a loud word for the truth. A plan has been proposed for instituting a new seminary in your State, near the River, in connexion with the 'Christian' denomination, for the purpose of multiplying preachers. Hardly any encouragement has been received yet; but perhaps, after agitating the subject a little longer, we may find the thing feasible. Doubtless many would be excited to such an institution, who are not within reach of Cambridge influence; and, by multiplying means, we should multiply men. Mr. Clough, an elder of the 'Christians,' a man of a good deal of talent and influence, has taken an interest in this subject, and, if he succeeds in effecting anything, will be a great blessing to his denomination."

This plan, it does not appear why, failed of its accomplishment. It is not likely, that two denominations whose members differed so entirely from each other in their education, habits and manners, social condition and associations, and in their modes of speaking and feeling on religious subjects, would ever have found it for their mutual interest to be so closely connected as this plan implied. However they sympathized in their doctrinal views of Christianity, there might have been found other differences between them, which would have proved a more serious obstacle to the success of the institution than even a diversity of creeds. My brother's earnest adoption of this plan, on its first proposal, grew out of his perception, expressed in the above extracts, of the great want of recruits in the ranks of the clergy. To this, indeed, he was constantly awake and frequently alludes. He had this further reason; the standard of education, the cast of manners, the modes of thinking and living, and consequently of preaching, of those educated in and around Cambridge, were such as, to a certain extent, to disqualify them for addressing certain classes of hearers, in such a manner as to make an impression favorable to liberal views of Christianity. He hoped that, in an institution like this, ministers might be trained, who would be adapted to such hearers.

His interest in this plan probably induced him to devise one for supplying the pecuniary wants of the school at Cambridge, and increasing its means of usefulness, which he put in execution the next winter. In the preceding year he had delivered, in the course of his Vestry services, a few lectures on the Geography of Palestine, for the purpose of conveying to his own parishioners more distinct views of Scripture facts. These lectures had been received with interest, and they had well answered their end. He proposed now to revise and extend them, to illustrate them by maps and drawings, and to deliver them to a public audience, at a moderate price, with the view of appropriating the proceeds to the education of young men for the ministry at Cambridge. His hope was to raise in various ways two thousand dollars for this object, of which he intended that the proceeds of this course should form the nucleus.

These lectures were given in an apartment in a building which had been recently erected by the Boston Athenæum, for the purpose of furnishing convenient rooms for public lectures and for the exhibition of paintings. The attention excited by the announcement of this course was far greater than had been anticipated. The introductory lecture, which was given in the last week of January, 1828, was attended by a great concourse; and, the number of persons who had bought tickets being greater than the room could accommodate, it was judged expedient to repeat them, and they were accordingly delivered to a second audience, the two courses going on at the same time. This unexpected success gave him very great pleasure, much more I think than if the object had been a personal one. He speaks of it thus in some of his letters to Mr. Allen and others.

"JANUARY 28.

"I do not yet know about the proceeds of my lectures. The Introductory was crowded and encouraging. I am told from every quarter, that I shall sell all my tickets, and, if so, I shall get about seven hundred dollars. But I have not expected, and do not expect, so much. If I can get encouragement to repeat them, I shall be rejoiced. I hope to go also to Salem; and, if I could do both, I should furnish my two thousand dollars this year."

"FEBRUARY 1.

"I have been busy, obliged to preach at dedication, lecture, &c. I gave my first lecture last evening, and feel happy and thankful for my success. I sold all my tickets, and might have sold more. But the hall was full. I have just been counting over my gains, and find in my hands six hundred and seventy-three dollars, and about ten more to be received from Hilliard. My expenses will be not far from fifty; so that I shall give six hundred and more to the Institution,—a very good beginning. Gentlemen urge me to-day to repeat, and I rather think I shall do it. If, by so doing, I could fill the hall, I should be right glad." . . . . .

"My Palestine Lectures have succeeded to my astonishment. They yield eight hundred dollars for the permanent scholarship, and one hundred and fifty dollars for the present year, besides my expenses." . . . . .

"My second course is about half as full as the first. I think people are interested, and the lectures are pleasant to myself, partly written and partly extempore. I am only cramped for time, as twenty lectures would not be half enough, and I give only five. I am going to Cambridge with them, and probably to Salem, and have been invited to Waltham. I shall thus get about twelve hundred dollars this year. How to scrape together eight hundred dollars more, I do not know, unless I should go to New York. How would that do?"

He was probably at no period of his life more busily engaged in every method of exertion, than during this season. He was literally crowded with occupation of every kind. Yet even in the midst of all this activity,—this unremitting devotion of himself to ordinary and extraordinary duty,—whilst he was actually accomplishing so much, and allowing himself so little time for relaxation or recreation as to excite the alarm, and call forth the remonstrances of his friends, he was frequently visited by a strong feeling of self-dissatisfaction. It often seemed to him, as if he did not accomplish all that he might,—as if he had within his reach means and opportunities of usefulness, of which he did not fully avail himself. One might almost hesitate in this case to give credit to the reality of such a state of mind, as that which dictated the following letter, did not the circumstances under which it was written afford the surest proof of its sincerity. It was dated on his birth-day, during a short visit to New York.

TO HIS WIFE.

"New York, April 21, 1828.

"This is my birth-day, and I was occupied yesterday, and last night, and this morning, in looking over my life, and into my character and heart. I would not dare to tell even you all that I have seen to mortify and shame me; and yet I have not been able to feel as I ought; and, what is worse, I fear that I am too inveterate to profit by my knowledge of myself, but must go on, one of that miserable multitude who 'see the right, and yet the wrong pursue.' I never yet was satisfied with my mode of life for one year;—perhaps I may except one, the first year that I was in Exeter. But since that, I have been growing worse and worse. I did think soberly, that, when I was settled down with you, I should turn over a new leaf; and I began; but, by foolish degrees, I have got back to all my accustomed carelessness and waste of powers, and am doing nothing in proportion to what I ought to do. In my standing and position, I have a great responsibility. I know what people, many of them, think, and what is the view of the public. I know that I have bestowed on me power to do a great deal, and a singular facility in doing some things useful, which lay me under an obligation; and I know that I do nothing in proportion to this ability and facility. Yet other people tell me I do a great deal, and I am stupid enough to take their judgment instead of my own.

"These, dear Mary, are the morning reflections with which I open my thirty-fifth year. Will the year be any better for them? I hope so, but I fear not; for I do not *feel* the weight and solemnity of these considerations, as they ought to be felt. My heart is hardened, and my conscience seared; and I expect to live and die as I am, and find that my whole reward is in this world. Dear Mary, I ask pardon for this strain; but I could not help it. Would to God I could feel all the gratitude I should for my singular blessings, and not turn them into curses. But, when I see how I use them,—in a word, I am afraid that, in talking to others, and going over the words and sentiments of religion and virtue, I have lost the power to apply them."

But it was the will of Providence, that he should be suddenly interrupted in the midst of these earnest and zealous exertions, by events which not only suspended his labors for a long period, but changed the aspect of his whole future life.

CHAPTER XIII.

SEVERE ILLNESS IN THE VILLAGE OF WARE—REMOVAL TO WORCESTER AND GRADUAL RECOVERY—ESTABLISHMENT OF THE PROFESSORSHIP OF PULPIT ELOQUENCE AT CAMBRIDGE—JOURNEY ON HORSEBACK THROUGH VERMONT, CANADA, AND NEW HAMPSHIRE.

1828. ÆT. 34.

In the last week of the month of May, 1828, he had been, as usual, much interested in the various Anniversary meetings, to which it is devoted. On the last day of it, Saturday, May 31st, he left home in order to fulfil an engagement to preach the next day at Northampton. This journey was then a very different thing from what it has since become. It was performed wholly in the old-fashioned four-horse stage-coaches, which left the city at one o'clock in the morning, and did not reach their destination till late in the evening. It was a hard and wearisome day's ride, even for a strong man. The day on which my brother went proved rainy and cold. He was exposed, and became wet, and on his arrival found himself already quite ill from fatigue and exposure. He passed a very uncomfortable night, suffered much from oppression at the chest and in breathing, and had a good deal of cough. Notwithstanding the continuance of these symptoms, however, he went into the pulpit and preached all day. In the evening he was no better; he passed another bad night, and in the morning was obviously very sick. Still he could not be persuaded, that he was so ill as to make it necessary that he should be confined at such a distance from home; and accordingly, after taking some medicine on Monday morning, without relief, he resolved to make an effort to reach home, and set out in the afternoon with this view.

He happened, most fortunately, to be accompanied by his friend, the late Mr. George Bond, who was on his return to Boston. They proceeded as far as the manufacturing village in the town of Ware, about twenty-five miles from Northampton, where they stopped for the night, intending to proceed in the morning. This, however, proved utterly impracticable. His powers of endurance had been taxed to their utmost, and he went to bed completely exhausted, and with every indication of an approaching fever. It was found, on Tuesday morning, that his disease was too firmly fixed to be kept at bay. He was compelled, though reluctantly, to yield to this conviction, and consented at length to have medical advice. The physician of the place, Dr. Goodrich, was called, who found him laboring under severe inflammation of the lungs. He was bled, and underwent other active treatment, which, with the rapid increase and severity of his disease, soon reduced him to a state of extreme prostration.

Mr. Bond left him on Tuesday morning, and in the evening brought the intelligence of his attack to his family in Boston. Starting in the next morning's coach, one of his friends reached him by Wednesday evening. The violence of his disease had not abated, but neither had it increased; and, upon the whole, his condition promised a favorable issue. He was as comfortably situated as it is possible for a sick man to be among strangers. He had large and airy apartments in an excellent hotel. Great interest was manifested in his case by the neighborhood, and offers of assistance in nursing and watching were made from many quarters. He had, indeed, all the alleviations of which such a sickness, under such circumstances, is capable; and, in addition to the attendance of his regular physician, had the advantage of the visits of his friend and classmate, Dr. Homans, then a practitioner in the neighboring town of Brookfield.

His case continued without any material improvement for about ten days. During this period, he suffered chiefly from fever, restlessness, and a very hard and harassing cough. He had the bloody expectoration usual in his disease, but in addition to it, on the fifth or sixth day, a pretty copious hemorrhage from the lungs, more so than is usual in similar cases. This, however, did not continue, and did not recur. The reduction of strength was much greater than is common in such attacks in persons of ordinary health, and he was exceedingly emaciated. Indeed, the entire and long-continued prostration resulting from this illness, which was certainly not one of extraordinary violence or duration, can only be attributed to that gradual exhaustion of the powers of his system, which had been produced by his unsparing application to his various labors, and which had rendered him totally unable to cope with a disease of even common severity.

In the course of a fortnight from his attack, his wife, who had been detained at home by the state of her own health, was able to join him; and he began gradually to improve, though his cough still continued to harass him. He was placed in a carriage and taken abroad, though still in a state of extreme tenuity and feebleness. As it was very clear that it would be a long time before he would be able to resume his duties, or even bear the fatigue of seeing his friends, it was judged inexpedient for him to return home; and lodgings were procured for him at Worcester, whither he removed, as soon as he was able, by easy stages, and there fixed his residence, with the intention of remaining through the summer.

In the mean time he had received the most gratifying assurances of the affection of his people, and of their lively interest in his welfare. These were exhibited not only by the deep anxiety manifested during his illness, increased as it was by the circumstances under which it occurred, but by the kind and prompt provision which was immediately made for the supply of his pulpit, so as to relieve his mind at once and entirely from all uneasiness on that account. Indeed, this event in his life, accompanied, as it seemed to be at first, by so much to render it one of peculiar trial and suffering, served to bring out expressions and testimonials of regard and sympathy for him, both at home and abroad, in quarters where he had no particular reason to look for it, to an extent for which he was by no means prepared, and in a manner to affect him deeply.

He remained in Worcester for about six weeks, his strength gradually returning, and his pulmonary symptoms subsiding. He was not able, however, to use his pen till the middle of the month of July. Extracts from letters subsequently written, will exhibit in the best manner the progress of his recovery, and the state, during it, both of his body and mind. The following, addressed to a young friend engaged in the study of divinity, who had written to him on the subject of a visit to Germany, was one of the first which he attempted.

TO MR. WILLIAM BARRY, JR.

"WORCESTER, JULY 12, 1828.

"It is such an effort to me to use the pen, that I shall be obliged to reply to your interesting letter very briefly. This I the less regret, as you appear, not only to be decided as to the course of expediency and duty, but also to have reflected so maturely and seriously on the only doubtful part of the question, as to render any warning on the subject unnecessary. I need, therefore, only say, that I view the advantages to be derived from a visit to Germany as so great and decided, as to make it a matter of congratulation that you are able to undertake it; not doubting that you will avail yourself of them to the utmost.

"As to the perils, your being perfectly aware of them arms you against them; and I should never fear to trust a man of sober and habitual religious principle and devout affections to a contest with mysticism and skepticism. My best wishes for your health and improvement go with you. May a good Providence keep you from all evil to body and to soul; and may you come back to us, thoroughly furnished for every good work, and zealous to devote your acquired gifts to the service of the churches, and the cause of truth and righteousness. Do not fail to remember, that I desire to be remembered with your correspondents, and to hear from you from time to time."

TO MRS. WILLIAM WARE.

"WORCESTER, JULY 13, 1828.

"I know that you will be anxious for the earliest intelligence, and therefore I write to you immediately, that Mary is safely the mother of a fine boy. She is apparently doing very well. This is another in the train of our blessings, which have been so singularly dispensed, that we almost feared that there must be here an interruption. That very event of my being taken ill away from home, which seemed so untoward, has proved to be the most kind appointment; first to myself, for I have doubtless recovered much faster than I could have done in Boston; and then to Mary, who was thought to run some risk in coming to me, but has been gaining strength, health, and flesh, daily, and is now in a situation quite as propitious, to say the least, as if she were amongst the crowd of friends in Boston. She has been my driver, too, till now I am able to drive myself, and can do without her aid.

"When our hearts are softened by sickness, and quickened by deliverance, how visible is the hand of Providence. In few circumstances of my life have I traced it with so much admiration, as during the last six weeks. Who would have thought, that I should have had the comfort of being attended, first by two brothers, and then by my wife; when I had no reason to expect either, least of all, the last? And, if I were to tell you how I felt, and still feel, about the truly fraternal visits of John and William, you would think me foolish. But so it is. I find that severe and solitary sickness opens floods of feeling; and makes even the little, every-day kindnesses of those around appear great and important. It will teach me to value more, and more willingly make, my visits to the sick; for, if apparently worthless in my own eyes, I shall know that they are inestimable in the view of the patients.

"I still gain daily, and begin to believe that I may hope for a thorough restoration. I hope to take horseback exercise this week, and, as soon as both Mary and myself are well enough, shall start for the White Hills. My earliest prospect of returning home and preaching is October."

"My feelings," he says, July 14, "are those of

health, excepting weakness, which is great. Within a week my voice has greatly mended, and I feel but slight uneasiness at my chest. I ventured to meeting yesterday morning; and, as I rode going and returning, and did not stand at all, I suffered no fatigue. It was a great enjoyment." July 25.—"I returned yesterday from a little jaunt of three days to Andover. Brother Allen drove me; and, though it was much more than I had previously ridden, I feel much better for it. In reply to your queries, no one can perceive that I gain flesh, but everybody remarks on the improvement of my countenance. I have walked a quarter of a mile, and this is as much as I have yet been able to do at once; but I can do it several times, that is, I have done it twice in a day. But, having usually ridden during all the cool hours of the day, I have made less progress in the power of walking than I might have done. I still keep open the blister, but it contracts in size. Further, I am not sure whether the uneasiness which I sometimes feel in my chest is within, or belonging to the external sore. But I am sure that I bear very little use of my voice, and have not gained in this particular for a fortnight." "I have received a long letter from ——, containing a solemn and pathetic argument and exhortation on the state of my case, urging England, and a year's relaxation, &c. I should be perfectly ashamed to go to England."

TO MR. GANNETT.

"The long letter, which I proposed writing, was chiefly to be a lecture on health, with personal application to the younger bishop of Federal Street. But I will give you two sentences instead of an epistle. I have long been concerned at your mode of life, which appears to be a careless, reckless throwing away of a chance of longevity; and, since I have been suddenly cut off in the midst of a similar career, I have thought of you much, and been anxious, like Dives, to send you a message, lest you also come into this place of torment. I refer not to work, but to imprudence; for it is nonsense to suppose that either of us works too much, whatever friends may say. Other men there have been who have done more. But we work imprudently, and I think very much alike. Want of method, late and irregular hours, neglect of regular exercise of body to balance every day the fatigue of the mind, and sometimes violent exercise, as if to do up the thing by the job. No constitutions can stand such a life. I am ruined by it, and yet I feel sure, that, by a right course, I could have done more in my profession than I have done, and yet kept my health. For me, it is too late; for you, it is not. And I am deeply anxious that you should act prudently from my experience, and not wait for your own. It is not health, only; it is the power of usefulness; and the sin, which weighs upon the mind and depresses it, takes away the consolations of a sick bed, embittering the heart with the thought, that we are suffering the just punishment of our folly and the neglect of duty.

"And there is no little sting added to the mortification, if, meantime, friends are attributing the evil to undue earnestness in duty. I would not have you feel this as I have felt it. It is the only drawback which I have had, amidst the many comforts and abundant blessings of my illness. A singularly kind Providence, a multitude of good friends, and everything which earth or religion could furnish for consolation and satisfaction, have made these few weeks of trial, weeks of peculiar blessings, which nothing has occurred to mar, except the intrusion of thoughts of self-reproach, because I had brought the evil on myself by negligent imprudence, after previous warning. I beg you to think on this subject, and *act*. You are endowed with powers of doing good, which not many possess, and which you ought not to trifle with. In these days they are needed."

The following is an answer to a letter from the same friend, proposing a missionary tour into the interior of the State of New York.

TO MR. GANNETT.

"WORCESTER, AUGUST 17, 1828.

"I received your letter yesterday, on my return from a ride to Ware, where I spent a night, revolving over in my mind the hours of my sickness. I drove myself in a chaise, which may show how far my strength has got. As to your plan, I see no objection to it; but, on the contrary, many things to recommend it. It will be of service to yourself; and I think it quite time, that the people of that region should have an opportunity of evincing the truth or falsehood of the assertion so often made, of their readiness to hear Unitarianism. I doubt whether you could accomplish it in a month, though in that time you could preach once in the principal towns. But might it not be more profitable to stay in some one place till, by repeated services, something like a permanent interest could be excited, and the embryo of a society possibly be formed? This may be worth considering. The present month is probably less favorable for such an experiment than the next,—especially than October; though, on second thought, the people in the large towns are not engaged in the wheat harvest, and it may therefore matter little. Mr. Pierce could inform you. Finally, I hope you will do it. On reaching one of the towns, you could in some way appoint one meeting, and at that it were better to name a second. At that time you could determine whether it were advisable to do more. Of course there are some hazards in preaching extemporaneously, but for such a purpose I am persuaded the advantages are such as to put all risk out of the question. It is a great matter to be able to change the subject and mode of treatment, and adapt and modify, according as experience or occasion shall suggest. Your facility is such, that you would apprehend nothing, and would only have to guard against your tendency to too great impetuosity, which sometimes might hurry you into indistinctness both of language and utterance. If you will bear in mind this single caution, you may be assured, I think, that you will do better to speak extempore, than to take any of your written sermons.

"I see no reason why the Executive Committee should not make an appropriation toward this object. It would certainly greatly favor our operations, to make a little excitement all along that road.

"You are right in your allusion to the proofs of Divine Goodness which have attended me. I have felt as if they were singular, and have looked at them in the train and development of events, very much as Jacob must have done, when he saw the end of his trials. Some of the most apparently adverse circumstances have ripened into great blessings; and I pray that I may come back to my place better fitted, as I may be and ought to be, for some of its duties. I feel now as if I could go to sick chambers with some confidence that I can give comfort and do good, which I never have felt yet."

During this summer a plan for establishing a professorship of Pulpit Eloquence and the Pastoral Care, in the Divinity School at Cambridge, was carried into effect. The want of a teacher in this department had been long felt, but I am not aware that any serious movement had been previously made for supplying it. The general feeling of the friends of theological education had been directed to Mr. Ware, as a suitable person to fill this place whenever it should be created, both on account of his hearty devotion to the duties of the pastoral office in his own person, and his well-known and deep interest in the education of young men for the ministry. His present sickness and its probable continued influence on his health, as well as the extent to which this had been previously impaired, rendered it desirable that he should be relieved from a situation in which he was constantly under temptation to continue a course of life which had already so much exhausted the powers of his constitution. The influence of this consideration on the minds of many of his friends doubtless hastened to maturity the plan for the establishment of a professorship at this time; and they took a strong interest in it from the belief, that it would be the means of removing him to a sphere of action, in which, while his duties would be less arduous, his usefulness would be at least not diminished.

Of this project he received early intimation, though no direct or official communication. It became necessarily, therefore, a subject of serious consideration with him; and he sought, in a confidential manner, the counsels and opinions of some of his friends, as to the course which it would be best for him to pursue, in case the proposal were directly made. He thus writes on this subject.

TO HIS BROTHER JOHN.

"WORCESTER, AUGUST 14, 1828.

"I got your letter to-night. I am surprised that the proposition is so old to you, for I had no idea that it had been heretofore hinted. The suggestion is almost new to me, except as I have sometimes fancied, in looking at the state and prospects of religion, that I had some notions which would do good at Cambridge. I think as you do, of the essential importance of that place. I have long seen what ought to be done; and, if it is said by those whose place it is to judge, that I am the person to undertake it, I should feel that I ought not to decline the task. A great undertaking it would be, and I could not engage in it without anxiety and fear. But I must say, that the duties would be more to my taste than any that I can think of; and, feeling the immense consequence of them, and having seen, by experience, what is needed, I should carry to the work an engaged mind and an earnest desire to effect something; and I have always found this one of the most essential qualifications. I have heard of it only through Mr. Higginson, who communicated the doings of the Directors and their conference with the Corporation, and that their determination is to make the appointment this fall, if they can get the funds. Means are to be taken for this end at once, and he says they are confident of success. In truth, the Institution cannot go on till it has a reinforcement. But my feelings respecting a parish, which has come round me as ours has, and has always treated me with such exemplary candor and kindness, will render the struggle not an easy one.

"Of course nothing will be said of it till the appointment is made. I am very glad to have your so full expression on the subject;—it makes me more sure that I am not wrong."

Towards the end of August, he had so far recovered his strength as to render it safe for him to undertake a journey alone on horseback, a remedy which he had before found so beneficial.

The following notices of the route, incidents, and other circumstances connected with this journey, are selected from letters, chiefly to his wife, written in the course of it.

"*Templeton, Monday, August* 25, 1828.—Dined in company with two —— ministers, one of whom complained that brandy was put on the table, and went on to gormandize meat, pudding, and pie, three cups of strong coffee, and two tumblers of bottled cider. The other ate, as I did, of but one dish. The day was excessively hot, but a good breeze till about five, P. M., when the afternoon became still, close, and uncomfortable. I reached Winchendon, seven miles, about seven o'clock; miserable inn;—milk set on the table in an old broken white earthen washbowl, and a tea-cup to dip it out;—crackers, baked at least two years ago. I think my plan of two meals a day will answer very well. As yet, I feel finely. I shall seek to ride, as I did to-day, from six to nine or ten, A. M., dine at twelve, and take milk in the evening. Being nowhere at the breakfast hour, nobody is distressed at my going without a meal, and I ride far more comfortably.

"*Thursday.*—Rode thirteen miles to Walpole, and from here shall despatch this letter. My thoughts go to you, and fancy that you may be quite sick, and half suffocated in your hot room, while I am here enjoying myself in the wide and free world. But I will not doubt that you are doing well. What perverse creatures we should be, if, after all the past, we could not take quietly and with confidence, any course of events. . . . . .

"*Woodstock, Vt., Sat. Eve., Aug.* 30.—This hot weather has been really terrible. For myself I have not greatly suffered from the heat, except through the sufferings of my horse, who has so wilted under it as to retard me in my way. I was yesterday weighed, and have gained two pounds since I was at Ware, five weeks ago. This is a very pleasant, well-built village, about as large as Worcester, lying directly in the midst of very high hills, which crowd upon it on every side. It is very striking, after riding among the mountains for eight miles, with here and there a little, one-story house perched on the hill-side, to enter suddenly on a town like this, crowded with people and bustling with business. You wonder where they can have come from. Saturday is the day when the neighboring farmers throng in to buy and sell; when I arrived, the streets were literally full of men and wagons and horses, as thick as I ever saw them on the Common at Commencement.* The country in this State strikes one finely;—noble hills covered with cattle and orchards, here and there a beautiful valley, richly cultivated, and everywhere little mountain streams with their mills. I find, too, that Vermont gains in population faster than Massachusetts.

" *Sunday Eve.*—One never knows who may be near him. Here I was glorying in my incognito, and fancying I might do any mischief and no matter, when, lo! a gentleman this morning calls me by name, and I find it to be Mr. Ward, of Worcester, just returning from Quebec, and he introduces me to Mr. Atkinson, who knows me well by sight. Then, on returning from church, the first sight is Miss Storrow entering the tavern with other ladies, and she leads me up stairs to her uncle's apartment, and introduces me to a host, and so I am at home at once. . . . . . I have heard the Calvinist and '*Christian*' ministers to-day. Both pretty well; the latter quite ingenious in a parallel between Joseph in Egypt and Jesus Christ.

" *Monday, Sept.* 1.—Went fourteen miles over a most wild road, through a region resembling the Catskills, the road oftentimes formed on the side of just such precipices as we saw at the Catskill water-falls. Very few houses; here and there a little interval between the mountains capable of cultivation. I am drawing nearer and nearer to the highest mountains. I stopped at noon at the only tavern, and found a very pretty family;—two rather handsome daughters, who wait on travellers,—very modest, proper, and well-behaved. One might hatch up quite a romance here. I had intended going no further than this, as there is no decent stopping-place under fourteen miles; but, as the day was cloudy and cool, and I in a hurry for my letters, I started and went right up hill for seven

* He refers to the days of his boyhood, when the spectacle exhibited by the town of Cambridge on the day of this anniversary was very different from that which is now witnessed.

miles. This is crossing the Green Mountains; and, if you can fancy a road just twice as bad as that which we mistook in going to Trenton, you will have an image of what I passed. A shower overtook me at nine miles, and I stopped at a poor tavern for the night, very near Killington Peak, which used to be thought the highest of these mountains, but has been lately ascertained to be, I think, the third in altitude. It stands very majestically before this house, and is this afternoon wrapt in very thick and dignified clouds. The name of this place is Mendon;—only *sixty families* in the town, and only one house in sight of this. The landlady is a genuine scold, the first I have heard for a long time; and her poor husband looks so sad and drooping, and her four children are so cross and impudent. . . . . .

"*Thursday Eve.*, *Sept.* 4.—Conceive of my fidgets, impatient as I am to be at Burlington and hear from you, to be obliged to stay at Brandon all day yesterday, and only make out to-day to dodge between the drops seven miles to Salisbury. The land is all afloat."

The time which he was thus obliged to consume on the road, was not wholly lost. His mind and pen, as we shall see hereafter, were now occupied during his moments of leisure in the preparation of a work which he had in contemplation; and the following poetical epistle to his wife, written at the same time, shows by what kind of thoughts his idle hours were employed.

"TO MARY.

"Dear Mary, 't is the fourteenth day
Since I was parted from your side;
And still upon my lengthening way
In solitude I ride;
But not a word has come to tell
If those I left at home are well.

"I am not of an anxious mind,
Nor prone to cherish useless fear;
Yet oft methinks the very wind
Is whispering in my ear,
That many an evil may take place
Within a fortnight's narrow space.

"'T is true indeed; disease and pain
May all this while have been your lot;
And, when I reach my home again,
Death may have marked the spot.
I need but dwell on thoughts like these,
To be as wretched as I please.

"But no,—a happier thought is mine;
The absent, like the present scene,
Is guided by a Friend Divine,
Who bids us wait serene
The issues of that gracious will,
Which mingles good with every ill.

"And who should feel this tranquil trust
In that Benignant One above,—
Who ne'er forgets that we are dust,
And rules with pitying love,—
Like us, who both have just been led
Back from the confines of the dead?

"Like us, who, 'mid the various hours
That mark life's changeful wilderness,
Have always found its suns and showers
Alike designed to bless?
Led on and taught as we have been,
Distrust would be indeed a sin.

"Darkness, 't is true, and death must come;
But they should bring us no dismay;
They are but guides to lead us home,
And then to pass away.
Oh, who will keep a troubled mind,
That knows this glory is designed?

"Then, dearest, present or apart,
An equal calmness let us wear;
Let steadfast Faith control the heart,
And still its throbs of care.
We may not lean on things of dust;
But Heaven is worthy all our trust.

'*Salisbury and Vergennes, September 4th and 5th.*"

"*Burlington, Sept.* 6.—I cannot tell you how I felt on getting your letters this afternoon, and learning how you had been all this time. You are a good creature to write so fully, and I am as happy as a prince. I never will be a fortnight again without hearing. I have tried it this time, and it is enough. . . . . . The rains have been tremendous,—torn away bridges and made gullies, so that many places are dangerous. You see on the other page how I employed myself yesterday and to-day. There is no great poetry in the thing, but a great deal of truth; and, as it was a pleasant exercise to me to fashion it, I hope you will not find the reading of it otherwise. It is as sincere as if it were prose. . . . . I expect to spend next Sunday (14th) in Montreal; from Montreal to Quebec in the boat, and ride back; then take the boats through Lake Champlain, and again at Albany, and so go down to New York, whence by land home. This seems to be the most feasible plan, and may bring me home by the first of October, when I trust I may find you in our palace in Sheafe Street, and a happy day it will be. I have no doubt from appearances, that I may preach then a little, and, by making head-quarters there, and driving round the country week days, get through the fall very well. In which said drivings I shall have sometimes your company, which I have often sighed for, and which would have made many of the sights and scenes I have been passing far more interesting. But all in good time. To-day I shall be much by myself, and hope to enjoy it. It is singular, that each of these three Sundays there should be very particular causes making it uncommonly desirable I should preach, especially at Princeton and here. At Woodstock the '*Christians*' would have been glad to have me, and it was an opportunity to be much prized. I really feel this deprivation not a little. But yours is still greater in not being able to attend worship at all. May it be more than made up to you in private and in other blessings.

"*Monday Evening.*—Swanton, eight miles. This is the last town in the United States. The Canada line is about seven miles from this. A fine place for smugglers. Many fine mills and large water works for cutting and sawing marble. Training-day; a militia company abroad in all its glory,—some with bayonets, some without,—some shouldering ramrods instead of muskets,—one with a stick of wood, of the sort called *cat-stick*,—and one marching majestically, with both hands in his breeches-pockets,—their whole deportment corresponding. It was all of a piece with the court which I saw this morning, where the lawyers were eating apples, and actually more than one continued eating while addressing the judges. Weather a little more moderate to-night. Only twenty miles to-day, when, if my horse had held out, I might have gone forty;—twenty is not enough, especially as I can much of the time only go on a walk or a jog but little faster. I need more exercise; I am sure, therefore, that I shall quit the horse. Miserable accommodations here. I am in a room twelve feet square, with a bed, a chair, and a wash-stand;—I am writing on the wash-stand. Having set the basin on the floor, I have taken out the drawer and laid it bottom up on the top, and lo! an elegant writing-desk. But I am as well and as happy, as if I were master of the palace of Versailles, and possessed the power and luxury of its owner. I hope you are so too;—would that I possessed the looking-glass of the fairy tale, by a peep into which I might see you as you are.

"*St. John's, Wednesday Evening.*—Leaving Swanton this

fine, beautiful, and cool day, I have urged my Rosinante vehemently till he has fairly brought me thirty-five miles, by which I gain more than a day. I am not sensibly tired;—the road has been level all the way. After about six miles I came to a spot where the lake had overflowed the road for nearly half a quarter of a mile, and I was obliged to ride through the waves two and three feet deep. Then a small river, from which the bridge had been washed away, over which I was ferried by a girl of blooming sixteen, without stockings,—who made a very interesting Charon, and wet her beautiful ankles in the cause. Soon after this, I crossed the Canada line, and fairly entered his Majesty's dominions. The frontiers on both sides are miserable;—thinly peopled by poor settlers in shabby log-houses. The first village was at Misisque Bay; after leaving which, the road winds round the head of the lake within twenty feet of the water for nearly two miles,—a deep sand mixed up in a rough style with stumps and boards, so as to make it almost impassable. The boards are brought into the lake from the various streams on which saw-mills are situated, and then are washed on the shore at this northern extremity. The recent freshet has deposited hundreds of cart-loads of timber, and boards, and sawdust. The road is therefore an unamalgamated mixture of those things. The next village is Henryville, twelve miles from St. John's; and here begins a wide road, straight as an arrow and level as a canal. You might see the whole distance, nay, to the north pole if it were not for the sphericity of the earth. I never saw anything like it. It tires one to look at it. It is now, after the rains, bad, but it is usually excellent, as I could see from certain passages. It is lined along the whole distance by rows of log-houses, or rather timber-houses, all of one size and shape, about twenty or thirty feet square, with one door and three windows; some very neatly whitewashed. The people seem poor and dirty. I could see into their houses as I passed; there is but one room, and this often has two beds in it; cooking seems to be done out of doors, and there the oven is sometimes built over the pigsty. The land is hardly cultivated at all. I find that the road runs along the River Richelieu, perhaps a mile from the bank, but the river is nowhere visible. I crossed it at this city over a fine wooden bridge nearly as long as West-Boston bridge. This is a shabby town, not very large.

"*Montreal, Thursday*, 11*th*.—I left St. John's at about nine o'clock for La Prairie, eighteen miles, a small town on the St. Lawrence, which derives its name from its situation and the neighborhood.

"One vast plain as far as the eye can see, not fertile or much cultivated. Everything like a foreign land,—strange manners, dress, and language. Every boy I have seen had on John's old, torn, straw hat, and almost every woman too. At half past one took steam-boat for this city, and came over in an hour, nine miles,—not right across, but down stream. I was disappointed at finding nothing at the post-office,—yet perhaps ought not to be. The first view of the city is better than I expected;—streets narrow, but houses of substantial bluish stone, well built. The mountain gives the town a picturesque air, as it often may be caught in glimpses as you pass the streets. The handsomest thing I have seen was a Highland soldier, keeping guard at the Government House. I had no conception of so rich a dress upon the breechless fellows. The cathedral is truly grand,—nearly enough finished on the Gothic model to give you a good idea of the whole. I have been into one of the churches, but not to examine the pictures. It is pleasant to me, I confess, to see the church standing open, and people passing in and out to their devotions, and men, women, and priests all engaged there. There were not a few; six priests variously employed, the oldest nearly eighty, and the youngest a handsome, happy-looking youngster of nineteen or twenty. The various styles of crossing with the holy water amused me. I went and looked into the font; it ought to have a great deal of spiritual holiness, for it has a vast deal of carnal dirtiness. The buildings of various sorts belonging to the church are of immense extent, and give an idea of its wealth and influence, which I was not quite prepared for. One of the first things that strikes your eye here is the number of men dressed in religious habits, whom you meet in the street, and the number in military apparel,—the army and the Catholic church. I came in the stage-coach from St. John's, having left my horse to be cosseted. I shall save seven days of time by it at least, and probably a little in expense too. This, however, is not quite certain. I am now just where I long to have you with me; I shall omit seeing many things till you come. I wrote to William, and to the Parish Committee too, within two days past. I am more truly tired to-day than since I left home,—standing, waiting, and walking.

" *Steamboat Richelieu, River St. Lawrence, September* 13.

. . . . . . My last was written on Thursday, the evening of my arrival at Montreal, and contained my first impressions after a four hours' visit. I put up at the Mansion House, a fine place, where were none but regular boarders, to one of whom I had a letter, Mr. Handyside, whose wife is sister of Mr. Adams of Burlington. They dine together in great style at five o'clock, but meet at no other time, breakfasting and teaing as they please. Yesterday morning, I arose at six and walked abroad to the city, having a direction to the principal buildings. I breakfasted alone at half past eight, and then immediately took a saddle-horse and rode round the mountain; not a very mighty mountain, but high enough to afford a very extensive view of a very flat and peopled country. The air was unhappily thick. Having crossed over, I went a few miles into the country and returned by another road around the southern base, passing many fine gentlemen's seats and delightful situations;—vast quantities of apples and crab-apples, but scarcely any other fruit. It was half past twelve when I returned; so, having eaten my lunch, a necessary part of Montreal life, I sallied out again to see the town. I looked at the pictures in the old cathedral, which do not seem very extraordinary, though two sufficiently pleased me. I tried hard, but unsuccessfully, to get entrance to the English church and hear the famous organ, and passed an hour in a very entertaining way in court, where the French and English languages are used promiscuously. And never did I witness a more disorderly scene, not even excepting the shabby court at Providence. The lawyers talked two at a time, interrupted one another, interrupted the judge, rushed from their places, and acted the part of angry men, with most vehement noise, and all sorts of gesticulation; meanwhile their clients often broke out aloud, contradicting their counsel, and the witnesses gave their testimony in long orations, emulating the tones, and shrugs, and eloquence of the lawyers themselves. Several causes were carried through while I was there, and all in this way,—all French; and I did think his Majesty's judge and barristers might visit the States and get a lesson of decorum and dignity from brother Jonathan. Then I went to the post-office, but no letter. Home to dinner at five o'clock, to tea with Mr. and Mrs. Handyside at seven, and aboard the boat at eight, for I have seen all the outside of Montreal and have no means of seeing the inside. Ten,—I am glad to be off. The night was dark and rainy,—the day is the same, and I am shut up in the cabin. I keep my eyes turning to shore, but see nothing interesting yet in low and level banks. We expect to reach Quebec at five o'clock.

"*Evening, Quebec.*—Conceive of me here, dear Mary, on this romantic spot, actually in a garrisoned town, where almost all you see and hear has to do with war and military affairs, and common conversation is just like what you read in books,—at least so it has been this evening. One of our boarders (we are but four gentlemen and two ladies) is a colonel, who has seen service, and is still connected with the army. I have already had from him many anecdotes of the late war, in which he acted a part. The house is close by the barracks and parade-ground, where I hear music and other martial sounds constantly. We arrived at half past five in the midst of the rain, which compelled me to buy an umbrella as soon as we left the boat, and has prevented my walking round the town at all. The arrival is quite imposing. You see the hill on which the city stands, when approaching it two miles distant. The river-banks for that distance are very high and steep, very like the banks at Trenton Falls. When within a mile, you see a cluster of houses on the shore under the bank, and great quantities of lumber. This is Wolfe's Cove, where he landed and climbed the precipitous banks to the Plains of Abraham, directly above. Passing this, you come upon the Cape, (which is a continuation of those high banks,) at the spot where the river St. Charles joins the St. Lawrence. On this point is the town. You see a town below the bank on the very water's edge, but nothing above till you turn the corner;—then comes in sight the real city, hanging fearfully on the very verge of the precipice as if it would fall off. You land amidst buildings, and ascend by a narrow, crooked, and steep street, most compactly built, till you enter the huge gate near the top of the hill. Our house is near this, and further I have not seen. I find, however, that it is a much more crowded place than I had supposed, not less so than Boston, with nearly half as many inhabitants, and about a thousand fewer than Montreal. The latter is much more loosely built. There is great intercourse between the two places, ten steamboats running there daily, or nearly so, and the fare but two dollars,—one hundred and eighty miles.

" *Sunday Night.*—I went out for my walk before breakfast for an hour,—a bright cool morning,—and took the compass of the town. I passed through three of the gates and saw the thickness of the walls, in one place fifty feet. I have, however, no distinct notion of the thing, and, if I had, would not try to describe it on paper. Immediately after breakfast. I again went forth, and in the Catholic cathedral heard the sermon to the troops and the English, by a young man ; and an uncommonly fine discourse, on the obligation to make our lives consistent with our profession,—an elevated piece of composition, lucid, forcible, and earnest. Thence I went to the English cathedral, and heard the service for troops there, (for that is the stated place to which they are marched in a body,) very poor and dull. Then went to the Romish cathedral, and heard the conclusion of a very animated French sermon, and witnessed high mass,—three bishops, and thirty or more other clergy, and the big building jammed with people. Thence to the regular service of the English cathedral, where I heard the bishop of Nova Scotia give an exceeding good preachment,—his manner simple and solemn, and, bating a bit, his discourse good. In the afternoon I heard a Scotch Presbyterian scream out a poor sermon to a thin audience. Rather a dissipated day, you will say ; but I have gratified a good deal of not irrational curiosity, and can truly say, that I entered into the spirit of much of the liturgy, and did not lose my time. But how glad I shall be of another quiet Sunday, in my own home and amongst my own people. The market was open and thronged till nine o'clock or later this morning ; and, at four this afternoon, the troops were paraded and reviewed, and half the city was out to see them. This is done every Sunday. The new governor I saw at church, and mean to attend, if possible, his first levee, held to-morrow.

" *Monday Night.*—I sallied out to the drill of the troops before breakfast, and after breakfast passed out of the principal gate of the city, that of St. Louis, on an excursion to the Plains of Abraham, where Wolfe's battle was fought, about a mile from the city, now a race-course. I saw the spot where he fell, and passed on to the bank, up which he led his troops; clambered down the steep; and, coming to the water's edge, entered the lower city over the spot at which Montgomery fell. It seems to me that his was a most insane expedition. I do not see how it is possible for any troops to force a way into Quebec. I then took the ferry across the river to Point Levi, which affords the finest view of the city; and, after staying half an hour returned, traversed the whole length of the lower town, and got home at half past two. Took a nap and went out again over some portions of the fortifications which I had not seen; returned to dinner at five; at seven attended for an hour the meeting of the Wesleyan Missionary Society; took tea at half past eight, and am now in my room just fit to think of home and go to sleep, while the music from the barracks is just far enough off to soothe me. To-morrow I hope to visit the Falls of Montmorenci, the citadel, and the armory, and in the evening start for Montreal. I must tell you what affected me a great deal this evening. I went to the Wesleyan chapel at six, thinking it the time of meeting. The candles were lighted, the house was empty, and I saw in an obscure corner a soldier with his cap off, kneeling down at his devotions. I could not help contrasting it with the probable employment of a great majority of the garrison, who are so peculiarly exposed to temptation and dissipation.

" *Wednesday Afternoon.*—On board steamboat *John Molson;* none of them to be compared to ours; less neat and orderly. Yesterday's visit to the Falls was a failure; I missed my road and came away without seeing them. However, I had a pleasant ride;—on the whole a very pleasant visit, though I have seen less of the inside than I might have done under other circumstances. The new fortifications of Quebec, which are very astonishing, I regret not being allowed to visit, and some of the religious houses I would like to have seen. But I shall never despair of coming again. Take it for all in all, the situation and vicinity are more charming than any spot I have known. As to an army taking it, it seems to be impossible; and, as to a blockade, there are always kept on hand two years' provision for twenty thousand men, so that the place cannot be starved. But, if I see it again, you shall be with me.

"*Sandy Hill, Sunday, Sept.* 21.— . . . . . . Only consider that I am now three hundred and twenty-three miles on my return, and so much nearer home than on last Sunday. In about ten days I shall be with you, unless things change; and, in reasoning about the matter, I am really at a loss to know what would be best. I feel able to be doing something, and I know there is something to be done in the parish which I can do. I do not doubt that I might now preach half the time without danger. . . . . . It is very desirable to be near enough to the people to attend to their affairs, and show them some sympathy, and seem to be caring for them. I really see no cause why I may not do it now; and I will promise to preach only one half the time and to be extremely prudent. . . . . .

"The preaching in this village,—a pretty large and handsome one,—is by Methodists and Presbyterians alternately. To-day was the Methodists', and I have been quite gratified by two good sermons, in a very plain, energetic, affectionate manner; in the morning, on the value of the soul and the danger of neglecting it; in the afternoon, on the character and security of the disciples of Christ. It was a pleasant day, even to the nasal psalmody which vented itself in the ancient fuguing tunes of my boyhood. We have a talkative, inquisitive woman from Boston here; who thrust herself on me to wait upon her to church. She inquired of a boarder on her return, why he did not go. He replied, that he did not like to hear the Deity abused, and he heard him worse abused in the pulpit than by any mob on the Common;—they attributed to Him their malice, revenge, selfishness, and many gross vices. This led to further conversation; and it soon appeared, that, though he had heard enough to justify him in this, yet he knew nothing as he should do, for he quoted some of the most offensive sayings of Calvinism as parts of the Bible. When I assured him they were not, he said he thought they were, and left the room. Yet he was setting up for a champion of the Divine Character! I had quite a pleasant talk with a Methodist and his wife, on board the boat, who, finding I was a Unitarian, from Boston, were very anxious to learn the nature and quality of my faith. He appeared very kindly disposed, listened candidly, and, when I offered him some tracts, promised to read them carefully, which I doubt not he will do. This woman, whom I have just mentioned as boarding here, has done her prettiest to find out who I am. She asked where I did business, and at last, when she could hold out no longer, asked plainly my name. However, I chose to evade her; but she is sure she has seen me somewhere. She is quite an original, and amuses me much. She has just offered to wait on me to the Falls, and it will require some generalship to get rid of her. After the bustle and hurry of the last ten days, I greatly enjoy this quiet retirement. I hope you enjoy the day too. Peace be with you.

"*Stillwater, N. Y., Sept.* 22. *Monday Evening.*—Mary tells me that you have sent to me at Montreal; which letter, as I shall not receive it, there is more need that I acknowledge. You will have learned, that I hurried on my way through Canada, and am hastening home, having gained daily, I think, in strength, and being not far from my usual state of health, excepting a considerable and not diminishing expectoration, and an aptness for hoarseness,—my voice, I think, not clear at any time. I have tried my strength in running over the Saratoga battle-ground,—with a good deal of interest, but not entire satisfaction. The truth is, that the ground is so extensive that it would require several long visits to acquaint one's self with the several localities, and fairly understand the matter. And, besides, the old guide, a man of eighty-four, who was in the battle, states things very confusedly, and does little to help you make out the very distinct account of Wilkinson; sometimes he contradicts it. But even the general idea I have brought away, of the form of the ground and of the position of the armies, is something. We (namely, I, Mr. Cornelius, lately of Salem, and Dr. Parker, of the British army, who happened on the ground) all went first to the British lines, which, beginning at the River Hudson, may be traced through the meadows up the hill, and two miles into the interior. The American lines were just opposite, and may also be traced for the same distance. These we did not visit, as the battle occurred on the British line. We then went to the head-quarters of Burgoyne, a house of one story and only two rooms. There we saw where General Frazer died, the very spot; and all the circumstances of that pathetic scene, as described by Madame Riedesel, were realized before us at once. This was near the edge of the river, two miles from the scene of conflict, (which was at the extreme British right,) but exposed to the fire of the American party, stationed on the other side of the river. In front of the house was a steep hill, and on the top of it a redoubt, in which Frazer requested to be buried, and where he was buried at about dark, during the heat of the engagement, and where the funeral procession was fired upon, as it went up the hill, and while the service was reading at the grave. The place is easily distinguished, and I went to it. A most beautiful prospect presents itself; the river, the fertile meadows, the hill beyond, and the canal winding at your feet,—all these, joined to associations of the place, made it one of the most interesting spots I have ever stood upon. Indeed, I scarcely know any scene so touching, so pathetically and poetically striking, as that of Frazer's funeral,—and a rare subject for either the painter or the poet. And yet an artist must fall short of the effect produced by the simple, artless narrative of Madame Riedesel. I have been reminded to-day of what I have often thought, how excellent it would have been, if Byron had travelled over these places and given us a Canto of Childe Harold. The whole route of the fashionable tour is full of poetical subjects. What would he not do with Niagara, Trenton, Quebec, the Plains of Abraham, West Point, Saratoga? and the funeral of Frazer would have given birth to one of the most beautiful productions of his pen,—a subject just suited to him. Anybody, who can write poetry, cannot do better.

"*Waterford, N. Y., Tuesday Evening, Sept.* 23.—My Monday's ride was on the banks of the Hudson, and cheek by jowl with the Champlain Canal, but there is nothing interesting or beautiful in the scenery. Some places of antiquarian interest I passed, as Fort Edward, and the tree beneath which Miss McCrea was murdered. My object was to reach the Saratoga battle-ground, twenty-five miles, in time to traverse it; which, as you have learned by my letter to John, I effected; and you may judge a little of my strength by my being able to walk and ride, mostly walk, over rough ground for four hours after such a ride, and then spend the evening till after nine in writing. It is very singular, that I should have made this visit with Cornelius, and that we should not have detected each other till just before we parted. He tells me, that I bear a striking resemblance to Parsons, the missionary. Truly mine must be a most accommodating face. Last week I was taken for Hoffman, the Baltimore lawyer. I came near being hurt during this excursion. My horse, who sometimes stumbles, came upon his knees, while going rapidly; but, thanks to my excellent horsemanship, in which I seem to outdo the Duke of Wellington, I kept my seat and remained unhurt.

"This morning (23d) I went round, about eight miles, in order to see the great aqueduct by which the canal passes over the Mohawk, well worth seeing, and the Cohoes Falls, which are very beautiful; distinguished from all other Falls in this, that the water touches the rock during all its descent, and is a brilliant, broken cataract of white foam, not rushing nor dashing, but quietly and majestically rolling down the steep. I believe the height is about eighty feet. There is very little water now, and there is a beauty quite unique in the thing.

"*Friday Afternoon, New York.*—Never take a man's word for it that he keeps a first-rate house, etc. I went to Waterford, Tuesday, in such a simplicity of faith, and very much because the fellow advertised a Reading-room, with papers from every part of the country, and I longed to see some from Boston. But, alas! his Reading-room was shut; the house big; full of pretension and discomfort; and I was put to bed with two companions, both of whom were so troublesome, that I killed them before morning. On Wednesday, I went to Albany, through Lansingburgh and Troy, and yesterday the boat put me in here.

"*New York, Sunday, September* 27.— . . . . I shall be at home Tuesday forenoon, and could jump for gladness at the very thought. It is quite time that I were there, if I may judge by my feelings; and I long to see for myself how you do, and just what progress you have made, and to show my acquisitions to you. I think you will be satisfied with them, and I do most earnestly hope and pray that I may not be forbidden to preach immediately. If I am, I cannot stay in Boston. I cannot live there, appearing well, as I certainly do, and yet do nothing. I must either go another journey or take a dismission. . . . . .

"Dr. Flagg was at church this morning, and brought me later news from you than I have heard. He says I never looked better. I do not pretend to say how I long to be with you. Home, home, home! a blessed place! but there are no words to tell how precious. Heaven keep you well, and give us a happy meeting.

"*Tuesday, September* 30.— . . . . . . The storm detained me yesterday (at New York) and I have had thus, by compulsion, a charming long visit, and enjoyed it very highly. To-day has been perfect, and I have ridden twenty-eight miles, to Sawpitts, a poor little village."

"*October* 1.—Twenty-eight miles to-day, to Fairfield, rather a large and pleasant village, which I reached, by my good star, just at five o'clock, and at the moment when a violent storm began. It threatens a long rain, whereat I shall be sadly impatient; and nothing else, I think, can prevent my being home next Wednesday. I found yesterday, at New Rochelle, in a charming house where I dined, and where the daughter's piano and album gave token of education, and the landlady's manners were lady-like and polite, the 'Life of John Urquhar' and his writings. I ran over them with great interest. He died at the age of eighteen, having already devoted himself to the missionary cause. A most extraordinary mind, and a most excellent character. He seems to have possessed the maturity of intellect and of goodness which belong to fifty years. To-day I met, at Norwalk, the 'Memoirs and Writings of Carlos Wilcox,' a Connecticut minister of just my age, who died a year ago; a poet, who lived for his imagination, and struggled with ill health and worse spirits for years. Perhaps you have seen his 'Age of Benevolence' —rather a mediocre poem, but the man's whole soul was given to it, and his character and letters are very interesting."

"OCTOBER 2,
[the birth-day of his wife.]

"'THE dawn is overcast, the morning lowers,
And heavily in clouds brings on the day;'
The roads are miry with continued showers,
And rain and mud deter me from my way;
And yet to me it all looks fair and bright,
For on this day my Mary saw the light.

"Many returns to you of this sweet day,
And each return more happy than the last;

Peace to your heart, as thoughtful you survey
  The various fortunes of the chequered past;
And bright and glorious be the visions given,
That clothe your coming years in hues of heaven."

END OF VOLUME I.

MEMOIR

OF THE

LIFE OF HENRY WARE, JR.

BY HIS BROTHER,

JOHN WARE, M. D.

IN TWO VOLUMES.

VOL. II.

NEW EDITION.

BOSTON:
AMERICAN UNITARIAN ASSOCIATION.
1874.

Stereotyped by
GEORGE A. CURTIS;
NEW ENGLAND TYPE AND STEREOTYPE FOUNDERY.

CONTENTS

OF THE SECOND VOLUME.

CHAPTER XIV.

CHAPTER XV.

CHAPTER XVI.

CHAPTER XVII.

CHAPTER XVIII.

CHAPTER XIX.

CHAPTER XX.

CHAPTER XXI.

CHAPTER XXII.

CHAPTER XXIII.

LIFE OF HENRY WARE, Jr.

CHAPTER XIV.

IMPROVED HEALTH—RENEWED ATTACK OF DISEASE—CONTINUED INDISPOSITION—PASSES A WINTER IN BROOKLINE—PROPOSES TO RESIGN HIS PASTORAL CHARGE—ORDINATION OF A COLLEAGUE—ELECTION AS PROFESSOR AT CAMBRIDGE.

1828-29. ÆT. 34-35.

Between August 24th and October 4th he had ridden eleven hundred and seventy-eight miles. He had improved very rapidly and steadily, and, at the last date, arrived at the house of his friend, the Rev. S. J. May, in Brooklyn, Connecticut, where he spent the ensuing day, which was the Sabbath, and whence he wrote as follows to Mr. Allen.

"I wonder if you have heard of my various pilgrimages and fortunes,—turns, twists, and conveyances,—strides, flights, and stumbles,—through all of which, adverse and prosperous, I have at length found my way safely to this port, and indite this epistle from brother May's table. Three weeks ago to-night I was in Quebec, the next Sunday at Sandy Hill, and the last in New York, where I spent three days, and was detained a fourth by rain. I have come through Connecticut by way of Middletown, and feeling pretty well, ventured to preach half the day, of course extempore, having no manuscript with me. I held forth for thirty-five minutes without any considerable inconvenience, brother May doing everything else. I am pleased to have tried; as I must, if I stay in Boston, preach at least half the time. I feel quite well, have my old looks, face brown with air, and whiskers; flesh about as usual, and a husky voice. As to my plan for writing, which I spoke of, alas! travelling has too much distraction in it. The first part of the time was too debilitating from heat, and the next portion too busy and fatiguing from the new and strange objects. I have however latterly done something, and shall bring home between fifty and one hundred pages of something; but a very different affair it proves from what I intended. Indeed, I have been unable to get my mind back to the same train in which it was, and have less confidence in my ability to do the work. However, I shall submit it to you, and, if you say go on, I will not flinch."

Of the above-mentioned visit I have the follow notice in a letter from Mr. May to Mrs. Ware.

"LEXINGTON, FEBRUARY 15, 1845.

"His letter of October 17th, 1828, brings to me a very vivid recollection of the delightful visit I received from him a few days before the date of that letter, on his return from his long journey on horseback. He came to my house apparently in good health, certainly in fine spirits. He insisted upon preaching for me. He did so, and preached a most impressive extempore discourse on the Beatitudes. Both his sermon and prayer were much longer than he intended they should be. His heart was so full, he could not refrain from pouring out his thoughts and feelings at greater length than he ought to have done. Still he did not appear to be fatigued. We kept up an animated conversation until after eleven o'clock. He seemed to feel sure that he had recovered his health, and should be permitted to return to his place, and labor as he was wont, for the redemption of man. He detailed to me his plans of future usefulness; and talked particularly of several books he hoped soon to prepare for the press. I am inclined to believe that the plan of his most popular work on the 'Formation of the Christian Character,' was definitely conceived that evening.

"The next morning he proposed to take my chaise, as he was impatient to reach Boston sooner than he could do on horseback. He was in high spirits, was sure that his public speaking the day before had done him no injury, and again recurred to his intended work.

"It was in October, you remember. The morning was cold. I begged him to take my great-coat, but he would not. 'His spencer would be enough.' He started about nine o'clock to ride to Providence, thirty-one miles.

"I took my seat by his side in the chaise, and rode seven or eight miles with him, until we met the stage coming from Providence, in which I returned to Brooklyn."

But the course of events after his return was far less favorable, than he thus sanguinely anticipated; and the sudden reverse in his prospects was the occasion of one of the hardest trials he was ever called on to endure. He reached home on Tuesday, October 7th, but, even before his arrival, had experienced symptoms of serious indisposition. Ten days afterward, October 17th, he gives to Mr. May this account of himself. "My preaching for you was not so innocent a procedure as I hoped. On Monday evening I began to feel an inconvenience which increased during Tuesday, and issued in the raising of blood on Wednesday morning, since which I have been confined to my house,—blooded, blistered, physicked, with other troublesome applications. I am now better, and to-day shall ride out. This of course changes the complexion of all my plans, and I am not yet sure that I shall not be obliged to pass the winter in another climate. You may easily believe, that I feel this disappointment not a little; and

I am glad, on your account, that I have nobody to blame for my imprudence but myself."

It was supposed at the time, that this recurrence of disease was mainly owing to the effort made in preaching. Subsequent observation and reflection, on his case and those of others, has led me to doubt whether this view of his relapse were perfectly correct, and, in general, whether the simple act of preaching, in clergymen laboring under affections of the lungs, be attended with so much peril as is commonly supposed; whether it be so often the principal cause of disease among them, as has been imagined. In the present instance, although the exercise of preaching was undoubtedly injudicious, and probably prejudicial, yet the severity of the attack, and the very serious consequences which ensued, may with more probability be attributed to the fatigue and exposure to cold and wet, which he underwent in his journey home. He was far too confident of the restored condition of his health, to exercise due prudence in his mode of travelling.

But, however this might be, the result was, that, although he speedily recovered from the immediate pressure of disease, his general health did not return, he did not regain his strength; his whole system, and especially the nervous system, was left in a very prostrate and unbalanced condition. From this he gave no indications of rallying; and it soon became obvious, that there was no immediate prospect of his return to his parochial duties, or of his being able to assume those of an office at Cambridge. Being incapable of exertion of any kind, it was judged advisable that he should, for the time, be placed out of the way of all temptation to it; and accordingly, in the beginning of the month of

November, he left his house in town, and took up his abode in Brookline, at the country-seat of his friend, Mr. Guild, which had been most kindly offered to him. Here he remained through this winter, by no means in a state of idleness, but quite incapable of any very serious or continued exertion.

On the 5th of November he writes:

"It is thought best that we leave town, and Mr. Guild has very kindly offered us his house and furniture, and we go into it without moving our household stuff. Much love to you, and I pray you send me a letter once in a while to help pass away my idle hours; for, being so retired and having no occupation, I shall need the word of friends sometimes to help me off with the winter; and I have reason to be thankful for the many and constant kindnesses which I receive from them. I sometimes think it is pleasant to be sick, for the sake of feeling and knowing how much goodness there is both in heaven and earth."

The establishment of the professorship at Cambridge was still a matter not definitely determined upon, and, although there was no reasonable doubt that it would be instituted, and would be offered to Mr. Ware, no official communication had been made with regard to it. In this state the affair remained through the season. It was his predominant feeling, however, that, even independently of any such new sphere of duty, his health would probably be, in future, such as to prevent his continuing his duties as a parish clergyman. He writes to Mr. Allen, November 23d:

"We are safely at home in Brookline, having abandoned our house in Boston, not without many regrets like those of Eve on leaving Paradise. I cannot realize that my pastoral life is so probably ended, and that I shall never again preach to a people of my own. I assure you there is more melancholy in the thing, than you would easily believe; and a quantity of self-reproach for opportunities neglected rushes upon the mind, which would make the prospect of a future account dreadful indeed, if we could not look to a merciful as well as righteous Judge. But I hope yet to be spared to do some good in the world. My place in Boston I think will be easily supplied. As for health, I have improved since I saw you. I find the freedom of the country very favorable. I use a great deal of exercise, and begin to do some hard work; but I am not yet capable of much mental exertion."

TO HIS BROTHER.

"DECEMBER 25, 1828.

"DEAR JOHN,

"The salutations of the day to you. I have been exercised, as you may well suppose, not a little, by the peculiar situation in which I am placed with regard to my people. I can do nothing for them; I probably never shall do anything more; they must have another minister. This should be done with the greatest possible unanimity; this unanimity is jeopardized by every week's delay; nothing prevents their acting but my being with them. As my work is entirely done, there is no good reason why I should stay with them. I have, therefore, made up my mind, that I ought to ask a dismission at once, and next Sunday, being the close of my twelve years, is a fit opportunity. I have looked at the thing fully, I believe, on all sides, and see no good reason for not doing so. I only wish your judgment and father's. Pray think of it, and give me your cool opinion. I do not wish it to be whispered, however, to another soul, until wholly decided.

"It *must come* to this at last. A delay would *do no good* to anybody, and I think *would injure* the Society. Is it not then a plain case?

"I have not said above, what is true, that it is perfectly impossible for me not to feel oppressed and anxious so long as I know there is a great deal to be done in the parish, and nobody doing it. If I were free, I should be easy. I am sure, that what I have done the last two weeks has affected me unfavorably; and I fancy it would have been just as bad, if I had thought over it all the time, and not done it."

In accordance with the resolution here expressed, a communication was read to his parish on the next Lord's day, in which he proposed to resign his pastoral charge. As furnishing the best history of this part of his connexion with his Society, and illustrating the mutual feelings which had grown up in the intercourse of pastor and people in the twelve years during which this relation had continued, the greater part of the several papers concerning the transaction are here inserted.

" *To the Second Church and Society in Boston.*

"My dear Brethren and Friends,

"As the present Sabbath closes the twelfth year of my ministry, I have deemed it a suitable occasion for making a communication which the state of our affairs seems to call for.

"It is now seven months, since it pleased Him who orders all things, to take me suddenly from my active duties, and suspend my intercourse with the people of my charge. I will not dwell upon the season of trial, which, severe as it has been, has been accompanied by many striking tokens of the divine blessing, and, I humbly trust, will not pass without profit both to you and myself. I had hoped, before this time, to be able to resume, in part at least, the discharge of my office; and I have recently made an effort to engage in some pastoral cares, but was soon compelled to relinquish the attempt. I am perfectly satisfied, that I shall be unable to do anything for you for many months; and you are aware that circumstances exist, which render it possible that I may never do so.

"In this state of things, I have anxiously reflected on the situation and prospects of the Society, and have been solicitous to know what part I ought to act. Is it my duty, feeble and incapacitated as I am, to keep my hold upon a place which needs and deserves the constant labors of vigorous health? Or ought I not to withdraw from the post, since God has taken from me the power of doing its work? These questions have exercised me much and earnestly. They have agitated my mind by night and by day. And, however painful the result, I have at length come to it decidedly, that I ought to bring the subject before you, and ask you to consider, whether, in the circumstances now existing, the welfare of the Society does not demand that our connexion should be dissolved.

"So long as the present state of things continues, you are altogether as a flock without a shepherd. And, when I consider the evils that must inevitably result from this, and to which a parish so situated is always exposed; and reflect, too, that very probably I may never return to you again, I feel that I ought to hesitate no longer. I ought to relieve you from the uncertainty and trials of your present condition, and give you the opportunity of obtaining a more efficient ministry. And I ought to relieve myself from solicitudes and cares on your behalf, which do not avail to your benefit, and which are unfavorable to my restoration to strength.

"Under these impressions, I do now, at the completion of my twelfth year, resign my office into your hands, and ask that our connexion may cease on the thirty-first of the present month.

"In doing this, I perform one of the most painful acts of my life. My situation has been one of many privileges, and such as perfectly to satisfy every wish of my heart. I cannot look back upon the years I have spent amongst you, without an expression of gratitude for the happiness, which, as a minister, I have been permitted to enjoy. Other men may have labored more faithfully and successfully; but no one can have ever looked back on twelve years of a happier connexion. The ties which I have formed are not to be broken without a pang, and I had fondly trusted that death only should dissolve them. But the few last months have changed the aspect of things. Their experience has warned me, that I may probably never again be equal to the labor of much public speaking, and that, having become useless in my present situation, I must consent to relinquish it. Meantime, you need an active pastor; and I trust and pray, that you may soon be united on one who shall do more and better for you than I have done, though he never can feel toward you more than I have felt.

"Brethren, I commend you affectionately, with all your present and future interests, to the favor and blessing of Almighty God.

"Your friend and pastor,

"Henry Ware, Jr.

"*Brookline, December* 27, 1828."

REPORT.

"The Committee to whom was committed the communication of the Pastor of the Second Church and Society, read on the 28th of December, 182S, have deliberated on the subject and beg leave to submit the following Report.

"It having pleased God, in his afflictive providence, to stay our Pastor in his course, by visiting him with severe sickness, and depriving him of his strength, so that, for many months, he has been unable to minister at the altar, or teach and guide his flock, he has been led, after anxious deliberation, to resign the office he has held, and ask that the connexion between us may cease.

"The solemn question is then before us, Shall we accede to this proposal, and consent that the connexion between us and him shall be dissolved?

"He tells us, that he is no longer able to fulfil his duties towards us, that he has attempted to perform some part of them and his strength has failed him, that he sees us as sheep without a shepherd, that he is, by night and day, anxious on our account, while his anxiety avails not to our benefit, and only adds strength to his own disease.

"We know his character and feelings. We understand what he refers to, when he speaks of duties he is no longer able to perform. We have had him before us for twelve years, and we cannot soon forget the example he has set of the pastoral character.

"He, indeed, hears instruction given us, and prayers offered for us, on the Sabbath. But he asks in vain, as we ask in vain, Who fills his place in the chamber of the sick, by the bed of the dying, and in the house of the poor, the widow, and the fatherless? Who is there to go about, as he did, doing good among our families, rejoicing with those who rejoice, and sharing the sorrows of those who weep, bringing to our firesides and to our domestic circles an example of the Christian life, and showing to all what a cheerful and blessed thing it is to be religious after the religion of the Gospel.

"While these offices are not performed, we, who know our Pastor's sense of their importance, cannot be surprised that his solicitude on our account should be unfavorable to the restoration of his strength.

"He speaks of the happiness of his connexion with us for twelve years, and of the ties which he had hoped that death only should dissolve. We can bear our testimony to the faithfulness and success of his labors during that period, and feel that these ties are as binding upon each one of us as upon him.

"For twelve years he has given his strength, his time, his powers of mind and of body, by night and by day, to us. We believe, that, in sincerity, in fidelity, in constancy and disinterestedness, his services have been without example. He has always cared for us, for our families, and for our children, more than for himself. He has spared himself no trouble ; he has omitted no occasion of doing us good. He has worn himself out in our service. And now, when his health is gone and his strength has failed, he comes to render back his office into our hands, and asks to depart in peace, that, as he can do no more for us, he may not come between us and our welfare, and we may be relieved from the burden of his support.

" In this state of things, we believe we give utterance to the single and universal feeling of his people when we say, that we cannot consent to the separation. 'We are not yet willing to give Mr. Ware up.' We therefore unanimously recommend, that our Pastor be desired to remain with us ; and that measures be taken for the choice of some person of piety and ability, on whom we may unite, to be his colleague ; to assist him in the discharge of his duties, and share with him the burdens of his office.

" This sentiment was strongly and repeatedly expressed, when the letter from our Pastor was read. 'We are not yet willing to give Mr. Ware up,' was said by some of his oldest and most constant friends, and was responded to by the hearts of all present.

" We are willing to wait until it may please Him, who has deprived him of health, to restore it.

" We are aware that there is danger, as he himself tells us, that he may never again be equal to the labor of much public speaking. If that should prove to be the event, or he should be called, in the Providence of God, to a situation in which his talents, character, and example may be of higher good to the great cause to which his life has been consecrated, then, and not till then, shall we consent to bid farewell to such a friend, as we may never meet again." . . . . .

" All which is respectfully submitted by your committee.

" P. Mackintosh, Jr., Chairman."

'*To the Standing Committee of the Second Church and Society in Boston.*

"GENTLEMEN,

"Having received from you a report of the proceedings of the Society in relation to my communication of the 27th of December, I beg leave to transmit through you my reply.

"The Society has been pleased, instead of consenting that our connexion shall be dissolved, to request that I would still retain my place, and allow them to appoint a Colleague Pastor, who shall take upon himself the active duties of the ministerial office.

"The manner, in which this measure has been proposed, is so full of kindness towards myself, that I cannot refrain from expressing the grateful feelings it has excited; and I am anxious to do what shall convince the Society, that I fully appreciate the spirit in which they have acted. In order to learn whether I ought to accede to their proposal, I have again considered the reasons which had induced me to ask a dismission from my charge. These were principally, that, under the present situation of affairs, the Society is suffering all the inconveniences of a destitute condition, and that my continuance in the office serves to prevent the remedy by the settlement of an able minister, without doing anything to advance my recovery. But I perceive that the measure now proposed will effect the beneficial objects which I had in view, and I therefore gladly and gratefully assent to it. I can imagine no objection to it, except that it will do nothing to relieve the pecuniary burdens of the Society. But this may be readily obviated, as I shall, of course, relinquish a certain portion of my salary on the settlement of another minister. I trust, therefore, that this happy event may be speedily accomplished. I shall rejoice to be thus spared the pain of suddenly breaking the bond that united me to you, and to be permitted, if I must withdraw at last, to do it gradually. In the mean time, I am happy in the belief, that Providence has been kindly preparing the way for your continued prosperity, and that you will readily unite on one, who is every way fitted to answer the reasonable expectations of a faithful and affectionate people.

"I am, Gentlemen, affectionately,

"Your friend and pastor,

"HENRY WARE, JR.

"Brookline, January 9, 1829."

On the 11th of January Mr. Ralph Waldo Emerson, who had for some time supplied the pulpit of the Second Church with much acceptance, was elected Colleague Pastor, in conformity with the recommendation contained in the report of the Committee, and was ordained on the 11th of March.

Some of Mr. Ware's letters written during the remainder of this season, will give a sufficient account of his condition and his occupations while at Brookline, of the plans which he formed for the spring, and of the circumstances which ultimately determined his destination.

TO MRS. E. B. HALL.

"BROOKLINE, DECEMBER 23, 1828.

"I creep along so, so, am stouter than I was a month ago, and, with occasional vacillations, make head way on the whole. I sometimes get nervous and cross, and am capable of very little close application of mind; but I read some and think more, and have built some of the finest castles, and projected some of the most splendid works, that air or earth ever knew. But, alas! of what use? All I can do is to eat and drink and sleep, and wait and hope. I trust you are more actively employed, and busy now in works of usefulness, before the evil days come and the years draw nigh, in which you shall say, you are able to do nothing. This brings me to the three heads of the epistle I promised you,—a very Cerberus, you will say. Well, never was a fitter time for the barking of the beast that keeps the portal of the unseen state; for you will receive it just between your birth-day and the new year. Pardon this confusion of figures.

"As there is no natural connexion between the three aforesaid heads or topics, I hardly know which to begin with. Proximity of time, however, suggests that which you suggested to me when I last saw you, and when I was just weak enough in body and mind to have it worry me, and keep buzzing in my thought, like one of the flies that Cowper complained of. (By the way, if you never have read the last volume of his Letters, you have a great treat before you.) You were saying then, you may remember, and Lucy amazed me by joining you, that you never would ride down hills again with an infant, but would get out and walk. Now I beg you to consider, whether you would be any safer in so doing, and whether also you have any right to do so. Are not you just as likely to stumble and fall as the horse? Remember, that, in riding with your child, you are either doing right or wrong. If wrong, stay at home. If right, then you have no right to quit the ordinary mode of conveyance and seek another, because, by so doing, you evince a distrust of Providence, take the care of your babe out of God's hand, and assume it yourself; and you must not be surprised if the consequence be, that your foot trips and you fall upon him and break his neck. Do you remember how S—— T—— was punished for her unreasonable distrust? And how many such cases are there, to teach us, that we ought not to go out from the common course of events, as if, by so doing, we could gain a security which Providence might otherwise have denied us. I assure you it would not surprise me at all to hear, that a woman persisting in the course you spoke of, had fallen down the first hill, and broken her child's neck, and her own arms. . . . . .

"Thirdly and lastly; I ask your serious and candid attention to what shall now be offered on a point which formed a subject of one of your letters months ago,—not to me, but to a much better person,—but on which I hope it will not be esteemed impertinence in me to animadvert briefly. You complained of the difficulty of doing your duties as lady of the parish, and the unsatisfactoriness of your feelings in regard to your intercourse with the people. This is a point on which I can sympathize with you fully and feelingly; for indescribable is the torture which I have undergone from that very cause. I came to my parish, as you have gone to yours, young, inexperienced in the world, and wholly a stranger to all that intercourse, which I knew to be expected, and in which I longed to be useful. But tongue cannot tell what I suffered. And, what is worse, I permitted my feelings sometimes to get the better of me, and, through dread and sickness of spirit, I left undone what I ought to have done. I shrunk from duties important and not really difficult, in the same state of mind in which Cowper shrunk from his post in Parliament. But this brought me no relief,—how could it? It only made the matter worse. It increased my sensitiveness, and added to it the pangs of a guilty conscience. I am not, even yet, wholly at my ease; but my experience may perhaps help you, and I do entreat you, manfully to use it as if it were your own.

"1. Resolve resolutely that *nothing whatever*, either in your feelings or circumstances, shall deter you from doing what you think you ought. This determination of mind is a great point, I can tell you. Never stand and think about it and dread it, but go at once and do it, and have it over. You remember the coward dies a thousand deaths in fearing one. I have died ten thousand in the agony of these fears;—but there was no need of it.

"2. Persuade yourself that you are *somebody*, at least in the eyes of other people, and have a right, from your education and situation, to assume something;—which will be readily allowed you, if you do not act the upstart tyrant. Oh, how long it was before I found this out; or could believe that others looked on me as anything more than little Henry Ware, or were ready to receive kindly and with deference whatever I should say.

"3. Be sensible that even the appearance of a wish to show kindness, the attempt to pay attentions and do good, are valued; and that oftentimes a slight favor, of which you think nothing, will be highly esteemed by others. You may think you have effected nothing, and therefore go home disheartened and sorrowing, when others may think you have done just what you should. I know all about this. And, since I have been sick, I understand how very sensible one may be to very slight benefits, and how great a kindness is the merest show of sympathy and a desire to aid. In your situation, you cannot make a call, or use a tone of sympathy and good-will, but it will be gratefully received, and remembered long after you have forgotten it. Is not this an encouragement? Do let these things move you. Be bold, for you have a right to be so; and it is only by pushing on, through difficulty and in spite of yourself, that you can ever arrive at anything like satisfaction. Give way to your feelings, and you only plunge deeper into trouble;—you make yourself their slave, and rivet their fetters so that they can never be broken off.

"Dearly beloved, the sermon is done, and the improvement of it made. Let me wish you joy on your birth-day, and a happy entrance on the new year. May you and yours flourish in all goodness and felicity. The love of all this household attends you."

TO HIS BROTHER WILLIAM.

"BROOKLINE, JANUARY 22, 1829.

"I think as you do about New Year's Day, and should not object to the introduction of the custom in Boston, but must remind you of your imprudence in giving heed to common Fame, who is an ancient, if not eternal liar,—and *my* fame requires that you tell those from whom you heard the story, that it is essentially false, with just enough truth in it to enable it to be told without blushing. In a word, it is a tea-table 'Romance founded on Fact.' And it had its origin in the circumstance, that your Reverend brother of the Second Church sometimes speaks in jest, and people think him so sober a fellow as to be always in earnest; whence having dissertated at a lady's house (not in the parish) on the beauty of the New York custom, and its desirableness, &c., it was said, 'Well, we 'll set the fashion New Year's Day, and you shall come and see us, and we 'll keep house.' January 1st was a dreadful snow storm; a journey to Boston would have cost me two fingers and a toe; and I had enough to do to keep myself comfortable by my own fireside, without conjuring up the recollection of a jest which I had forgotten for months. But I was 'all struck up of a heap' some time after, to hear that the dear lady had made her cookies, and boiled her coffee, and set out her decanters, and kept the hearth and the doorstone swept clean of ashes and snow all the morning, waiting for the minister to begin the fashion, as if it was a fit day for setting out so unruly a plant as a new custom."

TO THE SAME.

"FEBRUARY 7, 1829.

"Your project is a grand one. I say so because I have been conning over the very same thing for years, and know all its capabilities. I have laid down my plan for this very work, only after the resurrection, and the scene of it in Antioch, but with the very same design. And again I have arranged it for a poem, both epic and dramatic, drawn my characters, and sketched my plot; and, finding that I never should write it, have been all winter about proposing it to Hillhouse. You must not lose sight of it. It is a glorious theme, and would be a useful work, exceedingly pleasant to do, and you would do it well. First study the whole thing, fill your mind with the times, and then write it just as you write your letters, in the same style. Don't let me die without reading it, and I shall live only five years."

TO MR. WILLIAM BARRY (IN GERMANY.)

"BROOKLINE, FEBRUARY 22, 1829.

. . . . . . "As for any hazard to principle or character from the new influences of opinion and custom to which you are exposed, you have only to regard them (which you appear to do) in the light of moral discipline, to render them not only harmless but serviceable. Principle and character are universally of worth in proportion as they have been tried. It cannot, to be sure, be very pleasant to live amidst those who run counter in their daily notions to our own habitual views of decorum and right, to find our quiet Sabbaths turned into riot, and clerical proprieties set at defiance; but one may resist, and by resisting render old prepossessions still stronger, and home and country still dearer. Your opportunities of study are truly enviable, if we may innocently say so. It might almost make one sigh to think of your listening to Blumenbach and Heeren, (of whom we hear so much, but are condemned to know nothing personally,) and perfecting yourself in a language, which is to be the key to many stores of delightful literature and sound learning, to which we have no access. Well, you must remember it is endowing yourself with another talent; and your object will be to possess it in just that form, which shall render you most useful on your return. Much is to be done to elevate and extend both our literary and theological character; and your advantages will give you the power, if you will cherish the disposition, to be a public good, and to do something to lead the way in improvement.

"Having gained little or nothing this winter, I am directed now to quit this region during the spring weather; and I intend sailing for Charleston in the course of a month, my wife with me as nurse. There we shall take two horses and ride home. This seems more likely to give strength, if anything will do it, than a voyage to Europe, which in itself would be much pleasanter. But as I only seek health, I feel that I have no right to choose the pleasantest, unless it be also the best. I have the great satisfaction of leaving my people well provided for, as they are about ordaining Mr. Emerson as colleague; and, as they have conducted towards me in the most generous and Christian manner, I should have felt unhappy to have left them destitute. I have been able to do nothing for them for eight months. A few weeks since, I entered on a course of parochial cares; but was soon compelled to relinquish it, and have passed a most useless winter. Yet I live in hope of being restored to labor again; but, if there is no more work for me in the world, I hope that this long season will have helped to make me ready for labor elsewhere.

"I do not know that our religious affairs have anything worth communicating. Boston is more tranquil than for a few years past. Controversy continues, and in some instances with a most deplorable disregard to decency and truth. The worst features of party spirit have become canonized and holy. This violence, however, is seeming to work its own cure; a moderate party is beginning to show itself, and I trust will do something to heal the disgraceful divisions, or, at least, put down the shameless and unchristian doings, which now characterize too much the sectarianism of the day. 'The Christian Examiner' is to be withdrawn in part from this 'dreadful trade,' I trust, as it is undergoing a change of plan."

TO HIS BROTHER WILLIAM.

"BOSTON, MARCH 23, 1829.

. . . . . . "We quitted Brookline on Saturday, P. M., having packed our things for Charleston. When we reached town, the first thing that met us, was the appointment to Cambridge, unofficially communicated, but with the salary to begin immediately, and leave of absence in Europe. The next thing was a letter from Mr. Guild, saying that our friends, anxious that we should do the best thing possible, had made a purse of one thousand dollars and more, and begged we would go to England. To England, therefore, we go. Our present plan is to come to New York, and sail for London, it being far best to take the south of the Island first, and to be in London at this particular season. If we do this, you will see us on Saturday morning. This is, however, very uncertain, as we may be determined to sail from here.

"My parish refused, you know, to diminish my salary; but I have now communicated to them the fact of this appointment, and told them, that, as I am paid for another service, I consider them released from all obligation. They, I know, will not think so,—for never a people behaved better or more kindly; but just what they will do, I cannot tell. But, in any event, we shall have abundant means to spend six clever months in England and France.

"My colleague has begun his work in the best possible spirit, and with just the promise I like. The few, who talked of leaving the Society, are won to remain, and it is as flourishing as ever. We have given up hired singing, and employ our own men and women. I had a very interesting parting service at communion yesterday, admitted ten to the church, and did half the service without harming myself, I believe."

At this time the following communication took place between Mr. Ware and his Society, occasioned by the circumstances recorded in the foregoing letters.

"Boston, March 27, 1829.

"*To the Second Church and Society in Boston.*

"Brethren and Friends,

"Since my last communication to you, and the happy result of it in the settlement of another minister, two circumstances have occurred, which render it necessary for me again to address you.

"The first is, that it has been thought advisable for me to try the effect of a voyage upon my health, and I am consequently preparing to embark for Liverpool on the first of April. You will readily understand the gratitude and satisfaction which I feel, in the knowledge that you are not left unprovided for, and that neither the public nor private ministration of religion will suffer through my absence.

"The other circumstance, to which I refer, is the appointment which I have recently received to a professorship in the Theological School at Cambridge. Of the probability of this appointment I have been for a long time aware, and have had opportunity to reflect deliberately on the propriety and duty of accepting it. I do not know that there is any situation, connected with the interests of religion and of our churches, so important as this office. For it is the most responsible and influential in the Theological School, and that School is the nursery of our ministers, on whom the character and prevalence of religion depend. It seems to me, therefore, that whoever should have been appointed to this place ought to accept it at any sacrifice. Every other interest should give way to this. In my own case, the way seems to have been so providentially prepared, that I think neither you nor I can hesitate a moment as to our duty. I have become in a great measure unfitted for the public duties of the ministry, but may hope to become strong enough for the more retired and quiet duties of the new office. There is reason to believe that the removal would be advantageous to my health, and, without diminishing my opportunities of usefulness, would afford me a longer life. And as to the Society with which I have been so long happily connected, Providence has kindly sent to it another minister, and we can have no fear that my removal would be detrimental to its interests. I therefore do not doubt that I ought to accept the appointment.

"I should esteem it as a most happy circumstance, if I might be permitted still to retain my relation here, in connexion with the office at Cambridge. But such an indulgence will not be allowed. It will therefore be necessary, that we consent to a dissolution of our present relation. This, however, I do not design to ask at present. For, in the first place, the appointment is yet to be acted upon by the board of Overseers, whose concurrence is necessary to the confirmation of the choice; and, besides, it may not be permitted to me to return to my country; and, in that case, it would be a satisfaction to me to die as your minister. Or, if God should bring me back in safety, it would be a peculiar pleasure to be welcomed by you as my people. But in the mean time, as my support is provided from another source, I consider you as released from all obligation to continue my salary. I am virtually withdrawn from you and engaged in another service, and of consequence you are virtually freed from your engagement to me.

"And now, Brethren, being about to leave you upon an uncertain absence, I bid you and your families an affectionate farewell. I shall not cease to think of you with interest, and to sympathize in all your fortunes. The bond which unites us is connected with eternity; and, whatever may be our future relation upon earth, let us pray and hope, that, in a bet ter world, we shall meet and rejoice together again. Peace be with you.

"Your friend and Pastor,

"HENRY WARE, JR."

ANSWER OF THE SOCIETY.

"BOSTON, MARCH 29, 1829.

"REVEREND AND DEAR SIR,

"At a meeting of the Proprietors of the Second Church and Society, held this afternoon immediately after divine service, your communication of the 27th was read, and the following vote was unanimously passed:

"'That the subject of Mr. Ware's communication be committed to the Standing Committee, that they may return a suitable answer, and inform him, that the proprietors confirm their vote passed at a former meeting, continuing his salary to the first of July next, and request him to receive it.'

"In making known this vote, we beg leave to repeat the full and hearty concurrence of respect and gratitude, of which it is meant to be the expression. We rejoice, that the connexion between us and yourself is not yet to be dissolved. We rejoice, that the sacred relation is still to subsist, which has been so happy to all of us, and has wrought to us inexpressible good, which we trust will be eternal. While this relation continues, we are bound to you by a bond stronger than the ties of kindred. We feel ourselves near to you, although the ocean may roll between us. And, though a faithful servant of God needs no other and can have no higher reward, than the testimony of his own conscience, and the hope of his Master's approbation, yet we are sure that it will be grateful to you to know, that you carry with you the best wishes and the prayers of your people. Wherever you may be, it will be the greatest satisfaction to us, that we may still regard you, and that you desire us to regard you, as our

Pastor. We pray, that He who preserveth the stranger may keep you in safety on the ocean and in foreign lands; that the air of other climates may be made the balm of health to you; that you may not die, but live, and declare the works of the Lord; that we, your people, may welcome you to your native shore, and hear from your own mouth the good things that our God has done for you.

"We feel that you have done right in accepting the appointment in the School at Cambridge. We confess, that we do not relinquish, without a mixture of pain, the prospect of having you again among us as our minister. But that higher service has a stronger claim upon you and upon us; and it is an alleviation of the sorrow which we feel, that you will be useful in your new office, before it will be safe for you, with your first returning strength, to resume the arduous duties which you have always looked upon as belonging to the office of a Minister of the Gospel. We rejoice that one, who has such high views of that sacred office, is to have influence over those who are preparing to enter upon it.

"We most cordially reciprocate your kind wishes, and, in behalf of all your people, we bid you, dear and reverend Sir, *farewell.* May God be thy keeper; may he preserve thee from evil; may he preserve thy going out and thy coming in, from this time forth.

"With you also be peace.

"Peter Mackintosh, Jr.,
George B. Emerson,
George A. Sampson,
for the Committee."

I transfer from the Sermon of Mr. Robbins, to which I have been already so much indebted, an account of the last attendance on public worship and at the communion service, to which he alludes in one of the foregoing letters.

"The last Sabbath before embarking for Europe, he was present in this desk; but in so enfeebled a state, as to disqualify him for taking any other part in the service, save the reading of two stanzas of a favorite hymn. But the devotional breathings of the inimitable lyric poet, which are embalmed for immortality in those beautiful verses, expressed what was then passing in the heart of the reader, more clearly and happily, perhaps, than any discourse which he could have delivered. The aged friend, who has pointed out to me this hymn, and who bears the occasion in clearest remembrance, has told me, what I can easily imagine, that its reading was listened to by the whole congregation with tears.

"'May peace attend thy gate,
And joy within thee wait,
To bless the soul of every guest;
The man who seeks thy peace,
And wishes thine increase,
A thousand blessings on him rest.

"'My tongue repeats her vows,
"Peace to this sacred house!"
For here my friends and brethren dwell;
And since my glorious God
Makes thee His blest abode,
My soul shall ever love thee well.'*"

This change of destination was in all respects a most agreeable one. His original plan, as stated in his letters, had been to sail for Charleston with his wife, early enough in the season to enable him to avoid the harsh

"* I have been informed, that at the communion, which was administered on the day alluded to, Mr. Ware, although positively forbidden by his physician to risk the effort of speaking, could not restrain his desire to say a parting word. He made a brief address, which, to use the strong expression of my informant,—who alluded to the description I had given of the effect of the hymn upon the congregation,—'was heard not with tears only, but with sobs.'"—*Mr. Robbins's Sermon.*

and repulsive weather of a New England spring, to take horses there, after a sufficient delay, and travel homeward at a very moderate rate, following the mild weather on to the North, and reaching home after all the severity of the season had passed. But his desire to visit Europe had always been very strong. He had not only that desire for it, which must be felt by every man of taste and education; but he was perhaps even more strongly influenced by the wish to form an acquaintance, and establish an intercourse, with the ministers of his own denomination in Great Britain. He probably made his visit to Europe more of a professional one, than most of his brethren; and it did much to excite a spirit of familiar inter-communication between the Unitarians of the two countries, to make them acquainted with each other, and to create a reciprocal interest in each other's welfare and progress.

He sailed with his wife, in the ship Dover, Captain Bursley, on the first of April, and remained abroad nearly seventeen months, returning in the latter part of August, 1830. During his absence, he visited England, Holland, Italy, Switzerland, and France, spending the winter in Rome. During this period, although he enjoyed a great deal and gathered materials for enjoyment in all his after life, he also suffered a great deal. He had much to contend with, both bodily and mentally, from failing to find that speedy improvement in health and strength, which had been anticipated for him. At times, indeed, his condition was such, that he not only was forced to the conclusion that he had gained nothing, but he felt that he had strong reasons for the apprehension, that he was never to be better. From this cause he fell occasionally into a state of great depression at the prospect, which he was obliged to contemplate, of returning home, a weak, broken-down, and, what was worst to him, a useless man. Nearly up to the period of his embarkation for home, it remained a matter of considerable doubt, whether he had derived any benefit from his travels. His health had fluctuated from time to time, but on the whole he exhibited fewer indications of renewed vigor, than on his return from his excursion on horseback in October, 1828. On the passage home, he suffered from a very severe and painful, and, in his situation, alarming attack, which was thrown off with considerable difficulty, and reduced him much. He, however, completely recovered from this before his arrival home. From this period he continued decidedly to improve, and it was soon obvious that his health, if not perfectly established, was at least so far restored as to render him competent to the labors of his new office.

There would be no special interest in a detail of the events of this period of absence. The account of it will therefore be confined to such extracts from his letters and journal, as indicate the state of his health, his occupations, his movements from place to place, and his intercourse with interesting persons.

CHAPTER XV.

LETTERS ON HIS PASSAGE TO EUROPE—ARRIVAL IN LIVERPOOL—VISIT TO MR. ROSCOE—TO MRS. HEMANS—TO MR. MAURY—VISIT TO MANCHESTER—TO THE LEASOWES—PREACHING OF ROBERT HALL—PAINTINGS AT BURLEIGH HOUSE—VISIT TO WORDSWORTH—SOUTHEY—IRELAND—MISS EDGEWORTH—HOLLAND—PASSAGE UP THE RHINE—MASS IN THE CATHEDRAL AT STRASBURG—GENEVA—INTEMPERANCE FROM WINE—TREADING THE WINE-PRESS—CARDINAL MEZZOFANTI—FLORENCE—STATUARY—PAINTINGS—LETTERS FROM ROME—COLISEUM BY MOONLIGHT—RAFFAELLE'S CHAMBERS—HOLY WEEK AND SINGING THE *MISERERE*—GREENOUGH AND THORWALDSEN—STATE OF HIS HEALTH.

1829-1830. ÆT. 35-36.

TO THE REV. RALPH W. EMERSON.

"Ship Dover, April 15, 1829.

"My dear Sir,

"We are a little more than half way upon our passage; and a quiet day, relieving me from sickness and the ship from its tossings, invites me to send homeward, in a visible form, some of the thoughts which have been haunting me, of those I left behind. Amongst these are of course to be numbered my people, who have been a chief object of my care for years; and yourself, as the bond which now binds them together, and the heir of my solicitudes and duties. I have been thinking much, and with great gratitude, of the kindness of Providence in bringing our affairs to just this issue; so that, when compelled to quit my place, I have been able to resign it, with complete satisfaction, into the hands of one who seems both qualified and disposed to do all which ought to be done, and in the most successful way. If you will continue perseveringly in the way and the spirit in which you have begun your work, you may confidently look forward to a happy and useful ministry. I do not know what time and absence may do to diminish my interest in this Society; but I feel at present, as if it could never be lost, and that I shall watch its welfare with as great anxiety as ever. But I am henceforth separated from all active concern, and shall feel no right to intrude myself into its affairs. I mean, therefore, while I am absent, as occasion may offer, to transmit to you a few farewell sayings; some of which may be useless, but some possibly may help to guide you in following the thread of events, as far as desirable, and in changing the course pursued, wherever it can be done to advantage.

"One of the first things, perhaps, which will strike you in getting acquainted with the parish, will be, the inequality with which I have labored. I have never been so sensible of this, as since my sickness last summer, when I have had time to look back deliberately on my course; and I mention it now to warn you against it, as the source of much future regret and remorse. I will instance in the attention I have paid to the children, which has sometimes been very systematical and thorough, sometimes greatly neglected. Various causes have led to its neglect for some time past. And yet, if there be anything which gives satisfaction to a minister, and is a visible testimony of good, and a reward in hand for his toils, it is this. In eight or ten years he finds young men and women around him, whose characters he has helped to form, and who become the companions and helpers of him in every good undertaking. I long to see the children of our Society again brought under the constant superintendence of the minister."

TO HIS FATHER.

"SHIP DOVER, APRIL 25, 1829, just off the Irish Coast.

"MY DEAR FATHER,

"It is one of the alleviations of this horrible business of going to sea, that a quiet ship and a quiet stomach are once in a while enjoyed, as a sort of luxury; a luxury which I happen to possess this evening, and mean to share with you. Since last Sunday we have had foul weather, and, for the last two days, a violent gale ahead, which has driven us to our berths, dashed our dinners from the table, and kept us all miserable, without the sense of making any progress. This afternoon we have had a fine view of the Emerald Isle, a beautiful scene, under any circumstances, and especially so under ours; not to mention the poor Irishmen who ran up the rigging to see it, and got dashed by the spray for their pains. The lulling of the wind sets all to rights, and stomachs and tongues are in good humor once more.

"I have had few, very few, hours like this; the whole voyage has been a succession of sicknesses and ill feelings. However, even in lying in bed, sleepless and foodless, I have had some seasons of comfortable and happy thought; for an empty stomach is an excellent suggester of visions and exciter of reflection, and, in the past and the future, I have found some recompense for the evils of the present. But, among all my musings, it is a little strange, that I have never yet been able to feel that I am actually on the ocean, and embarked on an expedition of so much uncertainty. I have thought it over and over; considered, weighed, and repeated to myself in every form, the momentous nature of my undertaking, and its various risks and perils. But, after all, I have felt no otherwise than I should do if I had merely started on a journey to New York; whether it be insensibility, I know not. So it was too, in taking leave of friends; many were very much affected, but I never was at all. I could not *bring it home* to myself. I dare say you observed this, when I parted from you at Cambridge. I knew it was possible, that I never should see you again; but I went away as if only for a day. Just so it is still; and yet I believe, that I have given my mind to every view of my situation and every possible result of it, which becomes a religious and accountable man, and, by so doing, I hope to be prepared for it.

"I do not think that any one has more reason to contemplate with gratitude and admiration the dealings of Providence, in his past life and present situation, than I have. From my earliest childhood, through the various stages of my education, entrance on life, and success in life; and especially in the events of the past year, I have traced a guidance from above, which gives me a trust and hope, which, I think, have prepared me for anything, and in which I cannot believe that I am deceived. I have, of course, had a great deal of time to think of myself and review the past; and the great impression prevailing in my mind is, that of astonishment at the lot allowed me, accompanied by a feeling, that it is all the gift of Heaven, and none of my own deserving or acquiring. I am puzzled to understand how it is possible, that I should possess the favor in society, and the confidence, which have been extended toward me, when a fair survey of my private history and character always mortifies me for my negligence and ill-doings, and I know that I have done much less than I might and ought to have done. Yet, because of certain natural gifts, I have easily reached a point which I see others, of greater fidelity and diligence, fail of attaining. I take, therefore, no credit to myself, and hope that this feeling will save me from any improper self-confidence and presumption in the new duties to which I am called. It is among the wonders of my life, that they should have been put upon me as they have, when they are more suited to my taste than any others I could name; and I fancy that the interest which I shall take in them will enable me to be, to a certain extent, successful in them. I have a strong confidence that I shall survive all peril and sickness, and be permitted to enter on them, a tolerably strong man. You will not wonder that I should have it, when you think of the peculiar circumstances which have attended the whole affair; everything being so ordered as if on purpose to secure this result.

"Perhaps you cannot see it as I do, and will think it all presumption. It may be so, I acknowledge; but it is a state of mind favorable to a feeling of responsibility, and, so far, it may be a right preparation for duty. The manner in which I have been sent away, has, in this point of view, affected me deeply. The earnestness with which the generosity of friends was pressed upon me; the large provision which was spontaneously made, in order that I might go abroad under the best advantages; the letters that were sent to me from various quarters, (about fifty, where I did not ask for one,) and the kind messages and testimonies of interest, which came to me during the last few days, all combine to make me very thoughtful, and feel that I have laid upon me a weighty burden of obligation, which I can only repay by devoting myself to myself, while I am gone, and working with new vigor when I return. I should be most ungrateful if I did not feel, to the bottom of my heart, the kindness which I have experienced; and I wish that you and all my friends should understand how great it has been, and how much we shall owe to others if I come home safe and well.

"I am afraid this is hardly such a letter as you expected from across the ocean; but I did want to pour out to you some of my musings, that you may know what is passing in my mind; and it is not often that I get an opportunity of venting my egotism into your ears. I would tell you, if I could, how I am always tracing back every blessing of my lot to your early cares. Whatever is good in my habits and principles, and prosperous in my professional career, I see its beginning in your discipline, when I was young. And I feel as if

I ought, once in a while, to let you in, a little more nearly, to the mind and heart you have trained. I would rather show by my actions, than by words, my gratitude; but, if we should never meet again in this world, I shall be glad to have left with you one expression of it at least."

STORM, AND ARRIVAL IN LIVERPOOL.

(From his Journal, April 28.)

"On Tuesday morning, toward daylight, I overheard a boy say that we had passed Holyhead; and, at seven, I was wakened by the rushing of the waters into the cabin through the windows. Our state-rooms were soon afloat, and the confusion which ensued, in swabbing up the water and removing the carpets, delayed breakfast till nine o'clock, when there was so much motion from the increasing wind, as to render eating and drinking a very troublesome undertaking. But we were in fine spirits, expecting confidently to be in Liverpool by three o'clock. Signal was made for a pilot, off Point Linus, (Ælianus,) and, at about eleven, the boat rode by us, tossed about on the white waves, and seemingly in danger of being swallowed up. A dozen men in her, dressed in their storm coats and hats, made a fearful show, and, in their anxiety to direct us, all talked at once with such confusion of tongues, that it was impossible to understand them. It was now blowing a most violent gale, and we were standing obliquely towards the Skerry rocks. We were so near, that the objects on shore were distinct to the eye. When the pilots found that we could not hear, they addressed themselves to us by gesture, waving hats and hands with the utmost vehemence, and one of them earnestly running up the shrouds.

"The impression on the minds of all the passengers was, that they warned us off the shore, and their earnestness seemed to indicate some immediate peril. We were anxious enough, and, for a few minutes, the countenances around me betrayed as much horror as I ever saw expressed. The san-

tain still, however, stood on toward shore, till our uneasiness had reached a point to be borne no longer; he then gave orders to tack, and stood out to sea. We then felt easier, but the impression did not wear away, and the day was a horrible one. The gale became a hurricane, and we were driven to and fro about the cabin, without ease or security in any position. Meantime the pilot boat hovered about us, like a guardian angel, as Mr. T—— said. At about four o'clock we made the signal, '*Will you come on board?*' The boat dashed by us, and so near that we caught the directions given for preparing to receive them. The sails were trimmed accordingly, and an unsuccessful attempt was made to board. She bounded off again, and again returned. Nobody can describe the intense interest of that moment. It was a case of life and death. It seemed as if the little sloop must be crushed, like an egg, by the rolling of our ship down upon it; and as if to step from one to the other, during this horrible agitation, must be certain death. Two pilots lost their lives in such an attempt last winter, as we were told. And, therefore, as we watched these exertions, the two vessels side by side, now thrown apart, and then thrust together by the rising and falling of the sea, and, at each meeting, the pilot attempting to spring on board, while all his fellows stood by, each with a life-buoy in hand to throw to him in case he should lose his footing, our hearts throbbed violently; and, for myself, I felt almost faint, and could look on no longer.

"By and by, at a happy moment, I heard the cry which announced his success. A great John Bull, of three hundred weight, stepped upon deck. Every soul seemed to draw a long breath. 'I thank you, sir!' cried the captain, in his heartiest voice. The little sloop shot ahead, and was soon lost in the distance. This was just at eight o'clock. It was beginning to be dark. Never was greater relief felt than by our whole ship's company; we felt safe for the night. The wind became less violent, but was still fierce. I went to bed and slept soundly; and, when I awoke in the morning, found the ship just entering the dock at Liverpool."

TO HIS BROTHER JOHN.

"LIVERPOOL, APRIL 29.

. . . . "There was great anxiety, and not without reason. Three ships near us went ashore, and one was wholly wrecked, with the loss of every soul. They do not remember a severer gale in this place. So that we have not only the common incitements to gratitude, which are felt after a voyage, but a peculiar call to it, as having experienced peculiar deliverance. To-day's paper contains a particular account of the gale, which for some hours put an end to all business at the docks, and drove chimneys and tiles about the streets. As to myself, of whom you will expect a report, I cannot tell whether I am better or worse for the voyage. I have lost flesh, but not during the last ten days. I have felt the want of exercise, but, for the latter part of the time, have lacked neither appetite nor sleep. I have taken two or three slight colds, and always found my lungs unpleasantly affected by exposure to the sea air on deck. It produced greater expectoration and a sense of weariness in breathing. The excitement of yesterday, and of landing this morning, produced an excessive lassitude, with rapid pulse; but a warm bath, and lying down three or four hours, removed it; and I have walked abroad this afternoon and feel the better for it."

VISIT TO MR. ROSCOE.

(Journal, May 4.)

"We then drove to Mr. Roscoe's, about a mile further. He lives in a small, retired house, with but the shadow of his former comforts and elegancies around him; yet, even in this diminished sphere, you could not but observe the air of refinement and cultivation. After some conversation with Miss

Roscoe, we were invited to the old gentleman's chamber, a privilege we had hardly ventured to hope for. We found him feeble; but he rose to receive us, and showed the appearance of a most venerable, gentlemanly person. He has long been confined to his room, by a paralytic affection, I think; but it was delightful to find that he had been able to beguile the time by useful and interesting occupation. He told us that he had just brought to their conclusion two works, which he had been anxious to finish before his death. The first is a Catalogue of the Library of Manuscripts, (a very rich and extensive one, especially in the classics and the Scriptures,) belonging to Mr. Coke, of Holkham, which he inherited from the Earl of Leicester. The other is a splendid work on Botany, which has been his amusement for a long time. This he showed us, and a beautiful work it is. He also caused his daughter to read to us the Inscription, which he had just written, to be printed on the back of the title. Mary asked for a copy, and he allowed her to take it, saying, it was his farewell to the Muses.

"'INSCRIPTION.

"'God of the changeful year! amidst the glow
Of strength, and beauty, and transcendant grace,
Which, on the mountain heights, or deep below
In sheltered vales, or each sequestered place,
Thy forms of vegetable life assume;
Whether thy Pines, with giant arms displayed,
Brave the cold North, or, wrapped in Eastern gloom,
Thy trackless forests sweep, a world of shade;
Or whether, scenting ocean's panting breast,
Thy odoriferous isles innumerous rise,
Or, under various lighter forms impressed
Of fruits and flowers, thy works delight our eyes;—
God of all life, whate'er those forms may be,
Oh, may they all unite in praising thee!'"

VISIT TO MR. MAURY.

(Journal, May 3.)

"Mr. Maury, the venerable consul, twice called; once in company with his daughter. I passed an uncommonly pleasant hour with him at his office. He is old and very active, and attributes his fine health, in no small degree, to the daily use of the cold bath. He cited his old friend, Charles Carroll, as another example of its efficacy, and of rigid systematic temperance. He spoke much of Jefferson, with whom he was long a school-mate under his father's instruction; represented him as being, from childhood and through life, a person of wonderful industry; and showed me a very interesting letter written a few years since, in answer to Mr. Maury's inquiry after his age, which closed in nearly these words:—'As for myself, my frame is feeble, and my powers of body and mind decay; and I shall meet with welcome the hour, that shall once more reässemble the scattered members of our class with their venerated head.'"

VISIT TO MRS. HEMANS.

(Journal, May 8.)

"She gave me a hearty welcome, and I spent two delightful hours in various and animated conversation. In her appearance and manners there is everything pleasing and easy, but nothing striking. Her countenance disappointed me from its want of intellectual and poetic expression, and her air has nothing of that pensiveness, which the character of her works would lead one to expect. There was rather a remarkable brightness and vivacity about her; and, in the course of conversation, I found this to be the style of manner and character which she prefers. Her conversation was rapid and lively, not brilliant, nor often poetical, but full of fine thought and sentiment. She spoke with warm interest of America and her American friends. On the whole, I have seldom had so delightful an interview, and came away perfectly satisfied."

TO HIS BROTHER JOHN.

"MANCHESTER, MAY 13.

"On Saturday I saw Messrs. Robberds and Tayler, two of the four Unitarian ministers, and took tea with the latter; heard both preach, and exceedingly well too, on Sunday, and dined with them and the other two ministers on Monday, at Mr. Brooks's. I saw a great deal of them and enjoyed the intercourse very highly. They seemed gratified to see an American, and expressed a strong interest in all that relates to us. They are acquainted with almost everything we publish, and Dr. Channing is quite a classic with them. Indeed, I find that he is read and admired by all denominations. I wish to make it a point to see all the ministers of our connexion, who fall in our way; and thus far the acquaintances I have formed, have been highly gratifying. Much remembrance to kind and numberless friends. Tell me everything that takes place amongst them, and let me hear whatever relates to the parish and its concerns, and all who are interested in them. I find that I care more for them than for anything else."

THE LEASOWES.

(Journal, May 16.)

"We turned aside at Hales-Owen to see the Leasowes, Shenstone's seat. It has been wholly neglected for years, and is now in ruins. One would scarcely guess that the hand of man had ever been upon the ground. The house is finely situated, on a most commanding eminence, the path to it winding round the ascent. We found no one to accompany us; but taking the best direction we could get, we passed back of the house, and followed the faint traces of the ancient walk. It led us first down to a little pool, and then by the side of what seemed the dried-up bed of a small stream, beneath a walk of trees, and brought us to where the path turned to the celebrated urn. A falling tree has started it from its place, but it is still whole. The inscription has been renewed several times, and the effect of time has been to present a part of several of the successive renewals, so that nothing is seen but a confused mass of letters. But I am not sure that the effect of the whole scene is not more beautiful and touching, from the dilapidated condition of this and all the other memorials of its departed author.

" Turning to the left, we continued to ascend, and found the walk of trees becoming a grove. At the top of the hill are the ruins of a small Gothic temple, built of brick, and covered with mortar, entirely filled with the sparkling refuse of melted glass. In front of this, there had evidently been left an opening amid the trees, through which was seen a very extensive prospect of a various and rich country, with the village of Hales-Owen. We passed on a little further, when the grove ended, and a row of trees led us down the hill by an abrupt turn to the left, and we soon crossed the field to near where we entered it. We here encountered the stream again, and found the remains of a fine bathing-house, now covered with ivy. We had been walking an hour, had probably discovered all that was best worth seeing, were tired, and therefore returned to the carriage.

" We could not help expressing our displeasure, that such a place should have been allowed to become a desert; and we remarked, with a good deal of interest, that the elegant taste of a retired man, who probably looked no further than to his own amusement and the occupation of his leisure, should have imparted to this little spot so permanent an interest, that for seventy years it has continued to be a place of pilgrimage."

ROBERT HALL.

(Journal, May 24.)

" The congregation was assembled, but no minister. By and by a poor-looking body, from a pew on the left of the pulpit, rose and gave out a psalm. It was only when the last verse was singing, that a minister appeared. He was a large man, bald, with a gray head, and heavy frame and countenance. He began the service with reading the Scriptures, in a low, weak, thick voice, which he often was obliged to clear, and which he seemed to exert with difficulty. Then followed the prayer, in which was nothing striking; and it was nearly finished before I could make up my mind that this was Robert Hall, and then only by reasoning, that in such a chapel I should be likely to find no one else so simple and so perfectly correct in the use of language. His sermon was from the text, 'Lead us not into temptation,'—a plain, unpretending talk, without any attempt to quit the most obvious topics, or to adorn them with any flights of rhetoric or imagination. He merely spoke right on, pouring out a most rapid torrent of well-selected words, and exhibiting a superior mind only by the richness and accuracy of this spontaneous expression, the perfect lucidness of the whole arrangement, and the completeness with which every part was finished, so as naturally to introduce the next. His manner is very quiet; no action;—he lifted his hand but once, I think, and then but just raised it from the cushion. No effort to manage his voice; no looking about; but sometimes he turned his eye a little, and those who can see it say it is strong and impressive.

"On the whole, nothing could be more different from the idea which I had formed. I thought that his elevated style of composition indicated the *ore rotundo* in delivery; and I had dressed him out with a loud voice, and a great deal of flowing, energetic action. True, I did not hear one of his great efforts; but I was told his manner is never different. So uncertain a thing is eloquence, and so differently does it display itself in different persons. It was delightful to hear the strong terms of admiration in which Dr. and Mrs. Carpenter speak of him, uninfluenced by the violent abuse which he has lavished on

Unitarians. I have seen a good deal of this candor in England."

PAINTINGS AT BURLEIGH HOUSE.

(Journal, June 22.)

"The multitude of pictures was amazing, and Guido, Dominichino, Rembrandt, Raffaelle, Salvator Rosa, presented their beauties and wonders at every turn. But the glory of all was lost in the head of the Saviour, by Carlo Dolci. This we stood and looked at, as if it were really the holy person present; such truth and reality were in the whole thing. The idea is taken from the letter of Lentulus to the Roman senator. The figure represents the blessing of the bread and wine; the cup is in one hand, the loaf in the other, the eyes uplifted, and the mouth open. I never before believed that a figure of the Saviour could be drawn so as to satisfy me; but I found it here. I never before saw a picture which made me *feel;* but I found myself in tears as I looked at this. I experienced the same sort of thrilling emotion, which I have felt sometimes at an eloquent discourse. Mary agreed with me; and we were convinced, from the manner in which the attendant retired and left us to contemplate it in silence, that the effect upon us was not singular. Indeed, it is a miracle of art; it has revealed to me a power which I did not suppose art to possess; and the perfection of the work is such, that, like the Madonna at Cambridge, which I mentioned before, it may be approached within a few inches without destroying the illusion. Even the eye remains a living eye."

WORDSWORTH.

(Journal, July 13.)

"Mr. Wordsworth lives at Rydal Mount, a small but steep hill about a mile from Ambleside, offering beautiful and picturesque views of the lake, village, and hills, and being on the whole as pretty and appropriate a retirement as a poet would choose. Himself, wife, son, and daughter made the family; and they received us very pleasantly, to a pleasant and copious breakfast. He is a venerable, gray-headed man, of a good head and face, very small eyes, and pleasant smile, which he does not often use. His conversation was, as has been represented, flowing and rich, running on copiously, and sometimes enveloped in so many intricacies of speech and parenthetical members, as to be quite obscure, as is somewhat the case with his poetry. But he has a great deal of fine diction, as well as lofty thought, and the three hours passed away delightfully and rapidly.

"He spoke with interest of America and its institutions; and was particularly anxious to know whether the provisions for religious instruction were adequate to the growing population, and what would be the consequence of leaving it to the voluntary contributions of the people. He seemed inclined to rather dark views of the prospects of England, and spoke freely of errors of government, of the deplorable want of right education in the higher classes, and the sad deficiencies of the Universities. Though he allowed that something better is doing in them than in time past, still he thought it was too much in general, and not enough with a view to the qualifying for the actual callings and exigencies of life. That everything relating to education should be connected with religious principle, and should regard man as an immortal being, is a thought he dwelt upon earnestly.

"He talked a good deal of the superficial character of modern literature, and of the comparative advantages of the Italian and English languages, as regards poetry; saying that the natural music of the former had tended to satisfy their poets with little thought and sentiment, and the roughness of the latter had driven them to compensate, by weight and richness of thought, for the ruggedness of the diction. Dante was the only Italian who had not suffered from this cause. And it would be quite as difficult to translate English poetry into

Italian, as Italian into English; for example, they had no *words* which could convey Coleridge's 'Ancient Mariner.' He had much to say of the old institutions of England, both in Church and State, and evidently holds them very dear. When I spoke to him of our early acquaintance with 'We are Seven,' he said it was frequently mentioned to him. He has a great quantity of manuscripts ready for the press, but says he cannot tell when he shall publish; poetry is a drug, and readers are not ready for anything solid."

SOUTHEY.

(Journal, July 13.)

"About seven, we went to his house, called Greta Hall, half a mile from town, standing on an eminence, about as great as that on which Mr. Norton's house stands, and having a path to it through an extensive nursery-garden. The site is very commanding, overlooking the whole vale and affording noble views of the high mountains which environ it; Skiddaw rising near it just behind. It is, however, more like the elegant villa of a wealthy gentleman, than the romantic seclusion of a poet. We found him, unfortunately, at tea with several friends; however, he took me to a sofa in one corner and devoted himself entirely to me.

"Southey is fifty-five years old, (he showed me a portrait of himself taken at two years of age,—fifty-three years ago,—a round-faced, bright-eyed child, with a tremendous bush of hair, —he seems to have been always an Absalom in this respect); he looks ten years younger; was dressed in white pantaloons; has a most aquiline nose, bright eyes, thick, bushy hair; is of middling size, blushes easily, and has a very sensitive face; his eyes filled with tears several times during our conversation. He does not *dissertate*, nor at all attempt to show off, but talks on easily and naturally, in an affable and gentlemanlike way.

"He did not, any more than Wordsworth, disguise his partialities in politics or religion, and, as regards the Catholic question, declared that he would sooner have laid his head on the block, than have voted for the late measures of government. Wordsworth had put it on this ground, that the discontents of Ireland did not originate in the religious disabilities, and therefore could not be removed by removing them. From Ireland he (Southey) came to America. He spoke in terms of friendly interest; rejoiced that the more frequent intercourse was removing ill-will and jealousies; and said that he had more friends in Boston, than in any city of the world, excepting London, and that, if he were a younger man, he should visit America, and see for himself the condition and prospects of society.

"In speaking of his situation, I remarked that he seemed to be both in retirement and in the midst of the world. To which he replied, that, for the three summer months, he was full of company and saw all his friends, and for the other nine was wholly secluded; and that he could not desire a happier arrangement; that the summer days were too long for study; he could work only by candle-light, and if he could have three hours, from half past six to half past nine, he would not care what became of the rest of the day. Something led him to speak of writing by dictation, and he said he never had done it, neither was ever able to employ another person in any way about his works, except some trifling copying. I asked if he was in the habit of copying for the press, or if he sent his first draught. He said he generally copied, always what was important, and that it was only in making the copy that he paid the slightest regard to style. He then showed me his 'History of Brazil,' in the progress of its manufacture; bound up in six manuscript volumes, containing, first, the notes and materials put down while reading for the preparation, and, secondly, the history as first written. The copy which the printer used was destroyed. Then he showed me 'Thalaba,' the second draught; the first was written on scraps; these were copied into a book, on every other page, corrections made on the page opposite, and a copy from this sent to the printer, and destroyed. 'Madoc' and 'The Curse of Kahama' are in the same state; the latter has three different beginnings in three different sorts of verse.

"Then he showed me his unfinished American Poem, called 'Oliver Newman,' which is promised to Mr. Ticknor; and he bade me report progress to him. He read me a passage, which I liked much, but we were interrupted in the midst. He reads with a very peculiar intonation, which is, however, favorable to the metre, and not a bad specimen of poetical recitative; and occasionally he gesticulates with his arm. I afterwards read the opening canto, and thought it very beautiful,—as beautiful as the first in 'Thalaba.' I asked him by what process he built his stories; whether he laid out the whole plan first, or invented as he went on. He said, that he made the story complete at first, and altered as he went on, just as they build cathedrals."

SECOND VISIT TO SOUTHEY.

"I found him in his room, reading letters; a room stored with books, as I believe all in his house are. He has the largest library, it is said, of any private man of his fortune, in Europe. Many books are curious and rare; there is especially a large collection of Roman Catholic works. Our conversation turned much, this morning, on the state and prospects of the age, about which he is fearful and doubtful. He looks with great hope to the improving education of the lower classes, in which he differs from Wordsworth, who fears that they are raised too fast, unless you first elevate the mental and moral cultivation of the higher classes. He read to me a letter from Dr. Gouch, the King's Librarian, detailing a new project just commenced by the poor for their own improvement. They subscribe a certain sum annually, which is laid out in land and workshops, upon which they employ their own labor and realize a profit. Thus their means increase every year by the profits of work and by subscriptions. Seventy such associations are in prosperous operation, and are fast extending their influence.

"He read me a letter from the author of 'Zillah,' disclosing a fact worth knowing in the history of modern literature. Southey had objected to the work its too great bustle and over excitement. Smith replied, that it had been his endeavor to avoid this by introducing views and descriptions of Jewish society and manners; but that all this had been stricken out by the supervisors whom the bookseller employs, and who allow nothing to pass which is merely instructive. A pretty piece of despotism, truly; and so the taste of readers is not to be amended! I was glad to hear this, however; because I had opened the book with the hope of finding these very things, and had thought it a great error, that they had been neglected. But I think Smith should employ another bookseller. Southey's publisher writes to him respecting his late work on '*The Prospects of Society*,' that the sale has been good; but wishes he had omitted the consideration of *Politics* and *Religion*, as the sale would then have been ten times greater. Good! the prospects of society discussed, and no notice taken of Politics and Religion! A modest request, says Southey.

"As the Unitarians have accused Southey of misleading Dr. Channing in regard to them, I was desirous of inducing him to speak of them. He seemed, however, unwilling to say much, merely observing, that those whom he had known were most excellent men; that the system in England was Humanitarianism, and a very cold one; and he seemed surprised to hear that there are many Arians in London. He had allowed, that there has been great improvement recently in the character and manners of the clergy of the establishment; and I assured him, that I had found the Unitarians sensible of a similar improvement among themselves. When I remarked on the want of institutions for the express education of the clergy, I was surprised to hear him say, that they thought it best in England not to give them a peculiar education, lest it should create too much of an *esprit de corps*, and make them feel themselves a privileged order. I little expected any such objection from so zealous a member of the establishment and so determined an upholder of its immunities."

TRAVELLING IN IRELAND.

(Journal, August 8.)

" The road from Newry to Dublin, sixty-two (or fifty Irish) miles, is run daily by one-horse cars, carrying six passengers; or any one may post it in these cars at any time, a fresh horse every eight miles, by paying the full price of the six seats, that is, twenty cents a mile. These cars are the most exquisite Irishism we have seen, and, being such as are used in place of chaises by gentlemen and families, richly deserve description. A jaunting-car, then, is of two kinds, the Inside and the Outside; of which two let me gravely speak in order.

" The Inside-Car is most genteel, but far less common. If designed to carry four persons, it is of the shape and dimensions of a large washing-tub, with seats on the opposite sides, so that the passengers sit facing one another, and with their sides to the horse. If to carry six, the shape changes to that of a huge dough-trough, wherein careful housewives knead for the baking; and they are arranged three and three, face to face, as before. The driver is placed on a little *dicky* in front. But the Outside-Car is Paddy's glory, and hardly any other is seen on this road. The wheels are as small as the front wheels of the little wagon called Dearborn among us. Above them is suspended the vehicle, which, being like nothing else that ever went on wheels, must perforce be compared to a creature of some other element. Imagine, therefore, (to use my wife's similitude,) a dining-table, turned upside down, the legs cut off, and swung above the aforesaid wheels, and two or three ragged Irishmen seated on the topsy-turvy leaves, with their legs dangling down over the wheels. Or suppose (which is *my* similitude) two settees placed back to back, over the wheels, and the said Irish legs dangling down as aforesaid. I can think of nothing else, that will give nearly so correct an idea of this machine, in which so many of this jolly land are daily shaken and joggled, to the imminent danger of being pitched forward upon their pates.

"Behold, then, Mary and I hoisted up on one of these table-leaves, each grasping an iron railing with one hand and the cushion with the other, like John Gilpin in the poem, and grunting at every shake, which threatens to shake us out into the street, while the driver occupies the opposite scale as a make-weight or counterpoise, and leaves his own lofty seat unoccupied. Thus we rode over fifty mortal Irish miles, up and down, between eleven in the forenoon and ten in the evening; at which hour we were landed at 'the best inn in Dublin,' as the driver assured us, bruised and sore, to be eaten by fleas while asleep, and to be wakened twice before morning by watchmen and quarrels in the street. This said driver was apparently the identical Larry of 'The Absentee'; at any rate as like him, as the image of himself which poor Rip Van Winkle saw, when he came home from the mountain. When he had once driven us furiously over a rough passage for half a mile, and almost made us breathless with the agitation of head and legs, he slackened as he came to a hill, and, turning to us just like Larry, said, 'Was not that a pretty bit of a drive?' He talked of himself and his horses in most good-natured eulogy, and, when he proposed going with us himself into Dublin, told us 'we might find a man *dacenter dressed*, but we could not find a *pleasanter*, he was sure.' I think he spoke the truth."

TO PROFESSOR NORTON.

"DUBLIN, AUGUST 14, 1829.

"I think you will be pleased to hear from me, that your kind letter to Miss Edgeworth has procured for us a ready welcome and a delightful visit. We enclosed it to her, and sent it from Belfast, with a request to be informed whether she would be at home; as we thought it not worth while to drive sixty miles into the heart of Ireland with the risk of 'finding her absent,'—an old College bull, which very properly presents itself at this moment. Her reply was a very gracious one, and we passed nearly two days at Edgeworthstown this week, she seeming pleased with the attention, but the other members of the family still more so, as they seem to be more proud of her than she is of herself; and we were exceedingly gratified by everything we saw and heard.

"Her manners are easy and animated, without being striking; her conversation very lively and rich, with a great variety of fine sentiments carelessly thrown out, and perpetual illustrations and images, sometimes highly poetical, sometimes humorous, sometimes, perhaps, a little far-fetched, but always apparently accidental, and always rendering her talk delightful. She is too rapid and earnest to talk in set phrases, or to have any affectation; and, as to a masculine way, which some have ascribed to her, it seems to me there is nothing anti-feminine about her, unless it be to talk a great deal, and occasionally to laugh heartily. But she does not talk loud and boisterously; and her laugh so 'rings from the soul,' that even I, who laugh seldom, and am apt to be put out of countenance by a violent ebullition of that human peculiarity in others, could yet entirely sympathize with Miss Edgeworth, and wholly enjoy it;—for she has the discretion withal never to laugh long, (a discretion, by the way, to be recommended to all who would make their mirth acceptable,) and does not laugh from habit, but only when rightfully excited by sufficient cause.

And I am sure it would be hard to find fault with *her* for laughing, who has occasioned so much exercise of that sort to others.

"I was pleased to notice perpetual proofs of great strength of feeling, and that of the most amiable kind. She drew us to her by this trait, and fairly compelled our love. It was not infrequently, that we observed her eyes fill at the expression of a generous sentiment, or the relation of a touching anecdote. When I told her that, on my saying at my father's that I intended to see her, little Charlotte immediately clapped her hands and said, 'O give my love to her!' the water came to her eyes at once;—and it is plain, that she has practically all the love for children, and solicitude for their good, which are expressed in her works. She evinced it constantly in her treatment of her younger brother. Then we were very much struck and pleased with the manner in which she spoke of other authors,—so kindly and generously, so free from all petty feelings of jealousy, or whatever other evil emotion there may be; saying only what was kind, and taking pains to tell Lady Morgan's story in such a way as to apologize for her affectations, and give us a better opinion of her character. Of Scott she had much to say, and read to us several of his very interesting letters. On the whole, not to prolong, we were highly gratified and satisfied, and not the less so, because we found we were the first Americans, if we rightly understood her, who had paid her a visit at her own house.

"This is only one chapter out of a very interesting tour which we have made in Ireland. No part of our journey have we enjoyed more. Belfast and Dublin were full of business and excitement to us, owing to the present state of religious parties, and the organization, which is now making, of the Unitarian body. There is a great deal of talent and zeal coming into action in the best way, and I feel myself favored to have been on the spot at this moment. One particularly interesting occurrence has been my visit to Mr. Armstrong, once a clergyman of the establishment, who has thrown up his living because of his growing dislike to Orthodoxy. I found a letter from him in Dublin, inviting me, as an American, a Unitarian, and a friend of Dr. Channing, to visit him; and, as his house is but twenty-five miles from Edgeworthstown, we took it in our route. He is a fine scholar, and a man of talents, frankness, and ardent zeal,—aged about forty,—intimate with American history, partial to our country, and enthusiastic in his admiration of Dr. Channing, who can tell you more about him, as he has written to him. It is wonderful what a sensation Dr. Channing's writings have made in these realms. Everybody talks of them with enthusiasm; and, among his most ardent admirers, I have found a minister of the Scotch kirk and an Episcopalian lawyer. The latter declared, that to Dr. Channing he owes it that he is a Christian, and that he knows many of whom the same may be said."

TO HIS BROTHER JOHN.

"Dunshaglin, Ireland, August 15, 1829.

. . . . "In my last of July 18th, I believe I was complaining of feeling ill, &c.; I can now speak more favorably. I fancy that I have fairly taken a step in advance, and, as well as I can compare, am about where I was when I did myself mischief at Brooklyn. But I have, with advice and consent of council, fully determined not to come home this fall; and I believe that my friends will need few words to convince them that I am right. I am as anxious as any one to be at home, and at work again; and, perhaps, I might go on with my duties this winter tolerably well. But I am sure that I could not do my best; I could not devote myself to the office with the diligence which would be necessary for the best and the successful performance of its duties, and I might ere long break down again. By continuing my present course, there is a possibility that I may become quite strong; and I think it would be better to go to my work with my full powers a year later, with the prospect of a longer life, than to do work feebly during that year and perhaps shorten life by it. I have no ambition to be a martyr in any sense. I have as many reasons for wishing to live as most men; and I do not think that those, to whom I am accountable, will think that I am wrong in my present determination. I certainly owe a great deal to others, and I hope I may be permitted to live long enough to pay something of the debt."

TO THE REV. DR. CARPENTER.

"LONDON, AUGUST 24, 1829.

. . . . . . "Every part of my tour has given me pleasure, and I have hardly experienced a disappointment, excepting that of finding too much rain in the Highlands, too much cold everywhere, and Walter Scott not at home. I have seen as much of our religious brethren as I possibly could, have been most kindly received by them everywhere, and have been most favorably impressed by them in general. It would be idle to say, and no one would believe me if I should say it, that I have seen nothing which I could imagine might be better; but I have been most truly gratified upon the whole, not only with the present state of sentiment and feeling, but with the prospects of improvement, which are evident. I passed a fortnight in Ireland with great satisfaction. The state of things among our brethren is full of interest and life, and I believe they are wide awake to the call of the times, and fully equal to the emergency. There are fine spirits among them; and I shall be greatly disappointed if the action which seems to be beginning there, do not have most salutary influences both in England and America. The Irish are very favorably disposed towards their brethren in both countries. I mean the leading men; for you are aware, that the multitude have rather held back from English communion, under the idea that Unitarianism here is exclusive and *ultra;* and this feeling is yet to be removed. The principal men are doing what they may to remove it; and, when it is found that the English are seriously abandoning the narrow interpretations of Unitarianism, and look complacently and with brotherly kindness on Arianism, then will be seen a cordial union and coöperation. This is most devoutly to be wished."

TO HIS BROTHER WILLIAM.

"UTRECHT, SEPTEMBER 3.

"I write to you for once, not only with a Dutch quill, but with Dutch ink, on a Dutch table, and by the light of Dutch candles. You have heard of our pilgrimages through 'Fatherland,' and how, from the circumition of Scotland and Ireland, we returned to the overgrown City on the 21st of August. There we passed a week in preparation for our winter's campaign, and in visiting our few friends whom the summer had not rusticated. This being done, our supernumerary and wayworn clothing, &c., being packed away, that we might not '*ingredi Italiam impediti*,' our new and appropriate dresses provided, our maps purchased, and our French accent re-burnished, we sailed in the good steam-ship *King of the Netherlands*, (a packet which is half as large as the smallest on Hudson river, and very indifferently appointed,) on Saturday, August 29th, at ten in the forenoon. Our passage was one of the roughest, and we were two of the sickest; but we reached Rotterdam about dark the next evening, were quietly suffered to slip through the custom-house, and remained till next day, at four in the afternoon. Our first impressions of Holland were extremely pleasant. The houses are high, of small bricks, neatly painted, and with large windows. Canals pass through the centre of many of the streets, filled with vessels and business. The streets are paved with small square stones, flanked with brick, but no curb-stone. There are large trees on the sides of the canals, from end to end of the streets, having a most pleasant and cheerful appearance; and a kind and degree of cleanliness throughout, such as I never saw elsewhere, or had formed any idea of. Your first and perpetual remark is, 'How clean! how neat!' I never saw a clean house or clean street before. I did not know what cleanliness meant. This is particularly the case at Rotterdam and the Hague. Amsterdam is less remarkable; indeed, in great part, is very like the dirtiness of other great towns.

"We passed through Delft, to the Hague, Monday night, in the canal-boat, drawn by one horse, at four miles and a half per hour. The canal is one third wider than the New York canal; is thronged with boats,—sail-boats as well as others, —and its banks are beautifully dotted with gentlemen's seats and plantations. I had letters to two gentlemen at the Hague, but did not stay long enough to see them. We went to Leyden in a post-chaise the next morning, and here, it being vacation, and the Professor to whom I had a letter, being absent, I was greatly disappointed in not seeing the appurtenances of the University. I barely got admittance to some of the Lecture-rooms, and the outside view of the Library. In the afternoon we rode in a post-chaise to Haerlem. The roads are excellent, not wider than those which lead through avenues to gentlemen's houses, paved with bricks, laid edge-wise, very smooth and even, and lined with trees in such wise that you might think yourself driving through some fine park.

"At Haerlem, we were vexed to find that we could neither see nor hear the organ, except on public days, without the payment of a most extravagant price; and, as we had neither the leisure nor the money, we were compelled to leave this wonder unvisited. We saw some fine paintings; and I was permitted to say a few words, without sitting down, to an old gentleman to whom I had a letter. Left Haerlem on Wednesday morning in the diligence, twelve inside and three horses abreast, for Amsterdam. Here, too, the gentleman, a distinguished minister, to whom I had letters, was absent; and, after an amusing interview of bad French and blunders with his daughter, I was forced to cast myself upon a *valet de place*. We walked about the city, whose finest street is a row of palaces indeed; and visited the King's palace, once the Stadthouse, an immense and splendid structure, opulent in marble rooms richly carved, adorned with sculpture and painting.

"This morning, Thursday, we came in the canal-boat to this place. The route was exceedingly beautiful, the banks lined with country-houses, plantations, groves, and gardens, with interspersions of wide, green meadows, crowded with herds of black and white cattle. This is the only town we have yet seen, which lies out of the water. It is on a hill at least thirty feet high. Mr. Scheltema, the historian, to whom I was introduced, speaks as little and as bad French as I do, and is much more scared at his own blunders. So, after a short and most ridiculous scene of grimaces and attitudes, he rushed over to a neighbor's and brought in a young man, son of a Burgomaster, who has travelled, and speaks English. He proved to be very intelligent and gentlemanly, and, with his father, devoted himself to us for the afternoon. We saw the library of the University, in what was once Lucien Bonaparte's ball-room,—thirty thousand volumes; some ancient manuscripts; the Museum also of natural history and anatomical preparations, and wax figures in comparative anatomy, quite copious and very curious. We also saw the new barracks for four thousand five hundred men, just built by this same Burgomaster, and showed to us by him, just as a young mother shows her first child.

"Holland has delighted us, little as we have seen of it. I wish we had more time for it; and, if Mr. Van Polanen's letters had been received, we should have seen it under much greater advantages. As it is, we could not receive them, since our plan to visit Holland was arranged only very lately; and I regret it the less, because our time is so extremely limited. We are in great haste to be in Switzerland, so as to see something of it, and cross the Alps, before snow; and everybody says we are already full late, if we mean to stop at Geneva, which it is certainly a great object to do. We accordingly hasten up the Rhine. After eight weeks of incessant cold and rain, the weather begins to be more propitious, and we hope a fair autumn."

FEEDING HORSES IN HOLLAND.

(Journal, September 4.)

"In the midst of the last stage, which was a long one, the bits were taken from the horses' mouths, not, as with us, by stripping the bridle from their ears, but much more sagaciously and kindly, by unbuckling one side of the head-stall, and letting the bit drop down of its own weight. A large brown loaf was taken from the coachman's box, and a large jacknife from his pocket, and, after a draught of water, he proceeded leisurely and gravely to slice up the bread and put it into the mouths of his cattle."

PASSAGE UP THE RHINE.

(Journal, September 9.)

"Coblentz has about ten thousand inhabitants, and is strongly fortified on every side. On the opposite bank of the river is the fortress of Ehrenbreitstein, situated much like Quebec, and said to be stronger; rebuilt since the peace of 1814. The whole scene, as we parted from it the next morning, was most imposing,—the town on the left bank, with its ancient palace stretching its long row by the water side, and its cathedral and church towers, while on the hill behind rose the extensive lines of Fort Alexander. Across the river stretched the long and trembling bridge of boats to the village opposite, which lay beneath the hill like a little bunch of white houses; and on the steep hill above towered the new and strong castle, whose topmost battlements were just shining in the first rays of the rising sun. Here began the high lands and the picturesque scenery of the Rhine. It was a clear, bright day, occasionally clouded and showering for a few minutes, and we enjoyed highly an uninterrupted succession of varying heights, sometimes wooded, sometimes bare and rocky; thickly planted with vines, many of them even to the highest point; every few miles surmounted by the ruins of some ancient castle, while at the foot of the precipices which they overhung, were gathered towns and villages of a peculiar and foreign aspect. The natural scenery is of itself full of the most various beauties; in some passages it might be compared to that of the Highlands on Hudson river. The latter, from their superior height and darkness, are perhaps rather more grand for a short distance; but the narrow pass of the Rhine is constituted of more wild and abrupt crags, and in no other portion of the course is there any comparison to be made. The Hudson is tame by the side of the Rhine. The latter river is crowded on both banks with a succession of memorials of olden times and feudal ruins. On every most inaccessible cliff is perched some mouldering castle, and in every fertile gap which opens through the hills, stands an old but flourishing town. The hill-sides are waving and green with vineyards, many of the steepest thrown up into terraces, and the vines appearing in little green patches among the rocks, where you would think even a goat would hardly go to browse. Then there are no fences amid all this to break the landscape to pieces; a fine road runs along the water-side and on the edge of the precipices, to give you a view of the queer diligences and other travelling equipages, which slowly traverse the banks. Little boats, crowded as I never saw any before, shoot down on the rapid stream like meteors; lazy ships toil up by the side, drawn heavily along by two or six horses; and self-moved ferry-boats swing like pendulums across from side to side."

MILITARY MASS IN STRASBURG CATHEDRAL.

(Journal, September 13.)

"We witnessed the military mass, where six thousand soldiers are marched into the nave, and perform worship to the word of command, and to the music of their band. It was the merest and saddest mockery imaginable. The officers sat directly in front of the altar, and the men, who stood below, could of course neither see nor hear what was going on. They were very much engaged in talking and laughing. A party of some hundreds drawn up in the centre performed various evolutions during certain parts of the service, and at certain points all the drums were struck with violence. The band, in a gallery above, played incessantly. A large concourse of spectators was standing around, or walking to and fro. This lasted about twenty minutes. Then the service of the day ended, and the military departed. No sermon, no instruction; was there any worship? A separate mass was performing at the same time, at least in one, perhaps more, of the little corners of the building."

INTEMPERANCE FROM WINE.

(Journal, Geneva, October 12.)

"Our physician (Coindet, Senior), is a man of sixty, sensible, clear-headed, well-reputed, and speaks English; we are greatly pleased to have such a man by us. Speaking of the extraordinary season he rejoiced at one consequence, that, by destroying the crops, it will render wine dear. He says, there can be no greater curse to a country than cheap wine; wine countries are always poor; excess and drunkenness always accompany abundance. No mistake, he says, can be greater, than to suppose there is little or no intemperance among the peasantry of wine countries. I told him that he was contradicting a favorite notion of our country, and he assured me that we should rue the day when wine should become common and cheap. I have before heard the drunkenness of Switzerland remarked by several travellers, but have seen little of it myself, except so far as it has been indicated by the crowds which assemble in the bar-rooms and wine-shops. I saw a few men drunk in Strasburg; and, on questioning my guide, he said they had been drinking something stronger than wine, —beer. Dr. Coindet is a warm advocate for beer. 'Not ale, nor porter, but beer.'"

TREADING THE WINE-PRESS.

(Journal, October 30.)

"We have seen to-day a good deal of the treading of the wine-press. In Vicenza, huge tubs stand on carts in the street, into which the grapes are poured; and one or two men without trowsers walk about over them and stand upon them, while the juice runs into vessels below. In many cases there are no tubs, but the wagons themselves are used as vessels. The grapes are red, and we now understand perfectly the allusions to its resemblance to blood in the poets and ancient writers. These men looked, for all the world, like so many butchers. And strange is it, that men will be so wedded to their old ways as to continue so tedious, disgusting, and insufficient a mode of operation, in preference to the clean, rapid, and thorough work of the screw-press."

CANOVA'S HAND.

(Venice, November 3.)

"In the Council-Chamber of the Society of Fine Arts, over the President's chair, is placed against the wall, a little vase or urn, containing Canova's right hand preserved in spirits of wine, with this inscription, 'Canovæ dextera.' Beneath this is supported, on two little hooks, the chisel with which he wrought; and underneath is a neat marble slab, thus inscribed in golden letters, 'Quod mutui amoris monumentum, idem gloriæ incitamentum siet.'"

DR. (NOW CARDINAL) MEZZOFANTI.

(Journal, Bologna, Nov. 9.)

" The Librarian is Dr. Joseph Mezzofanti, a pleasant man of fifty, with a benignant, self-complacent countenance, who speaks English like a native, and, as my guide says, is equally conversant in all modern tongues, of immense learning, and sought after for his conversation, far and near. No titled or royal person passes through Bologna without sending for him. He showed himself a most intelligent person, and surprised me by his acquaintance with American matters. The Indian languages are of great interest with him. He showed me the only manuscript of any value in the library, a good copy of Lactantius, of the fifth century."

ITALIAN SUNSET.

(Journal, November 12.)

" Saw Florence in the distance at the fifth mile stone. As we descended thence to the valley, enjoyed a glorious sunset; —gorgeous purple clouds in the west, and light rich pink flying over the heavens;—the mountain-sides being of a blue purple, such as we have seen in pictures and never credited."

STATUARY IN FLORENCE.

(Journal, November 13.)

" My first two visits were given exclusively to the statuary; and my chief impression was that of wonder, and a sense of pleasure, from the entire ease of every figure. The attitudes and postures are so natural and unconstrained, and, at the same time, so various and graceful, that your eye rests on them with the same sort of feeling as when you look on children asleep; with the added sense of astonishment at the skill of the artist. This continued to be the prevailing feeling to the last. The Venus de' Medici is placed with four other prime figures in a small octagonal temple, devoted to certain chefs-d'œuvre, and, although not seen with so great delight as you expect the first time, grows upon you at every visit, and wins your whole approbation, and all your heart, at last. I am sure it never could have been designed for Venus; it is too merely sweet and modest, and wholly free from all air of voluptuousness. The arms and hands do not agree with the rest of the figure, and yet I cannot, for the life of me, guess how the original artist disposed of them. No one can form any notion of the statue from casts. Its peculiar beauty seems incommunicable. And I suppose that this is the case with all the finest works of art."

RAFFAELLE'S MADONNA.

(Journal, December.)

"There we saw and admired Raffaelle, especially his famous Virgin and Child, (*della Seggiola*,) of which everybody knows the engraving; but of this I say, as of the Venus, no copy can give you the finish, the soul, of the original. Everything about it is true, suitable, and heavenly. To me the greatest charm was in the infant Saviour, the expression of whose face, especially his eye, has a thoughtful and spiritual cast, which is perfectly fascinating, and, though seeming almost more than earthly, is so singularly fashioned as not to appear inconsistent with infancy. I have seen copies, called equal to the original, which do not approach this indescribable something, which is the charm of Raffaelle's work."

RELIGION IN FLORENCE.

(Journal, December.)

"Florence has the reputation of being the most devout city in Italy. The streets are full of priests and priestlings, and monks; the bells are perpetually ringing, night and day, and holy processions are frequent. I saw many, in which the host was carried to the sick; and certainly a more singular mixture of the imposing and the ridiculous could hardly be desired. Day or night, there is a large number of persons in white frocks, dirtied and rumpled, bearing large wax-lights, and lamps in glass lanterns. The priest, with the host, walks under an umbrella, and over that is a spreading canopy, borne by six men in white. In some instances there is also a guard of soldiers. One attendant bears a little bell, which he rings constantly, and, at the sound, all passengers uncover, lights are put up at the windows, and the street is thus illuminated as they pass. A crowd follows them to the house, where part of the procession remains chanting at the outer door, waits for their return, and accompanies them back to the church.

"I once, just after dark, did the same. I found, in a large church, that at least five hundred people had collected, and were on their knees at the seats and in the alleys, all joining, in a loud voice, the anthem sung by the priests, as they returned with the host, and proceeded to the altar. There were no lights except those at the altar and those borne by the procession. When all had collected at the altar, the effect was magnificent. The blaze of light in one spot of the church, shining on the glittering ornaments around, and the white and showy dresses of the priests surrounding the altar, the vast building with its arches and pillars, and recesses, dimly shown in the reflected light, or shrouded in thick darkness; the throng of kneeling figures, from whom arose a loud chorus, now sinking low, and now swelling to a tremendous shout, interrupted by occasional pauses, in which there was dead silence for a minute, or only the low muttering of one priest kneeling on the steps,—all together formed a scene of solemnity and grandeur, well calculated to impress and affect the multitude, and whose influence I could not help feeling. It continued, perhaps, ten minutes; then the priests and attendants abruptly rushed from the altar, like boys broke loose from school, and with hurried steps left the church. The lights were instantaneously extinguished, except those which are always kept burning, namely, six small candles; and two or three ragged boys sprung to the altar to scrape up the wax which had dropped upon the steps. About half the people left the church, and the remainder continued motionless on their knees, as if absorbed in devotion.

"Adapted as all this is to produce effect, I wonder that the charm is not broken, even on the minds of the most ignorant. The indecorum and indifference of the priests and their attendants, during the whole, are striking; and nearly every holy torch-bearer is anxiously engaged, as he walks, in contriving so to hold his huge candle, that the melting wax shall fall upon a paper held to receive it by a ragged boy, of whom a number always accompany the processions to collect the wax from these accommodating devotees, and sell it."

. . . . . "Of the people and manners of Florence, I of course can say nothing, as I had no means of intercourse with them. I am passing through Italy, as some men are said to pass through College, 'without touching.' Ignorance of the language, and no letters of introduction, leave me to grope my way along, looking at the outside of the country and the cities, but really coming in contact with nothing. I grieve at this sorely, and beg that, if brother or son of mine shall ever visit the Continent, he may previously learn to speak readily the language of the natives. It will not be difficult then to associate with any persons whom they may desire to know."

TO THE REV. RALPH W. EMERSON.

"ROME, DECEMBER 27, 1829.

"As for tidings of myself, I have none. I am well enough to enjoy life a good deal. I am deep in Roman antiquities, and Italian niceties. But I strongly apprehend, that the actual visiting of these celebrated spots tends to destroy the romance and break the charm, which our younger days have attached to them. It is a sad thing to be in old Rome, and yet find that rooms, tables, candles, and victuals are just what they are everywhere else; and that, in fact, day passes after day as it does elsewhere. Once in a while you touch a spot, or see a relic, which makes your heart jump; but, in general, you do not 'realize' that you are here. It requires the same study to persuade yourself that this is in truth the very place you have read of in history, that it does to persuade yourself that St. Peter's is any larger than the Boston State-House;—your *eyes* testify to neither fact. Yet it is a high enjoyment to stroll about here; and the knowledge of localities, thus picked up, will be very valuable in future reading.

"As for the modern paganism of the city, I think worse of it than ever, and fear that my tolerance of Catholicity will be wholly gone before I return home. It makes me sick to see the splendid temple of St. Peter employed for no worship, (comparatively) except the adoration which is paid to an ugly black statue of the Apostle, which is devoutly kissed and caressed by all the faithful who enter the aisle. The illuminations and other theatricals of this week, I have only partially seen; but Mrs. Ware beheld the wax exhibition of the manger and the nativity, and the remnants of the real cradle enshrined in solid gold. We had appointed an hour to-day for going to see the heads of St. Peter and St. Paul, which are up for exhibition at the Lateran Church, (it is thought sufficient for St. Peter's Church to possess their *bodies*, and the Lateran shares a divided honor by keeping their heads,) but accident prevented. I cannot say that I much regret it. I have seen one dead saint laid out in gold and precious stones,—I have looked at a variety of relics, real and spurious,—I care little to witness any more such mockery;—it is half barbarian, and half impious. We have worship near us in an English chapel; and while cut off from what we should prefer, we are able to enjoy highly the unexceptionable portions of that magnificent liturgy. But we look with longing souls for the return of our own simple forms and hearty worship."

TO HIS BROTHER JOHN.

"Rome, February, 1830.

"You say that I am not particular enough about my health. I do not want to be always mentioning it; for there is nothing particular to be said, unless I should detail all the fluctuations and changes. These are perpetual;—now better, now worse; now, for days, perfectly well and strong, and then filled for days with lassitude and depression. At Naples, for two or three weeks, I was miserable; then I brightened, and came from there here principally on horseback. Here again, I am not quite so well. But the sum is, that I have a better winter than the last, but do not think I have gained anything since October, and am almost frightened at the idea of being at home and going to work again in five months. You expect to see me, you say, in June. It is impossible for us at present to form any definite plan, and we wish you would have no definite expectations. I have several things to see and arrange in England, after seeing Paris; and I do want the utmost length of absence which can be afforded me. The utmost with which I flatter myself, is to be in season for the fall term at Cambridge; and I hope I shall not be unable to enter on it with some vigor. But really it will demand so much, and a sickly man, without energy, and obliged to be continually leaving his work half done, is such a burden to himself, though his kind friends forgive it, that if I make no more headway than I have done, I shall almost feel ready to abandon the cause. However, I do not despair; the winter is now apparently over; a glorious spring is brightening and blooming all around us, and five months of more favorable weather may do me a good which has not yet been done. Especially do I hope something from pursuing the plan I commenced at Naples, of riding one of the carriage horses as much as possible. Your letter was brim-full in the best way, and, together with Brother Palfrey's budget, (just such an one as I love, tell him,) has made me quite master of the state of things at home. I only want to see 'The Examiner,'—why will you not send me the latest numbers by the packet of the 1st of April, to meet me in Paris?

"We had a charming visit at Naples, in spite of the bad weather,—very quiet and pleasant. Eight or ten good days, some of them too lovely by half, were sufficient to show us the beauties and wonders of the vicinity,—Baiæ, Cumæ, Pompeii, and Pæstum;—and the city itself has nothing to be seen but the Museum, which could be visited in any weather. It is a miserably insignificant place, of narrow, dirty streets, mostly meanly built, and thronged with a filthy, noisy population, whose clamor and rags beggar all description. But our lodgings were within forty feet of the very water of that beautiful bay,—and in all weather, good and bad, it was luxury itself to look out upon it. There was no exhausting its beauties, and there is no describing them. Come and see for yourself, or you never will believe that we could be induced to prolong our stay from three weeks to six, in the midst of rain, wind, and hail, day and night, almost exclusively by the singular pleasure of living in a room which overlooks the Bay of Naples. Then the vicinity is full of romantic and classic interest, and the day's excursion to Baiæ was alone worth the voyage.

"I wish I had power and time to make visible to you the scenes of Naples, and the Italian mode of travelling. Suppose you should engage in Boston a coach with two horses, and a saddle-horse to accompany, to take you and your wife to Northampton, and the man should drive up to your door the largest stage-coach in the town with four horses,—a big, lumbering thing for ten passengers, and after all you should be obliged to take it, and be joggled and jolted in it all the way? the saddle-horse being one of those four bony, uncurried beasts, taken from the traces when you wish to ride, and you astride of him with his bridle unchanged, and a string of bells about his neck? In just this style did wife and I travel our one hundred and fifty miles from Naples to Rome, and it is a perfectly fair specimen of the dealing and the manners of the land. Mr. and Mrs. R—— and Mr. and Mrs. G—— accompanied us on the road; and we enjoyed the weather and the scenery highly, notwithstanding our fantastic equipage. But the only possible comfort in the carriage was found in lying down on the seats."

TO THE SAME.

"ROME, MARCH 11, 1830.

"Last night we visited the Coliseum by moonlight, and all the extravagant speeches, which have been made about the effect, are not a whit beyond the truth. The evening was fine as possible, and we wandered about amongst the arches, studying the picturesque appearances of light and shade in every possible position. While we stood on the top and looked around, a small company of gentlemen appeared in another part of the ruin, and made it echo with solemn songs well sung, then with a trumpet-like instrument. Meanwhile, in the dark arches was wandering a cowled monk, bearing a candle, which had a striking effect as it appeared and disappeared in the distance; then presently an owl hooted from the top; then a fife played sweetly from Cæsar's House, on the Palatine; and presently many of the bells of the city rung from a distance, making a beautiful addition to the circumstances of the scene.

"After this we walked slowly through the Forum, which looks solemn and grand by moonlight, with its heaps of columns and arches, far beyond what it does by day. Constant excavations are going on there, and in many spots the old pavement is left bare, and you may walk upon it in the very steps of Cicero and Trajan. For a considerable distance by the Forum the street has been restored to its former level. The earth had accumulated from twelve to thirty feet; the pillars and triumphal arches were sunk that depth in the ground, which ground is but a mass of ruins, in digging through which they are constantly turning up shafts of columns and other antiquarian remains. Indeed, this is true of all Rome, the soil is many feet above the ancient level, and full of precious ruins; so is the Tiber."

TO HIS BROTHER WILLIAM.

"Rome, March 12, 1830.

"You want to know about Raffaelle's Chambers, &c. In the first place you know they are in the Vatican, a huge palace, 'a mighty maze, *and built* without a plan,' piled together anyhow, around twenty-six courts, eleven thousand five hundred and twenty-seven rooms of all sorts and sizes, and, together with St. Peter's, which adjoins it, covering, within a trifle, precisely the same ground which is covered by Turin, a city of one hundred thousand inhabitants. The galleries trodden by strangers, are said to measure, in all, two miles of extent.

"Raffaelle's Chambers are four rooms, up three pair of stairs, painted in part by his scholars; they have no furniture, and are used solely by artists to copy, and by foreigners to gaze upon; the Romans rarely look upon them or any other curiosity. The paintings cover every inch of the walls, and consequently bewilder you. They are much injured by time, and it takes many visits to look them wholly into shape, and understand and feel their excellence. Each is a long study, and you have to pursue it standing in most uneasy positions; the best, you must contrive to peep at through the stagings and scaffoldings of the army of painters who are copying. It is very difficult, under all these disadvantages, either to judge fairly, or to get up any enthusiasm, especially as you have further to contend with the ridiculous and shameful violations of chronology and costume, and the outrage of all decent taste, which fill the Catholic paintings, and from which even Raffaelle is not exempt. For example, he paints the Almighty at full length, creating the world; he brings in Stephen and another martyr, to the scene of the Transfiguration, and a pope is ushered in, in state, to the Temple of Jerusalem, to witness the punishment of Heliodorus. It is difficult to delight in pictures which set truth at defiance thus, and there is hardly a first-rate picture of holy subjects in Italy, which does not in this way bear a lie on its very front. Still, the genius of Raffaelle conquers; and it is a comfort to know, that he put these shameful blots on his works, not from choice, but by command.

" Of the particular pictures, you certainly will not expect me to give you an account. You already know more about them than I can tell you. Some please me little, others much. Many of the subjects are of a kind not to suit my taste, but no one is without some one object, at least, to strike and fix the eye. It is amazing, in the almost countless multitude of figures, how he could imagine such a variety of exceedingly difficult, and at the same time exceedingly fine heads; the same of the attitudes. He seems never to repeat himself. He is wonderful in his children. I suppose I have seen hundreds of his children, all graceful, natural, beautiful, and yet scarcely even a family likeness between them. He charms me in nothing so much. His portraits are sometimes wonderful; nobody but Titian does so well, and he sometimes better, that is, if better be possible. I think no one can dispute the general opinion, that Raffaelle's Transfiguration is his greatest work. I look at it in amazement; it wants nothing but to be cut in two, and the lower part preserved, while the upper is burned. The latter is stiff, forced, unmeaning and false; the former, living, active, nature and truth itself. How could the same hand do so stupid a thing as the first, and so transcendently perfect a thing as the last! I can only account for it by the fact, that genius dictated the one, and the

Pope the other. At the bottom of the right hand corner is a little pool of water, which you may not have observed in the engravings, but which is alone, in the original, worth a day's journey to see. You see I have become a convert to Raffaelle's fame; it took time and familiarity to perceive his eminence; the first things I saw did not satisfy me, and still you will believe he really left behind him some poor work.

"You ask me about Correggio. Very rare are his works. We have seen but few. But those few are certainly unequalled in a grace and loveliness peculiar to themselves. Delicate beauty is their characteristic, it seems to me. I have this very day seen the only one of the size of life, which we have met with, in the Borghese palace, Danaë and Cupid, with two little Cupids in the corner sharpening their arrows. Nothing can be imagined more exquisitely beautiful, especially the figure and head of Cupid, and the two cunning loves in the corner. You will, one of these days, see a very exact copy of this Cupid, which Peale has been making.

"Of Rubens we have seen something, and invariably laugh at him. He colors the flesh in blotches of red and white, so that his figures look as if they were flea-bitten. He draws abominably. In every picture you see something wrong or distorted, and long to put a finger or a leg into some possible position. His women are all fat, very fat, and their clothes hang about them in the most dowdy way imaginable. Yet no doubt his coloring is rich, and he produces splendid effects by the disposition and glow of his drapery. They say, too, that Italy possesses none of his best works. I wish it did.

"I sometimes fancy, that I like statuary better than paintings; but this does not always last. It has a distinct and peculiar charm, and never gives me the dissatisfaction, which I often feel at pictures, on account of the multitude of crowded figures thrown into them. I dwell with more complete delight on a piece, canvass or marble, of one or two finished figures, than on any more numerous company. It is more simple and less bewildering. I fancy that painting can be more successfully copied than sculpture; though I am sure that some chefs-d'œuvre, even of the pencil, are wholly uncopiable. I will not give you a dissertation on statues here, though I could do so if I had room; but, respecting the moderns, I believe no one comes to Rome without discovering that Thorwaldsen is a man far superior to Canova;—more strength, nature, and truth, with occasionally, and whenever the subject demands, quite as much beauty and grace, and never so much of an artificial air. Canova studied grace and beauty only; studied for them even when they were out of place, and has given his figures, too often, the appearance of having been taken from posture-masters and stage-dancers, who were *trying* to be pretty and graceful. They seem to be conscious of being looked at, and to be saying to themselves, 'I wonder what they think of me?' Thorwaldsen has nothing of all this,—is far above it; his works are simple, easy, natural. He is just completing the Saviour and Twelve Apostles, for a church in Denmark; (I wish you could see them; they would astonish you;) also, for the same, John the Baptist, preaching; his attitude and look, and those of his hearers, are perfect. He has just finished a statue of a Polish officer, which cannot be outdone in elegance and manliness. Why cannot we have something of such a man in America? Why do we give twenty thousand dollars to a second-rate artist for two tame things (one of which I have seen) to adorn or disfigure our Capitol, when, for the same sum, or less, this great genius would have been proud to send us two of his immortal works?

"It amazes me to find so little of Michael Angelo's works. Some buildings we have seen, and half a dozen pictures and statues, that is all. What did he do in his eighty years, that Raffaelle in his thirty-six should have left us one hundred for his one? His famous 'Day of Judgment' I have not seen; indeed, from the badness of its position and the holy smoke of years, it has become almost invisible."

TO HIS BROTHER JOHN.

[Written on the occasion of the birth of a daughter in Rome, on the 23d of March, 1830.]

. . . . . "We are in possession of every comfort which we could have at home, and want nothing;—convenient, comfortable rooms, four in number;—many friends, American, English, and Italian,—a very good English nurse, speaking French and Italian, as we need;—and, if our Boston friends could look upon us, they would say, that we should not be better off at home. So look upon us as perfectly happy, and as pretty a little quiet domestic circle as ever Rome has seen since the days of the twin founders. After which of the long list of her worthy women we shall call the infant lady, it is hard to decide. If there had been two boys, the designation would have been obvious, and Romulus and Remus should again have risen to fame. As it is, there is great room for hesitation between Egeria, the first female name, I believe, on the archives of the Eternal City, and Lucretia and Virginia, the heroic virgins, and Cornelia, the mother of the Gracchi, and Agrippina, and Julia, &c., &c.

. . . . . "I have nothing to say about things here; neither description, history, nor dissertation; or, if I had, I have no heart to say it. I am full of self-dissatisfaction. I am weary of this miserably idle life, and yet I am fit for no other. I am afraid to go home, because I know I shall only be able to do half the requisite work, and to do that not more than half,—yet to stay away is altogether out of the question; and so I have before me the dismal prospect of going back to a languid, inefficient, discontented existence. If I were free from engagement and obligation, if I were at my own disposal, I should not think of going home this season; and Mary rather insists, that, as it is, I had better resolve to stay away, as, she says, full strength and longer life are worth more to her and to the public, than this year of duty. But, having flung away two years on the vain pursuit of this perfect strength, and wasted the charity of friends, I have neither courage nor conscience to do more; my lot seems cast, and I will abide by it. We have talked over this matter together, and the only relief, which Mary is able to suggest, is, that I should state my case exactly, resign the professorship, so as not to be a burden or hindrance to those for whom I care more than for myself, send her home from Havre, and spend a year in travelling Europe on foot and on horseback. This might be done at a very small expense, an expense which we could meet without taxing College or friends. She would go to some quiet retirement and take care of the children; and I, as the past year proves, could do perfectly well alone, and do not require a nurse.

" So much for what we have thrown out in our talks. You may ask, 'What is the matter, and what leads to this?' In reply;—I am doubtless better than when I left home, and at times have thought myself greatly gaining, but have frequent pull-backs, and since January have had an almost perpetual lassitude upon me, (with occasional turns of vigor,) which has resulted in loss of strength, so that instead of walking for exercise as I did, I have been driven, from weakness, to take to the saddle; and am obliged occasionally during the day to lie down, which has not been the case before. I tell you here the worst of it; and you may easily conceive that this disheartens me a little, at the time when I am thinking of a return and beginning to prepare for it. Yet, at the same time, I am not low-spirited, nor nervous, as I was at Brookline; and, when in company, I am apt to get excited to a very unusual degree,—as I never used to be,—which I look upon as part of my disease, and which observers account to be vigorous health; so that, if you inquire of any who have seen me here, they would probably say, they never saw me so well in their lives. But enough for the present;—you know, a man likes to talk about himself, and, besides, you ought to know all that passes with us both in body and mind. I do not wish you to do anything in the premises, nor say anything, except so far as may be necessary to prevent disappointment among our friends, and the friends of the College, at my returning a weak man. I shall be nothing else, and should be sorry to have them expect anything else. And yet, it is so difficult to say anything which shall not be stretched into the most exaggerated misrepresentation, that perhaps it is best to hold your tongue."

TO THE SAME.

"Rome, April 17, 1830.

"You must not expect from me an account of the ceremonies of Holy Week, which everybody crowds to see, and repents of having seen. I was wise enough to avoid everything but a few of the chief exhibitions, leaving it to others to lose sleep, and meals, and temper, in rushing from church to church, and from procession to procession, for three days and nights. I should have gone to see the procession and the pompous mass at St. Peter's, where it not that the present Pope is 'lame of one leg,' or of two, and cannot stand, and therefore makes no public show,—a lucky man. I heard the three *Misereres* on Wednesday, Thursday and Friday, and can only say, that, after all which has been said of them, I was not disappointed. The music differs from all other that I ever heard, having no marked time or rhythm, but being a succession of swelling and dying harmonies, more like the Æolian harp than anything else I can compare it to, and sung by voices which resemble no human sounds,—something partaking of the voice and of a wind instrument, but finer than either. But we were so jammed together in a Calcutta hole, in the dark, hot chapel, and compelled to wait two and a half previous hours, amid such a villanous chorus of chanting priests and talking and perfumed Englishmen and Germans, that we were in a very unprepared state to *feel*, though we were delighted to *hear* it.

Then, on Wednesday and Sunday, the Pope was brought out in his high dress to the balcony of St. Peter's, to bless the kneeling people. Except at the laying of the corner-stone of Bunker-Hill Monument, I have never seen such a crowd.

"On Sunday evening, the church was illuminated with its forty thousand lamps and torches; such a beautiful, magic, brilliant, bewitching sight, cannot be imagined. On Monday evening, the religious services of the occasion were concluded with a show of fire-works from the Castle of St. Angelo. Description would be poor to tell you the splendor and sublimity of the scene. Thus ended the holy work of these solemn days; and you may guess how far they are calculated for religious edification, and to do honor, in men's minds, to the name of the holy and simple person whose death and resurrection they contrive to commemorate with all this mockery of noise and tumult and theatrical parade. Many things which I did not see were perfectly profane; it is a great merit of what I did see, that it was simply worldly.

"No sooner had the last rocket spent itself, than Rome began to empty itself. Carriages were standing ready, and many went off immediately. The city looks thin."

SINGING THE *MISERERE*.

(Journal, Rome, April 10.)

"Wednesday, Thursday and Friday, I attended at the Sistine Chapel in the afternoon, standing in the dense and suffocating crowd two hours and a half, listening to the recitations of the priests, for the sake of hearing the *Miserere* at the close. Of course I was too tired, when it came, to enjoy it fully; but I cannot say that I felt any disappointment, especially in Allegri's on Wednesday. The music is most peculiar, not arranged in any perceptible rhythm or accent, so as to form what we call a tune; but a succession of modulated harmonies and cadences, swelling and dying, changing and intertwining, more like the singular and beautiful music of the Æolian harp than anything else to which it can be compared. The voices were of wonderful tone and power, not like human voices, but more liquid, clear, and piercing. No accompaniment of instruments, and the whole was apparently warbled out without articulate words. Each *Miserere* was of kindred features, twenty minutes long; and a short piece at the commencement of the service, called *Tenebræ*, was in the same style, and nearly as fine. The service closed with a few words, uttered by somebody whom I could not see, and a loud noise to mimic thunder, or, as some say, the rending of the veil of the Temple. Fifteen candles, to typify the disciples and the three Marys, are burning at first, which are extinguished one by one, to show their desertion of the Saviour, till only the Virgin is left, and she is carried and placed under the altar. Then the other twelve candles on the altar and the railing are put out, and the *Miserere* is sung in the dark. Formerly it was forbidden to make known the notes of this music; but, Mozart and others having taken it from the ear, copies got abroad, and no secret is made of it now. But it can be sung with effect only by those who have learned the traditional method at the Vatican. The bare notes are inadequate guides, and both in Germany and England the first performers have tried it in vain."

TO HIS BROTHER WILLIAM.

"SPEZZIA, MAY 6, 1830.

"To begin at the end, I saw Greenough two days ago in Florence. He had made quite a satisfactory model of Dr. Kirkland, which unluckily met with an accident, and he must do it again. He has other works enough on hand, and is doing them beautifully, and has such fine and high notions that I am sure he will be a great artist. His two Cherubs will be exhibited in America and will delight you. He has just taken a likeness of Mr. G——'s niece, five years old, and everybody says it is perfect.

"But the glory of all statuary, modern and ancient, is found in the works of Thorwaldsen. I saw nothing in Rome so much, and, the more I saw, the more I admired. To some of his works no approach has been made by other artists; and no impartial person sees them without joining decidedly in the unanimous voice of the artists, which places Thorwaldsen far above even Canova, and without feeling indignant that fashion and circumstances should have given the latter a false preëminence. The truth is, Canova was an elegant and accomplished man, personally known and beloved by the principal literati of Europe, who looked at his works and spoke of them with the enthusiastic partiality of personal friendship; and, having the voice of the press in their power, they, from Mad. de Stael to Lord Byron, could make it speak their feelings, and give to the whole reading world their own bias. Thus he became the fashion, while poor Thorwaldsen, with all his excellence and worth, has no accomplishments or acquaintance, comparatively speaking,—'has forgotten his own language, and never learnt any other,' as Greenough has it,—and has been obliged to rely singly on his silent merit. Besides he came seldom into direct observation, because his great works have been done for Denmark, whose king has the high honor of having so patronized Thorwaldsen, as to have called into being the two grandest things ever done in marble.

"But the artists have always done the man justice; and they even revenge themselves on the injustice of public opinion, by affecting to speak slightingly of Canova, of which there certainly is no need. Canova was exquisite in a certain line of beauty, but he could not go out of it. He had no variety, he repeated himself forever, and has done nothing more than make a great family of brothers and sisters, with a striking family likeness, who had all been brought up by dancing-masters and posture-masters, and could not sit, stand, or look, except by rule. In one word, he was artificial. Thorwaldsen is natural. He copies, not from certain conventional rules of beauty and taste, which he has in his mind, but from the various models of nature. Consequently he does not repeat himself, and presents a variety of forms, and expressions, and attitudes, that astonish you almost as much as those of Raffaelle. Like his figures, too, they are easy and free, without constraint or artifice. It is one of Raffaelle's distinctions, that you never see anything like stage effect; no attitudinizing, no strutting, no showing off of hands and limbs. A stranger may go into his Chambers and decide at once which of them he did not draw, by this criticism; the other pictures are not representations of the real persons and scene, but of the persons and scene as represented on the stage,—not Constantine, &c., but certain pompous actors playing the part of Constantine. Now Thorwaldsen has fully this eminent excellence of Raffaelle; and it is one no small proof of his greatness.

"To illustrate all this, and more, I ought to be able to describe to you his two great groups, but I cannot do it. Both were done for a church in Copenhagen, by order of the king of Denmark; the one in marble, colossal statues of Christ and the Apostles; the other in bronze, John the Baptist and fifteen or seventeen figures listening. The figure of our Saviour is one of the very few attempts to represent that holy person, at which you can look with pleasure. It is noble and sublime, sweet, simple, sad, in attitude and look. The Apostles are a glorious company of venerable men, so variously arranged, in attitude and drapery, that you detect no similarity, and yet with a severity of simplicity that cannot be surpassed. I think, that out of all the Apostles, of all the masters of painting, that I have seen, it would not be easy to select twelve which should be altogether superior.

"But the other group is my favorite; indeed, that I have spoken of is not a *group*, as each figure is to stand in a separate niche. John the Baptist is truly a group, to be placed in the pediment of the church. The only thing in antiquity to be compared to it, is the celebrated and admired group of Niobe and her Children. Now I do not admire that; it doubtless displays great skill, but it wants simplicity and nature. It is not a copy from nature, but from the stage,—a group of ballet-dancers; Niobe herself is careful to hold her garment gracefully in all her woe, and the children are thinking of displaying their postures, and holding up the folds of their drapery tastefully, instead of being absorbed by the terrors of the moment. Nothing like this in the group of John; all is easy, unembarrassed, unaffected, unconscious nature. The Baptist is a thin, haggard man, filled with his subject, and uttering himself vehemently; his hand raised powerfully, not gracefully, and his eye fixed, as if his mind were working with all its might. The people around him are just those whom you might suppose to be present at his preaching. They describe various classes and ages of hearers, and each may be said to be a model of its class. I cannot remember the order of the whole, but it was something like this: On his left hand stands a huntsman, leaning on his pole, with his dog at his side, which takes up the attention of two little boys just behind him, one of whom is pointing to him, and the other, a little older, seems divided in attention between the dog and the preacher. Then stands a fine noble soldier in his armor; then a figure whose description I forget (it was standing apart in another room, and I saw it but once); then a mother sitting with eye intent on the speaker, with her arm embracing a little child, who is leaning his head sweetly on her lap; then a young man, reclining at his length, and looking over his shoulder at the preacher. On his right hand you see, first, a young man with his arms folded; then an elderly man, with a young man behind, leaning on his shoulder; then a mother, kneeling, and a child, of eight or ten, looking over her shoulder; then an aged man, sitting, his knees rather raised, and both his hands resting on his cane, and his head on his hands. Here, you see, is almost every age, each in its characteristic attitude, and each with its peculiar expression of attention. Perhaps the finest things are, the old man, on one side, and the mother, with the child's head in her lap, on the other; though one hardly ventures to say. I am sorry that I did not study it with a view to describe it to you, as I could then have been particular. I was sorry to find, that it is impossible to procure casts of it, or of any of its figures. It was only the day before leaving Rome that I discovered it had been engraved, and I made two vain attempts to procure it. I hope still to procure the engraving. If I had not said so much, I could tell you of some of his single figures; but enough for the present."

TO HIS BROTHER JOHN.

"GENEVA, MAY 9, 1830.

"In my last, I only spoke out more plainly, what has for some time been my conviction, that I am gaining nothing; and I simply wished to have you prepared for a proper reception of my *Miserability* when I should return. I regret having hinted at a longer stay, because it was only a transient thought, is a thing impossible to be done, and could be of no advantage. Since writing, I have been better and worse, and, on my journey, am still in the midst of changes. My worst thing is an insufferable lassitude of body and mind, so that to do anything, even to read, is a burden, except at moments; and, as for my pulse, I have not detected it doing its duty with proper deliberation for many weeks. They try to persuade me, that all has been owing to the Sirocco winds of the Mediterranean; but I know better. The extreme heat of the weather, for the last ten days, has prevented my taking all the exercise I intended; but I have ridden on horseback or walked part of the distance every day. I hope in this way to realize some benefit."

TO THE SAME.

"PARIS, MAY 30.

"You will have seen, by my letter from Rome about eight weeks ago, that we have here gone through very much the same course of thought with yourself; your views, (I mean of the uncertainty of my case,) are not new to us, and we only thank you for speaking plainly. I am sure I need not stay away; I am sure I am not fit to do any hard work; I do not think I could edit 'The Examiner.' But I will come home by the packet of July 20th, and you shall judge. It will be the hardest of all I have yet done to abstain from Cambridge, especially as Mr. Norton vacates his place, and there is the more need of other laborers. And, for myself, I think on the whole I had better do what I can there, than attempt anything else, unless the friends of the Institution can at once supply my place, which, if they will do, I will cheerfully give way. I certainly cannot fancy anything more to my mind than the duties of such a place; but, as I care for the Institution quite as much as for my own gratification, to say the least, I would not on any account be a hindrance to the appointment of some active man who can do what I cannot do. But of this when I get home."

The following letter, which he received from his father during his absence, was occasioned by his own, written on the outward voyage.*

"CAMBRIDGE, JUNE 13, 1829.

"MY DEAR SON,

"Thursday Morning, June 11th, I first heard of your safe arrival at Liverpool, and, half an hour afterward, had the additional and unexpected delight of finding your letter of

* See page 34.

May 1st, in the post-office. We participate, faintly, indeed, but sincerely, in the joy and gratitude which you must have felt, upon finding yourselves carried safely through such unusual scenes of suffering and danger. That you should be feeble, after such extraordinary excitement, was to be expected. I hope and trust, that the excitement of a very different kind, which followed your landing on the coast of Europe will soon have restored your strength, and enabled you, before this time, to feel some of the benefits of your voyage. I receive great satisfaction from the courage, and hope and trust in Providence, which you express. No one has certainly more peculiar cause than you have, to trace the hand of a kind Providence in sustaining you through trials, and pointing out the course of duty. That you are not more exhausted than you are, by so rough a passage, both in body and spirits, seems to me a reasonable ground for hope, that your health will be improved by the voyage, as soon as you shall have recovered from its immediate effects. It certainly gives much relief to my anxiety for you (more of which I felt than I was willing to express, when we parted); and I cherish the confident hope, that you will be permitted to return to us, and, in a life of labor and usefulness, have an opportunity of expressing the deep sense which you feel, of obligation to the kindness of friends, and of the good opinion and confidence so extensively extended to you by the community.

. . . . . "You speak of the influence of early discipline upon your character and prospects in the world. Whatever that influence may have been, you must carry your thoughts to a higher source than you seem to do. Very little is to be attributed to any exertions of mine. If you, or any of my children, are under any obligations to me in this respect, it is rather for what I *have not done*, than for what I *have done* for you. Few parents, in similar situations, have probably done less, in the way of instruction or of discipline, than myself. I have sometimes had severe visitings of shame and regret, for having so much neglected my duty towards those whom Providence had entrusted to my care and guidance. But, at other times, I have been led, by the result, to think it was better for you, than if I had forced upon you more instruction, and a more exact discipline; that a kind Providence has done better for you, than, by distrusting its care, and endeavoring to take you out of its hands, I could have done myself. At any rate, I see few of those parents who have been far more liberal in their expenses, and far more abundant in their cares, instruction, restraint, and guidance, than myself, who I think have more just occasion for gratitude and satisfaction in the result."

CHAPTER XVI.

SEPARATION FROM HIS PARISH—ENTRANCE ON HIS PROFESSORSHIP —STATE OF THE DIVINITY SCHOOL—INTRODUCTORY ADDRESS—NATURE OF HIS DUTIES AND HIS MODE OF INSTRUCTION—TRACT ON "THE FORMATION OF THE CHRISTIAN CHARACTER"—HE RESUMES PREACHING—EXCURSION TO THE WHITE HILLS—SICKNESS AT CONCORD, N. H.

1830-31. ÆT. 36-37.

It had been desired by many of Mr. Ware's friends, that his connexion with his people in Boston should continue after he had assumed the professorship at Cambridge, with the hope that he might still perform some of the duties of their minister. It was obvious to him, however, that this would be merely a matter of form; and to a mere formal connexion of this character, where no corresponding duties or obligations were implied, he had the strongest repugnance. Before removing to Cambridge, therefore, he asked a dismission from his parish. His letter closed with the following words.

"In thus seeking to dissolve a bond which has so long united us, it is a high gratification to remember, that it has been so happy a one, and to feel that we separate as Christian friends, who will still retain an interest in each other. I look back with grateful recollection on your uniform liberality, kindness, and indulgence. I feel grateful, that I am not to leave you alone, but have seen you already provided with an able administration of the word and ordinances. And it is a particular pleasure to feel, that I shall still be near you, and enjoy the opportunity of sometimes exchanging with you the offices of Christian friendship."

In acceding to his request, the parish, through its committee, conveyed to him the following expression of the feelings to which the occasion gave rise.

"In reviewing the circumstances of our connexion, we look back upon the events of many years, endeared to us and to our families by the memory of your kindness, your sympathy, and your Christian fidelity.

"In sickness and sorrow, how often have you come to us with the comforts and hopes of the gospel. In the day of our prosperity, how has the value of the good granted us been increased by your rejoicing together with us, and leading us to make it the occasion of a greater good hereafter. How often, in our afflictions, have we leaned upon you, and, while we have been comforted, have been taught to put our trust in Him who is able to save. How have we seen the eye of the dying, when the light of life was fading from it, turned upwards to that brighter light from heaven; and the heart of the mourner set upon that better mansion, which our Master has gone to prepare. If occasions have sometimes occurred in which we were divided in opinion, and had begun to be alienated in feeling, how have our differences ceased when you have come among us, in the spirit and with the influences of the Gospel of Peace.

"It is pleasant to us to dwell upon these recollections. They are deeply seated in our inmost hearts; and, mingled as they are with the image of your truth, and love, and faithfulness, they can never leave us.

"We had hoped that many such years were in store for us. Those of us, who are tottering upon the verge of life, had hoped, that you might be by us in the last trying hour,—that the prayer for strength in the dark valley, might be offered by you. Those of us, whose ties to life are strengthened and renewed in our children, had hoped for your aid and counsel in leading them to the fountain of life; we had hoped to see them formed under your influence, and to be able to point them to your example. All of us had hoped long to walk with you, to hear your voice in the pulpit and at the altar, and to enjoy the privilege of a relationship, which we felt to be of a better and higher character than that of common friendship.

"The wisdom of Providence willed it otherwise. We saw you worn out and fainting in our service. We anxiously watched the progress of your disease, and saw you depart for a foreign land. Our prayers have been answered in your return to your native shores, with health in some measure restored. And, while we lament that you have not yet strength to enter again upon those duties, from the discharge of which we had promised ourselves such large benefit, we thank God that you are not to be lost to the church, but that you have been called to an office in which your powers will be employed in awakening in others, who have taken up the cross of Christ, the zeal, devotion, and self-denial, which may fit them to become his faithful ministers.

"We pray, that, in this work and in all the relations of life, you may be blessed.

"We should do injustice to our feelings, if we failed, on this occasion, to make mention of her also, who has laid us under such obligations by her devotedness to you, when we looked upon you as belonging to ourselves, and who, though not long with us, had already taught us how highly to value, and how deeply to regret her.

"We thank you for the kind interest you continue to feel in our welfare. We are grateful, that you do not leave us alone, but that our common wishes have been gratified in another pastor, in whom we are happily united, and who is able to take your place in the administering of the word and ordinances.

"While we listen to him, we shall not cease to remember you; and we rejoice that you will be near us, and trust we may still have the privilege of calling you our friend.

"May the blessing of God be always with you."

He was desirous of preaching a farewell discourse; but, this being manifestly inexpedient, he contented himself with the delivery of a short address to the congregation, in addition to the usual services of the next Sabbath, from which the following extracts are made.

"The bond between minister and people is close and peculiar. It ought not to be formed inconsiderately; it must not be broken rashly. Strong, deep, fervent affections are bound up with it; tender and intimate feelings surround and hallow it. When confirmed by time and intimacy, if it should be rudely ruptured, many hearts are torn; even when gently severed, many hearts bleed. *Our* separation (blessed be He, who in judgment always remembers mercy,) is not sudden nor abrupt,—is not the consequence of dissension, dissatisfaction, or division,—has not been sought or desired on either side. It is the gradual result of circumstances, ordered not by man, but by an uncontrollable Providence, which arrested the minister in the midst of his labors, when he was engaged in them with more than usual satisfaction, and more than usual encouragement:—a Providence, which, having withdrawn him from your service, presented to you at once a man on whom your hearts could rest, and provided for him another sphere of duty. We separate, therefore, in unbroken good-will; and commend each other to God as we part, not only from a sense of Christian duty, but with a warm sentiment of brotherly affection. It is a reason for devout gratitude to-day, that, with all the trials which have borne upon us, and introduced this event, we have been spared that bitterest of all,—alienation and dissension.

. . . . . . "If I were to mention all that I discern in the past of error, negligence, unfaithfulness, on my own part, I should only unnecessarily pain you, and perhaps seem to be making an exhibition of humility. But some of you will understand me when I say, that I feel I need their forgiveness for instances of what must have seemed to them culpable remissness; and I cannot be at ease, except by hoping that they have granted it. Indeed, no one who has not experienced the difficulty of always doing all that is to be done in the complicated and trying walks of the pastoral office, can guess with what bitterness a minister is sometimes compelled to reproach himself, and how the kind approbation of his friends serves only to humble and rebuke him under a consciousness that he ill deserves it. For you,—you have borne with my weakness, overlooked my neglects, been liberal to my necessities, candid to my faults. I can only thank you for that indulgence which has made my path pleasantness and peace, and beseech you to cheer the way of my successor with similar kindness.

"Yet, whatever may have been my failure in executing the plan of my ministry, with the plan itself I perceive no reason to be dissatisfied. Being persuaded that the private duties of personal and pastoral intercourse are at least as important as the public exercises of the pulpit, and in fact necessary to their efficiency and success, it has been my wish and purpose to give much of my time and affections peculiarly to this sphere of action. If I have done any good, I attribute it almost entirely to the opportunities and power which I have in this way gained. That I have done no more, I feel now to be mainly owing to remissness, irresolution, and want of exact method in prosecuting this, the most difficult as well as important department of the minister's labors.

. . . . . . "Brethren, my work among you is ended.

Such as it has been, it is over. For you, and for me, the account is sealed up for a solemn judgment. The day is coming which will try it as with fire, and disclose to us its true character, with all its lasting consequences. Join me, brethren, in the prayer, that God will show mercy in that day!

"Meantime we are to finish our mortal probation apart. Yet I cannot feel that I shall be separated from you. This house will long seem to me my own religious home, and those who worship here, the members of my own religious household. Still, as returns the hallowed day, my spirit will come up among you, as it has done from across the ocean, and amid the worship of strange lands, to join in your praises, and bend with you at the mercy-seat. And when the day shall arrive, that these temples have mouldered, and all earthly worship ceased,—when the scattered congregations of the saints shall assemble together with the church of the first-born in heaven,—then, too, it is my hope and prayer that we shall be found side by side in the worship of eternity, and accompany one another still in that career of infinite progress and spiritual glory, which we commenced together here.

"In this hope, I bid you,—as your minister,—farewell. I rejoice that I do not leave you alone, but to the guidance of able hands, and to the instruction of faithful lips. God bestow upon your minister and upon you the choicest of spiritual blessings! May he lead, support, encourage, cheer, and save you! May the spirit of Christ dwell in you richly with all wisdom; and the peace of God, which passeth all understanding, abide among you and sanctify you always!"

Thus terminated his course as a Minister of the Gospel. He now discontinued the special exercise of that function which had always been held in his regard as the highest, the holiest, the most desirable on earth. To fill well the office of a minister of Christ had been the dream of his childhood, the determined purpose of his youth, the object to which he had devoted the whole heart and head of his mature life. So far as reputation, character, influence in his profession were concerned, he had met with a success far beyond his most sanguine expectations; and, so far as he had in view the better purpose of doing good to his fellow-men, he had the best reason for believing, that, whilst his labors had been always acceptable, they had also been useful. The relation of a minister in our communities is not confined, however, to the people of his particular charge. He maintains a certain connexion, also, with society at large; and, as I cannot venture to speak in my own person of the estimation in which my brother was held, or the influence he exercised at the time of his leaving Boston, I am happy to be able to do it in the words of one who knew him well, and had been for many years his highly valued fellow-laborer.

FROM A SERMON BY MR. GANNETT.

"I have often thought, that, in him of whom we are speaking, might be seen an example of the force of character in commanding influence. During the latter part of his ministry in this city, I suppose no other person possessed so entirely the confidence of our citizens. Always acceptable and highly esteemed as a preacher, yet his gifts in public discourse were not of that extraordinary kind which makes their possessor an idol or a sovereign with the people. His modes of life were unostentatious, and his personal manners tinged with an appearance of abstraction or indifference. He did nothing to court popularity, or secure the favorable regards of any class of people. Yet he was, beyond all doubt, at the time to which I refer, the one man in Boston on whom men of all parties and all denominations and all classes bestowed unqualified esteem. Does not the universal regard in which he was held, and of which we have been reminded by various proofs since his death, show the worth of a character in which no one can detect a blemish?"

He removed to Cambridge in October, 1830. His health, in the interval which had elapsed since his return, had very much improved. By his journeying, and also probably by his long escape from wearing and exhausting labors, a favorable impression had obviously been made on his constitution, which had not even yet shown its full effects. But, though thus rejoicing in his own renewed capacity for duty, he was destined to undergo a great degree of anxiety for some months of this and the following year, on account of the health of his wife, who suffered severely, and for a long time, from serious pulmonary complaints. This anxiety was in no slight degree aggravated by the reflection, that her illness was, in part at least, induced by the exposure, fatigue, and anxiety, which she had undergone during his own protracted sickness. He had the happiness, in the ensuing spring, of witnessing her complete recovery.

It has been already stated, that, for a long time before the establishment of a regular school for theological instruction in the University in Cambridge, many persons, especially graduates of the College, had been in the habit of residing there, during a part at least of the period of their preparation for the ministry. Before the organization of the School, they had been unofficially under the superintendence of the Professor of Divinity; but, at the time of Mr. Ware's accession to the professorship, the theological department was in operation, and was recognized as a part of the regular course of instruction in the University. It was under the charge of his father, then Hollis Professor of Divinity, and of Mr. Norton, who held the office of Dexter Professor of Sacred Literature. With them he was therefore at once associated in his new duties; and from such a connexion he had reason to anticipate, not only an intercourse most agreeable and instructive to himself personally, but the most happy results on the prospects of the Institution. No one could enter upon an office with a more deep feeling of its importance, and of the great responsibility he assumed; for, looking on the calling of a clergyman in the light he did, he would of course regard the place of him, who was to be engaged in preparing individuals for it, as of a still higher and more responsible nature.

The views with which he entered on the duties before him were embodied in an 'Introductory Address,' which was delivered to the members of the School in October, and published at their request. The subjects of this Address are thus announced:

" These two branches [the Eloquence of the Pulpit and the Pastoral Care] go together, and sustain each other. The minister is the better preacher for having his heart warmed by intercourse with his hearers in private; and he goes to them in private with the greater influence and effect, because he carries with him the sacredness and sanction of the Pulpit. The full power of the Christian ministry can be known only where both departments are exercised with faithfulness; and he entirely errs, who fancies he may neglect either, and yet command the best success in the other. It is to the union of the two, that we must look for the efficient and complete minister. And I think we cannot better introduce our labors in this department than by attempting to illustrate this important truth."

By the Eloquence of the Pulpit, as a thing to be taught, he does not mean " that high and singular gift, that extraordinary combination of powers and attainments, which the books describe as the property of the orator; for men so splendidly endowed are but few in an age; and the church, if it must depend on them, would soon perish for want of advocates. It is not this, which our institutions propose to teach, or which our students aim to acquire. What we propose is, simply, the power and habit to select judiciously, arrange clearly, and express forcibly and fervently, the topics suited to the pulpit; and to utter them with that distinct, correct, and pleasant elocution, which shall ensure for them the attention of the people. Thus much is capable of being learned; and this is what we mean by Pulpit Eloquence, when we propose it as something to be attained."

" By the Pastoral Care," he goes on to say, " we understand that duty towards individuals and families, which consists in personal acquaintance and intercourse for the purpose of knowing the character and condition of the flock, that so the minister may be ready to derive opportunities of usefulness among them, in either their temporal or spiritual relations, by giving counsel, instruction, reproof, encouragement, consolation, according to situation and character. We do not regard it as consisting in what appears sometimes to be understood by the term,—the custom of simply visiting as a friend, or making calls from house to house; much less ceremonious or party visiting, or social tea-drinkings. Some ministers have much intercourse with their people, or rather with a certain portion of them, in this way; but this is not doing parochial duty. Social visiting is well. It has its uses; indirectly, its religious uses. But pastoral visiting has *directly* its religious uses. The pastor goes ' from house to house,' like the Apostles, with an expressly religious object; and he executes it, not only in sympathizing with the joys and sorrows of his people, and administering advice in sickness, and comfort in affliction; but also in communing with them on their religious interests, and applying himself to their spiritual ignorance, trials, doubts, perplexities, and progress. It is to this that we especially refer, when we speak of the advantages he must derive as a preacher from the discharge of his duties as a pastor."

The remainder of the discourse was occupied in illustrating at large the necessity and importance of this connexion between the two branches of ministerial action, and the support which each furnishes to the other. It concluded with the following passage:

"I have now said what I designed, to show the mutual dependence and reciprocal influence of the Eloquence of the Pulpit and the Pastoral Care. It is the union of these which forms the complete and effective minister. It is such ministers that we desire to send forth to the churches; 'eloquent men and mighty in the Scriptures;' who shall carry into the pulpit the best gifts of utterance and persuasion, and the most affectionate zeal for the salvation of men; and who shall move amongst their people with the kindness of friends, and the cheerful gravity of men of God. That *you* may become such, is to be the object of your and my unceasing and solicitous study.

"You are called to be Preachers and Pastors. It is for this that your whole discipline is to prepare you. The learning and exactness of the study, the musings and devotions of the closet, the watchfulness and discipline of daily life, all are to combine in fitting you for the solemn function of preaching God's truth to a sinning and slumbering world, and of guiding and counselling men in the most interesting concerns of the human soul.

"Let me exhort you, then, to look forward habitually to the day when this charge of souls shall be actually in your hands, and to consider by what preparation you shall be able to acquit yourselves in it satisfactorily and acceptably. Contemplate the Pulpit, from which you are to speak to God in behalf of the congregation; and realize with what devotion and elevation of spirit you should be imbued, in order rightly to carry up the general offering of praise and supplication;—the Pulpit, from which you are to address men on the loftiest themes, and awaken their dull hearts to the spiritual things from which a sensual world is constantly enticing them; and realize with what holy earnestness of deep conviction, with what suavity and vehemence of utterance, with what clear and energetic reasoning, with what intimate knowledge of Scriptural truth, of Providence, and of human nature, you must be filled and glowing, in order worthily to execute so vast, so various, so delicate, so responsible a trust. Bring this thought before you. Keep it before you. Weigh it, feel it, understand it. You will then cheerfully devote yourselves to the severest toils which shall be requisite to accomplish a thorough preparation.

"Look also to the Pastoral relation. Consider what it is to be the religious counsellor of hundreds of souls, in every most trying and momentous crisis of their being. Consider what prudence you must study, what wisdom and discretion you must cultivate, what readiness, what patience, what forbearance, what affection, what zeal; above all, what need there is of a spiritual habit of mind, a fondness for religious thought, a heart always alive to sympathy with man, and ready to rise in devotion to God. You will then comprehend with what diligence you are now to cultivate your affections, and live as men of faith and prayer, that you may not then be strangers to the most spiritual part of your labors, but may go to them as to an accustomed and welcome occupation.

"Understand, therefore, the importance and dignity of the work you are to undertake. There is no more momentous trust committed to human hands. There is no higher honor to which man may aspire on earth. Office more responsible no one can bear. Duties more weighty and trying, no one can assume. They are the office, trust, honors, and duties, which once were borne by the Son of God. To esteem them lightly, to prepare for them sluggishly, is the extreme of folly and of sin. It is to seek and deserve disappointment, failure, and contempt. It is to dare the displeasure of Heaven, and darken the prospects of the soul. Be persuaded, then, to set your standard high. Act from elevated and disinterested principles, with a lofty aim, and a vigorous perseverance. In attainments and in character press on to the *aliquid immensum infinitumque;* or, in words more solemn and exciting still, 'to the mark for the prize of your high calling of God in Christ Jesus your Lord.'

"It is to help you in this arduous and almost fearful preparation, that I have come among you. I truly feel that I could receive no more interesting or important charge. And what power God has given me, what skill and knowledge experience may have taught me, may be more than occupied in the responsible task. I will do what I can. May God grant his blessing! I only ask of you to second my exertions, and give me your prayers."

No one of his writings conveys so lively an idea, as this, of my brother's views of the character and duty of a minister, and of the principles and feelings which should actuate him in his labors among his people. It may be regarded as an embodying of the results of his own experience in the office, an exposition of the principles by which he had been himself governed, deriving confirmation of their justness from the success which had attended their application in his own case. It particularly dwells upon and enforces, what he always regarded as lying at the foundation of a pastor's usefulness, and thought of and talked of the more because it was so often overlooked, the necessity of a personal intercourse between the pastor and his people, and of a personal sympathy between them.

This address was republished in England, and from some of his friends there he received the most cordial expressions of their favorable opinion.

FROM MISS JOANNA BAILLIE.

"In addition to your former very gratifying remembrance of me, from which I received great pleasure, I have now to thank you for a copy of your excellent Introductory Lecture to your course on Pulpit and Pastoral Duties, which cannot fail to make a strong and salutary impression on those who are fortunate enough to be your pupils. What a happy pastor and nappy flock they would be, whose ministers should follow the perfect model you so eloquently set before them! Some of the good old Presbyterian clergymen, whom I have heard of in my young days, the immediate successors of those who had so bravely withstood the persecutions in Charles and James the Second's times, resembled what you would have your pupils to be, with some lack, however, of that liberality, regarding the opinions of others, which your followers will always entertain. May you go on prosperously in your honorable and important task! and may it please God to spare you many years, and give you health to fulfil it!"

FROM MISS EDGEWORTH.

"The books you were so kind as to send me by a countryman and namesake of ours, have been safely delivered to us, and I return you sincere thanks for the pleasure you have given me in so many ways. I was in the first place truly gratified by your remembering your too short visit here with so much satisfaction. It was indeed a most pleasing visit to us. We felt that you suited our domestic habits, and that the more we had seen of you, the more we should have esteemed and liked your character.

"The books you have sent confirm me in this conviction. The 'Introductory Address' on the connexion between the Duties of the Pulpit and the Pastoral Office appears to me to be admirably well adapted to its purpose. I cannot conceive any young man reading it, much less hearing it, without being moved to good, and moved steadily and permanently. The Address is itself the example of all it recommends with such pious, such benevolent, such persuasive eloquence,—eloquence in the highest, best sense of the word.

"I think even in Ireland, and at this moment of the delirium of party spirit, such a pastor would be loved and respected, and would even be paid his tithes.

"I particularly like what you say of the influence which the pastoral character has, even on the mode of delivery. It is a new and perfectly just observation. The being in earnest at once cures affectation and all the defects of delivery which have any hurtful influence on the congregation in distracting attention, and all other defects are of little consequence. I have observed, that preachers who have been very defective in pronunciation, accent, provincial accent I mean, have nevertheless, when thoroughly in earnest, commanded the minds of their hearers more than the most eloquent speakers. Dr. Chalmers is an example of this.

"When Mrs. Edgeworth had finished reading your New

Year's sermon on 'The Duty of Improvement,' she exclaimed, 'I think it is the best sermon I have ever read.' I had refrained from telling her what I thought of it, being anxious to know whether we agreed in opinion. Her exclamation delighted me.

"In the volume on 'The Formation of the Christian Character,' I particularly like Chapter the Fifth, on 'The Religious Discipline of Life,' the guard to be kept over the principles and the habits."

It did not lessen his sense of the weight of responsibility which rested upon him, and of the difficulties of his new situation, that he knew very well that much was expected of the influence, which he was deemed capable of exerting on the pupils of the School in that part of their preparation which was his particular province. I cannot doubt that he felt sometimes oppressed by this consideration, and fearful that there might be disappointment at the want of greater results, than there was any reason to anticipate. From letters written at this time I extract the following passages, which, besides containing allusion to this point, give an account of the mode and spirit, in which he entered on his task.

TO MR. ALLEN.

"CAMBRIDGE, NOVEMBER 26, 1830.

"Things are promising, and an excellent spirit prevails My duties are in the highest degree pleasant. I attend the Senior and Middle Classes once a week in the composition of sermons;—not formal lectures, but free discussion amongst us, in which they take part with spirit,—criticizing sermons,—and bringing plans and skeletons for examination. I attend also the Senior Class once a week in *reading*, by Porter's

'Analysis,' as a text-book, and once a week in declamation. On Wednesday evening I have three or four to take tea, and talk with me, (this recently). And the student who officiates in preaching on Friday, Saturday, and Sunday evenings, comes to breakfast the following morning, and I go over with him his sermon, as thoroughly as possible.

"You may form some little judgment from this, what my course and quality of employment is. Another term I shall do more. I have far more power of application than I expected to find, and think I am gaining strength. I use a good deal of exercise; go to bed early and rise early; and, if Mary were but well, so as to give me the sort of help which I hope from her, I should be only too well satisfied. But we must always have some drawback.

"This account I send in reply to your request that I would tell about the School and myself. When I see you, I can go into details, and hope to get from you some hints to help me."

TO HIS BROTHER WILLIAM.

"CAMBRIDGE, JANUARY 1, 1831.

"You ask about my routine of duties, to which I reply thus. Friday evening, the two upper classes in rotation preach extempore. I follow the preaching with remarks, more or less particular, which I enter in a book on reaching home, and thus lay up a series of papers on preaching, &c., of which I may perhaps make use at some future time. Saturday and Sunday evening, the same classes preach before the whole Faculty; and, if I say anything worth the while, I record it. Then, once a week, I hold an exercise with the same classes, (Tuesday and Wednesday,) on the art of making sermons. I assign certain topics and questions, and point out authors to be read; and the hour is passed partly in conversation, and partly in lecturing. I think it most useful to make them think and talk as much as possible, because they thus become much more interested and excited on the subjects, and enter into them more fully, than if I merely read or spoke my own opinions. I have had great success in leading them to talk, and it is a very interesting exercise.

"In a similar manner, I spend an hour with them on the art of reading and speaking,—drilling and practising; and, after the extemporaneous preaching on Friday evening, we often stop and have declamations. With the Senior Class the lecture on Sermonizing will soon be exchanged for an exercise on Pastoral duties. I ought to have stated, that they bring to me plans and skeletons, once a fortnight, on given subjects, which I criticize; and I sometimes require them to write out at length one of the heads, for example, the Exordium or the Conclusion. Also, once a term at least, they are to bring up a complete sermon, besides those which they preach in turn.

"With the Junior Class, I have no exercises at present, and shall not have, except perhaps in reading, during the last term. I have, however, become acquainted with them, by inviting them to tea, three or four at a time, on Wednesday evening, when I have an opportunity of learning something of their characters, and giving them advice. This I find very pleasant, and, I hope, useful. Also, the preacher of Friday, Saturday, and Sunday evening breakfasts with me the next morning, and we go over together very critically his performance, both as to matter and manner; and, if the sermon be faulty in any special particular, he is told how to mend it, and required to do so, and then to show it to me.

"This is about the whole; not a very laborious, but a sufficiently constant employment, and thus far pleasant, as I am met by the best dispositions on the part of the young men; and, though it is too soon to judge whether I am actually exerting a good influence or any influence at all, yet I have good and encouraging hopes. If anything would damp my hopes and destroy my courage, it would be the expressions, which come to me from many, very like those in your last letter, seeming to imply an expectation that I must effect a great and perceptible improvement at once. It is fearful to think that such a task is expected of me; and all that I can do is to do my duty as well as possible, and leave the consequences to the candid and considerate judgment of men. I hope they will judge kindly. I see that much is to be done; that a change ought to take place. I think I know what it is. But is it possible for me to bring it about speedily? Is it reasonable to expect it of me? And, if I should fail, ought I to be censured? Do not be too sanguine, and do not allow others to be so. It is, you know, far easier to know what is to be done, than to have the wisdom and skill which shall effect it; and, when we effect so little by preaching to men and women, how can we expect to do great things with young men?"

TO MR. ALLEN.

"CAMBRIDGE, MARCH 7, 1831.

"I am pretty well, but quite lazy. I seem to have done nothing this winter, and yet perhaps have done as much as I ought. My absolute duties are not laborious, and I think I have had some success. I think some serious impressions have been made; I am pleased with the disposition to give more attention to the more serious views of character and duty. I have turned the exercise of extempore preaching into an extempore discussion, which acts much like a conference meeting. I propose a subject, of a practical character rather than speculative; four speak upon it from the pulpit in order; then all are at liberty to speak from their places. It proves interesting, and I flatter myself it tends to promote personal religion. Our subjects have been, 'What is Religion,' 'Power of Conscience,' 'Method of Cultivating Conscience,' 'The Inferences to be drawn from the Parable of the Prodigal Son;' and the next time will be, 'The Example of Jesus, as a Preacher of Retribution.' This is at present my favorite exercise."

TO THE REV. DR. CARPENTER.

"CAMBRIDGE, NOVEMBER 12, 1831.

"Mr. Shute will tell you, that Mrs. Ware and myself are in perfectly good health, and have just removed into a house which we have been building, and from which we hope not to be removed until we go to our final home. It is within a few rods of our Divinity Hall, which renders my intercourse with our young men easy and constant. You can readily judge how interesting a work it is, that engages me, and perhaps may understand, too, how difficult it is to satisfy one's self in the performance. Our number this year is thirty-three; among them are individuals of rare promise. The spirit which reigns among them is excellent,—all that it should be. You would be delighted to witness their industry, seriousness, and ardent interest in the labors of their profession. It is particularly gratifying, I think, to witness so little of the spirit of sectarianism. They seem to be anxious for Christianity as a religion of benevolence and power, not of a party, and cherish an enlargement and generosity of view, which it would do your heart good to observe.

"They have recently formed among themselves a Philanthropic Society, of which all, I believe, are members, whose object it is to collect information respecting the various benevolent projects of the day, to excite an interest in their own minds respecting them, and to prepare themselves to act understandingly, when they shall go out into the world. This society meets once a month, when a report of some committee on a specified subject is read, and a discussion takes place. The subjects already taken up are, Prison Discipline, the Reformation of Juvenile Criminals, Foreign Missions, the Wants of Seamen, and the Amelioration of the Condition of the Blacks. A good deal of excellent fruit is already growing on this young stem. Several of the young men, from three to six, walk to the next town every Sunday, to give religious instruction to the prisoners at the State penitentiary. They are engaging, also, in a similar enterprise in the County jail. So that we hope they are training up to be active and benevolent, as well as learned, ministers of Christ. This is a delightful prospect. There is, also, a good deal that is cheering in the prospects of religion in the community, notwithstanding the events which accompany the storm of fanaticism that is now driving over our land. Our own societies are flourishing; there is less of a sectarian spirit than formerly among them, and an increasing desire for plain and serious instruction on personal religion. I have been led to observe this in the eagerness, with which a little work of mine on the Christian Character has been sought for, and other similar works are multiplying and circulating.

. . . . . "Our affairs here are prosperous, and we are particularly gratified with the signs we witness of increasing regard to the Christian religion as a practical and spiritual system. Works of a serious and devotional character are earnestly sought for by our people; and the issue of our long controversy seems to have been to revive and quicken, rather than destroy, the love of earnest and deep feeling in the pursuit of personal religion. I am sure you will rejoice with us in this. It is a proof, I hope, that our controversy has been conducted wisely, and that we have a right to increased confidence in the worth and truth of our views."

The following letters, also to Dr. Carpenter, although written some time afterward, will be read with more interest here, as giving his own account of the nature and extent of his occupations, and the manner in which his department was conducted.

TO THE REV. DR. CARPENTER.

"CAMBRIDGE, AUGUST 20, 1833.

"My duties in the School, in which you express so much interest, grow more and more delightful to me. The last term was one of peculiar gratification. We have just dismissed a class of twelve, who have gone out to their work in the finest spirit, and with preparation of mind and heart which cannot fail to fit them for useful action. Besides the regular instruction of the School, they have formed among themselves a Philanthropic Society, whose object it is to inform them respecting the various benevolent projects of the day, to excite an interest in these, and to prepare them to act in relation to them. Their meetings have been highly valuable, and have tended to foster a practical turn, which is greatly to be praised. We needed something of the sort, to qualify the speculative and scholastic character which is so inevitably the consequence of seven years spent within the walls of a university.

"You have expressed a wish to know something of the routine of my office. I will try to give you some brief notion. 1. At the opening of each term I deliver a written lecture to all the classes, on some topic of personal and professional character: e. g. *Importance of Piety in a Minister*,—*The Spirit of the Profession*,—*Clerical Prudence*, &c. This is the only course of written instruction, except that I have begun a pretty extensive course of lectures on Preaching, to be delivered year after year during the summer term. Otherwise my exercises are carried on in free conversation. I assign topics, direct them what books to consult, and then we *talk together* about it. I fancy this method more likely to excite their own thoughts, and interest them deeply, and secure lasting impressions, than if I simply told them what I think myself. Besides that, I thus learn their difficulties, and can apply myself more certainly to their state of mind. Hence I find, that the same subjects require to be differently treated before different classes, which could not be if I only rehearsed a set of written lectures. Then, 2. The courses of instruction treated in this way are as follows: In the second year, the *Art of Composition*, including, first, the finding of thoughts, or the art of discussion; secondly, arrangement; and, thirdly, style. This is followed by a course on the *Composition of Sermons*, accompanied by criticisms and remarks, and by exercises of the students in drawing up plans and arranging skeletons. A course on *Prayer and Public Devotions*, designed to guide them to the profitable and true manner of conducting that exercise. A course on *Pastoral Duty*, embracing the whole of a minister's private relations to his flock, the principles on which he should conduct himself to all classes, and the various efforts to be made for their general and individual religious improvement. These several courses occupy two years, one afternoon each week. 3. Instruction in *Elocution*. Once a week we spend one evening in declamation, and generally close it with remarks, and criticize the speaking of individuals in private. Those who most need instruction, read to me privately. 4. There are two other exercises. On Sunday evening, one of the Senior Class preaches. The members of the Faculty remark on his performance. I take his sermon home and examine it; he breakfasts with me Monday morning, and I criticize it and advise him. On Friday evening, I hold an exercise to promote *Extemporaneous Speaking*. Four persons in order, from the two older classes, speak on some question previously assigned, after which any one may rise and speak. This proves a very delightful and useful exercise. 5. On Saturday evening, I hold a meeting, at which those who please attend, for purposes of devotion, and conversation on topics of personal religion. This has been held rather irregularly, but has been very useful, and will not hereafter be irregular. 6. Besides this, during part of the second year, the class reads to me pieces of their own writing, for purposes of practice in writing and speaking; and, during the last year, sermons are written and brought to me for criticism.

"So much for a bird's-eye view of what belongs to me in the theological department. Besides this, I attend prayers at the University chapel every morning during the year, my father attending in the afternoon; and I preach in the said chapel every Sunday afternoon, for half the year; Mr. Palfrey preaching the other half-year, and my father always preaching in the morning.

"I shall be greatly obliged to you for any hints on these several subjects, and on the best manner of conducting instruction. Your experience in the art of teaching, and your interest in these subjects, must enable you to say what would essentially aid me."

TO THE SAME.

"CAMBRIDGE, JULY 28, 1834.

"MY DEAR SIR,

"I have, within a few days, received by Dr. Tuckerman your little letter of June 5th. You ask me to tell you further of 'the developement, success, and failure of my plans' I can say nothing yet very definitely beyond the fact, that I feel encouraged. In general, I think that I have met with success, and that failure has taken place only in minor points; and then, I suspect, it may be attributed to my own negligence. We have just dismissed the first class, which began its course after Mr. Palfrey and I came here; and we have the satisfaction of believing, that the friends of the institution are content with what has been done. The day on which the class took leave of us, was one of most deep and gratifying feeling. How you would have enjoyed the serious, ardent, elevated, spiritual tone of their dissertations, and felt to your heart's core the expression of their sweet singing. This was in the forenoon. Then, in the afternoon, their *Philanthropic Society* held its anniversary, and was addressed by several of the ministers, at their request. It was a most rich occasion. The topics of remark were,—*How shall be obtained a supply of devotional works?*—and, *What is the true character of preaching for the times?* The latter brought out a great deal of powerful and moving remark. Mr. Walker, of Charlestown, especially, spoke from the depths of a strong and thrilling emotion, which moved us all, as we seldom are moved. Not more than two or three times in my life have I witnessed so much emotion in a speaker and his hearers. Many of the hearers, since that day, are unable to speak of it with dry eyes; indeed, it was a marked day, and must give a complexion to our preaching henceforth. It was an outpouring of the spirit. We all came away disposed to 'thank God and take courage.''

During the fall and winter of the year of his settlement at Cambridge, 1830–1, he was engaged in completing, and preparing for publication, his tract on the "Formation of the Christian Character," the work by which he has perhaps been most extensively known, and probably most extensively useful. This he had had in contemplation for a long time. There are some notices of his plan as far back as 1827. It was a frequent subject of his thoughts and conversation during his long confinement in 1828; and he seems, by keeping the subject before him, and constantly revolving it, to have filled himself with suitable thoughts, and nearly completed their arrangement in his mind. So intent was he on this object, and so ready with his materials, that he began the composition of it at an inn in Princeton, Massachusetts, at the close of the first day of the solitary journey which he made in August and September, 1828, as I find by an entry of the date in the original manuscript. He continued to work upon it at short intervals during the whole of his absence; on some days writing only a few lines, but on one, accomplishing fifteen pages, apparently at a single sitting. The last entry was made at Pawtucket, Monday, October 6th, on his way home from Brooklyn, and after he had begun to experience symptoms of that indisposition which laid him up the whole of the ensuing winter. He had then written as far as the third section of the fourth chapter, concluding the subject of "Meditation." It was at this point laid aside for a long time. During the winter he seems to have felt entirely incapable of any serious and continued application. No further attempt was made to go on with the plan till the next November, (1829,) when he wrote a little at Florence, and afterwards, during the winter and spring, at Naples and Rome, in this way completing the fourth chapter before his return home. The concluding chapter was added after he was fixed at Cambridge, and the whole was revised carefully and published in May, 1831.

This work proved extremely acceptable to the religious community with which he was associated, and was even received with considerable favor by many of other denominations, who had no sympathy with the doctrinal opinions of its author. It obtained, and has continued to have, a wide circulation in this country, and has gone through fifteen editions of a thousand copies each. It was also speedily republished in Great Britain, and has been there also extensively circulated. He received from many quarters very warm assurances of the approbation of those whose opinion he valued, and, what was still more grateful to him, the strongest evidence of the favorable influence which it had exerted on the religious character and progress of many who had read it.

When absent in attendance on the ordination of Mr. Fox, at Newburyport, he wrote thus:

TO HIS WIFE.

"NEWBURYPORT, AUGUST 3, 1831.

"I am surprised to see how seasonable my little book has been, how widely it has been circulated, and how strongly people feel about it. They speak to me of it with tears in their eyes. It seems just to have met the wants of the crisis. You will sympathize in the pleasure and gratitude I feel. Few things have ever given me so sincere and hearty pleasure, as the perception, that, in this thing, I have actually done something to aid men in the most interesting circumstances of their life. I am only astonished, that I do not feel more humbled and ashamed at my own miserable inconsistency, and that I can look without compunction at the careless life I lead. I hope I am not hardened forever. But, however it may fare with myself, I do rejoice and feel thankful, that I am able to do something to save others from the fate to which I am hurrying myself. Is not this strange?

"I have searched myself pretty thoroughly, and I do truly believe, that not a particle of personal vanity or literary pride enters into the gratification I feel. I am sure that I look on it with a religious pleasure only, and that it is too much mingled with the sense of my abuse of powers, by which God enables me to do good, and therefore *commands* me to do good, to allow any inferior satisfaction. What obligations are mine, and who does so little in comparison with what he ought to do? And yet so I live on, and do not do it. But I ought not to be thus croaking to you, dear Mary; I only meant to ask your sympathy in my pleasure, and my pen has run on with my feelings, which had better be kept to myself."

His health had regularly improved after he began to reside in Cambridge, and in the spring of 1831 was remarkably good. In February of this year he preached for the first time for nearly three years, with the exception of the single instance at Brooklyn, in December, 1828. It was on the occasion of the death of Mrs. Emerson, the wife of his colleague and successor in the ministry. Notwithstanding his improved health, however, it was not regarded as expedient for him yet to resume his labors in the pulpit; and accordingly he did not make another attempt until the 2d of October of the same year, when he began and persevered in his regular course of duty as one of the preachers in the College chapel. No particular evil to his health was the result of his preaching in either case, nor, so far as can be judged, at any subsequent period; and it seems very probable, that more influence in producing and keeping up the complaints under which he from time to time labored, had been attributed to his efforts of this kind, than was fairly due to them.

In the spring of this year he was well enough and strong enough to make an excursion on foot to Northborough and Worcester, in company with his eldest son, then a lad about fourteen years of age. In the beginning of August he made a still longer one, partly in the same way, accompanied by Mr. Angier, a member of the Divinity School. After attending an ordination at Newburyport, on the 3d of August, they made their way toward the White Mountains of New Hampshire, sometimes on foot, and sometimes in the public conveyances.

TO HIS WIFE.

"Centre-Harbor, Lake Winnipiseogee,
"Sunday Evening, August 7, 1831.

"My dear Mary,

"I wrote to you from Newburyport, and to John from Dover, which place we left on Saturday morning; and, having walked three miles, took the stage, and rode through a very rough country, over a rocky road, fifty miles, and then walked five to this place, which we reached just at sunset last evening. The weather has been cool every day, and we have enjoyed it much. We found here two Mr. Davises, from Boston; one of them joined us this morning at five o'clock, in an excursion to the Red Mountain, a height which overlooks all the country,—not very difficult to ascend,—and giving a fine view of a wild, mountainous region, and the full quality of the Winnipiseogee Lake, which is a very ugly lake, be it said with submission. To my mind it looks just like a great meadow overflowed with water, with a few tufts of grass sticking out here and there. The shores are generally barren. We were absent five hours, and had a fine appetite for breakfast at half past ten o'clock. I never felt better.

"There is no place of worship here, there being but a few houses; so we have been obliged to keep quiet. The old woman inquired if we did n't know her grand-daughter in Boston. I should think Red Hill about the height of Mount Holyoke, and I have not felt so finely, so bright and ethereal, since the day I went over the Swiss mountain with you,—the Brunig. On the top, Mr. Davis pulled out Milton from his pocket, and we took off our hats, and read his grand hymn,—'*These are thy glorious works.*' I would hardly have believed it could be so applicable to our situation there. Two Cambridge scholars, pedestrians, have just arrived. The old man who keeps this house is quite a man; and his two daughters are genteel, well educated girls, who have been singing very sweetly with Angier and me.

"*Monday.*—Glorious day. Nine miles to Sandwich to breakfast, by a route among the hills, very like some pretty spots in Switzerland. The Sandwich mountains on our right, the Ossipee on our left,—not a rich or much cultivated valley. Nine miles further, to a house in the corner of Ossipee, where we took a wagon thirteen miles to Conway, principally through a pine wood,—beside six miles of pond through Eaton, in leaving which we had a noble mountainous prospect.

"If pleasant, we shall reach the mountains to-morrow, and we hope to be at Concord next Sunday, intending to pass home by the banks of the Merrimack. In this case we shall reach home by the middle of next week. I should be sorry to be longer absent. I think that I have something to call me to Cambridge, and at that time only two weeks of vacation will remain.

"I see, in looking back, that I have omitted an essential item in the history of Sunday,—viz.: that we went to meeting at five o'clock, where Mr. Angier and I did all the singing, to the astonishment of the natives; and in the evening we sung a good deal with our host's daughters."

During this excursion, as on others, he was not satisfied to pass, without occupation, those odd moments. which usually hang so heavily on the hands of travellers at public houses in the intervals of motion. He was always provided with means for employing such intervals profitably. On this occasion he busied himself in composing a poetic description of the incidents of the tour, and of the emotions excited by the wild and sublime scenery in the midst of which he was travelling.

He had engaged to preach on his return at Concord, N. H., on Sunday, August 14th. They had completed their tour through the Notch of the White Mountains, had visited the Mountains at Franconia, and passed through Plymouth on their way homeward, when, after walking on Thursday morning for some distance, they obtained conveyance in an open wagon to Boscawen. Unfortunately, they had become heated by their previous exercise, and my brother became quite chilled by exposure to so free a current of air whilst in this excited state. Soon after reaching Boscawen, he became severely ill.

The next day he was able to reach Concord, but could get no further, and was there speedily joined by his wife. She found him laboring under a high degree of fever, with great exhaustion. It was a kind of attack from which he had frequently suffered before, but the present was more than usually severe. He had himself regarded his sickness as of a very unfavorable character, and entertained serious anticipations of its results, as appears from letters written to his wife and children. Contrary to these expectations, however, his symptoms yielded readily, and in the course of a few days he was able to be conveyed home. But, though he threw off thus speedily the acute symptoms of his disease, his system did not rally from the subsequent effects of it so readily as in former years. He was left for some weeks in a very depressed and nervous state, languid and prostrated, and totally incapable of any exertion. He left home, indeed, in the latter part of August, from inability to bear the excitement and bustle of Commencement week. Still he was able to resume his regular duties at the beginning of the term in September, and, as has been already said, began the exercise of his office as one of the college preachers, in October.

I am happy to have it in my power to add an

account of this expedition, with which I have been favored by the Rev. Mr. Angier, his friend and companion.

"WASHINGTON, NOVEMBER 10, 1845.

"MY DEAR SIR,

"I have with me a copy of the 'Pedestrian Journey,' composed by your brother, on our walk to the White Mountains, in the summer of 1831. I have taken a melancholy pleasure in reading over, again and again, the fragments of which it is composed, and which so vividly recall scenes and incidents to which they relate. I see him now, equipped, as he describes himself at the opening of the journey,

'Like Cæsar for his conquest;—my hope
Before me, anxious cares thrown by,—my thought
Free to expatiate undisturbed, and take
Its tone,—cheerful or grave,—devout or gay.'

"And well do I remember, how entirely, though often evidently suffering, he redeemed, on his part, the pledge contained in these lines:

'Now then, my one companion, go we forth,
Pledged to be cheerful alway, and content,—
To find all pleasant, or to make it so;
Without restraint, but such as kindness claims;—
If silent, unsuspected, unreproached
For sullenness of mood, and free to do,
As ready to allow.'

"And,

'So, up the hill-side, down the valley, we
Nearer and nearer to the lake draw nigh,
And cast our knapsacks down in Alton's bay.
Hail, lake! with form as rugged as thy name,—
Hail, Winnipiseogee!'

"And here were the scene and occasion of one of these fragments, 'Red Hill,' which, together with those, at least, entitled 'The Avalanche,' 'Mount Washington,' and 'The Echo,' I hope to see preserved in the memoir you are about publishing. It was after sunset on Saturday evening, when we arrived at Centre Harbor. Sunday morning, by sunrise, there being no religious service where we were, we set out, accompanied by Mr. Thomas K. Davis, of Boston, on a walk to the top of Red Hill. After we had spent some time in gazing upon the extensive and beautiful scenes before us, Mr. Davis took from his pocket a copy of 'Paradise Lost,' and, opening at Adam's Morning Hymn, handed it to Mr. Ware, with the request that he would read it. 'With the words,' breathed forth in those sweet, low, and earnest tones, which had so often penetrated them before, I *know* 'our hearts rose up,' as he went on, the tones of his voice becoming more deep and fervent, as he felt the inspiration of the poet. The *spiritualization* of the scene, all the hallowed associations of the hour, conspired to make us feel that, though there was no preface of 'Let us praise God,' or, 'pray,' yet this was something more than a gratification of taste,—it *was* an *act of worship*, as sincere, as *heart-felt*, as any we ever engaged in. We instinctively uncovered, and 'reverently bowed our heads and stood.' Well does he say, 'Such Sabbath is not lost.' It was one of the happiest, one of the best days of my life,—most enjoyed when present, most pleasantly remembered when past, —never to be forgotten, always to be remembered with gratitude.

"As my pen runs on, many scenes and incidents and conversations arise to my remembrance, most pleasing in the retrospect, and illustrative, often, of those characteristic qualities, for which Mr. Ware's memory is so affectionately and reverently cherished. But I must draw this letter to a close; not, however, till I have recalled, with mingled feelings of regret and pleasure, the last two days of our pleasant journey.

About sunset, Friday evening, we arrived at a little tavern in the town of Peeling, on the banks of one of the branches of the Merrimack. It was a lovely close of a most beautiful and happy day. We made our ablutions at a trough in front of the house, and soon after supper, being somewhat fatigued, I retired to rest,—the more willingly as we were to rise at three o'clock in the morning to ride the next day to Concord, it being Mr. Ware's earnest desire to spend the Sabbath there, and give Mr. Thomas a labor of love. But your brother was less prudent, or less self-indulgent, and more inspired with the scenery we had beheld, than I. He sat up writing till twelve o'clock! though he must rise at three. The movement he made in the room, on retiring, awoke me; and, at my request, he read me what he had been writing. He then folded it up, and, from that night, I think, it was never opened again till at least five or six years afterwards. We got a man to drive us in an open wagon, in the morning, as far as Plymouth, where we were to take the stage to Concord. The morning was cool, —a dense fog on the banks of the river. Your brother was chilled through. Then in the middle of the day it was very hot and dusty; the extremes of heat and cold, with previous want of sleep, prevailed against the little strength he had, and by the time we reached Boscawen he was too ill to proceed. Here I stayed with him three or four days; but, there being no prospect of his getting well enough to go home as soon as it was necessary for me to go, I left him and brought the intelligence of his illness to his family and friends in Cambridge."

The following are some of those portions of the poetical Journal of this tour, which are referred to in this letter. They received little subsequent correction or polish, but retain nearly the form which was given to them at the time.

"RED HILL.

"Then reverently we bared our heads, and stood;
And from that holy bard, whose sightless eye
Beheld the wonders of the Invisible,
We raised the hymn so worthy Paradise,
In its pure early worship. With the words,
I trust our hearts rose up; the morning wind
Bore them, like incense, upward, and there seemed
A soul of deep devotion breathed abroad
On all the things we saw; they heard the call,
The eloquent call, of Milton and of God,
And uttered praise. The sun and clouds in heaven
Heard, as they rose above us, and replied;
The lake responded with her thousand isles;
The mountains that encompassed us around,
Near and more distant, seemed to bow assent;
The birds joined harmony, the lowing kine,
The waving trees, the lowly herb beneath
Our feet, with burden of rich fruit, and last
The scattered hamlets, whose ascending smokes
Showed human life awaking to the day;—
All seemed to hear and join the act of praise.
So to our hearts it seemed, so full, so warm,
So loud, the burst of holy praise, rung forth
In words that reach and rouse the inmost soul
Of Nature, as of man,—the general soul
That fills and vivifies whate'er exists.

"'T is well to worship where the pomp of man
Intrudes not. So infirm are we, so bound
In chains of sense, that crowded chapels, throngs
Of dressed adorers, bursts of choral song,
The formal, eloquent routine of praise,
Sometimes excite, sometimes distract, confound,
Or dissipate the soul.
'T is well to know that piety
Draws its best nutriment from solitude,
Withdrawn from man, in secret intercourse

With man's Creator; on the mountain top,
Beside the waterfall, within the dark
And silent forest, on the midnight bed,
Within the chambers of the secret mind,
Where no eye pierces, no ear listens, save
That of the indwelling spirit, which pervades,
And moves, and blesses all. Then worship grows
A holy, heavenly thing; the unfettered soul,
Emancipate from earth, no more disturbed
With others' thoughts, nor bound to tread
The path by others signified, springs free,
Exalted, spiritualized, and carries back
To earth and life a fragrance and a strength,
That earth gives not, and that prepares for heaven.

"Such Sabbath is not lost; and, from the mount
When we descended, with the little flock
That gathers in a humble upper room,
Like that perchance wherein Paul preached, we too,
Were found. A touching sight, thus far from home,
Amid the wild hills, to behold a few,
Summoned at call of Him who rules the earth
As king, and numbers millions for his own,
In every age and nation, bending down
In prayer, and listening to the word of life; —
A fragment of the universal church;
Pondering upon the thoughts which make the joy
Of spirits in heaven, and urged to find, like them,
Their happiness in glorifying God.
How truly came from Heaven a messenger
Like this, — how surely leads to Heaven."

"THE WILLEY HOUSE.*

"Here pause upon this ruin; what a tale
Of grandeur and of woe is written here!

* The particulars of the event referred to in these lines are fresh in the memory of those living at the time of its occurrence; but many readers of the present generation may be ignorant of them. The "Willey House," so called

He, whom we think not of, because his power
Leads all things gently with the cords of love,
Doth sometimes teach us with a startling blow,
That wakes our senses to his majesty.
He touched the trembling mountain and it fell,—
Fell, with its burden of rent rocks and trees
Of giant growth, a fearful avalanche,—
Fell, amid storm and tempest, while the clouds
Dropped down in floods, and angry lightnings flashed,
And thunders echoing rolled. It seemed as God
Descended in his terrors, as of old
On Sinai, wrapt in darkness, clouds, and storm.
The mountain felt him near,
And trembled from its base; the swelling streams,
Each with its own commission, carried forth
The message of destruction, bidding man
Tremble, adore, and think upon his God.

"Behold this house; thus near the horror came,
A few short feet, and stayed, and left it safe.
Oh, had its panic-stricken tenants stayed,
They had been safe; but in their fear they fled,—
Fled from their shelter to the very death

from the name of the unfortunate family who perished there, is situated in the Notch road of the White Mountains of New Hampshire, several miles from any other habitation. In the autumn of 1826, this family resided there, and had had reason to apprehend, from certain signs, that a slide of earth was likely to take place, from the mountain in the rear of their habitation. They had accordingly provided a camp, in a spot, as they fatally fancied, of greater security, to which they might retreat, should the danger seem to threaten them more imminently. The events of the night are described in the above extract. A fearful mass, of rocks, earth, and uprooted trees, descended from the mountain in the direction of the house, but, instead of overwhelming it, divided into two streams, which, passing on each side, united again at some distance in its front. The house was found the next morning just as it had been hastily left by its terrified inhabitants, and a flock of sheep, unharmed, were quietly feeding on the green before the door. With the exception of a single slight article of clothing, which was probably caught by the bushes as they fled, no relic has ever been discovered of this unfortunate family; and the fearful character of this catastrophe, as well as the mystery which attaches to it, have invested the spot, in the minds of travellers, with a romantic and melancholy interest.

They feared. The morning saw them in their tranquil home,
A family of love; the mother smiled
Upon her five young mountaineers, and joyed
To aid them in their sports, and lead them on
To better things than sport. The drizzly rains
Confined the father too within, and much
They talked, perchance, and marvelled at the storm,
That, seemingly exhausted, still poured on
Floods inexhaustible, and gathering
Blackness and fury ten-fold, as the day
Passed on. Yet what felt they of fear, or why?
Were they not sheltered in a quiet home?
And what but pleasure, from their nook secure,
To look abroad on this sublime display
Of Nature's glorious and unusual pomp?

"So came the eve, and with the eve came fear;
The tumult thickens, fiercer winds arise,
More copious torrents fall, the mountain groans,
Signs of unwonted dread are heard abroad.
But what do they portend,—the danger what?
The safety, where? in quiet or in flight?
Oh, horrible suspense! and, at some sound
Of ominous import, forth at once
Wife, husband, children, in distraction rush.
Again the sound terrific, like the crash
Of earth's last wreck, burst on their frightened ear,
And the descending ruin bears them down.

"They sleep in peace; and, humble as they were,
Few of earth's honored sons have monument
Magnificent as this.
To form it, this perpetual hill did bow,
These hoary rocks forsook their ancient base,
And here, while time shall last, the funeral pile
Shall tell where they repose. The crowds that come
To worship at this mountain, countless tribes
With numbers yearly growing, shall be found
Seeking their sepulchre, to learn their names,—

To hear the story of their fate, and speak
One word of pity at the awful tale.
Sleep, then, in peace; unwonted death was yours,
Yours an unwonted monument, and yours
Funereal pomp that kings have never known.
Here, in the embosomed depth
Of these your native mountains, sleep in peace,
Till the last tempest rend the mount again,
And call you from its bosom into light."

During the remainder of this year and the next, his bodily condition was uncommonly good. He was, it is true, far from possessing now that degree of health which he enjoyed during much of the period of his ministry; but he was uniformly able to attend to all the calls of his office, and was not forced to absent himself from home for the purpose of physical restoration. He went through, however, with a trial of much anxiety and affliction, in the long-continued and alarming sickness of his wife, terminating happily at last in her complete recovery; and in the sickness and death of his second son, a child about three years of age.

CHAPTER XVII.

PUBLICATION OF THE "SUNDAY LIBRARY"—HIS "LIFE OF THE SAVIOUR"—"SCENES AND CHARACTERS ILLUSTRATING CHRISTIAN TRUTH"—SICKNESS IN 1833—LETTER TO MR. ROBBINS—PREPARES A "MEMOIR OF THE REV. DR. PARKER"—HIS CONNEXION WITH THE ANTI-SLAVERY CAUSE—HIS TRUE POSITION WITH REGARD TO IT—LETTERS RELATING TO IT.

1831–1835. ÆT. 37–41.

NOTWITHSTANDING these calls on his time and his feelings, he was engaged in several other enterprises beside his regular duties. He superintended the publication of an edition of the "Life of Oberlin," and prefixed to it an Introduction written by himself. He printed a Tract entitled, "An Outline of the Scripture Testimony against the Trinity." He delivered also an Address before the Cambridge Temperance Society, entitled "The Combination against Intemperance explained and justified;" illustrating the necessity of this combination; defending its principles, especially that which demands the pledge of entire abstinence; and stating distinctly the results which it aimed to bring about, namely, the extermination, the absolute, perpetual extermination, of ardent spirits as an article of drink. Of this Address two editions of ten thousand copies were published and distributed, one of them at Albany, at the instance, it is believed, of a very distinguished and persevering friend of the cause of temperance.

He projected, also, during this year, the publication of a periodical series of volumes, under the name of "The Sunday Library." Among the wants of the religious public, which were the constant subjects of his thoughts and purposes, he had long felt one to be the want of suitable books for the Sunday reading of young persons,—of those who are old enough to think, and consequently to need instruction, on religious subjects, and who are so young as to render it necessary that the form in which they are presented should be made attractive. Indeed, every one who has had the care of the young at any age must have been aware of this want, and have experienced the same difficulty, namely, the difficulty of finding such employment for them, as is not at variance with the sacred nature of the day, and yet has in it sufficient relish for the tastes and habits of mind at their time of life.

In order to fill up this deficiency, he proposed to issue, at short intervals, a volume of two or three hundred pages, on subjects calculated to excite the interest of this class of readers, and written in a manner adapted to their tastes and capacities. In pursuance of this plan, he laid out a series of subjects, and, in the course of the year 1832, wrote, as the first volume, "The Life of the Saviour," which he published in January, 1833. This was received with much approbation. A second edition was called for in the same year, and several others have been published since. It was also reprinted in England, and still continues in circulation there, though, it is believed, without the author's name. Its circulation, and the approbation it received, even in this country, were by no means confined to those of the author's own religious denomination.

This volume was followed by "The Life of Howard," written by Mrs. Farrar, and intended as the first of a subordinate series of "Lives of the Philanthropists." Subsequently appeared, "The Holy Land and its Inhabitants," by the Rev. S. G. Bulfinch, and a "History of the Reformation," by the Rev. T. B. Fox. These works were well received by the public, their circulation was extensive, and their sale such as to afford to the writers a sufficient remuneration; still, at the close of the fourth volume, the work was discontinued, simply from the difficulty, notwithstanding the strenuous efforts of the editor, of finding writers willing to contribute their aid, and the impossibility of his carrying it on alone.

In the next year, 1834, while this work was in progress, and, as he supposed, in successful progress, and the labor necessary for its continuance committed to other hands, he projected another publication, having somewhat of the same general purpose, namely, to provide interesting reading of a moral and religious kind for the young. It was entitled, "Scenes and Characters illustrating Christian Truth." In carrying out this plan, he in the first place selected a variety of topics, which seemed to him capable of suitable illustration in the form of tales or sketches, and then endeavored to find, among those of our writers who had distinguished themselves by compositions of this kind, persons who would be willing to assist him in his undertaking. In this attempt he was less successful than was to have been wished or expected. He was able to prevail on but six of those to whom he applied, to aid him, and the work therefore only reached the sixth Number. The first Number, "Trial and Self-Discipline," was written by Miss Savage; the second, "The Skeptic," by Mrs. Follen; the third, "Home," by Miss Sedgwick; the fourth, "Gleams of Truth," by Dr. Tuckerman; the fifth, "The Backslider," by Mrs. George G. Lee; the sixth, "Alfred," by his sister, Mrs. Edward B. Hall.

This attempt fell short of its object solely from the want of contributions. The Numbers which were published, were well received, some of them were very popular; the public were interested, and the purpose was so far fully answered, but it was found impossible to procure the requisite materials for its continuance. It might seem, that these enterprises were too much for the time and attention of one man, already sufficiently occupied with the labors of his place; but it should be stated, on the other hand, that it was not the expectation of the projector of these works, to take any part in the details of their execution, but merely to lay out the general plan, to furnish subjects, and trust to others for the treatment of them. His experience at length convinced him, that it is easier to obtain promises of assistance, than their performance.

The history of these projects is noticed a little out of the order of time, from their natural connexion with each other. But, to go back to the personal history of our subject; in the beginning of 1833, he was again confined by long-continued, though not very severe, illness. He had had a slight attack of ill health in the summer of 1832, but, with this single exception, that year had been marked by peculiar exemption from his usual maladies, and by unusual capacity for exertion, as is sufficiently shown by the fact, that he had, in the course of it, beside performing the regular duties of his professorship, composed and published the several works already mentioned, namely, "The Life of the Saviour," the edition of "Oberlin," the Temperance "Address," and a Tract on "The Trinity." No doubt he had, by these unusual labors, drawn too largely on his stock of health. The effects manifested themselves not so much by an attack of distinct disease, as by the existence of a state of great and unaccountable exhaustion and prostration. This was so considerable, as to confine him to his house and, during much of the time, to his chamber, for a part of the months of January, February, and March, in 1833. This confinement was attended by a greater degree of depression of spirits and of incapacity for exertion of any kind, than was usual to him even when subjected to disease of considerable severity. The winter and the first month of spring passed without any appreciable improvement; and, despairing of it at home, he set out at the end of March for the South, and began so immediately and rapidly to amend, that he returned to Cambridge in about four weeks, almost completely renovated. It was truly remarkable to observe, on this and many other occasions, how very sensible was his constitution, so long as anything of its original elasticity remained, to the invigorating influences of change of place and air, and of an interest in new scenes and objects; and how rapidly his health improved when he was freed from the pressure of those occupations by which he was burdened when at home. How probable is it, that a more equal distribution of his efforts, and a more careful adjustment of his labors to his ability to accomplish them, might have retarded for a considerable time the progress of disease, and protracted the term of his life and of his usefulness.

In December, 1833, he was called upon to assist in the ordination of another minister over his old parish, his immediate successor, Mr. Emerson, having relinquished the charge of it, and Mr. Chandler Robbins having been invited to fill his place. He preached the sermon on this occasion, which occurred on Wednesday, December 4th. As a mark of the continued interest which he felt in this Society, as well as of his personal regard for their new pastor, the following letter is inserted, written on the Sabbath following the ordination:

TO THE REV. CHANDLER ROBBINS.

"CAMBRIDGE, DECEMBER 8, 1833.

"MY DEAR YOUNG FRIEND,

"My thoughts are so much with you to-day, that I think I must send some of them to you. I well remember the solicitude and trembling with which I passed through the first Sabbath of my own ministry, on which so many interests of so many persons were depending; and I deeply sympathize with you in the same mixed trial of feeling through which you are passing. May it be peculiarly blessed to you, and no prayer that you offer be unanswered. And will you allow me, in consequence of the interest I take in your people, as well as in yourself, to express a few of the thoughts which are passing through my mind?

"In the first place, you are to be congratulated on the circumstances in which you have been called to the Second Church. Yet, at the same time, they constitute a peculiar trial. The cordiality and unanimity of feeling among the people, while gratifying, is yet founded upon a very slight personal knowledge, and probably exists with some coloring of their own imaginations. Now I say, that these circumstances will constitute a peculiar trial, making it perhaps more than usually difficult to come up to expectations, founded not wholly on personal knowledge, but in part on public rumor, and in part also on imagination. I have no apprehension on this score, provided you be aware of the truth, and able to direct yourself accordingly. But I have seen some instances of the evil arising from a young man's beginning at the top of the ladder, as it is phrased, and would gladly put you on your guard, so that you may hold on and not fall off; which is oftentimes much more difficult than to climb up from the bottom. In connexion with this, is to be recollected the state of your health, which deprived you of much of the time which would have otherwise been given to laying up resources, and which may render laborious exertions difficult for you, if not dangerous. For this reason, I hope that you will attempt nothing in the way of vestry meetings or any extraordinary labors this winter. By all means, run no risks beyond the necessary toils of a new preacher, pastor, and house-keeper. It is always a great evil, that the new minister rushes into such a crowd of engagements; he should not needlessly multiply them.

"Then, I cannot help feeling a great interest in you as a minister in the city, where a great deal is to be desired from the general influence of the clergy on the public mind, and where I think the clergy have been in the habit of exerting less than they might and should. But I do not mean to enlarge upon this point. I would say only, that, unless times have greatly changed, the North End affords a field of local influence beyond any other part of the town; and from local to general influence the advance is not difficult. As a citizen of the North End, sharing the local interests, and aiding the improvement, of that section, you may soon find yourself valued, and, I hope, be able to restore your Society to its old local character, and cause it to be constituted of the people of that part of the town, rather than of the distant sections.

"Then, when I remember what a city minister's life is, its exactions, and trials, and exhaustions, and interruptions, I feel extremely solicitous, that you should have the wisdom, from the first, to adopt that course, which will enable you to meet all without failing or breaking down ; and, for this reason, I wish to urge on you the necessity of plan and method in all your arrangements of time, and modes of life. I do not know what your habits are, and therefore, perhaps, all I may suggest is wholly unnecessary. But I do know what a Boston minister's habits ought to be, if he would have comfort, success, or improvement; and, unless he start with them, he can never hope to attain them. I venture to speak of this with the greater emphasis, because you are beginning your family arrangements at the same time with those of your ministry, and may and ought to have a regard to the same interest in both plans. If I were now to go back to Boston, knowing what I do, I should adopt and adhere to a plan somewhat like this: To secure four hours of absolute retired study in the morning, and never leave my house before twelve o'clock, except in cases of necessity;—to devote four afternoons in each week to pastoral duty, one to other friends, and one to recreation. By adhering to this, I might hope to keep my business in order, and not greatly fail of any duty. Otherwise, I should expect my life to be one of perpetual confusion and vexation. And, though I never would be a *slave* to my method, yet I should feel it essential to my peace, that I should deviate from it as seldom and as little as possible. Otherwise, my time, my health, and my conscience would be at the mercy of other men.

"The cheerful and confiding temper, with which you begin your work, is an augury of success. May God grant, that nothing may occur to damp your spirits, or repress your ardor. But you must be prepared for discouragement of various sorts, and prepared to meet them without allowing them to depress you. I know of no recipe, beyond that of a devout faith, for meeting such things without depression, better than to keep in good health, and *never be hurried;* that is, never let one's business get behindhand; have the accounts of every day squared at its close. '*Haud inexpertus loquor.*'

"I feel that you will excuse these suggestions, on a day like this. How much depends upon it! How much do you feel of the weight and magnitude of your coming cares and their consequences! Yet it is impossible, that, without experience, you should have a feeling of responsibility, at all approaching that of one who has already been in the midst, and made himself acquainted with the whole. You may judge, then, that it is no common interest which prompts me to speak to you to-day. May it be the beginning of an active, effective, and happy ministry, in which you shall always seek and always find the blessing of Heaven."

During the few years, which have been now gone over, of his residence at Cambridge, there are several letters written at different times, having no special connexion with the narrative, and miscellaneous in their subjects, which are here subjoined. The following was addressed to Mr. Allen in reply to a request for advice concerning the manner of managing the meetings of Associations of ministers.

TO MR. ALLEN.

"CAMBRIDGE, NOVEMBER 10, 1831.

"DEAR BROTHER,

"I wish I could meet the Association at your house. I should delight to spend another day with that body. I remember my three days with them, with peculiar pleasure. As to your subject, I had talked it over a little with Mr. Hill, who mentioned it to me. I can see no objection to the plan you propose. When several ministers are present in a public congregation, who meet in that way not very often, why should the whole word be monopolized by one?

"1. If the object be to *warm each other*, certainly it will be best effected by several speaking.

"2. Or, if instruction, the same.

"3. The meetings would be more *interesting*, both to ministers and people.

"4. Besides, it would be going back to *the beginning;* for I suppose, that, in the earliest Christian churches, they did not dream of being all silent but one.

"5. Have not all of us felt, that the formality and uniformity of our meetings for public worship tend to render them cold and unimpressive? and what better way of remedying this evil, than such a change in the form of these extraordinary occasions, as you propose.

"I hope, therefore, you will recommend and urge, that, after the sermon, (if you have one,) the other ministers should be expected to speak; and, further, that the custom should be universal, on *all occasions*, when more than one minister is present, that those who do not preach should be asked if they have not a word of exhortation, and, if so, be bid to '*say on.*' I think it would be a salutary thing.

"By the way, the subject of Mr. Hildreth's Address is one excellently fitted for a beginning of this practice, which I hope you will introduce.

"As to remaining together two days, I dare say you might make it profitable. Much may be said in its behalf, and I believe that an impulse would thereby be given to all your plans of public improvement, schools and Sunday schools, libraries, and various associations. I have even thought, and I think I mentioned it to you, that we should do well to meet thus with lay delegates, in a sort of convention. Why not suggest this, and discuss it? No harm, if it is thought premature; it will be brought about at last. I should doubt, however, whether the Association had best meet less frequently. The ministers should see each other often, for many reasons; and, if it be too much to spend two days together once a month, yet they should at least meet for a day as heretofore. I am glad you are stirring in this matter. I am persuaded that we have much to learn respecting the best modes of operation and influence, and that we have to be convinced of these two things,—that ministers are to take an *active lead* more than formerly, and that they are to be less *fearful* of using or hazarding *influence* in the promotion of new objects for the general good."

TO THE SAME.

"CAMBRIDGE, MARCH 23, 1832.

"We had a delightful and exhilarating evening at the School last week. The Philanthropic Society, being engaged in inquiries relative to the improvement of seamen, invited Mr. Taylor to attend the meeting; an invitation was given to our friends in Cambridge, and the Chapel was well filled. The first evening he was unable to come, but we had excellent speaking; and, adjourning to the next night, he came and spoke excellently well, and has done real good by his visit. Such seasons for warming us are good. Our young men acquitted themselves well; and Taylor said, in his address:—'I am astonished; I had heard you were all cold Christians, philosophers, who would make the world stop to hear you think. But there 's fire amongst you,—there 's fire amongst you.'"

TO HIS BROTHER WILLIAM.

"CAMBRIDGE, MAY 17, 1832.

"By the way, why won't you write sermons in precisely the brief, pithy, broken, dialogue style of this letter of yours? It would be prodigiously taking and lively, and would inevitably do good to your delivery. Try it on some passage of your next sermon. We want greater variety of style; our hearers' minds want to change their postures as we proceed;

and this should be a matter of calculation and effort with us, just as much as the plan of the sermon. When we always keep up the same sort of talk, always equally dignified, solemn, and exact, no wonder people gape and think it a long half-hour.

"A really excited, extemporaneous actor does not do this. He changes his key,—goes quick and then slow,—asks questions,—answers them,—exclaims,—reiterates,—speaks by hints,—by short sentences,—by single words; and, through this variety, not only *sustains*, but *increases*, the attention and interest. Passages done up like your letter, thrown in toward the close of a sermon, would electrify. You could come down on your hearers like a storm, and so make a peroration that would send them away trembling, and never to forget. Try it,—try it. We don't consider the secrets, the mysteries, the power of style, that is, of words and phrases. They have a mastery which we are strangely insensible to; and we, who have to live and work by them, are inexcusable in not studying the thing more; making experiments, trying new combinations, arrangements,—*artifices*, if you will. But all artifices (conducted by a judicious man) are only experiments to ascertain what is natural; experiments which sometimes fail, unluckily; but which sometimes succeed;—and then, what a gain! I have a great deal to say on this point. I have thought of it, and made six lectures on it. I am ashamed to say, I have not much practised accordingly. But I have a little; and I flatter myself you may see an example of a good way of studying variety, in my Address and my Review on Intemperance. If I am not mistaken, (pray tell me if I am,) the styles of the two things are entirely unlike; that of the Review, judged on general principles, far the best; that of the Address, however, better suited to delivery. Is this accidental? No. A matter of intention and design; and, however I may have failed in fulfilling my intention, it serves to explain what I mean by striving for variety in composition.

"Now I hold, that the best style for one purpose may be the worst for another; also, that every discourse to be spoken is susceptible of a greater variety in itself, and that he who has to speak two a week, on all sorts of subjects, should know how to command all sorts of styles, and be as different from himself, at different times, as another man. The same in delivery. Why should he write or deliver a Thanksgiving sermon and a funeral discourse alike? or the argument and the exhortation of the same sermon? Is not this sound doctrine? Did you ever practise on it? Did you ever write a sermon in the manner of your letter? Try it,—try it,—and, my word for it, you will have found a jewel. Bah! what a homily I have made! No matter,—you sent me a dissertation, and here is one in return.

"How glad I am, you like Oberlin; and I agree with you about the book,—it ought to have been four times better. If I had read it before being in France, I should certainly have gone to Waldbach.

"Spring is just coming on, like a Russian summer, all at once. By the way, have you read Reinhard's 'Memoirs'? There's another man for you! What miserable pigmies we are! what idle cumberers of the ground! Reinhard and Oberlin do wonders; and we live along, and die, when we might be—not as useful as they, but less of nothingarians. We all need regeneration.

"Good night, dearest brother. God bless you. I rejoice with devout gratitude of soul in all the good I hear of you, the improvement you make, and your acceptable labors. Go on, and prosper. You have gained much; you are destined to gain and do more. Courage and onward. Oceans of love to all of you."

TO HIS SON.

[During the prevalence of the Cholera.]

"CAMBRIDGE, JULY 18, 1832.

"We have no apprehension of the disease *here*, and even in Boston, so admirable is the preparation, that I think it will hardly find any victims. In all this we have reason to rejoice and be grateful. But, while we think of it thus, we cannot help being impressed with the thought, that there are other dangers to life more near us, and other evils greater; and, if Providence delivers us from the pestilence, it ought to warn us to look at them. I have been thinking a good deal of this.

"I find that your two parents are in very frail health, frequently ill, and probably destined to a short life. You will perhaps, therefore, be left at an early age to take care of yourself; and I often ask myself, whether you will be prepared to go on in an industrious, useful, honorable life, and make your way well in the world. You will have nothing to depend upon but the talents God has given you, and your education. Those talents are equal to your necessities, if you rightly improve them; and I hope you are now so devoting yourself to study, that you will have a mind richly furnished and well cultured; so that you will be able to take care of yourself, do good to other men, and prepare both for this life and the next. Then, if we should live to see you become a man, we should have the pleasure in your prosperity, which my father has had in mine; and, if we should not live, but should leave you to yourself in the world, we should have the comfort of feeling that you will not fail to do your duty."

TO THE SAME.

"CAMBRIDGE, DECEMBER 30, 1832.

"I was glad to perceive, that you were interested in 'The Young Christian,' and that you allowed yourself to *think* of what you read. That is the only way to profit by it; and nothing can conduce so much to the formation of a right character and the securing of true happiness, as a fondness for thoughts and subjects of this character. Your notion about Heaven was a natural and rather a just one. It is a place as yet secret to us, except so far as we know it to be the dwelling of the good, and the centre of all bliss. It is wonderful, when we know it to be so, that we think of it so little. And especially, when we have good friends already gone there and waiting for us, it is strange that we do not feel always as if it were our true home, and prepare to go thither.

"*Eternity*, about which you ask, is used in two senses. When applied to God, it means *without beginning* and *without end.* You perceive, that, if there ever was a time when He did not exist, He never could have existed at all; because there is nothing which could create Him. Therefore He had no beginning. But when applied to *men*, it means only *without end;* and is commonly used in relation to a future life. So that *man's* eternity begins at death. This is a subject of very grand and mysterious thought. In 'The American First Class Book,' there is a noble piece by Mr. Greenwood, on 'The Eternity of God.' I beg you will get it and read it; read it over and over, and you will feel how wonderful and glorious it is.

"I wish it were possible for you to live without hearing anything about religious parties and disputes, for it is a great misfortune to a young person to know anything about them. But it cannot be avoided in the present state of society. Therefore, I am willing to answer your question about the Unitarians. They do not believe Christ to be the same with God, but just as different from him, as a son always is from his father. So that you perceive there is no such perplexity in the case as you seem to imagine."

TO THE SAME.

"STEAMBOAT BOSTON, [from New York to Providence,] DECEMBER 31, 1833. Evening.

"MY DEAR SON,

"As the last hours of the year approach, and I look back on the past, that I may thank God for its blessings, and may ask his pardon for its sins, it is unavoidable that I should think of you, and should wish that you too may make the best improvement of this solemn season. I ask myself, how I may help you do it? And I think the following is the best plan. Between this time and Sunday, reflect on the following questions seriously and deeply.

"1. What special reason have you for gratitude in the past year?

"2. In what respects have you made improvement?

"3. What have been, and are, your particular faults?

"4. What resolutions should you make for the next year?

"5. Are you willing to make them, and try to keep them?

"Write down, carefully and fully, your answer to each of these questions, and bring it to me Sunday evening.

"My wish is, to teach you to know yourself, and to help you in that greatest work of life,—*self-improvement.* While you think, therefore, every day on these questions, do not fail also to pray to God to bless you, so that you may learn and do your whole duty.

"Your affectionate father."

The next year, 1834, passed with very little serious interruption from ill health. I do not find, indeed, that he was detained by it from his usual duties for a single day. The letter, however, inserted below, refers obviously to an attack which took place while he was on a visit at Portsmouth. It contains statements with regard to his frequent returns of ill health, which were perfectly true, and exhibits a feeling on the subject with which every habitual invalid will heartily sympathize.

TO THE REV. MR. GANNETT.

"CAMBRIDGE, APRIL 17, 1834.

"MY DEAR GANNETT,

"I could not but feel grateful, though surprised and perplexed, at the manner of your speaking to me yesterday. Like many of my friends, it showed you to lie under a misapprehension, which is to be removed. I am tired of explaining, for people will neither understand nor believe me; and heartily sick of being obliged to think, act, and speak, with so much reference to myself; and it is one of the greatest evils of my oft infirmities, that they compel me to be misunderstood, and therefore blamed, in spite of all explanations. But I do wish *you* might see things as they are, and not be amongst those who misinterpret and censure. (The last man, by the way, who should pluck *these* motes out of my eye, would be the exclamation of your friends.)

"The long and short of the matter is this;—I am and have been constitutionally subject, from boyhood, to attacks of slight disease every four, six, eight, or twelve weeks. It used to be *sick headache*, lasting twelve or twenty-four hours. Since my serious illness, it has changed its form and become a mere obstruction of the digestive organs, lasting one, two, three, or four days, according as I may have succeeded in delaying its recurrence. Now this takes place just as surely when I am quietly and leisurely doing my little routine at home, as when I undertake anything extra. Yet, if so, it goes off without any eclat or exclamation, as it ought. But if, by chance, it occur when I have been preaching anywhere, or riding from home, or writing an article for 'The Examiner,' then I am sure to be scolded. Is this reasonable? Is it not hard to bear? and must I refuse to do anything beyond my daily round, because people will misunderstand this matter? I think not; and I think you will agree with me.

"As for this recent attack, I had succeeded by great carefulness in protracting the time of its recurrence unusually, and, in consequence, it was a little more severe than usual. But, if I had not been away from home, you would never have known it; for, when these turns occur at home, they are not matters of public emblazonment, though they are just as truly my sins.

"Now I beg you to allow this to pass for a sufficient vindication, and to make you my vindicator, and not my accuser; it being hardship enough for me to bear my trial without having added to it the reproaches of those I honor and love.

"And, finally, let me ask you to reflect, whether the *beam*, as big and as violently worked as a battering-ram, ought not to be plucked out of your eye, now that you have got the mote out of mine. There is no doubt, that you are fast overthrowing yourself, and are soon to be numbered among the crippled. It ought not to be so. The company of invalid pensioners is large enough, and the church cannot afford to have you taken from its active service and thrown into its hospital. I know that you will think and act for yourself;—but, if the four last years of my bitter, *bitter* experience could but warn and move you, and save you from premature decrepitude and uselessness, I should have one more reason to bless God for having allowed me to do some good.

"Yours, in all truth and love."

The visit to Portsmouth, just referred to, took place in the April of this year. He went there for the purpose of collecting materials for a biographical sketch of the Rev. Dr. Parker, who had died the preceding year; a man eminent in his public office, as a minister of religion, and deeply and widely venerated for the Christian virtues of his character. My brother had been selected and invited, by a committee of the Parish over which Dr. Parker had ministered, to prepare this Memoir, and the task was a peculiarly grateful one. As long ago as during his residence in Exeter, he had listened with great satisfaction to Dr. Parker's preaching; and there are among his papers several notices and analyses of his sermons; and, ever since his own entrance into the profession, he had always looked upon him as possessing and exhibiting in a remarkable manner those qualities and traits of character, which should distinguish the clergyman. He regarded him as a model-man in the sacred office. There are a few letters relating to this undertaking.

TO HIS SON.

"PORTSMOUTH, APRIL 8, 1834.

"Yesterday I spent the greater part of the day in Dr. Parker's study, writing and overlooking papers. I suppose that you know what my errand is, and I find it extremely interesting. It seems like a sacred work to sit in the chamber of a good man and see what he did while alive, and to hear from all about him of his usefulness and benevolence, and to witness proofs of his good influence on others. He was so good, so active, so disinterested, that everybody honored and loved him, and many speak of him as their greatest benefactor. And, while I see what he has done, and how deeply his people loved and now bless him, I feel that the ministry is the holiest and happiest work on earth, and a good man the greatest man; and I feel ashamed to think how far I have myself come short of what I might have been, and ought to have done."

TO MRS. PARKER.

"CAMBRIDGE, APRIL 17, 1834.

"MY DEAR MADAM,

"The kindness with which you inquired for me, during my indisposition at Mrs. Adams's, makes me certain that you will not be unwilling to learn from my own pen, that I am wholly recovered from it, and quite well again, excepting that I am rather weak; an evil, which every hour helps to remove. I found my household in a condition to call for strong feeling; and I have seldom been so deeply touched, as when I learned that our little boy, two years old, had been for six hours, on Sunday, between life and death, every gasp seeming to be his last, and twice his breathing so long suspended, that all supposed him to be gone. We feel toward him now, as toward one raised, like the widow's son, from the grave. I trust his life has been spared for some good end.

"I cannot help connecting this incident with the visit which I have just been making at Portsmouth, and feeling as if it were the design of Providence to strengthen in me the feelings and purposes to which that visit had given rise. I must repeat to you, that I consider it a privilege to have been engaged as I have been; and, should I fail at last of satisfying the wishes and feelings of the friends of our departed and lamented friend, yet I am sure that I shall myself be abundantly rewarded by the impressions and instructions which I have received. But I will try not to fail; and I am assured of the candid and considerate judgment of those most deeply interested."

This Memoir was not completed till the beginning of the next year. It was prefixed to a volume of Sermons, and was also published separately.

During this year, my brother's name became connected, in the public mind, with the movements of the

Anti-Slavery party, which about this period were becoming more and more a matter of interest and excitement, from the greater zeal and activity manifested by those who were engaged in them. No friend of humanity can fail to sympathize with, and wish success to, exertions having in view so noble an object as American Emancipation; and, in common with all enterprises intended for the amelioration of the condition of any portion of mankind, he felt strongly impelled, not only to bid God-speed to the undertaking, but to join heart and hand in promoting its accomplishment. With this feeling he engaged cordially in some of the earlier proceedings of the Abolitionists. He assisted in the formation of an Anti-Slavery Society in Cambridge, and was elected its president. At this period, as will be readily recollected, efforts of this nature were by no means looked upon with so tolerant a spirit as that with which they are now regarded. Mr. Ware gave much offence by the part which he thus took, and especially by his announcing an Anti-Slavery meeting from one of the pulpits in Boston after divine service. For his course in this matter, and especially for this particular act, he was subjected to animadversion in the public papers in a manner which would now be hardly considered possible; and many of his warmest personal friends, and friends of the University and of the Theological School, remonstrated with him very earnestly. It was seriously represented to him, that, whatever might be his individual opinions and sympathies on this subject, he was bound, as the servant of the College, as the servant of the public, designated by them for a peculiar function, to avoid any such entanglements with the exciting movements of the day, as would interfere with his exertions, or impair his usefulness, in that relation. Most of the expressions of opinion, which this subject called forth, were characterized by that kindness, forbearance, and respect, which were due to the unquestioned purity of his motives, and the sincerity of his convictions; but some, it must be confessed, were marked by a harshness, which could not but have been deeply painful to one of so mild and gentle a spirit.

Doubtless he gave to these remonstrances, so far as they related to a duty growing out of his connexion with the College, due consideration; but it is certain that he never recognized for a moment the right of the College, or of the friends of the College, to question him, or interfere with respect to the part he felt called on to take as to this or any other of the agitating topics of the times. It was reported, and believed by many, that the Government of the College had expressly made his silence in this matter a condition of his continuance in his office. He would not have held his office an hour on such terms; and I have the most direct authority for asserting, that such dictation was never dreamed of, and the supposition that it was possible, was repelled with indignation.

But, although he yielded a respectful attention to the entreaties of his friends on this point, it was not owing to any such external influence, that he did not continue to coöperate in a formal manner with the Abolitionists, and consent to be one of that body, which has since acted so prominent a part before the public. That he continued through life to sympathize most heartily with the great efforts which were made, and for the most part with the men who were making them; that he prayed most earnestly for the success of their enterprise; that he believed, in the main, that they were doing good to the cause,—I have the best reason for knowing. There was no want of hearty interest in their undertaking, and no indisposition to put forth his own arm in its aid, in a proper time and place; and the very last effort at composition which he made, was in the production of some verses on this subject.

The real cause of the negative support, which he was regarded as having given to the Anti-Slavery movement subsequently to this period, was mainly, as I believe, the difficulty which he had in sympathizing with the state of feeling which existed, and which it was deemed essential should exist, among those who devoted themselves to it, and his reluctance to join in the kind of measures which were judged necessary in carrying on their work. It was not in his nature, and it did not accord with his views of Christian feeling toward any portion of his fellow-men, to cherish and propagate that spirit of denunciation, of harsh construction of character, conduct, and motives; and that intolerant, persecuting temper (for intolerance and persecution are, in their essence, by no means the exclusive failing of a majority), which have too often distinguished some of the principal champions of Abolition, and have kept from, or driven from, their ranks many of the milder spirits, who otherwise would have rejoiced to join in the enterprise. He could feel, that the African was his brother, and desire and strive to impart to him an equality of privileges and hopes; he did not, at the same time, any the less feel, that the master was also the brother of each. He would have pleaded the cause of the slave in the spirit of love and not of wrath·

and would have entreated the master as a brother, and not arraigned him as a criminal. He believed, that great reforms in the face of society must necessarily proceed slowly; that great changes in the condition of large masses of men cannot be readily and safely effected at once. He was one who would have patience with Providence, and be content to be used as a means of promoting its purposes in its own way, instead of seeking to direct and control it.

But, even supposing the temper and spirit, in which the cause of Emancipation has been advocated, to be right and politic, my brother was not calculated, by his temperament or habits of action, for engaging in it. He had not that kind of nerve, which qualifies for a great work of reform in the external condition of things. His mission was to the internal man; his power was over the motives, the principles, the springs of moral and religious life in the individual bosom. He knew where his strength lay,—instinctively rather than by a direct analysis; and he wisely devoted himself to those objects, which were within the compass of the ability that God had given him. His views of the proper mode of managing this cause were probably expressed in the provisions of the Cambridge Society, which he drew up. These were such, that Dr. Channing said he should have been willing to subscribe to them; though, as is well known, he never identified himself with the great body of the Abolitionists, and, deeply as he felt the wrongs of slavery, and notwithstanding the great efforts which he made in the cause, never fully sympathized with their spirit, or approved their course and management.

This statement has not been made in my brother's

defence against any charge, brought forward now or during his life, of indifference to this great cause of humanity, or of a want of courage to maintain ground which he had once taken with regard to it. I have desired merely to give my own impressions of the course of his feelings and the motives of his conduct. Some will believe, that he erred in one direction, and some, that he erred in the other; but, whether he did or did not, none who knew him will doubt that he acted from a conscientious sense of right. And I suspect it will be found, when the subject is looked back upon, after the heat and passion, the turbulence and contention, of the times have gone by, that a course like that which he would have advised, and a spirit such as he would have cherished, might have produced as speedy, and perhaps speedier, results, and would have been in nearer conformity to the teachings and example of our great Master.

The above paragraphs were written when I had looked in vain for any other remaining expressions of his opinions and feelings on this very important subject, except those which are contained in the first two of the following extracts from his correspondence. I have since been so fortunate as to find a letter, the last of those subjoined, which contains a very sufficient exhibition of his sentiments.

TO THE REV. SAMUEL J. MAY.

"CAMBRIDGE, APRIL 29, 1834.

"I thank you for your letter. I am not quite sure that you will wholly acquiesce in my views and feelings, when you see me; but I think we shall do very well together, though I should object to modes of expression, at least, which you use.

I will not be timid or temporizing; but I will try to be inoffensive. Mr. Sewall has written to propose, that you should lecture here in May; and we should be very glad, for some reasons, that you should do so; but, on the whole, we feel that it will be best for the cause in this place, where it is new, that we feel our way amongst ourselves at first. This will be much safer than to attempt anything by addresses from any extraneous Society. It is, you know, the great misfortune of this cause, that it has been so advocated by some, as to prejudice the community against it. This prejudice adheres to the *very name* of *Society;* and we feel that we must privately remove that, before any agent of the Society can be listened to with good effect.

"I hope you will see the propriety of taking this ground here. I hope to see you when you are in this vicinity."

TO THE SAME.

"Cambridge, October 15, 1834.

"One point, on which I wished to talk with you when here, was, the character of 'The Liberator.' If you sympathize with it, and approve wholly of its spirit, it would be in vain to say to you what I wish. But, if not, if you feel how objectionable is its tone, how frequently unchristian its spirit, and how seriously it prejudices a great cause in the minds of many good men; then you will be ready to hear my question, —a question which has been agitated amongst a few of us here, viz.:—Would it not be possible to induce six or seven gentlemen, of calm and trustworthy judgment, to form themselves into a committee, each of whom should, a week at a time, examine all articles intended for 'The Liberator,' and induce Mr. Garrison to promise to publish nothing there, which should not have been approved by them? Is this possible? Would it not secure an unexceptionable paper, without injuring Mr. Garrison's interest? Would you be willing to aid in promoting such a scheme,—or can you suggest a better? Pray answer these questions at your first convenience.

"Dr. Channing is said to have given on Sunday a most powerful sermon on the subject of the late public commotions at Charlestown, New York, and Harvard College. According to Dr. Follen, his views on Slavery were so strongly favorable to the Emancipationists, as to make me wonder at what you told me of his interview with Mr. Abdy. Dr. Follen calls it an *Abolition Sermon.*"

TO A FRIEND.

[In answer to a letter of inquiry and remonstrance.]

"CAMBRIDGE, OCTOBER 23, 1835.

"Your letter is very kind, and I do not know what ——— means by calling it impudent. I am sure I thank you for it, though I do not see that any good can come of it. I have not seen the papers to which you refer, but they certainly err in saying that I am an officer of 'The Middlesex Anti-Slavery Society.' I did not know that there was such a body. But it would be of no use to say so, for I am, or have been, an officer of 'The Cambridge Anti-Slavery Society.' I am sorry that you, or any of my friends, should feel any uneasiness on this score; and you would not, if the truth were known; which cannot be, in the time of public madness, from newspapers. One must submit to whatever they choose to say. Why they so eagerly pounce upon poor me, I do not know. If for the sake of injuring the College, and if the friends of the College think it thus injured, it will be very easy to give me a hint of it, and I can stand out of the way. For, though you may be made to see the truth, the public cannot, so long as newspapers are what they are.

"But what is the truth?

"I, long ago, like other men, became interested in the subject of Slavery, and read and thought a great deal about it. I became persuaded that the dreadful evil never could be got rid of, unless it were so all at once, and by the force of public opinion. So far, I was an Abolitionist, and am still. When I saw how outrageously Garrison and some others were abusing this great cause, mismanaging it by their unreasonable violence, and by what I thought unchristian language, and a convention was proposed in Massachusetts, I joined a few gentlemen in Cambridge, in an association for the purpose of inquiring whether something might not be done to moderate the tone they were using, and prevent the mischief which we thought likely to ensue. We were foolish enough to imagine, that we might possibly exert some favorable influence. We attempted it, and of course we failed; for all who know Mr. Garrison, know that he is not a man to be controlled or advised. Our Society lived about a year, and has now virtually expired. I never belonged to any other. I have attended but four Anti-Slavery meetings, three in Boston, and one in Cambridge. I never had any acquaintance with Thompson, who, I thought, had no business in the country; only a speaking acquaintance with Garrison; and I was never in the Anti-Slavery rooms but once.

"So that, you see, I am not a very active and powerful agitator after all; and it is ridiculous to think that so poor a tool as I, should be one of those selected for the thunders of the press. The redoubtable editors would be quite crest-fallen, if they should find on what a nothingarian they have wasted their valor and decorum.

"You ask me, why not set them right? For two very good reasons. 1. I am in principle an Abolitionist. I see no other principle that can consist with Christianity or good policy; and, much as I disapprove a great part of the doings of the Abolitionists, so long as I maintain their great principle, I shall be held just as guilty. 2. I cannot bear the execrable tyranny of public opinion, and of the newspaper press, which is now exerted to put down all freedom of thought and opinion on this subject. It is perfectly execrable and detestable, and ought to be resisted. I cannot, even in appearance, yield to it, though by so doing I should save reputation and life.

"And, after all, no harm is done. This madness is temporary, and will pass away, and people will come to their senses. Meanwhile, I keep mine through all the bustle, and advise you to do the same."

It would seem as if this letter does not confirm, as to one point, the view which I have taken of my brother's sentiments, namely, where he speaks of the evil of slavery as one to be removed "all at once, and by the force of public opinion." Still, I have preferred to leave the statement as it was originally made, since I am confident that his general habit of thought on such subjects is correctly represented; and, although he might have believed that Emancipation must be an immediate and not a gradual process, he could hardly have imagined that the state of public opinion, throughout the whole country, which must precede such a measure, could be the result of anything less than a persevering and long-continued effort to enlighten it.

CHAPTER XVIII.

PUBLISHES A SELECTION FROM THE WRITINGS, WITH "THE LIFE AND CHARACTER," OF DR. PRIESTLEY—LIMITED SUPPLY OF MINISTERS, AND PLAN FOR THEIR INCREASE—FAMILY MEETING AT HIS FATHER'S—RELIGIOUS EXERCISES WITH THE UNDERGRADUATES —"SOBER THOUGHTS ON THE STATE OF THE TIMES"—SEVERE ILLNESS IN THE WINTER OF 1836—HIS OCCUPATIONS DURING IT—AFFECTION, AND LOSS OF THE USE, OF HIS EYES.

1835-1836. ÆT. 41-42.

In the course of the year 1835, he made a "Selection from the Writings of Dr. Priestley," which he published, prefixing to the volume a notice of his Life and Character, written by himself. There is no name among Unitarians which has been so uniformly assailed with obloquy and reproach; and many, indeed, of his own denomination, have been willing to shake off from themselves the unpopularity which attaches to his character, by disclaiming him as a fair representative of their opinions, or properly as a member of their body. With many of the opinions of this writer, on the doctrines of religion, the Editor sympathized very little, as little as any of his brethren; but his object in this work was partly to lay before the public a collection of writings, in themselves valuable as the productions of a pious and religious man, and partly, also, to do something towards placing in its true light the character of a man so much traduced, of one, to whose purity of life, strict integrity, unsurpassed sincerity in the pursuit of truth, and personal piety, even some of his most decided theological opponents have paid a willing tribute.

In the course of this year, also, his attention was specially turned to the subject of the preparation of young men for the ministry, whose pecuniary means, or whose deficiencies in early education, did not make it expedient for them to join the School at Cambridge. The number of preachers annually sent out by this Institution was smaller than the public required. There was frequently a difficulty in supplying the demands, made by newly-formed or by vacant parishes. In different parts of the country, many new Unitarian Societies were springing up spontaneously, some of them in small and remote communities; many attempts were made to form such Societies, which proved in the end abortive; and many were ultimately successful only after a long and painful struggle. Hence there was a demand for preachers beyond the usual supply, and, from the character and condition of many of the Societies, for preachers whose education, and habits, and views in life would render them willing to labor in a narrow sphere, and for a small compensation. The condition and wants of many of these parishes, and their increasing number, had often been brought to Mr. Ware's notice, as he was the person most frequently applied to for advice, encouragement, and assistance. His mind was thus naturally turned to the consideration of means for meeting this want, by increasing the number of students of Divinity, and also by making provision for education of a less elevated standard, than that of the Theological School. He now had some correspondence with regard to a plan for this object; but no steps were taken concerning it for some years afterward, though it continued to occupy his attention.

In the year 1837, it became anew a subject of very serious consideration, and several meetings were held, at which a regular plan of operations was proposed and discussed. It was proposed to form a school in some country town, where the expense of living would be moderate, for the education of lads from ten to twelve years of age preparatory to their becoming students of divinity, some of them to be carried through College and through the Divinity School, and some to be trained for the ministry without a public education. This school was to be under the direction of a clergyman, at the same time the pastor of a parish, who was also to have under his charge young men, who were preparing for the pulpit. Circulars were issued, requesting the opinion of various persons on the plan, and making inquiries for suitable pupils for such an establishment. The answers received were of the most satisfactory kind, admitting the necessity of the thing, approving the plan, and, in many cases, pointing out a considerable number of pupils. After a good deal of inquiry and discussion, the project was dropped for the time, not from want of friends or of means to carry it on, but chiefly because no suitable person or place could be readily found. It has, however, never been lost sight of; and recently an institution, having the same general object in view, has been established at Meadville, in Pennsylvania.

Another subject, somewhat akin to this, and one which occupied his thoughts a great deal, was that of the connexion of the Divinity School with the University. In common with many friends of both Institutions, he had great doubts of the propriety and expediency of this connexion; and at several times he made exertions with the purpose of bringing about a separation. He was, I believe, after very mature consideration and much communication with others equally interested in the cause of Theological Education, very clearly of the opinion, that the prosperity both of the College and of the School would be promoted by this measure; that, although some literary advantages unquestionably arose from the vicinity of the School to a great learned institution, yet that unfavorable influences on the manners, character, modes of living, and views in life, of the students, more than counterbalanced them. As far back as the year 1823, I find that his attention had been called to this subject, and he committed to paper some hints relating to it; for what use, if for any except his own satisfaction, does not appear. It continued to occupy much of his attention, and, indeed, to the very close of his professorship, the wants, prospects, and interests of the Theological School and of Theological Education, were among the principal subjects of his thoughts, and he never ceased to labor, and induce others to labor, in the cause.

During the year 1835, with a few slight exceptions, his health was tolerably good; at least it was such, that he was seldom prevented from attention to his customary occupations. In the month of March, he was taken sick at Providence, on his way to visit his brother in New York, (who had just experienced a severe domestic calamity,) and was unable to proceed. This did not, however, prove a continued sickness, and want of time alone made it necessary for him to return home without accomplishing his object. On this occasion he wrote to his brother thus:

"CAMBRIDGE, MARCH 28, 1835.

"Trouble is hardly so familiar a thing to you, as it is to me; and, if it has not made me insensible, it will help me to sympathize. I recollect your remarking, in a letter some time since, on your long continued prosperity, as if you looked on it with a sort of apprehension, and as if you could hardly hope to be saved, you said, without some of the discipline of adversity. I sometimes feel, that, with all that I have had, I am still needing some discipline to reach a spot which has never yet been reached, and to wake me up to the life which I ought to live. But, in either of our cases, it is not because Providence has not given us a wise and appropriate discipline, but because we have failed to make the best of it, that we are still so far from the mark.

"It is in vain to ask or to receive the visitations of Heaven, unless we sedulously labor to improve them; and that is not altogether an easy thing at all times. We are too apt to fancy, that they will do their work by their own inherent power. May you have more wisdom in using your afflictions than I have had, and so prevent the necessity of their being repeated to you. It is not difficult to find consolation during trial. The religious sentiments excited by it are so full of hope and peace and delight, that they lead to great enjoyment of mind, and help to make us specially acquiescent and happy. But to apply the discipline to a permanent improvement of our hearts and habits, is less easy. I hardly know how I have fallen into this strain; perhaps it is not that which you will most readily receive."

In the summer of this year, his domestic affections, always of the most tender character, and embracing not merely those who surrounded his own fireside, but all the members of that wide circle with which he was connected by the ties of kindred, were highly gratified by the happy accomplishment of a plan, which he had much at heart, for assembling them in a family meeting to be held at his father's house in Cambridge. An occasion of this sort is not one in which those, who are not immediately concerned, can be supposed to take any particular interest. Its chief value is to them who partake of it; its chief interest is in the hearts of them who meet. But the character of my brother was never exhibited in a more engaging light, than when he mingled, in a familiar and unrestrained manner, in a circle like this; and never, probably, in his whole life, was his heart more entirely full of filial, fraternal, and paternal love, than on the day of this meeting. It took place on the 20th of August, 1835. Four daughters, with their husbands; three sons with their wives; three unmarried daughters and three unmarried sons, with twenty-seven grandchildren, assembled and spent the day together. On coming together in the morning, the patriarch of the day was saluted, by the eldest of his grandchildren, with the recitation of the following verses, from the pen of his daughter, Mrs. Hall.

"We are coming! we are coming!
What a merry host we are!
Laughing, shouting, singing, drumming,
We are coming, Grandpapa!

"Here are Henrys, by the dozen,
Here are Marys, half a score!
Brother, sister, aunt, and cousin,
We are coming,—many more!

"We are coming! Willies, Lucys,
Annes, and Lizzies, two and two;

Frank and Robert, little *gooses*,
We can find no mates for you.

"We are coming! Edwards, Johnnys,
Harriet, Jairus, George, Louise,
Prentiss, too, without their cronies,
All are coming,—what a squeeze!

"We are coming! don't you hear us?
What a glorious noise we make!
Grandmamma, you well may fear us,
With your lemonade and cake!

"We are coming! O believe us,
Happy, joyful, *glad* we are!
In your open arms receive us
With your blessing, Grandpapa!"

Amounting, with a few other relatives, to fifty-two in number, they dined together in one room; of all ages, from the old man of seventy-one, to the infant a few months old. After dinner the present of a comfortable arm-chair was made to each of the parents of this group, by the whole company, and the remainder of the day and evening were spent in amusements and recreations, suited to the various tastes of the party. It was remarkable, that of so numerous a family, the members of which were widely scattered, and of such various ages, not one was absent; and of all this collection there were probably none, of an age capable of receiving impressions, who did not feel that they owed much, very much, to the subject of this Memoir, for wise and timely counsels, for kind and brotherly encouragement, and perhaps for reproof not less kind and brotherly; and, more than all, for support and comfort in trial and affliction, and for confirming religious faith, and brightening religious hope.

These lines were composed by him to be sung afte dinner.

"Children's children are the crown of old men,
And the glory of children are their fathers."

"In this glad hour when children meet,
And home with them their children bring,
Our hearts with one affection beat,
One song of praise our voices sing.

"For all the faithful, loved, and dear,
Whom thou so kindly, Lord, hast given;
For those who still are with us here,
And those who wait for us in heaven;

"For every past and present joy;
For honor, competence, and health;
For hopes that time may not destroy,
Our souls' imperishable wealth;—

"For all, accept our humble praise;
Still bless us, Father, by thy love;
And, when are closed our mortal days,
Unite us in one home above."

ust add, that to no one, among all those who gathered together, was this an occasion of more deep and heartfelt delight, than to the venerable head of the household, then in his seventy-second year, in the midst of a vigorous old age, his body unimpaired, his mind unclouded, and, above all, his heart warming, as it ever had done, to all the charities of life, and yielding as readily to all the tender and holy sympathies of our nature. It was no common satisfaction, to see flocking around him so many descendants, all prosperous in their lives, respectable in their characters, and happy in their families; two sons, and three husbands of his daughters, engaged heartily, honorably, and usefully in the same work, to which his many years had been devoted, to which he had led them, and for which he had helped to prepare them; all looking to him as one to whom they owed much, under Providence, of whatever was worthy and valuable in their lives. It was an occasion which none who were engaged in it can ever forget; and it left a lasting impression upon all their minds, of the good and happy influence upon life which may be made to flow from the maintenance and cultivation of the domestic affections.

Mr. Ware's attention was, during this year, directed particularly to the religious condition of the Undergraduates, with a view to increasing their own interest in it. This subject, indeed, occupied his thoughts a great deal during the whole period of his connexion with the University. With the exception of morning and evening prayers, and the preaching in the Chapel on Sunday, direct attempts were rarely made by any instructor to exert a religious influence on the pupils. This, however, was not the result of neglect or indifference. Interference on this point had been purposely abstained from, by those to whom such a duty would naturally have fallen, lest some color might in this way be given to the oft reiterated charges against the College, that it exercised an influence on the Undergraduates favorable to that particular sect to which most of those concerned in its government and instruction belonged. On this point he differed from his colleagues, and, among the rest, from his father; but, governed only by his own sense of what he thought right, he, in conjunction with Dr. Palfrey, made an attempt to interest the Undergraduates. He invited them, generally, to meet him on Sunday mornings before service, and engage in conversation on religious subjects, desiring them to state freely their views, feelings, and opinions. He usually began with a short extemporaneous address upon some particular topic, gradually bringing their minds to bear upon it, and then encouraging them to a free and familiar expression of their own thoughts.

These meetings excited a satisfactory degree of interest among a considerable number of the young men, and were also attended by some of the junior officers of the College. A most salutary influence was exerted on the minds of many of those who were present; and, on some, the impressions made were of so serious a kind, as to produce a permanent change of character, and lead them to select the ministry as their profession. There are no means of knowing how long he persevered in this plan. His numerous other engagements, his burdensome duties, especially the necessity of preaching on the Sabbath, either in the Chapel or abroad, combined with his frequent indisposition, at length rendered its regular continuance impracticable; and every one knows how certainly irregularity in matters of this sort ensures their being at last given up. He was so well satisfied, however, with the result of his first attempt, that he felt courage in a subsequent year to renew it; but the causes referred to rendered its continuance, as a permanent exercise, quite impossible.

In October of this year, he published without his name a pamphlet, entitled, "Sober Thoughts on the State of the Times, addressed to the Unitarian Community." It was not however strictly anonymous, the authorship being not only immediately suspected, but soon known. The object of this tract was to draw the attention of nis brethren, both clergy and laity, to the religious aspect of the times, as it regarded especially their own body, their relation to other sects, and the duties growing out of their peculiar position. The time at which he wrote was in his view a period of rest after a long controversial contest; a contest which had begun with the memorable passage between Drs. Worcester and Channing in the year 1815, and had continued, with little intermission, for the space of twenty years. And now, as it appeared, the combatants in this warfare had stopped to breathe.

"This, then," he says, "is the present aspect of our religious affairs. We have discussed with our differing brethren the doctrines respecting which we differed, and the questions are at rest. *The result is, we are a community by ourselves.* When we began the debate, we were members of the general congregational body, communicants at the same tables, and sheep under the same shepherds. (I speak in general terms.) Now a separation has taken place. We have our own congregations, our own ministers, our own institutions and instruments of religious improvement. It is a crisis of unspeakable interest to us. We are deeply concerned to know what is the character and power of those institutions, what the nature and operation of our distinctive faith, and how far we are faithful representatives, advocates, stewards, of that pure and glorious Gospel, on whose behalf we have been allowed to contend."

He proceeds then to pass in review the character of the Unitarian community,—the principles of truth and duty which it assumes as fundamental to its existence,—the *Idea* of Unitarianism. He next inquires how far its character conforms to or is a fair representation of this idea; whether the institutions of religion are faithfully supported; whether there is a proper practical apprehension of what are the requisitions of religion; and he refers strongly to some prevalent and lamentable deficiencies in these respects. He speaks of the standard of life, which the denomination should adopt, and by which they should live; and, above all, he lifts a voice of warning against a low and lax one, as not only false in itself, but even impolitic and inexpedient as to its effects on the success and standing of a sect. The whole constitutes an earnest appeal to Unitarians to be true to the great principles of the Reformation, to which they believe themselves more faithfully devoted than other Christians, and not to fail in their duty of carrying out in their lives the truth for which they have been so earnestly contending.

He was also interested about the same period, as one of a Committee of the Massachusetts Peace Society, in setting on foot a course of Lectures on subjects connected with the great objects of their association. The nature of the plan will be seen in the following sketch of the subjects proposed to be treated. But the course was not given till a few years afterwards.

"1. The Moral Character of War.

"2. The Bearing of the Doctrines of Political Economy on the Subjects of Peace and War.

"3. The Advocates of War answered.

"4. The Circumstances which show a Tendency toward its Abolition.

"5. The Means by which its Abolition is to be effected.

"6. Substitutes for War.

"7. The Relations and Duties of Free Governments."

He was laid up in the early part of the year 1836 by a long and severe fit of sickness, of the same general character with that which had disabled him in 1828, and which made still farther inroads on his already shattered constitution. He was attacked, in the beginning of February, with inflammation of the lungs, attended by repeated and continued hemorrhages in small quantities, which confined him to his room for eight weeks, and left him unable to return to his usual exercises in the Divinity School for some months. He did not resume preaching until July. Though he was greatly reduced in strength and flesh by this illness, and never, probably, recovered entirely from its effects, it was not attended with much pain or suffering, except that which may arise from mere debility; and he retained his cheerfulness and animation of spirits through the greater part of the time.

He had indeed a strong presentiment that he should not recover; but this feeling was not accompanied by anything like gloom or depression. On the contrary, the probability of such an event was the subject of free conversation, which was always of a cheerful and elevated character. There remained for a long time a good deal of doubt, even after some gradual improvement in his condition, whether his case were not about to terminate in a chronic and fatal disease of the lungs; and, during his slow recovery, his mind, escaping as it were from the grasp of those more serious interests which had engrossed it for so many years, seemed to go backward and yield itself to that strong love of poetry and poetical composition, which had been one of its predominant tendencies in early life. Apparently as the direct consequence of reading a newspaper in bed, while his wife was out of the room, he began to suffer at this time from a painful affection of the eyes, which rendered all use of them impossible, and he was obliged to depend entirely on others for reading and writing. He accordingly dictated to his wife, or wrote with a pencil in bed with his eyes closed, and in this way went on with his poem of "The Dream of Life," to which allusion has before been made, and composed, beside, several short pieces. At the same time he was desirous of hearing poetry read, particularly that of a religious and devotional character. He was especially engaged in the subject of Lyric Poetry, and not only so in poetical productions of this kind, but he also sought out works on its history and criticism. He became indeed so much interested, that he collected materials for, and made some considerable progress in, the preparation of Essays on English Lyric Poetry.

Of some of the tendencies of his thoughts, while thus gathering his strength through the days of a tedious convalescence, necessarily cut off much of the time from that refuge in books and writing to which he had been accustomed to fly, the following verses, composed at this period, give indication. They serve to show, that, however strong might be his hope and faith, and however readily and cheerfully he might contemplate the not improbable result of his disease, this state of mind was founded on no confident or presumptuous estimate of his own merits, or any undue reliance upon them for acceptance after death. The comparison which he drew within himself,—one which I believe he was always drawing,—between the judgment of his character and services formed by the world, and his own perception of what he ought to have been and ought to have done,—ending, as it often did, in a painful and humiliating sense of unworthiness,—was too uniform through life, and too indirect in its manifestations, to be the result of anything but the most entire sincerity and severe self-examination.

" IN SICKNESS. MARCH, 1826.

" FATHER, thy gentle chastisement
Falls kindly on my burdened soul;
I see its merciful intent
To warn me back to thy control,
And pray, that, while I kiss the rod,
I may find perfect peace with God.

" The errors of my heart I know;
I feel my deep infirmities;
For often virtuous feelings glow,
And holy purposes arise,
But like the morning clouds decay,
As empty, though as fair, as they.

" Forgive the weakness I deplore;
And let thy grace abound in me,
That I may trust my heart no more,
But wholly cast myself on thee;
Oh, let my Father's strength be mine,
And my devoted life be thine!"

LINES WRITTEN MARCH 29, 1836.

" IT is not what my hands have done,
That weighs my spirit down,
That casts a shadow o'er the sun,
And over earth a frown;
It is not any heinous guilt,
Or vice by men abhorred;
For fair the fame that I have built,
A fair life's just reward;

And men would wonder if they knew
  How sad I feel with sins so few.

" Alas, they only see in part,
  When thus they judge the whole;
They cannot look upon the heart,
  They cannot read the soul:
But I survey myself within,
  And mournfully I feel
How deep the principle of sin
  Its root may there conceal,
And spread its poison through the frame,
Without a deed that men can blame.

" They judge by actions which they see,
  Brought out before the sun;
But conscience brings reproach to me
  For what I 've left undone,—
For opportunities of good
  In folly thrown away,
For hours mis-spent in solitude,
  Forgetfulness to pray,—
And thousand more omitted things,
Whose memory fills my breast with stings.

" And therefore is my heart oppressed
  With thoughtfulness and gloom;
Nor can I hope for perfect rest,
  Till I escape this doom.
Help me, thou Merciful and Just!
  This fearful doom to fly;
Thou art my strength, my hope, my trust,—
  Oh help me, lest I die!
And let my full obedience prove,
  The perfect power of faith and love."

This affection of the eyes continued for more than a year, and for the whole of this period he was unable to read or to write. All his preparations were therefore necessarily made with the assistance of others, so far as reading and the making of notes were concerned, and his exercises in the Divinity School and his preaching were consequently extemporaneous. He now found a new evidence of the great value of the power of extemporaneous speaking, which he had taken so much pains to acquire. He did not use a written sermon again till the ordination of Mr. Bartol, as colleague of Dr. Lowell, in Boston, March 1st, 1837, nor afterward till he gave the Convention sermon in May of the same year. After this time his eyes were restored to a tolerable state, though they never regained their former strength. It does not appear, that preaching extemporaneously served to diminish the labor of preparation; the pains he took on each occasion to make himself familiar with his subject consumed, on the whole, as much time as would have been required to write out the discourse. And, even after this long experience, he did not have recourse to it more frequently than before his illness.

CHAPTER XIX.

EXERTIONS IN AID OF POOR AND DESTITUTE SOCIETIES—NEW DUTIES AT THE UNIVERSITY—HE PROJECTS A COURSE OF LECTURES ON "THE POETRY OF SCIENCE"—PREACHES THE CONVENTION SERMON—SERMON ON THE CILLEY DUEL—DEATH OF HIS SISTER, MRS. HALL.

1836-38. ÆT. 42-44.

His health after this last illness was never entirely re-established, and, through the whole of the year 1836 especially, he was very feeble, and hardly competent to the exertion required by his labors in the School. In the autumn of this year, he complains, in one of his letters, of his health, a rare thing for him; yet at the same time he was engaged sedulously in collecting statistics of poor and destitute Societies, with the view of having some measures taken for procuring a supply of their wants.

In consequence of facts brought to light by this inquiry, an effort was made, under the direction of the American Unitarian Association, to raise a fund for the purpose; and Mr. Ware subscribed, and pledged himself in some way to procure, five hundred dollars towards it. In order to accomplish this, he prepared a discourse, embodying the results of his inquiries, and stating the wants which existed in different quarters. He preached it, in the course of the year 1837, before a number of congregations in various parts of the State, making a collection in each case after the service. In this way he more than redeemed his pledge, and collected the amount of six hundred and ten dollars.

Encouraged by his success, towards the close of the same year he made a similar effort for the Evangelical Missionary Society, and raised for them the still larger sum of eight hundred and twenty-four dollars. It is right to say, in illustration of the character of these labors, that, at the very time he was making such extraordinary exertions to procure money for public objects, his own income from his professorship was so inadequate to the support of his family, that he found it necessary to undertake new duties at the University for the purpose of enlarging it.*

The advanced age of his father, but more particularly the failure of his sight at this time, began to render it difficult for him any longer to conduct the exercises of the Undergraduates in Paley's "Evidences" and Butler's "Analogy;" or to continue to serve as one of the preachers in the Chapel. These duties were now,

* In a letter written about this period, he thus expresses himself on this subject: "It will not be possible for me to continue in the office at the present salary. I have very reluctantly brought myself to say this; for I would both be and seem willing to labor in any important post without mercenary views, and even at some sacrifice. But, after trying it to the best of my skill in economy, I find it perfectly impossible to live here, as I am obliged to live, on the salary I receive. No professor with a family *does* it, or *can* do it. I have spent more, every year, to such an extent that I have been obliged to consume a large part of what I had laid by for age or emergency; and have been, so far, impoverished by my office. I cannot do this longer, because, by the end of the year, I shall have exhausted my funds.

"Meantime my constitution is so far reëstablished, that I am now capable of occupying a station which may demand more physical strength, and I have no fear of returning to the mode of life from which I was taken in a state of debility. For the kindness shown me in offering me this retreat, and in afterwards bearing with my partial and interrupted labors, I have always felt deeply grateful."

therefore, transferred to his son with a portion of the salary, whilst the father merely continued his connexion with the students of the Divinity School. This very materially increased the burdensomeness of his duties, not merely by the additional amount of labor he was called on to perform, but by the perplexing variety of occupations to which he was consequently subjected.

But all this did not tend to extinguish his love of active exertion; for we find him, about the same period, engaged in several other undertakings. In the fall of 1837, he began a voluntary course of Lectures to the Theological Students, on Moral Philosophy. How far the plan was pursued, and how complete his instructions were on this subject, does not appear. He also wrote the poetry for an Oratorio, "The Feast of Tabernacles," which was composed by Mr. Charles Zeuner, and performed at the Odeon, in Boston. He prepared, also, and delivered before many audiences in Boston and elsewhere, a Lecture on "The Poetry of Mathematics." The success of this production was so considerable, that it was suggested to him, that a similar mode of illustration might be extended to other branches of science, and thus an attractive and instructive *course* of Lectures be given on "The Poetry of Science." The plan struck him very favorably as having great capabilities, and want of time only prevented him from carrying it into execution. He was desirous of undertaking it at this time, from the wish to make it the means of filling up some arrears in his pecuniary means, which had occurred during those years in which his salary had fallen short of his necessary expenses. But, although this project was ultimately relinquished, it was a favorite one; and he entertained it so long as to find time to collect, in the course of this and the next year, a considerable amount of materials.

On looking over the notes which he made for these lectures, I must confess myself surprised, well as I knew the rapidity and activity of his mind, at the richness of the collection of facts, hints, and illustrations, which he had thus incidentally accumulated, on subjects with which he had been but slightly conversant. He knew too well to what he was competent, to venture out of his depth. He did not pretend to a properly scientific consideration of any part of his subject, but proposed merely to give a general sketch of the prominent features of each department of science, with a particular illustration and development of those which have a peculiar bearing on poetry and religion. This was a task for which his mind was most happily suited.

In May, 1836, he was chosen to preach the Sermon before the Convention of Congregational Ministers in the succeeding year, a privilege, of late years, but rarely conceded to the Unitarian portion of this body, by the majority. He delivered this discourse, June 1st, 1837. The state of his eyes had rendered it necessary, that it should be wholly written from his dictation; beside this, he had been confined to his bed by sickness, for the few days during which it was composed. His condition rendered it very doubtful whether he would be able to appear in public; but, extremely anxious to do so, he made himself familiar with the manuscript the night before. In the morning it was still a matter of very questionable prudence, whether he ought to make the attempt; but, feeling good courage as the hour approached, he dressed himself, was driven to Boston, and, having acquitted himself of the appointed task, returned immediately home, apparently uninjured by the exertion.

At the close of the Academic year, in July, he delivered two discourses, appropriate to the young men who were about leaving College, on "Education the Business of Life." They were published at the request of his auditors.

The two following extracts are from letters written about this period, although their subjects have no particular relation to it; the first, to a friend under an engagement to preach at Cincinnati; the second, to his brother, the author of "Letters from Palmyra," concerning the second of his works, "Probus."

"CAMBRIDGE, MARCH 31, 1837.

"I send you a few tracts, such as perhaps may be useful to you. When you reach Cincinnati, you may supply yourself from our depository there.

"As to preaching, it is not easy for one, who has never been upon the ground, to say distinctly what would be the sort of sermons desirable. The general position is, however, I think, very clear; let the aim be *Practical Godliness*;—build this on *Principles* and *Doctrines*;—teach the peculiar doctrines, openly, fearlessly, decidedly, but *gently* toward others, and always for the sake of their practical application; not as merely theological dogmas,—not controversially,—not as mere builders of a sect. Thus let it be seen, that we wish to establish the Christian church, and that the Unitarian system is only our instrument for that work.

"With this view, I should, in your case, prepare the most serious discourses I could, urging the severest and highest morality on the ground of the most liberal and rational principles. These principles I would state, expound, apply; but so that no one should have occasion to say, I did it for their own barren selves, but for the sake of the piety and goodness which are to proceed from them."

"CAMBRIDGE, MARCH 27, 1838.

"I am glad to find you are getting on with the book, and books. As for titles, it is a puzzle sometimes. I do not like either of your *aliases.* Why not 'Probus' alone?—or, it just occurs to me, add—'Rome in the Third Century.' Of the words '*Christians,*' or '*Christianity,*' I should prefer the former, if either; and esteem its plurality no objection; always provided the article *the* be not omitted. I do not know whether the feeling is to be regarded, but I have a feeling of reluctance at seeing this Christian purpose stuck upon the title-page. 'Probus, or Rome in the Third Century;' commend me to it, and it to you, as euphonious and significant, and committing nobody, yet taking all. As regards the Christian delineation, I think, from what occurred in former times, that your tendency may be to regard it too exclusively as a *Revelation of Immortality*, and too little as a *Remedy for Sin.* The former is the vein for speculative philosophers and for poets; the latter for real life and substantial influence, and that to which its whole power is due. The doctrine of Immortality, without its stern application to the *conscience*, and the other doctrine of the world's actual depravity, would have been worth little; and the New Testament, and all the history of the Christian progress, show the great fact of regeneration to be the chief thing of pith and moment.

"This accounts for the prevalence of the doctrine of atonement. Christianity roused first of all the consciousness of sin and consequent danger; *penitence* was the first emotion, and *reform* the first duty; not the solution of philosophical skepticism, and joy at the prospect of immortal life. I suppose, of course, that you will attend to this more than before; I hope you will not fail to make it prominent. There is no satisfactory view of our religion and its efficacy from any other point."

In the year 1838, he speaks of himself as better than he had been since 1828. But this was not actually the case, however buoyant he might have felt at his comparative activity and power of exertion at some particular moments. Still he was well enough to pass this year and the next in the performance of much labor. In January, 1838, he gave a Lecture introductory to a course of lectures under the patronage of the Peace Society, and was engaged otherwise in carrying on the cause. In April, he visited New York and Philadelphia, preaching the ordination sermon of Mr. Holland at Brooklyn, and preaching also at Philadelphia.

In the winter of this year, he partook, with the rest of the community, in the shock produced by the death of Mr. Cilley, a member of Congress, in a duel fought under circumstances of great atrocity, and outraging even the feelings of those who had, by usage, been rendered blind to the barbarous character of this custom. He availed himself of the excited state of the minds of all at this event, to lift up his testimony against duelling, and endeavored to produce a serious impression on the young men whom he was in the habit of addressing. His text was Prov. xx. 3, "It is an honor for a man to cease from strife." This discourse was delivered in the Chapel in the morning, and he was to preach in the City in the afternoon. After service in the morning, he received a note from the President, expressing his gratification with the sermon, and requesting him earnestly to repeat it in whatever place he should preach in Boston in the afternoon. He accordingly delivered it at the West Church. He received a note from one of the audience, written the same day, asking liberty to publish it, and to "present him with an edition of it;" and in the course of the next two days he received a further application on the behalf of several gentlemen of the congregation, proposing the same request. It was accordingly given to the public.

In the summer of this year, 1838, he underwent a very severe affliction in the death of his sister Harriet, wife of the Rev. Edward B. Hall, of Providence. The circumstances attendant upon her loss were of the most painful character. She had been, up to the day of her decease, in her usual health, and had ridden on Saturday, with her husband, from Providence to Grafton, where he was to preach the next day. The same night she was seized with apoplexy, and died the following morning. Her friends at home had even no intelligence of her illness, till her husband arrived at Cambridge, bringing with him the news of her death. Mrs. Hall was some years younger than her brother Henry, and, from this circumstance, he had been led to take almost a paternal interest in her education. She had exhibited in early life many strong and peculiar qualities, and had had many difficulties of temperament and of disposition to struggle with. He had watched her development, aided her by counsel, and sometimes by reproof, in her efforts to overcome faults, and had encouraged and cheered her in her intellectual, moral, and religious progress. The excellent qualities, which exhibited themselves as she advanced in life, had been to him a source of great gratification; and he had the satisfaction, for some years, of seeing her in a situation where she was at once happy and useful. This event coming upon him so suddenly, though met with entire submission, produced a deep impression on his mind. With the exception of the loss of his own wife, in 1824, no death of an adult member of any branch of the family had taken place for more than thirty years; and, whilst he had looked upon, and spoken of, this remarkable exemption with religious thankfulness, he had strongly felt that such an exemption from the ordinary lot of humanity could not long continue. But he had expected that he, as the feeblest of the flock, should fall the first. Little did he anticipate, that a blow was to strike down one so much younger than himself, and apparently the healthiest of the family-circle. At the time of this event he was in the habit of keeping a brief journal of passing occurrences, and from this I extract the following notices of it.

"*June 24th, Sunday Evening.*—On returning from Lecture, met Lucy at the door, with tidings of the sudden death of Harriet. Yesterday, well and happy,—this morning, dead in agony. We have felt and said for a long time, that this exemption of our family circle, for thirty years, could not be expected to last; but who would have looked for the bolt to fall there? Providence is a mystery; we see a little, and know nothing.

"*Monday, 25th.*—The family are gathering from all quarters; how different a meeting from that proposed for this summer! The disease proves, on examination, to have been apoplexy; and I find that disorder of the head has been not infrequent with her. What a bewildering and amazed day!

"*Tuesday, 26th.*—Yesterday was cloudy, with violent rains in the afternoon; evening clear, with a sweet new moon. To-day brilliant, with sunshine and all the glory of a most beautiful summer. We buried her at Mount Auburn, at twelve o'clock. Brother Parkman prayed. Who of us can forget the impression of that moment, when we stood at the open tomb amidst all the magnificence of Sweet Auburn's most luxuriant scenery?

"*Saturday, 30th.*—Lecture at half past eight; an old one, because too much absorbed in the events of the week to command myself to write. I do not yet find myself restored to a capacity for study or thinking;—unhinged, restless."

Who of us, truly, can forget the impression? To be so soon, indeed, renewed, but with what a contrast in the circumstances! She had been cut off in a moment, in the midst of health, spirits, and the reasonable expectation of a long life. Five years afterwards, the same group followed to the same resting-place his own remains, the shadow of his former self, the victim of slow disease, at the long-expected termination of a life of protracted infirmity.

CHAPTER XX.

DISCOURSE OF MR. EMERSON BEFORE THE DIVINITY SCHOOL—MR. WARE'S CORRESPONDENCE WITH HIM—FESTIVAL AT EXETER—RESIGNATION OF HIS COLLEAGUE, DR. PALFREY, AND OF HIS FATHER—STATE OF THE SCHOOL—EFFORTS FOR ITS IMPROVEMENT—LETTERS TO HIS SON.

1838-41. ÆT. 44-47.

HIS thoughts seem, from about this period, to have been almost exclusively directed to the state and prospects of the Theological School. This subject absorbed, for the most part, his attention during the remaining years of his life. In the same summer of which we have been speaking, Mr. Ralph Waldo Emerson was invited, by the graduating class of Divinity Students, to deliver before them the annual discourse. This discourse, while every one saw in it much to admire and approve, contained many sentiments concerning the supernatural character of Christianity, which were regarded by the principal friends of the Institution, as unsound, and of dangerous tendency. No one could feel more strongly on this point than Mr. Ware; and he had an opportunity on the evening of its delivery to hold some conversation with its author with regard to it, which is referred to in a letter to him, written the next day.

"CAMBRIDGE, JULY 15, 1838.

"MY DEAR SIR,

"I do not know how it escaped me to thank you for the volumes of Carlyle; to make up for which neglect, I do it now.

I am glad to have so strong a motive as this gives me for reading him carefully and thoroughly. I believe that I am not so far prejudiced by the affectations and peculiarities of his later manner, as to be unwilling to perceive and enjoy what he has of manly and good; and I would willingly work myself, if possible, beyond the annoyance of that poor outside. Indeed, I have always seen enough of his real merits to wish I could see more, and I heartily thank you for giving me the opportunity.

"It has occurred to me, that, since I said to you last night, I should probably assent to your unqualified statements, if I could take your qualifications with them, I am bound in fairness to add, that this applies only to a portion, and not to all. With regard to some, I must confess, that they appear to me more than doubtful, and that their prevalence would tend to overthrow the authority and influence of Christianity. On this account, I look with anxiety and no little sorrow to the course which your mind has been taking. You will excuse my saying this, which I probably never should have troubled you with, if, as I said, a proper frankness did not seem at this moment to require it. That I appreciate and rejoice in the lofty ideas and beautiful images of spiritual life, which you throw out, and which stir so many souls, is what gives me a great deal more pleasure to say. I do not believe that any one has had more enjoyment from them. If I could have helped it, I would not have let you know how much I feel the abatement, from the cause I have referred to."

To this letter, Mr. Emerson replied as follows:

"CONCORD, JULY 28, 1838.

"What you say about the discourse at Divinity College, is just what I might expect from your truth and charity, combined with your known opinions. I am not a stock or a stone, as one said in the old time; and could not but feel pain in saying some things in that place and presence, which I supposed might meet dissent, and the dissent, I may say, of dear friends and benefactors of mine. Yet, as my conviction is perfect in the substantial truth of the doctrine of this discourse, and is not very new, you will see, at once, that it must appear to me very important that it be spoken; and I thought I would not pay the nobleness of my friends so mean a compliment, as to suppress my opposition to their supposed views out of fear of offence. I would rather say to them,—These things look thus to me; to you, otherwise. Let us say out our uttermost word, and be the all-pervading truth, as it surely will, judge between us. Either of us would, I doubt not, be equally glad to be apprized of his error. Meantime, I shall be admonished by this expression of your thought, to revise with greater care the 'Address,' before it is printed (for the use of the Class), and I heartily thank you for this renewed expression of your tried toleration and love.

"Respectfully and affectionately yours,

"R. W. E."

It is unnecessary here to refer to differences and discussions growing out of this, and other expressions of opinions of the same character with those which were contained in the discourse of Mr. Emerson. The existence of such a controversy, in the midst of those with whom he had been associated, was to my brother a very painful thing, and he regarded it as a great evil; but he regarded it as a still greater evil, that opinions like these should obtain and hold their ground in a Christian community. He did not hesitate, therefore, on all suitable occasions, to express the very decided conviction which he felt. The very last sermon which he ever prepared for the pulpit, but which, as will be seen, he never preached, was composed with a view to the state of public feeling which grew out of this controversy; but the only public expression of his sentiments concerning any part of it is contained in a sermon on "The Personality of the Deity," which was delivered in the Chapel in the early part of the term following the delivery of Mr. Emerson's discourse, and was published at the request of the members of the Theological School. Of this Sermon he sent a copy to Mr. Emerson, with the following letter.

"CAMBRIDGE, OCTOBER 3, 1838.

"MY DEAR SIR,

"By the present mail, you will probably receive a copy of a Sermon, which I have just printed, and which I am unwilling should fall into your hands without a word from myself accompanying it. It has been regarded as controverting some positions taken by you at various times, and was indeed, written partly with a view to them. But I am anxious to have it understood, that, as I am not perfectly aware of the precise nature of your opinions on the subject of the discourse, nor upon exactly what speculations they are grounded, I do not, therefore, pretend especially to enter the lists with them, but rather to give my own views of an important subject, and of the evils which seem to be attendant on a rejection of the established opinions. I hope that I have not argued unfairly; and, if I assail positions, or reply to arguments, which are none of yours, I am solicitous that nobody should persuade you, that I suppose them to be yours; since I do not know by what arguments the doctrine, that 'the soul knows no persons,' is justified to your mind.

"To say this, is the chief purpose of my writing; and I wish to add, that it is a long time since I have been earnestly persuaded, that men are suffering from want of sufficiently realizing the fact of the Divine Person. I used to perceive it, as I thought, when I was a minister in Boston, in talking with my people, and to refer to this cause much of the lifelessness of the religious character. I have seen evils from the same cause among young men, since I have been where I am; and have been prompted to think much of the question how they should be removed. When, therefore, I was called to discourse at length on the Divine Being, in a series of College sermons, it naturally occurred to me to give prominence to this point, the rather as it was one of those, to which attention had been recently drawn, and about which a strong interest was felt.

"I confess, that I esteem it particularly unhappy to be thus brought into a sort of public opposition to you; for I have a thousand feelings which draw me toward you; but my situation, and the circumstances of the times, render it unavoidable; and both you and I understand, that we are to act on the maxim, 'Amicus Plato, amicus Socrates, sed magis amica Veritas;' (I believe I quote right.) We would gladly agree with all our friends; but, that being impossible, and it being impossible also to *choose* which of them we will differ from, we must submit to the common lot of thinkers, and make up in love of heart, what we want in unity of judgment. But I am growing prosy; so I break off.

"Yours very truly,
"H. WARE, JR."

The following is Mr. Emerson's answer.

"CONCORD, OCTOBER 8, 1838.

"MY DEAR SIR,

"I ought sooner to have acknowledged your kind letter of last week, and the Sermon it accompanied. The letter was right manly and noble. The Sermon, too, I have read with attention. If it assails any doctrines of mine,—perhaps I am not so quick to see it as writers generally,—certainly I did not feel any disposition to depart from my habitual contentment that you should say your thought, whilst I say mine.

"I believe I must tell you what I think of my new position. It strikes me very oddly, that good and wise men at Cambridge and Boston should think of raising me into an object of criticism. I have always been,—from my very incapacity of methodical writing,—'a chartered libertine,' free to worship and free to rail,—lucky when I could make myself understood, but never esteemed near enough to the institutions and mind of society to deserve the notice of the masters of literature and religion. I have appreciated fully the advantages of my position; for I well know, that there is no scholar less willing or less able to be a polemic. I could not give account of myself if challenged. I could not possibly give you one of the 'arguments' you cruelly hint at, on which any doctrine of mine stands. For I do not know what arguments mean, in reference to any expression of a thought. I delight in telling what I think; but, if you ask me how I dare say so, or, why it is so, I am the most helpless of mortal men. I do not even see, that either of these questions admits of an answer. So that, in the present droll posture of my affairs, when I see myself suddenly raised into the importance of a heretic, I am very uneasy when I advert to the supposed duties of such a personage, who is to make good his thesis against all comers.

"I certainly shall do no such thing. I shall read what you and other good men write, as I have always done,—glad when you speak my thoughts, and skipping the page that has nothing for me. I shall go on, just as before, seeing whatever I can, and telling what I see; and, I suppose, with the same fortune that has hitherto attended me; the joy of finding, that my abler and better brothers, who work with the sympathy of society, loving and beloved, do now and then unexpectedly confirm my perceptions, and find my nonsense is only their own thought in motley. And so I am

"Your affectionate servant,

"R. W. Emerson."

In the summer of this year Mr. Ware had an opportunity of reviving some of the most pleasant associations of the earlier part of his life, by a visit to Exeter, for the purpose of attending a festival of the alumni of the Academy, on the occasion of the retirement of his old friend, Dr. Abbot, from the office of Principal, which he had held for fifty years. In this he took a great interest; and, although not himself an alumnus, he was welcomed, as a former instructor, to a participation in the pleasures and festivities of the occasion, and contributed his share to the entertainments of the day, by making one of the addresses to the assembly, and composing a song for the dinner. Many of his old friends were still remaining to welcome him; and he was happy to find that the warm feeling of attachment, which he ever retained for the place and the people, was met by a reciprocal feeling among those with whom he had passed so many pleasant days.

"SONG FOR THE ABBOT FESTIVAL, EXETER, N. H., AUG. 23, 1838.

"Tune, *Sandy and Jenny.*

"FROM the high-ways and by-ways of manhood we come,
And gather like children about an old home;
We return from life's weariness, tumult, and pain,
Rejoiced in our hearts to be school-boys again.

"The Senator comes from the hall of debate;
The Governor steps from the high chair of State;
The Judge leaves the bench to the 'law's wise delay';
Rejoiced to be school-boys again for a day.

"The Parson his pulpit has left unsupplied;
The Doctor has put his old sulky aside;
The Lawyer his client has turned from the door;
And all are at Exeter, — school-boys once more.

"Oh! glad to our eyes are these dear scenes displayed;
The halls where we studied, the fields where we strayed!
There is change, there is change! but we will not deplore;
Enough that we feel ourselves school-boys once more.

"Enough that once more our old Master we meet,
The same as of yore when we sat at his feet;
Let us place on his brow every laurel we 've won,
And show that each pupil is also a son.

"And, when to the harsh scenes of life we return,
Our hearts with the glow of this meeting shall burn;
Its calm light shall cheer till earth's school-time is o'er,
And prepare us in heaven for one meeting more."

The next year was a very busy one, and during it he enjoyed better health than in any which intervened between his sickness in 1836, and his last disease. He remarks, on being prevented from preaching by illness toward the end of July, that it was "the third Sunday lost by illness since the beginning of the term, the middle of February. Less loss than any season since in Cambridge. *Laus Deo.*" In the spring he was engaged in carrying through the press a new edition of Mr. Buckminster's Sermons. This edition was chiefly a republication of the volumes which had already appeared. The only additions were, some notices of Mr. Buckminster's character, by Mr. Norton, which appeared in "The General Repository;" some occasional Discourses in the second volume, which had been published in the author's life-time; and some passages selected from his manuscripts, after his death, for insertion in "The Christian Disciple."

In this year, Dr. Palfrey, who had been his colleague during the whole period of his connexion with the School, resigned his office; and, in the autumn, his father, who had still continued to superintend some of the exercises of the theological students, was obliged, by the almost entire failure of his sight, to withdraw himself wholly from duty. The Rev. Dr. Noyes was elected to fill the place left vacant by the former; but the necessary result of this change was, that the labors, hitherto divided among three officers, were now to be performed by two.

My brother had always felt, that the labors of the Professors in the School, interrupted as they had been by the additional duties for which they were called on in the University, were not only greater than their number was adequate to, but more varied, and consequently perplexing, than could be performed by them in a manner satisfactory to themselves or the public. He had been oppressed by a feeling, that, feeble as he was, and exposed to frequent interruptions in duty from attacks of ill health, he did not himself do justice to the place which he occupied; and, failing to come up to his own standard of what the office required, he had more than once felt disposed to resign it to a more competent, if not a more willing, laborer. During the remainder of his incumbency, his life was, I will not say embittered, but harassed and rendered anxious, by considerations growing out of what appeared to him the unfavorable condition of the School.

In the success of the Institution, as must be evident from his entire course with regard to it, his whole soul was bound up. He had very elevated views of its importance; and of the great and salutary influence which a race of ministers, thoroughly and religiously educated, were capable of exerting upon the state of our country. It was the wish nearest his heart, that this

Institution should be so endowed, so placed, and so conducted, as to train up such a race of ministers. He believed that it was practicable to accomplish this; but he felt very strongly, that, in its condition at that time, the Institution did not do all, of which it was capable. The circumstances, which, in his opinion, stood chiefly in the way of its successful career, were, its connexion with the University; its situation so near the metropolis as to familiarize its members with a style and manner of living not the best suited to prepare men for a profession, that requires, in most of its members, simple, frugal, and self-denying modes of life; and the inadequacy of the means of instruction. While he remained in Cambridge, he, from time to time, joined with his friends in efforts to remove these obstacles. In the course of the year 1839, several meetings of gentlemen interested in the School were held, having this purpose in view. It was thought, however, that the conditions, on which the funds of the School had been intrusted to the Corporation of the University, did not admit of their being transferred to a separate body; and, this being the case, some of those most inclined to promote its prosperity were deterred from giving their aid, though still a large and liberal addition was made to its funds within the two or three following years.

It is only necessary to add, that, in the course of the last two years of his Professorship, the additional duty of teaching Ecclesiastical History, by a course of Lectures, fell to his lot, a work on which he was first engaged in the autumn of 1841. In further illustration of his feelings, his position, and of the condition of the School, the following extracts are inserted, from a letter addressed to the Rev. Charles Briggs, the Chairman of a committee of the alumni of the Theological School, chosen at their annual meeting in 1841, for the purpose of taking into consideration means for promoting its interests.

"CAMBRIDGE, JANUARY 15, 1842.

. . . . . . "I will not labor this point; but there is another which should have your serious attention. *The School has, in fact, less than two men devoted to it.* Let me ask the Committee to possess themselves of the facts of the case. I will state them. Dr. Noyes teaches the Hebrew to the Junior Class, an hour every day; the criticism, &c., of the Scriptures, Old Testament and New,—the Evidences of Christianity and Doctrinal Theology,—these branches occupy an hour and a half more every day. Look at that list, and say if it is possible for one man to do, in all those branches, the thorough work, satisfactorily to himself and to the friends of religion, which in such an Institution ought to be furnished.

"Then, for myself; my regular duty was, to teach the composition and delivery of Sermons, and the duties of the Pastoral office. This involved a great deal of time and drudgery, in the examination of written discourses, and in exercises in reading and speaking. It required Lectures also on Preaching, and on Church Polity; and exercises on Style and Composition, and Public Prayer. To do these things faithfully and well, would demand a great deal of time, and allow little else to be done. Besides this, I now teach Natural Theology, —in these metaphysical days no slight affair,—and Ecclesiastical History, which can be decently taught only by one who devotes his life to it.

"Yet, miscellaneous as all this is, and a source of perpetual dissatisfaction, because we are compelled to feel every day, that we can do no justice to the subjects, or our pupils, or ourselves, we yet might endure it with some equanimity, if it were all. But, after a week of anxiety and weariness, we are to preach on Sunday,—one of us a quarter, the other, half the time. That great work is thus committed to men with jaded spirits, and bodies needing rest, and minds whose whole attention has been engaged in a way not well suited to prepare for the pulpit. Ought the preaching in *that Chapel*, to *those young men*, to be left thus to accident, as it were,—to be provided by men, who, if they do their other duties, cannot prepare for this, and, if they prepare for this, must neglect some other duties? Yet such is the present state of affairs.

"And this is not all. We are also called upon to attend morning and evening prayers in the College Chapel, and in the Chapel of the School. The latter we intrust more than half the time to the members of the Senior class, and thus relieve ourselves, while we benefit them.

"Moreover, if any Undergraduates study Hebrew, Dr. Noyes must leave his proper studies and go and teach them. And, for myself, I am obliged to teach Butler and Paley to the Undergraduates, and to lecture to them once a week, for half the year, on the History and Criticism of the New Testament, to the great interruption of my proper duties in the School.

"The Committee will perceive, then, that, in point of fact, our Divinity School has far less than the strength and time of two men; and that, on these fragments of men and their time, are laid all the deep and large subjects, which in other institutions are divided between double the number of whole men, and some of which singly demand nothing less than the entire, undivided attention of one man, to do them anything like justice. The Committee will judge whether it be right and decent to leave, what ought to be the great school of Liberal Theology in the land, in such an unsatisfactory state.

"What, then, shall be done? This is for the Committee to consider, and I trust they will not lightly give up the attempt to do something.

"I will take leave only to suggest one consideration, which presses strongly on my mind and conscience.

"Very little provision is made for a religious influence upon the Undergraduates of the College; nothing but the Sunday sermons and prayers. Those young men ought not to be so left. It is to the last degree desirable, that they should be put under other and more frequent influences of Christian training. But how shall it be? I confess to you, that I do not see the possibility of anything being done under the existing pressure upon the religious teachers. What seems to me most of all things desirable, is the appointment of a College Preacher, who shall have the whole office of the religious worship and instruction; who shall preach on Sunday to the students,—shall at other times and in various ways be devoted to their religious and moral culture, as their minister and pastor, and in this way, may be an unspeakable blessing to them; who also shall be pastor to the families worshipping in the Chapel, that now live without the privileges of that important relation.

"If this could be brought about, I think it would be a great gain to the College, and it would so far relieve the officers of the School, that they could go on with comparative comfort. I should, for one, think this preferable to the appointment of another professor, who should, like us, be mixed up with both Institutions. Even then we should have a greater variety of things to attend to than we could do well; but it would be better than it is now.

"I send you these hints, because I know of no subject at this time more imperatively demanding to be attended to. There is no time to be lost. If anything can be done, we want the benefit of it at once. If nothing can be done, the sooner we know the worst, the better. I hope a good deal from your consultations and wisdom." . . . . .

We may here retrace our steps a little to introduce into our narrative a part of his domestic history, which contributed not a little to brighten the last few years of his life. In the earlier part of this Memoir, he has been seen in the relation of a son, receiving instruction and direction from his father in the formation of his own character, and in preparing for the conduct of life. We find him, as he advanced in years, performing the same office for his own offspring. His oldest son had graduated in 1838, was engaged in the ensuing year in teaching a school at Milton, and, in the course of the year, chose the profession of his father. The letters, from which the following passages are extracted, were written to him during his absence from home.

"CAMBRIDGE, DECEMBER 12, 1838.

"I have in fact been busier than usual this term. Besides the recitations at College, which require a great deal of time in preparation, I have written more sermons than I ever did in the same number of weeks, and with more care than I used to do when I was younger. I have now finished; having written a series on connected topics, discussing some grave questions, in twelve discourses. Most of them have some relation to the present state of the public mind, and the composition of them has been exceedingly interesting to me. Besides all this, and my common duties at Divinity Hall, I have employed an hour once a week in holding a religious meeting at College, (Wednesday evening,) when from thirty to forty collect together, as we did one year on Sunday morning. The plan, however, now differs in this; that several gentlemen, tutors, proctors, and divinity students, engage in it, and it becomes quite a conference. I hope some good from it. There are always some in College who are sufficiently men to understand the worth and the duty of a religious life, and it is a pity that they should not be aided; and equally a pity that others, who are so unfortunate as to be insensible and thoughtless on that great subject, should not be in the way of having their attention called to it.

"I have just been reading, with uncommon satisfaction, Dr. Channing's Address on 'Self-Culture.' It is a remarkably lucid and beautiful exposition and appreciation of some of the noblest and most generous views of man, adapted to awaken a lively interest, and to move one to effort for improvement. One rarely meets anything more just and true, and I think that Dr. Channing never printed anything more useful. I hope you will read it, and make yourself master of it by familiar and loving study. It is well worth it. If Mr. Angier has it not in the house, I will send it to you. I think, that, at your time of life, you will find it delightful to cheer and aid you.

"I am glad to find that you still pursue manfully the even tenor of your way; you will find your reward, I am sure, in the growth of your character, and in an increasing strength toward your future way of life. Self-knowledge, self-discipline, self-culture,—let these be your business, humbly and resolutely, and your opportunities will not be thrown away."

"CAMBRIDGE, DECEMBER 30, 1838.

. . . . . "Father's eyes are lately growing worse rather rapidly; he can hardly read a page at a time. I think that it affects his movement so as to make him appear like an older man, though I do not perceive appearances of age otherwise. I do not know whether I told you of a visit to him of his only brother (seventy years of age) ten days ago. He was very feeble from sickness, and they will never meet again. It was quite an affecting sight; and I have been looking round this evening, as the melancholy of the closing year steals upon us, to consider the number of aged connexions who seem to be just on the edge of life,—seven over seventy. In the course of nature a few years must call on us to surrender many of them, if we do not ourselves go first, which may very possibly be, for death is no respecter of persons.

"I wish I could help you to make your passage over this line of the year. And yet, perhaps, I could say no more than to urge you to do it thoughtfully and religiously."

"CAMBRIDGE, MARCH 8, 1839.

"The first part of your letter I answered to Mr. B——. I should have been glad that it might have been affirmatively. As regards your situation at Milton, I should judge, that, if desired to remain there, in such wise as to prove that your services are acceptable, it would be well to do so. It is a useful occupation of your time, and you are doing good; the unpalatableness of the thing will be diminishing, though the real satisfaction may be small; but this, I suppose, is true of the situation in which most men pass their lives. I think too, that you must have perceived, that a right use of the probation, to which it subjects you, may make it profitable enough to compensate for all its annoyances. These annoyances are superficial and temporary,—the moral advantages may be deep and permanent. Unless, therefore, an opportunity offer of taking a pleasanter school, of a higher order and smaller number, I think your true course will be to continue where you are.

"As to the other subject, it is of yet deeper and more vital interest. All the wishes of my heart would be gratified, and the highest purpose of my life fulfilled, so far as regards yourself, in seeing you truly and devotedly a minister; I could pray for nothing better on earth, than to see that hour. I have ventured to hope that I might see it; but my fears have always been strongest. Not, certainly, that I should be unhappy to see you otherwise engaged; for a good man in any calling is an honor; but I should prefer this; and you may judge then how readily I should encourage you in the purpose you are cherishing. I had not supposed that you could yet have arrived at the full determination; though I had hoped that a process was going on in your heart and character, which might result in it. I have seen some signs of that process, I fancy; but I had not supposed it had proceeded far enough to satisfy you, that you were ready to begin the work of preparatory study. If your resolution is not founded on erroneous views,—if you have made yourself fully aware of what is, and ought to be, implied in a dedication of yourself to this work,—then I am heartily rejoiced that you come to it so early.

"But I am very anxious, that you should not deceive yourself; that you should be fully awake to the whole meaning and consequences of such a step; that you *should count the cost*, as our Saviour said to his disciples; and should find yourself able and happy to abandon everything else, and devote yourself to this, not only as on the whole the most eligible profession, but as the choice of your soul, from which nothing could possibly tempt you. This is the state to which I wish to see you come; and I have a good deal to say about it. I hope, therefore, that you will deliberate and do nothing hastily. I feel sure, that, the more you deliberate, the more firm will be your purpose, if rightly founded. And, as I have no time to enlarge now, I just add one hint, containing an important principle by which to try yourself. To make a good and happy minister, a man must be such from taste and affection; he must be a *religious* man *first;* he must be a minister because impelled to be so by his religion, and not be religious because impelled to be so by his profession. I could be happy, therefore, in encouraging you to this great step, just in proportion as I had cause to believe, that an interest in religious things had become the chief and moving concern in your mind.

"I have delayed writing, partly because we thought it possible you might be here yesterday, and partly because my eyes are very bad, and I have not been able to use them more than just enough to get through my regular business. In this great decision, my dear boy, let us earnestly and daily seek guidance from Him, who is all light, and alone can lead us aright."

"CAMBRIDGE, MARCH 10, 1839.

"You will not wonder, that the great matter of your decision dwells on my mind, as I suppose it fills yours. You may judge from my letter (which I trust you received yesterday) something of my thoughts concerning it. When I know more exactly what is, and has been, passing in your mind, I shall be better able to judge whether I say anything suited to your wants or not. Meantime I wish to enlarge a little on the view which presents itself to me, and we can compare opinions afterward.

"Referring, then, to the general statement in my letter, I take it for granted, that your tendency to elect the ministry for your calling is accompanied by the determination to sustain that personal character which is consonant with it, and to give up those dispositions and tastes which are incompatible. For myself, this is the point to which I direct my whole regard; for, I do not doubt, as far as intellectual fitness is concerned, you will find no difficulty. I only ask, whether the habitual state of the affections, and the tastes for society and life, will conform. And, as in all cases this would be the first, second, and third consideration, so I will tell you why I am anxious you should give it an unusual prominence.

"I have seen many young men break away from the common routine of life, and devote themselves to theological study, with so slight a perception of the change they needed to undergo, that they never became what they should be,—never were equal to the proper work they had undertaken,—never found any satisfaction in it. I would not for the world have you such. It is hard to see others so mistakenly enter the service of the church. I could not bear to see a son do it. . . . . .

"Now, habit is second nature. Dispositions and tastes, habitually cherished for years, become our masters, and are even stronger than principle; so that they rule us in spite of ourselves, unless by a resolute and long-continued effort we subdue them. This is that change which the New Testament calls regeneration; and, unless a man go through it thoroughly, so as to be altered from the very bottom, (not superficially, not on the outside, for appearance' sake, but in heart,) he cannot be fitted to succeed, or be happy, in the ministry; nay, not as a Christian man. For sacrifices of taste and pleasure must be made, which he will be unable to bear, unless he have acquired a deep and hearty taste for those higher blessings of the soul, which spring from a reliious life.

"You perceive, then, to what my solicitude points. I think that your mind has been recurring to the same. What I wish is, to urge you to it with yet more earnestness; so that you shall not leave the matter, till you have probed it to the bottom, and, by reading, thought, and prayer, have deliberately made the work *thorough.*

"Then I look a step further, and I ask, supposing you have done this, and to be confirmed all the more earnestly in your purpose,—Would it be best to begin your professional course this fall? I think it premature to decide that question. I do not yet see how the balance inclines between the very good reasons which may be adduced on both sides. But I confess, that so much as this appears pretty clear, as I now see it, that it would be best to pass the first year in private study with some clergyman, and enter the School at the end of the first year of the course."

CHAPTER XXI.

DECLINE OF HIS HEALTH—VISIT TO NEW YORK—IS TAKEN ILL IN THE PULPIT—RETURNS TO CAMBRIDGE—CONTINUED INDISPOSITION—RESIGNS HIS PROFESSORSHIP—REMOVES TO FRAMINGHAM—HIS CONDITION AND OCCUPATIONS DURING THE AUTUMN AND WINTER OF 1842-43—LETTERS.

1842-43. ÆT. 48-49.

It only remains now to record the closing scenes of his life. From the period to which we have brought our narrative, there was a slow but sure decline. Accustomed to refrain from complaints about his health, and never willing to plead the state of it as an excuse for omitting any exertion which he thought it his duty to make, so long as it was possible to keep from his bed, he toiled on long after he should have relinquished all effort, and have given himself that rest which alone could have deferred the fatal event. His disposition for useful occupation, his interest in his work, never left him. Like the spent swimmer, who still hopefully contends with the current that is sweeping him rapidly onward to a certain death, he too struggled manfully, striving and hoping to the very last. It is quite probable, that an earlier retreat from his post might have done something to prolong his life; and our first feeling is that of deep regret, that this step was not taken. But what, after all, would have been to him, or to his friends, the reprieve of a few short months, or even years, to be spent in listlessness and inactivity, and perhaps despondency, whilst the maladies which were to destroy him were surely, and only more slowly, doing their work? There is scarcely any doubt, that, for several years, whilst the apprehensions of his friends were directed to the state of the lungs, from which he had through life suffered so much, disease was gradually and insidiously invading other organs, and exhausting the energies of life in another direction.

But the first very distinct indications of more deep-seated disease, and of a kind differing from the attacks under which he had before suffered, were seen during the autumn of 1841. He was at this time engaged in the preparation of his Lectures on Ecclesiastical History, a task for which he felt himself but poorly qualified by his previous course of study, and upon which he entered with but little courage. Indeed, amidst his other engrossing duties, so multifarious as well as laborious, he found this new field of exertion, not only burdensome, but perplexing and vexatious. He held on, however, to the close of the College term, in the second week of January, but then found himself in a state of great exhaustion. Early in this month, he was present at a large meeting of the members of the family in Boston; and, not having seen him for a long time, I was made anxious by his wasted and haggard look. Still he entered with his usual spirit into the enjoyments of the evening. The impression, however, was not effaced; and it was satisfactory to me to learn, that he had made arrangements to spend some weeks of the vacation in the city of New York, away from the occupations and interruptions which would attend him at home, and with no other care than that of filling the pulpit of the church of Dr. Dewey, then absent in Europe.

Of this visit he kept a brief journal. It was his plan to pass two Sundays of his absence at Baltimore and Washington; and he had also, as he records, made arrangements for preaching in New Jersey. Such were his habitual ideas of giving himself rest from labor.

He arrived in New York on the 13th of January, and took lodgings at the house of Mrs. Isaac Scott, a family connexion, in a remote part of the city, for the purpose of having his time much at his command, and of avoiding the distraction of mind and the fatigue, which would result from seeing many persons. On Sunday, January 16th, he preached twice, making this note in his journal: "Spoke feebly in the morning, better in the afternoon. Church not so thin as I expected, the day being snowy." Of this day he wrote thus to his wife:

"*Thursday, January* 20, 1842.—After telling you in the letter which I despatched to-day, that the mail disappointed me, I found your letter and John's at Francis's bookstore. Very, very welcome, I assure you; for I am pretty lonely, and have time to think of you much. It is a good deal for you to find the chance of writing so much, and I value it the more. The subject on which you particularly speak, is one that exercises my mind a good deal, but about which I despair of doing what is to be done, unless we can change our miserable, hurried, and bustling life; and, as you set it forth, it is a great reason for change. You want to know more about my Sunday. I do not remember what I have written, but I presume I have nothing to add, except that I preached the sermon on 'The Reality of Religion,' which you last heard, and in the evening 'The Sentence of an Evil Work.' I was not in good case; but am more than ever satisfied that my preaching powers have sensibly deteriorated. I am trying to write a sermon on the State of the Religious Community; and have written more than enough, but not satisfactorily."

Through the week he was much abroad in the open air, walking a good deal about the city, and visiting many of his old friends. The weather was for the most part fine and mild. He read also a good deal, and finished the sermon referred to in the preceding letter, in the preparation of which he was much interested. He notes during this time, nearly every day, some feelings of indisposition, showing that the state of his health was such as to call to it his frequent attention. He mentions particularly, as "quite a common thing with me of late," the occurrence of a headache on rising in the morning, which went off after breakfast.

On Sunday, January 23d, he makes only the following record. "Rose at eight. Very cold. Felt *quaverish*. Taken ill in church. Drs. Perkins and Revere visit me twice. Write home. Many friends call." He entered the pulpit this day for the last time. He began the services in the usual manner, but had proceeded only about half way through the first prayer, when it was observed that his voice faltered and that he coughed; but he still went on and finished the prayer, and then read the hymn. He then sat down for a while, but soon very deliberately rose, and stated to the audience, that he felt himself suddenly too much indisposed to go on with the services. He therefore dismissed the congregation and went into the vestry-room. Hither he was immediately followed by Dr. Revere, who has kindly given me the above account, and adds:

"I immediately followed and found him unusually pale, his hands cold, and his pulse thready, frequent, and unequal. I inquired the nature of his illness. He replied, that he had not felt so well as usual before church; but that, having coughed during the prayer, he found that he had spit up a quantity of blood, which he showed me on his handkerchief. Though his manner was quite calm and self-possessed, I saw at a glance, that he supposed that the hemorrhage was from the lungs, and was of ominous import. On examining his face carefully, I thought I could see a stain of blood on the upper lip, and desired him to blow his nose, which was followed by a considerable discharge of blood, by which he appeared to be assured."

It was the opinion of Dr. Revere, and also of Dr. Perkins, who soon after visited him, that the hemorrhage was not from the lungs, and was not in itself of serious import, which proved to be the correct view of his case; for he had no indications subsequently to this period of any disease of the lungs, and nothing remained the next day as the consequence of this attack except a state of utter prostration.

I subjoin, as quite characteristic, his own account of this attack, which he felt at the time to be of some importance, and which actually closed his career of activity, and put an end to his public life. He writes thus to his wife in the course of the day:

" *Sunday.*—A good day yesterday, but the change of weather affected me unpleasantly. [The weather, which had through the week been so mild, had on Saturday become cold and windy, and on Sunday morning was very cold.] Completed a sermon on the times, which I was anxious to preach. Did not feel very well when I rose this morning. (By the way, E—— came home in the night, to the great rejoicing of all.) I had a good deal of trial in speaking this morning; and, after I got through the first prayer, was a little startled at a show of blood in my mouth. I tried all sorts of experiments to ascertain where it came from, and soon decided, after reading the hymn, that I had better not go on. So I dismissed the congregation without a sermon. Dr. Revere came to me in the Vestry, and doubted whether it were from the lungs, and I began to think I had done foolishly; but he said, No, for my system was excited, and I should have hurt myself. So I went home, he with me, and Dr. Perkins soon came in; and they agreed that they could not tell whether it were a serious thing or not, but I must keep quiet and take medicine. This was two hours ago, and I write at once, that you may hear from me before the rumor reaches Cambridge. I trust that it is nothing of moment; but we cannot tell; and I have so long lived upon uncertainty, that, come what will, I am not greatly taken by surprise. I think you will not be. In opening my Bible, I just came to the verse,—'*He is not afraid of evil tidings; his heart is fixed, trusting in the Lord!*' There is a great comfort there. Mr. Eaton waits for the letter. I am still expectorating colored matter. Love and peace, dearest. I suppose that I must come home; and so end all my schemes. Well, so be it. A thousand loves to the children. I shall write again unless I am ordered home at once."

The same evening he wrote again:

"I have been much refreshed by sleep, and relieved by medicine. Dr. Revere and Dr. Perkins have both paid a second visit, and leave no further directions. They will not say whether I can go home at once, but, I suppose, will let me go on Tuesday. They say I cannot preach, if I stay. It is a grievous disappointment to me, as it puts an end to very fond plans, and changes my whole winter, if nothing more. I do not presume to look further. I presume that the attack is one, which, with due care, will pass away, and leave me to pursue my studies next term; but it would not be strange, if it should prove something worse, and were to drive me for a time from all employment. I shall try to bear with equanimity the prospect and the result; but, if I am to be so set aside, I do not know where bread is to come from, and the struggle will be severe. But I shall not look on the dark side. None of us must; let us wait,—have patience,—be trustful;—we have infinite causes for gratitude and none for complaint, and I hope we have faith enough left to receive meekly and cheerfully any appointment that is in store for us. Friends are very kind. Of course the circumstances and publicity make an excitement. This is painful and mortifying. I at some moments think it would have been better to run the risk of going through the service, and avoid the sensation; but I suppose the counsels of prudence rightly prevailed. Indeed, I am sure that I could not have continued to speak loud. But, to think of being exposed to such a public infelicity! It is a very trying part of it."

Immediately on the receipt of the intelligence of this attack, his wife left home to join him. She arrived in New York on Tuesday morning, and, leaving there the same afternoon, returned with him to Cambridge on Wednesday morning. There was at that time no further hemorrhage. He gradually collected a little strength, and had then once or twice a slight return of bleeding, but not accompanied by so great a prostration. Still he felt well enough to attempt the performance of his College duties; but, after a few days, he again gave way, and was seized with an acute affection of the organs of digestion, by which his labors were suspended for ten weeks, his strength even then being very imperfectly restored. This was accompanied and followed by other symptoms, which showed too well how fearful an inroad had been made on his constitution, and that the worst apprehensions of his friends were probably to be painfully realized.

It was now quite certain, that to persevere in an attempt to perform the duties of his office, would be to sacrifice the little chance which remained of his restoration. With his feelings about the School, his knowledge of its necessities, and his disposition to work, a continuance in the place without performing its duties fully would have been only a source of discomfort, dissatisfaction, and self-reproach. Either he would constantly have made, on every interval or alleviation of disease, some injurious effort, or else he would have regarded himself as a useless incumbrance in a post which should be filled by a sound and able man. He determined, therefore, to vacate the professorship at the close of the academical year in July, and to seek out some quiet and remote situation in the country, where, in entire relaxation from labor, his jaded system might possibly be recruited. He accordingly sent in his resignation to the President of the University. In accepting it, as an expression of their regard for his services, the Government of the College voted the continuance of his salary for half a year beyond his leaving the office.

After making excursions into various parts of the country with the view of finding a suitable place of abode, he at length selected one in the beautiful town of Framingham, about twenty miles from Boston; and thither, with his family, he removed in the latter part of the month of July. Notwithstanding his great bodily infirmity, he had assumed a portion of his accustomed duties about the middle of June. During the three last weeks of the term, he gave to the Senior Class one lecture a day, and to the whole School six lectures on Preaching. It had been his earnest desire to preach a sermon in the College Chapel on the last Sunday of the term; and it was with no small sacrifice of feeling, that he became at length persuaded, that it was the part of wisdom to forego the melancholy pleasure which this would have afforded him. He left the School, therefore, and the University, without any formal expression of those feelings of which his heart was full.

On this occasion he received from his pupils a parting testimony of their regard, in the form of a letter, from which the following passages are taken:

"We would not allow you to leave us, without telling you what we feel of the value of your teachings, and thanking you for your kind care and concern for each and all of us. We thank you for the interest you have taken in all our studies and pursuits. We thank you for the patience and candor which have marked your intercourse with us in the recitation-room, for your willingness and desire to hear all our doubts and questionings, to know the mind of each of us, and to give to all our opinions their full value. We thank you for all the important hints and lessons you have given us upon the various and difficult duties of the Christian ministry; lessons, which we trust our future course may show not to have been lost upon us. We thank you for the constancy in meeting us, which sickness and pain could not hinder; and for your singular diligence and earnestness in fitting us for our work in the world, we shall never cease to be grateful.

"But your exertions in improving and filling our minds are not the only, or the chief, subject of our gratitude. We thank you especially as our spiritual guide. We shall long remember the gentle rebuke, which called us, almost without our knowing it, to the stricter line of our duty. We shall long remember the mild admonition which checked without wounding, yet came so directly home to our hearts. And we shall never forget those needful and timely counsels, which made us feel, that, in our Professor, we had also a friend to our souls, and which deepened and strengthened our hope, and faith, and love.

"Your example, beloved Sir, even more than your instructions, has taught us the greatness and beauty of a Christian life; and for this we are grateful to the Providence which has permitted you so long to be with us. In your uniform cheerfulness, in your submission and contentment in the trials and vexations of your situation, we have seemed to recognize the true temper and spirit of the Christian. And, when we have seen your high confidence in God, our hearts have been encouraged to trust in him more fully. You have been our friend and brother in ways that you did not know; and we are sure, that, wherever you go, all will find in you such a friend and brother.

"Receive now, dear Sir, our affectionate *farewell.* You have long been with us, and joined in our daily and social devotions. Though *you* may no more be present at our altar, yet *our* prayers there shall go up for you, and our hearts shall be warm toward you, and we will be present with you in spirit. Here we may not meet you again, but we look confidently to a more intimate union hereafter."

Of his last interview with the School, his nephew, (now the Rev. Joseph H. Allen, of Jamaica Plain,) gives me the following account:

"It was Wednesday, July 13th, when he met the School for the last time in the Chapel. The lecture he gave that morning was one of a short course he had been delivering on Preaching. The subject of it was, 'Sentiment, the Relation of Truth to the Imagination and Feelings.' 'Preach *experimentally*, not as a discourser, but as a partaker. Have religious experience. Speak from personal knowledge; otherwise there is no heartiness, no distinctness. The preacher must have felt all; have met every struggle. Then there is no embarrassment, nor dread of mistake. *The power of the pulpit depends on this; and this is within the reach of all.*'

"This shows the substance and tone of his last instructions to the School. At the close of them he was silent for a few moments. Then he said a very few words in reference to the letter which had been addressed to him by the members of the School. I do not remember what he said; hardly anything is left on my mind but the general impression. He spoke of the partial and imperfect success he had met with, as if there were only one feeling with him,—regret that he had not done more. He was too much subdued by his own emotion to say much besides this, and he seemed as soon as possible to seek the relief of uniting with the School in prayer,—that last prayer, when the strength of the man whom we had seen steadfast and unmoved, patient and uncomplaining through everything, was bowed down as the weakness of a child for the moment, and then rose again, calm, unfaltering, and warm with heartfelt love. That hour can never be forgotten. We can only pray, that something of its spirit may dwell with us through our lives."

I insert also a sketch, found in his own hand-writing, of the short address above referred to, in which he gave vent to his feelings on this occasion, and took his leave of this cherished sphere of duty.

"And now the time has come that brings to a close my labors here. For nearly twelve years I have had close connexion with the succession of young men who, in this place, have pursued the most interesting studies, in preparation for the most important calling. They have been years of great anxiety and of great satisfaction. If I could look back upon them without any misgivings as to my own capacity and fidelity, I should say, that no life, except that of a parish minister, can comprise so various and great satisfactions. But, while I see much that I could wish to be otherwise on my own part, I must say, that, with the pupils of the Institution, there has rarely been any cause for the slightest discontent; and, for the most part, my connexion with you has been one of cordiality, confidence, and gratification.

"I am now to bid farewell to this pleasant scene; and I cannot do it without expressing to you something that is in my heart, as I think of the past and survey the present. I heartily reciprocate the kindness of the expressions, which, in your farewell letter, you have used. Let me thank you for that letter. I could have wished that your language had been less expressive on some points, on which my better knowledge of myself makes me feel it to be undeserved. But one stimulus to improvement always is, the mortification of the mind, when one feels humbled by the expression of an undue estimate on the part of others. But, as a token of your friendship, I shall always prize it; and you may be assured, that I shall never cease to look back with pleasure on the circumstances that have attended our connexion with one another. I can never cease to take an interest in your fortunes and labors. I shall follow you with my eye and my heart, wherever you shall go, and rejoice, as if you were all my sons, in whatever success and honor God may please to vouchsafe to you. May He crown you with his favor; may He give you that greatest satisfaction of seeing the fruit of your labors on earth, and of being welcomed to the presence of your Master in heaven."

The annual visitation of the School, which occurs at the close of the academic year, took place on the 15th of July. He had waited only for this occasion, and immediately afterwards commenced the work of removal. This occupied several days; and it was not till the 23d of the month, that he found himself really settled in his new home, and felt that he had indeed left behind him all his old occupations and interests,—that he was, for the first time, it may be said, since the days of childhood, entirely at leisure, without a purpose, without an aim, without some object of interest, to the accomplishment of which all his powers were to be devoted.

The condition in which he found himself was undoubtedly severely trying to his courage, patience, and hope. It was not merely, that he was separated from an institution to which he was from principle, as well as feeling, deeply attached,—with which he had identified himself,—to whose prosperity and usefulness he had been willing to devote his health, his life;—but it was a separation also from all active duty in that profession, which had in him swallowed up every other interest, and engrossed his whole soul from his very boyhood. It was not, therefore, as in the case of leaving his parish, the passing merely from one field of duty to another, in which, if his affections were not more deeply interested, he at least knew, that the sphere in which he was to work was a wider and a more important one than any single parish could be, and that therefore the opportunity for being useful was enlarged. But, in the present case, there was no such alleviation of the painful necessity which compelled him into retirement. It was an entire withdrawal, with broken health and shattered nerves, from all the scenes of active life; it was surrendering to other hands the post at which he had so long stood, from sheer physical inability to maintain it longer. He would have liked better, I do not doubt, to have kept on, were it possible, with even diminished capacities, till his last sickness should have found him still on the spot, and summoned him away in the midst of active duty; and it was a sore thing thus to leave his labors, with the prospect before him of months, perhaps years, of incapacity and inactivity, —living in the midst of a community, where so much was to be done, and so few as ready and willing as himself to do it.

In the village to which he removed, he found everything to answer his anticipations. Quiet and retired, it yet afforded a ready access to all his friends by means of the railroad, whilst it was at the same time sufficiently remote to prevent that constant pressure of company, to which he had always been exposed at Cambridge, and which had, in truth, been such, as to prove wearisome and burdensome, interfering with his necessary duties, and often with the desirable privacy of domestic life. He lived near the church and in the immediate neighborhood of the Rev. Mr. Barry, in whose education for the ministry he had been interested, for whom he entertained a warm regard, and whose ministry he hoped to be able constantly to attend. The inhabitants of the place, many of whom were acquainted with his character and had listened to his preaching, knowing his purpose in coming among them, refrained with a considerate kindness from breaking in upon that seclusion, which was now so necessary to him.

It was painful at this time to witness the condition to which he was reduced. His feebleness was such, that it required a very obvious exertion to go up the few steps which led to his house. He could walk only a short distance without fatigue; and, indeed, could engage in no occupation or exercise which implied the outlay of much muscular strength. Within a few years, he had gradually assumed the appearance of an age far beyond that to which he had actually attained. His countenance was pale and sallow, his body emaciated, his form bent, his gait uncertain and slow; so that he bore, in his whole aspect, the marks both of sickness and of years. He had hoped, when fixed in Framingham, to be able to resume the exercise of riding on horseback, which had formerly proved so beneficial to him; but he found himself inadequate to the exertion.

But, though he had sought retirement and repose, inaction, in the strict sense of the word, was utterly incompatible with his nature. To have some pursuit was an essential element of his life; and, in order to fill up the comparative leisure which he now enjoyed, he looked forward to several plans of occupation. Among them was the preparation of a Memoir of the life of the venerable Noah Worcester, the Apostle of Peace, which he had undertaken at the request of his family. In this task he felt a strong interest, from his deep sense of the eminent services, which had been rendered by Dr. Worcester to the cause of humanity. During this autumn and winter, he examined the materials which had been furnished, arranged the principal facts, and made considerable progress in writing. The result of his labor on this work so nearly completed his plan, and seemed, to those who had proposed the undertaking, so worthy of the subject, that, in the year after my brother's death, it was given to the public. A preface, many notes, and a concluding chapter, were added, by the Reverend Samuel Worcester, one of the sons of the deceased; but the chief portion of the work, which extended to about one hundred and fifty pages, was printed from the original manuscript, thus written under circumstances of much depression and discouragement, and, for the most part, "with great heaviness." It had been his intention also to superintend the instruction of his children; but he found it so difficult to command the steady attention this effort required, that it became necessary for him gradually to relinquish the attempt.

At the end of August he returned to Cambridge, and spent there a part of Commencement week, attending the various public exercises, and apparently enjoying them as usual. From some little minutes, which he kept while at Framingham, of his employments, we find, that, during the first three months, he had a constant succession of visitors from among his relatives and more intimate friends, but not in a manner or to an extent that burdened him. A few extracts will serve to convey some idea of the manner in which his time was passed. Of the period from the 3d to the 23d of October, he says:

"Out-door work and exercise occupied this time of a very beautiful season, spent not with much method, and with very little study. Attended the installation of Mr. Stone at Sherburne. Started for Pomfret; weather changed;—spent a day at Worcester and returned. Attended a convention of Unitarian friends at Worcester, October 18th, 19th, 20th;—interesting and profitable."

Of the period from this to the end of the year he writes:

"From this time a delightful fall. Our visitors gradually became fewer. We enjoyed health. Made two visits to

Cambridge and Boston. Association at Grafton. S Worcester spent a day and night, (November 7th,) preparing a Memoir of his father; finding no encouragement to print, I laid aside all preparation for the present. Did hardly any study; little power of application; great inequality and frequent derangement of health. Attention to children's studies interrupted and unequal; want of method, &c. Among the books read, I recall the following; some aloud; besides innumerable chapters and passages at random. Nothing could be more miscellaneous; a good deal of Latin in scraps; some French, some Greek, New Testament. *Studied* Hebrew with Belsham, Stuart, and Wakefield, Wrote Review on Peace for 'The Christian Examiner.'"

Here follows the list, of about forty volumes, to which he alludes, of works of biography, history, poetry, and fiction. Of the remainder of the season he makes the following record:

"The winter set in early in December. Have had good sleighing and equal cold for four weeks. To-day (25th) Pierpont preaches. I not well enough to be abroad; poorly for some time past. Laying plans of mental occupation for new year, in order to do something if possible; hope both disposition and ability may increase. My wish is to complete in January the Memoir of Worcester; and during the season to finish D. L. ['Dream of Life,' a poem], and either Xn. Pr. [his work on 'Christian Progress'] or E. on P. R. ['Essay on Practical Religion.'] I could do the whole, if tolerably well and tolerably resolute."

"The month of December cold, equal; and good sleighing till middle of March. Very miserable most of the time. Went once to Boston for two days. Never more oppressed and good for nothing, than for about four weeks. Utterly incapable of work. During this period wrote nothing but

Review of Greenwood's 'Sermons,' and four short Notices for 'The Examiner;' an Anti-slavery song; and, with great heaviness, a little of D. L."

During a part of the autumn there was a very considerable improvement in his condition; not, indeed, any sign of a permanent restoration, but an increase of appetite and strength, and a corresponding change in appearance. He was able to take more exercise, walked a good deal, drove around in his *carryall*, busied himself in various kinds of out-of-door work on his place, gathering vegetables and fruit, taking care of his horse, &c. He visited Boston in December, and attended the ordination of Mr. Smith as the Colleague Pastor of his friend Dr. Parkman. He certainly seemed to have gained a good deal in many particulars; but he had that about him which precluded a well-grounded belief, that he had undergone any radical change. He was still exceedingly thin; he had gained no flesh. He spoke particularly of restless and sleepless nights, occasional headache, frequent nausea, unequal appetite, and impaired digestion; but, above all, he complained of an unconquerable sense of fatigue and exhaustion, which, although resisted to the best of his ability, and not so overcoming him as to prevent much reading and some bodily exercise, was still a feeling from which he was never entirely free.

The following letters, written during this period, and, with a few exceptions, dated at Framingham, will serve to illustrate many points which have been already adverted to, and will aid in conveying some idea of the state of his body and mind, his views of his condition, his present occupations, and his hopeful anticipations of future profitable employment. In explanation of the first of these letters it should be stated, that it was well known, that, on leaving his professorship, he was casting himself and his family on the world, with very insufficient means of support. Soon after settling in Framingham, he received, from some generous friends in Boston, a liberal sum, which had been collected and invested for his family. Similar favors had been previously tendered him while at Cambridge, when the straitened condition of his finances had been suspected; but these had been firmly, though gratefully, declined.

TO ABEL ADAMS, ESQ.

"SEPTEMBER 8, 1842.

"When I last had the pleasure of seeing you, you informed me of the generous purpose of some of my kind friends, to do something toward the promotion of my comfort and the confirmation of my health. What I said at that time, was all that I could say; and I do not know that I can add anything to express my deep sense of the great favor which has thus been done me. Yet I will write one line, that I may assure others as well as yourself, that I accept their tokens of good-will with the heartiest gratitude. I cannot but feel humbled and mortified, when such large favors are again and again bestowed upon me, to reflect how poorly I have merited them, and I sometimes feel inclined to refuse them; but then I remember, that to do so would indicate a false pride. I ought not to be unwilling to receive, when friends say they are gratified to bestow; and I cannot deny, that it gives me pleasure, as it does them, to feel that their kindness will enable me to look with less anxiety on the prospect of leaving behind me a helpless and dependent family. They have done much to relieve my mind of a heavy burden; and I say from the bottom of my heart, 'God bless them!'

"Let me depend on your friendly offices to convey to them my thankful acknowledgments."

TO THE REV. CHARLES BRIGGS.

(Agent of the American Unitarian Association.)

"What should you think of twelve Tracts, of twelve pages each, made up of choice and pithy passages selected from the periodicals of past years, and from eminent writers?—narrative, doctrinal, devotional, &c., to be entitled, 'FRAGMENTS,' and numbered, '*Basket No.* 1, 2,' &c., with the motto on the title-page, 'Gather up,—that nothing be lost; and they gathered up twelve baskets full.' If the Committee should fancy it, I think I could undertake it."

TO HIS SON.

"NEW YORK, JANUARY 13, 1842.

"Among a multitude of other thoughts, thoughts of you have been busy with me since I left you, and I employ an early moment to tell you so. Almost my last occupation was with you, and in relation to two matters which are brimfull of interest. You may guess, but cannot know, what it is for a father to anticipate the near appearance of his son in the place of a minister; and your going so unexpectedly into King's Chapel makes me feel the reality as I hardly have done before. In the common eye, it is less than if you were going to *preach*,—but not in mine; it ought not to be in any one's; and I have been anxious that you should take care to make it a very real and substantial act of devotion, and so solemnize in a peculiar manner your first public ministry at the altar. Do not go 'to read prayers for Dr. Greenwood;' but go to offer a real sacrifice for yourself and the people, and make it a day of memorable religious worship to yourself. I shall think much of you;—may God be gracious to you."

"Of the other thing, too, of your sermon, I have been thinking. I am pleased with your wisdom in preaching from your own experience. In so doing, you are likely to strike the universal key of humanity, and thus call out a responsive note. I am greatly pleased, too, with the evident pains you have been willing to take; it gives promise and encouragement; and, if you will continue these two things,—*carefulness, and the practical use of your own self-knowledge*,—you may do a great deal to compensate for the disadvantage you were deploring the other night. No knowledge is so good for the minister, as that derived from self-study; many things have concurred to addict you to that, as I perceive; and you cannot pursue it without a reward, alike in personal improvement and in the power of affecting others." . . . . . .

"I trust and hope that you mean to be one of those wise and true men, who will make sermons a matter of self-application, and not think their work done when *others* apply them."

TO THE SAME.

"Framingham, October, 1842.

"I was very glad to get your letter, and wish I could meet you at Cambridge this week, to talk it over. Yet I am not sure that I could help you. Some things are very plain, some very perplexing; and nobody but yourself can strike the balance, so as to extricate the duty. If the duty were clear, I dare say you would have no hesitation. Now, to make out the duty, there seem to be these points to be considered.

"1. The great needs of the place.

"2. The strength and unanimity of their persuasion that you are the man they want; this fact must be ascertained clearly.

"3. Do other circumstances confirm or oppose their judgment in this thing?

"4. Is the case so strong, as to make it better for you to labor there, than to go on as you are doing?

' 5. Indeed, it is now a question to be decided, whether your improvement will be more consulted by continuing this attempt at solitary study, or by going into the midst of parish duties; and, if the latter, would it be better to assume a permanent charge, or to make experiment of a temporary engagement?

"I am much inclined to think, that you would now be a gainer by residence in a parish; it would present many forms of action to try and bring out advantageously your powers, as well as to make you feel that you are living to some use; but I should think a temporary engagement more advisable than a permanent one. Three or six months' residence at ——, if they would like it, might be well worth the while; it could be done in perfect consistency with your declining to be a candidate; it might end in your finding the place such a field as you would entirely prefer; it might end in a mutual conviction that it is not your post: at any rate, it would have the recommendation of showing, that you are perfectly disposed to meet all wishes, and have no merely selfish views. In a word, would not a few months so spent, there or elsewhere, be, on the whole, more satisfactory, than a continued residence at Cambridge; even for *study* would it not accomplish as much, might it not be as profitable for the society as a settlement, and still leave the settlement an open question? There is a great deal to be said and weighed, which I cannot hint at. In such cases one's mind settles by degrees, as time proceeds; and I dare say, that ten days on the spot will bring you to a conclusion, in which you will have no misgiving. Be candid, cautious, deliberate; throw aside personal preferences; and insist on making it a mere question of duty;—and may God lead and bless you.

"We had a most blessed time at Worcester; a happier, more hearty, more religious, and more improving season, could not be. Mr. Gannett's sermon threw a bright and glorious light about us, made a deep impression, and gave a most felicitous tone to the whole occasion. About sixty, clerical and lay, were present from abroad. Emotions were deep and fervent. The influence of Dr. Channing's recent death was evident. We all went home 'to thank God and take courage.'"

TO THE SAME.

(At Fall River.)

"FRAMINGHAM, DECEMBER 13, 1842.

"It seems to me, that, if I knew exactly where you are sitting, and what you are doing, and the shape and furniture of your apartment, I could more easily begin speaking to you. I seem now to be aiming at a nonentity, and talking to space; but, as you are somewhere, and 'Uncle Sam' knows how to get at you, I will make imagination do the work of knowledge, and feeling feel you out. About one thing I can make no mistake: the hours are long and solitary in that chamber of yours, and you sometimes get tired of your loneliness, and fall to reverie more than study. I remember my early days in Beverly, in Exeter, and even in Boston; and they were among the most wholesome, too, that I ever spent. Since then, I have had so much of the crowd and bustle of life, that I have been living on the nourishment I gained in those times of quiet self-companionship, as the bear lives in winter on the fat it laid up in summer; and I have become like the bear in spring, quite lean and destitute, needing the refreshment of another season to recruit my spiritual being. Now is your time for fattening, or more properly training, your soul, and for proving the truth of Paley's maxim, '*Live much alone.*' There is no such preparation for profitable living among men, as much living away from them. I am glad, for this, as well as for many other reasons, that you should have this winter's opportunity. It is shorter than Paul's three years in Arabia, but you will try to make it as valuable; and

I do not doubt you will aways look back on it, as containing many of your golden days.

"Two or three things let me hint to you. There is danger that you may over-use your eyes. Be careful and judicious; avoid too much night study; you can afford to do nothing by candle-light, if you use well your six hours of day-light. My early error in this respect has cost me very dear. Resist the tendency to non-activity of body. I spoke about it the other day; and, as I have suffered from this cause too, I am very anxious to save you from my error. Be as active as you have been. You may help your eyes, and your mind, essentially, by accustoming yourself to study, (that is, in thinking,) while taking your walks; and then you will avoid the feeling by which many excuse their neglect, the feeling that they are losing time. Ten minutes' study without book or pen, is worth as much as half an hour with them; and it adds to the exhilaration of a walk to be making orations meantime. I have been reading the lives of Richter and Wilberforce; and I am struck with the fact, that both loved to study in the open air, and to compose while walking, and recommend the practice. It is the habit of Dr. Beecher, and of Mr. Gannett, who thus prepare their unwritten addresses. This saves eyes and health, and disciplines the mind.

"This solitary winter may be invaluable, as helping to form the habit of making a reference to God in everything, and of living perpetually in religious communion;—the first, last, and chief thing, and yet that in which we are most of all apt to be remiss. It would be well worth six months' dwelling in a hermitage, like the old anchorites, if we could gain thereby the true life of God in our souls. Pray be wise enough not to throw away the advantages of this winter; when you have great help, too, in the fresh feeling of your newly-assumed responsibilities.

"We are all as well as usual; the children greatly enjoying the snow, and very busy in their studies. We are quite by ourselves, and learning to be systematic. My study hours accomplish little; I have very little power of application, and grow more and more sensible that I am becoming good for nothing. Perhaps it is doubtful whether I shall ever rally to any good effect. The recent kindness of my friends, in making provision for future days, is inexpressibly comforting to me, as I can live or die without any worldly anxiety on my mind. I hope and trust. All good be yours."

TO THE REV. RICHARD L. CARPENTER.

"FRAMINGHAM, DECEMBER 28, 1842.

"MY DEAR SIR,

"I have just had the pleasure of receiving the letters of yourself and your sisters, by Miss H——, (whom I have not seen, being twenty miles from Boston, in this my hermitage.) I beg you to give to them my heartiest thanks, and assure them that the satisfaction, which their friendly remembrance gives me, shall be made known to them under my proper hand and seal. By the present opportunity I must content myself with hastily acknowledging your kindness in writing to me. It has delightfully brought to me the image of your father, and makes me feel, that, even on this side the Jordan, I shall not be wholly separated from him. May you live to be what he was, and to supply all his places. Since I saw him, what a change in the circle that he and I loved! Himself, Channing, Tuckerman, Worcester, Follen, gone to the land of souls! How is their place to be filled? I do not know how it may be on your side of the sea; but here, I look about me, and see among our younger brethren many spirits worthy to follow such fathers, and gloriously preparing to carry on their work. Great activity of soul there is, and great eagerness; some restlessness, some folly of speculation; but there is also great soundness, steadfastness, and *true progress*, which it would rejoice you to witness, and which give assurance of increasing day.

"We, perhaps, never had a heartier confidence in the stability of our congregations than at this time; there is a development of personal religion and strong spiritual life, which is most truly comforting.

"I am mortified, that, after taking great pains to prevent it, I cannot succeed in hindering the Post-Office from laying its all-grasping hands on my packages. I have almost done sending anything to my friends. I think that some of my father's Dissertations will gratify you; though, as you observe, their subjects are of the elementary and familiar kind. He is seventy-eight years old, very nearly blind, somewhat deaf, subject, therefore, to great trial and infirmity; but, withal, greatly happy in a Christian's hopes, and with domestic blessings unusual. A numerous family settled all around him; two sons, one grand-son, and three sons-in-law, engaged in the ministry within a few miles. That grand-son is my oldest boy. How I should like, if it were possible, that he, and you, and your brother, should meet and know each other. Perhaps it may be. One of you may come hither; he may go to England; anything is possible, and anything may be hoped. Let us hope it.

"You kindly speak of my health. I have but a broken constitution, I fear. I have not preached for eleven months. I have retired into absolute rest at this village, and am, I think, recruiting. I hope to begin to write again in the spring. The College treated me with the greatest generosity, and enabled me, with the help of some admirable friends, to live on for a season in idleness. They have relieved me from all anxiety about my family's support; and, if perfect restoration is possible, have given me the opportunity. God bless them for their love!"

TO AN AGED RELATIVE.

"FRAMINGHAM, DECEMBER 20, 1842.

"We, in this our banishment, are in good condition, and enjoy ourselves. I believe that all but my own personal self have grown fat; we certainly are very happy here, though I do not become stout and hearty. When last at Cambridge, we heard of aunt S——'s visit, and could not but regret we were not there to take part in the pleasure. Having once left the old home in this way, we shall hope that we may see her under our roof as soon as we have a roof within reasonable reach of you. When and where that will be, God only knows No persons live in a state of greater uncertainty than we do. We are most strictly pilgrims and strangers now; and we have constant admonitions that the world is fast passing away and we growing old. How many of the family have come to such a length of years, that they stand on the borders of the region of perpetual youth, and must ere long exchange gray hairs and feeble limbs, for everlasting smiles, and vigor that cannot die. Father evidently fails, and may leave us at any time. Without sight, and with imperfect hearing, life would soon become a burden, if lengthened out."

TO THE REV. C. BRIGGS.

"FEBRUARY 17, 1843.

"I cannot express how unhappy your letter makes me. God knows I long to be at work, and should count it a great privilege to be put into such a field as Albany presents. And to be obliged to decline it, makes my spirit sink. I almost fear that I am never to be allowed to labor in the good work again. I have been in a very poor state for two months past, and the doctor says I must not hope to preach for an indefinite time; he even hints at *years* of comparative or absolute silence. What can I do? I hope to have faith and patience; but you see I cannot go to Albany. I have been recruiting during the last fortnight, and hope to revive with the spring. Blessings on you and your fellow-laborers."

TO MRS. FARRAR.

"FRAMINGHAM, JANUARY 14, 1843.

"MY DEAR MRS. FARRAR,

"Mary produces for me, from her bundle, a luxurious show of morocco and fur, into which she says I am requested to thrust my two lower extremities, that I may be as warm-footed as my friends are warm-hearted. On trial of their commodiousness, I pronounce them to be as snug as they are comfortable,—fitting close without pinching,—and prompting the wish (a New Year's wish) that the provider of them may, from the sole of the foot to the soul of the body, be enwrapt and defended in an equally pleasant and sufficient protection from all evil.

"It is sad to have no better tidings of Mr. Farrar's welfare. I feel almost a well man in my forlornest moments, when I think of his afflictions, and perhaps I sympathize with him, and think of him, all the more deeply and often, for imagining in those dreary moments that I may be following hard after him. At any rate, my best wishes and heartiest respects attend him. 'Sorrow may endure for a night, but joy cometh in the morning.'

"His and your proposal, that we should share the last resting-place together, is a most grateful one to me. I receive it with thanks and pleasure. You do not know, and he does not know, that I have some very peculiar recollections and associations, which make my whole feelings towards him peculiar. He did me two kindnesses in College,—slight to him, who was always doing kindness,—probably forgotten as soon as done,—but to me great, and leaving an ineffaceable impression; and his image has always been connected with them to the present day. I have a special happiness in having been cast so much with him on that account, and in finding him and his so thinking of me and mine, as to connect us in his arrangements when thinking of the great transition from world to world. I used to think I should never care at all where my bones should rest; and in one view I do not. But, as I draw nearer to the hour, I feel my heart fluttering at the thought of reposing by those whom I honor and love; and there is a certain satisfaction in the anticipation of a common and united repose. You will, therefore, make him understand how kindly we take this proof of his and your regard, and connect it, in our own thoughts, with that future rising which shall restore and reëstablish our friendship, where there will be no bodies to clog our full enjoyment, and make love anxious, as it is here.

"With hearty respect and love to you both,

"Very truly,

"H. Ware, Jr'

CHAPTER XXII.

VISIT TO BOSTON—REPEATED ATTACKS OF ILLNESS THERE—HE RETURNS TO FRAMINGHAM—JOURNEY TO PLYMOUTH, FALL RIVER, AND PROVIDENCE—IMPROVEMENT AFTER HIS RETURN HOME—IS SEIZED WITH APOPLEXY—HIS CONDITION AFTER THIS ATTACK—DEATH—FUNERAL.

1843. ÆT. 48-49.

In the latter part of January, 1843, soon after a short visit to Boston, he addressed the following letter to the writer of this Memoir.

"Framingham, January 28, 1843.

"My dear John,

"I left you suddenly and partly by compulsion, for I had determined to stay another day. I greatly wished more elucidation and direct advice. I have got to a time of life when this persevering ill-behavior of my body looks to me as an affair of growing seriousness, and it becomes a sober man to take observation of his whereabouts and his progress. I see that I have been foolish in some of my self-regulations, and am not to wonder if I pay the penalty. If I can retrieve what I have lost in any good degree, I ought to do so, and I wish to know how. I know much from my own experience, and shall guide myself by that; but I must have some light from the observation and wisdom of others. And as, in the uncertainties of life, a man should be equally ready for all things, and have the equanimity to meet every change cheerfully, and as this cannot be done unless he knows when severe change is approaching, and as the greatest change sometimes comes insidiously and without warning, so that a man falls over the precipice without being aware of his nearness to it; I want to ask you to deal very honestly with me, and, as soon as you are sure,—whether it be this year or thirty hence,—as soon as you are sure, that, by slow degrees or rapid, my life is coming to its end, you will tell me so. I covet the privilege of going home with my eyes open, and in a quiet state of conscious preparation, if it may be. I do not want to live weeks and days in a state of mere suspense, which tortures and afflicts without doing any good. Let me, if I am to have the languors of protracted debility, or the pains of acute disease, let me have with them the knowledge that I am approaching my end, and in sight of a world where I shall have no pain or languor, and so be enabled to bear the burden by the power of those elevating thoughts. I have got rid, through the kindness of excellent friends, of all distressful anxiety for the living of my family; I can leave them in comparative peace; in that sense, my house is set in order. I want now to be secured against the possibility of so great a misfortune as that of dying without the chance of a tranquil preparation of mind and feeling. I wish to be assured of early plain dealing, and I beg you will not refuse it to me. I am using too many words I see. It seems to me among the probabilities of which I should rationally and religiously take cognizance, that my system may run down without another reaction; it has been so with others,—it must be so with me sooner or later; why not now? and what a fool should I be, not to acknowledge it. But I also see, that there are many grounds for thinking, that it may revive, and that it may run on to a good old age. I want to do my duty, and be equally ready for either event. If you can aid me, do; and Mary and I will do our part.

"I still suffer oppression from all I eat, and a considerable sense of weakness. My nights are better; my days languid; and sometimes I fight against depression in vain. I shall be down again, I think, in a few days; for I think the jaunt was of service to me; and I want to do some things, which I had no time for. Till then, good-bye. Special love to Helen."

This letter, it is hoped, was answered in a spirit as sincere as that in which it was written. It was thought desirable for him to spend some time in the beginning of the spring in Boston, where the opportunities of out-door exercise are better than in the country; and, accordingly, after some delays, he came to my house on Thursday, March 30th. For a few days after his arrival, he seemed cheerful, was excited by new objects, and conversed with interest and animation. He went abroad and visited a number of his friends, and wrote a number of letters, among which was the following, addressed to a young friend abroad, engaged in study for the ministry. It is interesting, as exhibiting almost the last workings of his mind on the great themes, that so constantly occupied his thoughts, whilst the blow that was to prostrate him was even then ready to fall.

"Boston, April 1, 1843.

"I am glad to have a chance to write to you so directly, for there seems a natural propriety in our having some intercourse with each other; and it is strange, that you should have left home without my having arranged a correspondence with you. But in truth I have been too ill to be anything but selfish; and during the whole season I have had the miserable necessity of caring so much for myself, as to have little disposition to care for others. I am living very retired in Framingham, able to do and enjoy hardly anything, and my prospects for the future are very uncertain. A hard and savage winter has confined me; spring does not yet open; the country is covered with deep snow and ice; a heavy snow-storm last night. I am in Boston for a few days to consult my brother, the doctor; and, while so near the steamer, I feel near to you; therefore, I fulfil a long intention, which I have not had *spunk* for a few weeks past to execute, of sending you one word of old good-will and friendship. It was some time after ——— had received your letter of I forget what date, before I saw it; and some weeks have passed since I saw it, and should have followed my impulse to write at the moment. I hope and trust, that in the mean-time you have worked yourself into clearer light and a more settled feeling. Only time, reflection, self-study, and devotion can do any good to the dissatisfaction of heart which you describe. Counsel from a friend can do no good, except so far as the expression of sympathy does good, and words of encouragement. I can pretend to offer you nothing else.

"You want to feel, I think, that such experiences are not singular or very unusual; that men of thoughtful minds and sensitive hearts are apt to pass through such trials in the great effort to form their characters by the exalted standard which they see before them. A tremendous struggle it is, between early habits of thought and life which tend to keep a man down, and the riper aspirations which invite a man up; how justly described in Paul's account of the conflict between the flesh and the spirit; and only to be brought to a successful issue in the way that he prescribes, namely, an absolute and total surrender to the law of Christ. Nothing else can deliver him from the body of such a death. I suppose, that, in your case, the difficulties are greatly increased by the nature of the studies and speculations in which you have been fond of indulging. You have been hunting after wisdom in all the various departments of human philosophy, and the guesses of men, who lean on their own understanding, and think themselves competent to understand all mysteries and all knowledge. You have thus been led away from the infallible guide, from the true light; and now find yourself in uncertainty and discontent;

with an enlightened mind, but an unsettled heart; without assurance, calmness, and peace; ever learning, but not come to the knowledge of truth. You have gone hither and thither, following the vagaries of human wisdom; and I suppose you can find no rest to your soul, till you fling yourself with perfect simplicity and confiding, childlike, docility on the word of divine revelation. 'Lord, to whom shall I go? Thou hast the words of eternal life.' I feel sure, that, if you would escape out of the gulf in which you describe yourself as being, and arrive at substantial peace and self-satisfaction, there is no way but this; 'the peace and joy of believing.' I cannot but hope that you have already found it so. Cut yourself off from those secondary masters, who are fumbling about in the chaos of human opinions and uncertain conjectures, and take no master but Christ; you will find, that, weary and heavy laden as you may be, he will give rest to your soul.

"The greatest misfortune of this time, the greatest drawback to individual growth and social spiritual progress, I fear, is the substitution of Philosophy for Christianity, of Speculation for Faith; and I really have no wish for you, as a man and a minister, except that you may be heartily persuaded of this, and do accordingly. If you will, I venture to promise you a perfect deliverance from the evils you deplore. May God guide and bless you in the great work.

"I should be very glad to have a letter from you; the fuller the better. Let me know all about you. I do not hope to aid you essentially; but I should like to do anything that may have any, the least prospect of securing to you a true peace, and to the church an efficient servant."

On Sunday, he visited in the morning his old place of worship in Hanover Street, a privilege he never felt willing to deny himself except when absolutely necessary; but, in the afternoon, not being able to walk so far a second time, he attended service at the church in

Bowdoin Street. He appeared, on the whole, during the first days of his visit, better than had been anticipated; yet still his condition was most unpromising. He labored constantly under a sense of overpowering exhaustion. His weakness was such, that it was quite a painful effort for him to go up stairs to his chamber; his appetite was poor, and he was oppressed by his food. Some changes were made in his diet, and some remedies were administered; but he passed the week very poorly, and, for the last few days, did not come down stairs, and sat up but a small part of the time.

On Monday, April 10th, he was well enough to come down to breakfast, but was soon obliged to return to his chamber from increasing indisposition. Still, so far, no symptoms had occurred differing from those to which he was accustomed. In the afternoon, appearing somewhat better, he was left for a short time with one of his daughters only in the room. He soon spoke of feeling more unwell, described his sensations as those probably of approaching paralysis, and, anticipating speedy unconsciousness, desired the little girl to repeat carefully all he had said to her mother, should he not be able to do so upon her return. He did not, however, lose his consciousness, but, when the sensation he had experienced,—a numbness,—had subsided, went quietly to sleep. Upon awaking he remembered all that had passed, and gave a distinct account of it, but soon manifested some wandering of mind, and incoherency of language. Remedies were about being administered, when he was seized with a general convulsion, accompanied by entire unconsciousness. The convulsion subsided in a very few moments, but left him in a state of complete insensibility, with an apoplectic aspect and respiration. Dr. Jackson saw him in a very few moments after his seizure; but his situation was apparently one which did not admit of any remedy, and for some time it appeared probable, that the attack would prove speedily fatal.

In a short time, however, there was a slight, though very imperfect, return of consciousness and of the power of speaking, but not with any coherency; there was no proper restoration of mind. He slept a good deal, and, except that his sleep was accompanied by frequent moaning, the latter part of the night seemed to have been passed pretty comfortably. In the morning he was much restored, and his mind gradually cleared up. He was exceedingly prostrated by the attack, but it left behind fewer other ill consequences than were to have been expected. He improved very slowly in appetite, power of digestion, and strength; still he did improve, and, after a few weeks, was able to be got down stairs, and to ride abroad in a carriage. He was able also to see some company, to read a little, and to hear reading. On the 6th of May, he was seized, in a manner differing from any preceding illness, with an inflammatory affection within the abdomen, accompanied by hemorrhage and a great deal of pain, and followed by excessive prostration. For several days his symptoms were very alarming, and his disease threatened seriously to have an unfavorable termination. Gradually, however, he again rallied; his case seemed much more favorable than for some months before; and, although the loss of strength and flesh had been great, yet there was an improvement in his aspect, his spirits, and his hopes, and an appearance of elasticity and reaction in his system, which had not been anticipated.

He was confined by these two attacks for the greater part of ten weeks, and was not able to leave Boston till the 5th of June. During this period, his son, who had completed his studies the preceding summer, and had received an invitation to settle over a parish at Fall River, was ordained. It had been a fond anticipation, that he would gather strength enough to preach on this occasion; and, when satisfied that this was unlikely, he trusted he might find himself able to give the Charge; and, to the last, he clung to the hope, that he should at least recover sufficiently to be present. But one by one, very reluctantly, he was forced to relinquish the expectations he had cherished, of assisting in the consecration of his son to a work for which he had labored and sacrificed so much himself.

While thus confined to his chamber, he manifested the eagerness for occupation always characteristic of him. He wrote a good many letters, to some of which, addressed to correspondents in Europe, he received answers before leaving his room. He became particularly interested in the subject of music, and procured several works relating to it, which he studied with much satisfaction. His attention was excited also by all the prominent topics of the day; and especially by those which were discussed at the various meetings of the Anniversary week in May, many of the debates being of a very animated character, especially on the subject of Slavery. But the principal subject of his thoughts was a project, which he had entertained for some time, of becoming the Editor of "The Christian Examiner," and devoting himself for the future entirely to its management. This plan occupied his chief attention during the remainder of his life. He had hoped, from time to time, that he should be sufficiently restored to take charge of some small country parish, where the labor would be light, and the demands on his time inconsiderable. He had even fixed his eye upon a vacant place, to which he thought he might be competent. But the occupation of an Editor seemed, upon the whole, better suited to his probable condition, and was quite agreeable to his taste. "The Christian Examiner," as has been seen, had been formerly under his care, under the name of "The Christian Disciple," and had been ever since the principal, though not the accredited, organ of Unitarianism in the United States. For the few preceding years, it had been in the hands of his brother William, who now wished to relinquish it. In January, he had written to him thus:

"January 6, 1843.

"I am more and more inclined to take the work. I feel greater uncertainty about my ability to undertake a parish. My liability to ill turns would make the regular preaching almost impossible, and I should have to lie abed Sunday and yet be out Monday, and make terrible havoc, &c. So I think my best way will be to edit, and to preach occasionally. I hope not, for a parish is my heart's desire. But, *what we can, not what we would.* I have been for three weeks very second-best;—as near good for nothing as walking man can be. Somewhat better now. One reason for seeking 'The Examiner,' is, that I have on hand a great quantity of material, half-prepared, which I could work out to great advantage."

As it became desirable now, that some definite arrangement should be made concerning the work, he entered upon the matter with even more than his usual earnestness, and laid out quite an extensive plan of operations. His intention was to devote himself exclusively to this object. He proposed to unite in support of the work all the talent of the denomination, and to use vigorous means to secure it a very extensive circulation in all parts of the country. It was his purpose to give to it a high practical and devotional character, as well as to make it an organ for the defence of what he believed to be the truth concerning the doctrines of Christianity. It was his hope, also, as a result of an extensive circulation, to make it profitable in a pecuniary way, and to devote the whole income, beyond his own support, to the various important objects in which he was interested. In speaking of his intentions and views to the publishers of the work, he expresses himself thus at different times.

"*June* 7.—I wish it to be understood, that I undertake 'The Examiner' for the sake of the public cause, and with a view to do the utmost possible for the cause. On this account I shall think it a duty to make the best possible arrangement, so that the profits may go to the work and not to the Agents. Therefore, I shall feel bound to take up with the most advantageous offer; and I cannot in any degree feel myself bound to keep the work in your hands, if I can do more profitably elsewhere."

"*June* 27.—I explained to you my general design, and you know it to be my purpose to make the work, as far as possible, a great public instrument of spreading truth; and you are aware, that, in order to accomplish this design, it will be necessary to make the expenses of the work as small as possible, that its receipts may be as large as possible."

In pursuance of this design, he occupied himself a good deal of the time in various preparations for the management of the work. He laid out subjects which he wished to have treated; looked around for persons to be engaged as contributors, planned various modes of operation, and devised means for raising its character and extending its influence. Being in the city, and in an apparently prosperous state of convalescence during the week of the Anniversaries, he was in a very animated and excited state of mind on this subject, and conversed with several of his brethren concerning it. He also communicated his intentions and plans to the Berry Street Conference of Unitarian Ministers, who were holding their annual session, and by them they were favorably received. He met with encouragement in all quarters, and he was filled with hope, and indulged in ardent anticipations of still continued usefulness in this field.

There was unquestionably at this time something morbid in the state of his mind. He exhibited an almost delirious restlessness and eagerness of purpose, an over-sanguine estimate of his means and prospects. Still, his faculties were rather unbalanced, than overthrown. His mind seemed generally to act with its usual correctness, and, in ordinary conversation on common topics, little would have been noticed different from his usual manner. Even on this subject, with regard to which he was so much excited, his views were in the main sound and judicious, though on some points, and at some times, extravagant and wanting in that calm and subdued judgment, which usually distinguished him. But, if he indulged in some delusion, it was happy for him that he did. It prevented him from feeling, that he was condemned to spend the remainder of his days in inaction, a useless member of society. He continued to dwell upon this object and even to labor for it, as long as he lived; and the contemplation of it contributed not a little to vary with pleasant and hopeful thoughts the heavy and wearisome hours, through which he was still to pass before he arrived at his journey's end.

It is a painful characteristic of the disease, which was slowly invading his life, that it not only may lay in ruins the intellect of the unhappy subject of it, but often prostrates also the power of moral control. There is hardly a more trying and humiliating spectacle, than that of an individual whom we have been accustomed to revere for high qualities and capacities, reduced to a condition of imbecility of mind; wayward, irritable, perverse, or even idiotic;—to see the gentle become violent; the forbearing and considerate, unreasonable and capricious; and the calm and mild indulge in the most violent passions. Happily his friends were spared the worst part of such a trial. The effects of his malady were sometimes apparent in the operations of his mind; and for many months it rendered necessary a hard and sometimes an unsuccessful struggle to preserve that kindness and gentleness of feeling, and that placid, forbearing manner, which were so eminently his. But he never fell into that wretched condition, in which there is no struggle to maintain moral control, because the perception of moral relations is lost. Disease with him never even approached this dreadful extremity. To use the beautiful and expressive words of one whom I have already quoted: "It touched, but without rudeness, the springs of his intellectual life. It disturbed, but without violence, the fountain of his affections, the Siloam which had healed and blessed so many. But, disturbed as it was, the fountain flowed and sparkled still, for those who waited at its brink." *

The improvement, which, as has been said, took place after his last attack, went only to a certain point; his condition soon became at best stationary; and, in the beginning of June, weak and emaciated, impatient of a longer absence from home, and with the restlessness of body and mind belonging to his state, he left Boston on his way to Framingham. On Monday, June 5th, he went to Cambridge, and passed there some days. His father was at this time beginning to exhibit, as it has since proved, the early symptoms of the same disease which was bringing to its close the life of the son. Still, notwithstanding the infirmities of mind and body under which they both labored, they enjoyed some periods of most satisfactory and comforting intercourse. On Thursday afternoon, June 8th, he went as far as the house of his sister, Mrs. Edward Warren, in Newton, where he spent the night, and reached Framingham the next afternoon. In recording in his journal, which now contained little more than dates, his arrival home, he adds, as indicative of his heartfelt satisfaction at the event, his usual exclamation, "Laus Deo!" and this, except one or two unimportant remarks concerning the weather, was the last entry he ever made.

But the same uneasiness of body and restlessness of mind, that rendered him impatient of absence while abroad, rendered him equally impatient for some farther change when he was at home. His system was in that peculiar state of constant irritation from the malady within, which deludes its victim into the hope that his sufferings are owing to circumstances without, and

* Sermon of the Rev. Chandler Robbins.

leads him to expect in constant change, the relief which still flies from him as he seems to approach it. While in Boston, he had projected, when his strength should be sufficiently restored, a journey to Fall River on a visit to his son; and, though really incompetent to such an undertaking, he was not willing to defer it. Accordingly on the next Thursday after his return, June 15th, he set out in his carryall, accompanied by his wife, on this expedition. Journeying by short stages, he reached Plymouth on Saturday night. Here he was very unwell, and remained till the next Thursday, at the house of the Rev. Henry Edes, whose wife, for whom he had a great regard, had been one of the young women of his parish in Boston. On Friday he renewed the attempt to proceed, and went as far as Middleborough. While at this place, on endeavoring to step into a door a little more elevated than common, he failed from great weakness, fell helplessly backward, and struck the lower part of the spine with much violence against the ground. The blow was a severe one, and not only jarred his whole frame a good deal at the time, but left effects from which he suffered considerably afterward. He was, however, well enough the next day to resume his journey, and reached Fall River on Saturday night. He remained here till the Monday following, when, accompanied by his son, who was himself somewhat out of health, he went as far as Providence, to the house of his brother-in-law, the Rev. Edward B. Hall. Here his son became so much more unwell, that it was necessary they should hasten home; and, giving up their own conveyance, they took the railroad, and arrived at Framingham on Friday afternoon, the 23d of June.

He was not in a condition of body, during this excursion, to endure anything with tranquillity, nor in a frame of mind to derive enjoyment from those sources, which had always before served to render travelling very delightful. It was therefore neither a pleasure nor a benefit to him, whilst it was painful to the friends who accompanied him and those whom he visited. The same state of things remained for a while after his return; and he continued to experience some pain and difficulty of motion from his fall, but nothing worse. In no very long time, however, a very marked improvement took place in several respects, especially in the state of his mind; an improvement, of which he was himself sensible, as he had been keenly so of his preceding condition; and he spoke of it with heartfelt gratitude. It was in this state of comparative improvement, that I passed part of a day and night at his house in the beginning of August. The change that had taken place surprised and delighted me. He was tranquil and cheerful, entered with his usual animation into the common subjects of conversation, spoke of his plans for future occupation and usefulness, of the progress made in the arrangements for his taking charge of "The Examiner," and talked, with a good deal of interest, of a journey I was about to make through the interior of the State of New York, which he had several times visited, and under circumstances that had left a strong impression upon him. He spoke also, with much feeling, of the change in his condition, and of the great satisfaction it gave him. In the afternoon we drove for some miles around the neighborhood of his residence. He seemed to enjoy it much, and to be as much alive as ever to the beauties of the season and the scene. So striking was all this, that, notwithstanding his almost shadowy form, his thin and pale countenance, and tottering steps, it was hardly possible not to hope against experience, and anticipate greater changes, of which these were but the forerunners. Though such hopes were vain, there was yet to his friends much consolation in this short respite. It almost seems, on looking back, as if a veil, which disease had hung over his spirit, had been lifted up for a short period before the shadow of death settled upon it, that our last recollections might present him to us with all the endearing associations of his better days.

It was the last day of this interval of relief. His state afterward was one of great prostration; but there was no depression of spirits, and no return of that nervous irritability from which he had suffered so much. On Thursday, August 10th, though very languid, and doubtful of his ability to go so far, he went to Northborough, about ten miles distant, accompanied by his eldest daughter, driving himself in a carryall. He was refreshed by his ride, "feeling better every mile," as he said; and spent the day there, returning at night. As he was coming home, it rained heavily; he was obliged to get out on the way to adjust his harness, and thus became somewhat wet, but suffered no immediate inconvenience from it. The next day he was weary, felt very ill, and passed most of the time upon his bed. On the 12th, he revived a little, walked and rode, but was not able on the 13th, it being Sunday, to attend public worship as he had wished. On Monday, the 14th, he felt more bright, and passed a pleasant hour with his friend, the Rev. S. K. Lothrop, who paid him a visit. About one in the afternoon, while the family were at dinner, he lay on the sofa in an adjoining room, having just taken a little food himself. He called his wife to him from the table, and said that he felt very strangely,—that he believed he was going; but immediately added, as if to prevent unnecessary alarm, "not going to die, but to faint, I believe." He had at the same time a flush upon his countenance, and something like a convulsion; but this was only momentary, and he did not lose his consciousness. He closed his eyes, and never again opened them voluntarily.

So utter a prostration followed immediately on this attack, that he was not removed from the room in which he was seized. A bed was brought down into it, and from this he never rose again. He was faithfully and kindly attended, during his illness, by Dr. Whitney of Framingham; but his condition was now evidently such, that there was no longer the hope of even postponing the fatal event. For some days after the attack, he was extremely restless and apparently uneasy, rolling constantly from side to side, and frequently moaning aloud; yet, when asked of his sensations, he complained of little else than a feeling of excessive weariness. After the subsidence of this symptom, he lay for the most part in a state, apparently, of imperfect sleep. But from this he was easily roused, and was capable of attending to, and of understanding, what was going on around him. He knew perfectly well those who visited him, spoke to them, listened attentively to what was said, and often signified his attention or his assent, when incapable of the exertion of answering. He was, from the first, perfectly aware of his situation, as one that precluded all hope; he resigned himself to it at once,—not, obviously, from that feeling of indifference to the event, which is the result of long suffering, and of an insensibility growing out of an oppressed condition of the physical frame, but from that profound sense of the duty of entire submission to the will of God, which he had always cultivated, and always endeavored to exhibit, in circumstances of trial, danger, and sorrow. When once convinced that the time of his departure was at hand, he gave himself up entirely. There was no misgiving, no looking back to the world, as if he desired still to linger there. He, as it were, pressed earnestly forward,—not, as in times past, regretting the fields of labor he had left, and longing to be again engaged in his work; but, contented with his condition, his mind dwelt now almost exclusively on the world to which he was hastening.

As he lay on his bed, with his eyes closed, and with no manifestation of sensibility except an occasional tossing of the limbs, or change of posture, or audible moaning, he would have seemed asleep, or in a state too nearly approaching it to be conscious of trains of thought. But it was found, that at these times he was often occupied in active contemplations. "My mind," he would say, "is crowded with thoughts, precious thoughts of death and immortality." His mind occasionally wandered, and yet he could at no time be regarded as properly delirious. He sometimes fancied himself in another place, and could not reconcile together all the circumstances of time, place, and persons, of which his senses informed him. But there was no considerable or permanent aberration on any important particular.

He had interviews with many of his friends and relatives during the weeks which intervened before his decease, and with some of them he was able to converse with freedom and clearness. To his brother Allen, a few days before his death, he said: "My life has been singularly blessed. My success has been beyond my brightest hopes. But my work is done. I am going. It is all right. All is well." His friend Mr. Gannett, who also visited him, has given the following account of his interview. "Not a great while before brother Ware was taken away, I visited him in his sick chamber, not expecting that he would know me, but to my great surprise and delight, he raised his hand to take mine, with his eyes open, and said, in a distinct voice,—'I am glad to see your face in the flesh once more.' He spoke of the goodness of God, and the many mercies which he had enjoyed; alluded to his departure, but said he should be still with us; he 'could not believe that the church above and the church below were separated.' He spoke of his weariness, but said it was only weariness of the body. He spoke again of his connexion hereafter with us and our interests,—and, lifting up his hand and arm, said, 'It is only these inferior instruments that the separation affects.' I finally took leave of him; but when I reached the door, he called me back and said with inexpressible interest;—'Farewell. Peace and love to the brethren.'"

But generally, on occasion of these visits, he took no special notice, unless he was roused and his attention was directly called for. He then welcomed his friends, and seemed obviously to have been aware of, and pleased with, their presence, but too much overwhelmed by a sense of exhaustion to make the exertion to speak. Commonly he spoke as if it were a very great effort; but, when the effort had been once made, he would sometimes continue to talk on with considerable ease To one of his family, who asked him how he felt, he answered, "Quiet, contented, and happy." At another time, when he seemed as tranquil and easy as a sleeping child, he replied, "Very well, only so tired!" every word and motion indicating this feeling to be predominant. He inquired after his father, who had been seriously ill; it was announced that he was better. "He will follow on very soon," said he, and then expressed surprise that it had not been all over with himself before now. At another time, a fortnight before his death, during a visit from the same relative, he talked freely, spontaneously, and with less effort than ever before. Now and then he lost a word or a thought, but, on the whole, was bright and intelligent. His mind ran back to the peculiar circumstances of their long and intimate connexion through life. He expressed a strong wish, that he could bring all these circumstances together into a small compass, so that he might view them at once. Alluding to his own approaching death, which he often spoke of, and always as of an event which was certain to take place in a very short time, he said, that "this was a period when there were many reasons why one would not wish to leave the world, because there were so many things in progress, in which he was interested, and could desire to see the result of." It was said in reply, that at no time probably would this be otherwise, since there would be always new projects in existence for the improvement and happiness of mankind. "Yes," he said, "I suppose that it is so;" and then fell away without further remark.

But, even when his mind seemed to be most distinctly verging on delirium, the predominant character and tendency of his thoughts were for the most part the same. They dwelt upon his condition, his approaching change, his faith, his Saviour. On one occasion, he seemed to fancy himself to be about to administer the Communion. He called all his family about him, and spoke to them in words like those with which he was accustomed to address his own flock on such an occasion; and to those around he seemed as earnest, as collected, as devout, as when in the days of health he had actually stood at the altar of his church. "Warm and elevated expressions of gratitude to the Saviour, intermingled with affectionate addresses and counsels to his family, fell from his lips. His thoughts turned to the closing hours and acts of the Master whom he loved; and, speaking of the design of Jesus in instituting the Last Supper, as if inspired by the very spirit of his own boundless benevolence, he stretched out his feeble arms, saying, 'He intended it for all; he would gather all to his embrace.'" *

But his state, during the weeks of this confinement, was far from uniform. He seemed to have, in the course of them, two or three separate attacks of the same nature as the first, but less severe. These were severally followed by an aggravation of his symptoms, and, at some times, he exhibited signs of a paralysis of the left side of the body; but this was not complete or continued. In the intervals of these attacks he rallied, and took more notice, and exertion was less burdensome; he was able to take more food, and that even with some relish.

In the afternoon of Thursday, September 21st, he had in this way revived somewhat, and had taken consid-

* Sermon by the Rev. Chandler Robbins.

erable notice of what was passing. He asked his wife to read to him. His children had been on a visit to Cambridge, and had just returned. He spoke to them all, and asked how they had enjoyed themselves. He seemed pleased with their being in the room, and particularly noticed the buoyant spirits and happy playfulness of the youngest, a little boy about three years old. A few moments afterward his wife began to feed him with a peach. She had but just given him a piece of it, when she observed that he suddenly thrust the thumb of his right hand into his mouth in a very peculiar manner. She, supposing that there was something there which gave him inconvenience, took hold of his hand, asking him if it was so. He did not answer her inquiry, but said distinctly, though in a low tone, "I am losing all control of myself." There was a spasmodic movement of the hand, a slight convulsion of his whole body, and he was instantly insensible. His eyes closed, a profuse perspiration covered him, and he lost immediately the power of swallowing. For a few hours his breathing was as gentle as an infant's; in the course of the night it became somewhat laborious; but, at last, tranquilly and quietly as he had lived, without further convulsion or struggle, at half past six in the morning he "passed on." *

Late on Sunday evening, his body arrived at the house of his father in Cambridge, being conveyed from Framingham in his own carryall by his wife and son.

* It was said in one of the numerous notices of this event from the pulpits of his brethren in the ministry:—"It is the language of a gifted lady, who has just written to us, '*I see, Henry Ware has passed on.*' Passed on! Beautiful thought. He has not stopped, he has not ceased to be, he has passed on, in faith, and duty, and love, to higher labors and undefiled reward."—*MS. of the Rev. E. B. Hall.*

The funeral took place on the afternoon of the next day, September 25th, from the College Chapel. It was attended by the government and members of the University, and by many of his friends and former parishioners from Boston. The services were performed by the Rev. Dr. Parkman, his tried friend and former associate in the ministry, and by the Rev. Drs. Francis, his successor, and Noyes, his colleague, in the Theological School. The choir of the Chapel chanted the twenty-third Psalm, which he had asked to have read to him a few days before his death, and which was the last passage of Scripture to which he listened.

His remains were followed to Mount Auburn, and deposited in a sepulchre which had been presented to him by his friend, Professor Farrar, of which he was the first tenant. Here, just at the edge of evening, in the midst of a gentle shower, whilst the falling of a few of the leaves of early autumn was in solemn keeping with the melancholy ceremony, was left his weary and wasted form. He had grown old and died before his prime, worn down by those exertions, both of body and mind, which had been directed for thirty years to a single great object, an object to which he had devoted his whole spirit, with a constancy which knew no repose, till he was laid, like his Master, in this new tomb "wherein never man before was laid." But of the grief, the sense of loss, which must always attend such a separation, there could in no case be more satisfactory consolations. His life had been a pure, an active, a useful, and a happy one. There was as little in it for his friends to look back upon with regret, as is compatible with the necessary imperfections of the human character and condition; whilst there was much, very much, that could be contemplated only with, we will not say pride, but a sentiment of a higher and nobler sort. All the success which he wished, or was capable of enjoying, he had attained. He had striven unceasingly, and not in vain, in the only paths in which he desired to walk. He had enjoyed and he had suffered much. He had received multiplied favors from his fellow-men, and choicest blessings from Heaven. Gratitude to God and men was among the most cherished of his feelings. He had been tried by repeated afflictions, and by wasting, protracted, and painful disease. But he had submitted with patience and without repining. They had not dimmed the brightness of his hope, nor ever made him waver in his faith. He had always lived in the near expectation of death, and, when at last it came, he met it with unfaltering trust.

CHAPTER XXIII.

NOTICES OF HIS CHARACTER.

I DO not know that it is necessary to add anything to the foregoing pages, by way of further illustration of the life and character of the subject of this narrative. I have endeavored, as far as possible, to convey his history in his own words, and to display the qualities of his mind and heart by the unstudied expression of them which is contained in his own writings. Still there are some things, which, I feel, may be interesting to those who knew him; partly the result of my own recollections and impressions, and partly the expression of the recollections and impressions of others.

Those who were familiar with him, will need nothing to revive in them a remembrance of his personal appearance. Of the portraits accompanying this Memoir, the first, taken early in life, is a just representation of him as he appeared in his best days and under the most favorable circumstances; the second, taken after severe illness had broken his constitution, and left its traces even on the lineaments of his face, though in form and feature a tolerably exact likeness, still does not give a fair impression of his usual aspect, even under these circumstances. His countenance was always pale, and conveyed the idea of feeble health; but it did not, till late in life, bear a positively morbid appearance. Its expression was usually mild, thoughtful, and serious; rarely, if ever, gloomy; and very frequently, especially in society, cheerful. He was somewhat below the ordinary stature, and, in his latter years, he stooped, so as to take something from his actual height. In youth and in the beginning of manhood, he was full in his person; but, by the time of his ordination, he had begun to lose this plumpness, and became gradually thinner as he grew older. In early life he looked much younger than his years; towards its conclusion, much older. This was owing as much, however, to his bent form and feeble gait, as to change of countenance; whilst an entire inattention to dress, and to personal appearance in general, contributed to produce the same result.

His whole appearance and address, though far from imposing or dignified, usually made a favorable impression, excited attention, and inspired confidence. His former pupil, the Rev. John H. Morison, of New Bedford, writes to me thus of the impression he received on seeing him for the first time.

"On a drizzly October day, I think in 1826 or 1827, I, then a school-boy at Exeter Academy, had ridden to Greenland; and while I was there, at a comfortless hotel, the stage-coach drove up, and half a dozen passengers, or more, came in to warm themselves. As they were standing by the fire, one man, dressed in a dark camlet cloak, by his look of gentleness, purity, and heavenly-mindedness, so engaged my attention, though not a word was spoken, that, on my return to Exeter, I spoke to several persons of the stage passenger, whose countenance had made such an impression upon me. After a day or two, I learned that it was Henry Ware. I did not see him again until after his return from Europe, in the spring or summer of 1831; but his look went with me as distinctly as if he had been my father."

He always looked his profession; not because he assumed its air, or aimed to put on its external aspect; but probably because his thoughts and purposes were always in it and of it, and of scarcely anything else. This was especially the case in the pulpit, a place which he seemed never to enter without a profound appreciation of its solemn character and duties. An aged friend, who was only occasionally a listener to his preaching, said to me since his death, that "she always loved to hear him preach. She did not know what it was. There was nothing remarkable in his appearance or looks. He was no great of an orator, yet everybody was glad to see him come into the pulpit. There seemed to be something in him different from other men."

His manners were seldom very courteous, or, properly, cordial; sometimes the opposite, even at first repulsive. Still they were not permanently unpleasing, because they were natural and earnest. They never owed a favorable impression to their correspondence with the forms of society, but to their expressing correctly his own feelings at the time. They had not that equal blandness, which belongs to some men whose pride it is to be always polite; as they conveyed his feelings, they varied with his feelings. He might be sometimes *less* cordial than he felt, never *more* so. The lassitude and depression of ill health, as well as his natural shyness and reserve, often caused him to express less than he meant; a regard to conventional forms never made him express more. Hence he might be at first repulsive, because he was no formalist, and could not assume the expression of more cordiality than he felt; but this soon wore off, for gentleness and kindness were his predominant feelings toward all, and it was soon seen, that he was sincere, and felt always at least as much interest as he professed.

Though he loved human intercourse, yet there are few, who so seldom meet men for the mere purpose of meeting them. He enjoyed literary and refined society, yet he never directly sought admission to it. He perhaps, indirectly, rather avoided the ordinary social communication of this kind, especially while a parish minister. During this period of his life, he was brought so much into contact with his people and others, when obliged to meet them for some specific purpose, that he had no time left for other intercourse, and therefore seldom appeared in general society. After his removal to Cambridge, the same remark is generally, though less strictly, true of him. But he was always a most important member of the wide family circle to which he belonged; their friendly meetings were very delightful to him, and by his good humor, cheerfulness, and kind interest in all, he essentially contributed to their enjoyment.

Though most friendly in his feelings towards all, he was, properly speaking, on terms of close intimacy with very few, except those connected with him by the tie of consanguinity. Yet no one was more ready to perform the duties of a friend, even to those, of whom he knew little, and who had but a slender claim on his attention. There are few who have performed kind offices for so many, or who have so often forgot themselves in their desire to serve others. This disposition, in many cases, degenerated into a weakness, of which he was well aware. He frequently regretted a facility of temper, which caused him to be overburdened with occupation, too much of it in the service of those who had no right to his time; and which prevented him from saying No, when it was most clearly his duty so to do.

As a result of the reliance felt on his willingness to serve, as also of confidence in his judgment, he was constantly called on for advice by his brethren; and, having been engaged in the education of young ministers, they were accustomed to look back to him as a counsellor in circumstances of doubt and difficulty. The number of such applications,—coming, as they did, from his brethren in the ministry, his former pupils, persons interested in forming new societies in various parts of the country, vacant parishes in search of preachers, and feeble parishes struggling with insufficient means,—was so great as to form a serious addition to his other occupations. He became a sort of central point of the denomination, to which inquiries were directed, and from which aid was sought.

He did not hesitate sometimes, when he judged it necessary, and when he thought it became him, to assume the office of a counsellor and even of a censor. He not only offered his advice to those who seemed to be pursuing a doubtful path, but took occasion sometimes to administer reproof. It is remarkable, that, notwithstanding the freedom with which he did this, there was hardly any instance in which he gave offence, and there were very many in which his admonition was received with gratitude. The following are examples of his manner of addressing those whom he wished to influence; the first relating to the style of preaching of one in whom he took a great interest, and the second, to the publication, in a periodical work, of an article written in what he thought a wrong spirit, by one whom also he held in high regard.

"You encouraged me in one of your notes to believe, that my suggestions respecting your preaching would be welcome; and, as I am ambitious for you that you should preach as effectually as possible, I will venture a few words of criticism. I do not know, indeed, that I have anything to say beyond what I have said already; but, as you are rather peculiar in your peculiarity, which is a fascinating one, and likely to do you harm by being misunderstood, as you say it has been, I think it cannot be amiss to add a remark or two which have occurred to me, and this the rather, because there only needs a little modification and caution, to render yours the truest, most interesting, and most effective method. Your danger lies simply in this,—in neglecting the Scriptures, and making too little of the power of association over men's minds. This was evident from your mode of expression in your introductory sermon, where you spoke disparagingly of that preaching which is founded on texts and the exposition of Scripture phrases. How much you meant by this, I do not know; but the impression left on my mind was, that you meant all that I have now expressed. Now, if so, you are clearly wrong, and will infallibly defeat your great object. You wish to make preaching more effective by bringing to its service all subjects of human interest; and this is right; you cannot go too far, nor gather too widely. But another thing is to be done, namely, to secure men's attention,—their willing, welcome, respectful attention,—to what you thus present. If you do not this, all is vain. And this you will fail to do, if you give the impression, that you contemn or neglect that Book which to them is the great prime source of truth and authority, or that you are fond of irreverent, and, as appears to them, profane illustrations. If you would have them show respect to your mode of teaching, you must pay respect to their preferences and prejudices in these particulars. You must draw perpetually from the Bible, which is their supreme and sacred authority, and sanction and make sacred your illustrations from other sources, by connecting them with those of Scripture. Men have been so long taught, that nothing is religious but what comes direct from revelation, that it requires the greatest circumspection to bring them to a juster view; and it would be a pity to fail of so good an end, merely from unwise disregard of their established associations. You showed, in a striking manner, that much of our Saviour's imagery owes its sacredness to association alone; and this fact teaches, I think, decisively, how important it is to consult that principle of the human constitution, which is able to convert the common into the sacred, and make the innocent appear profane. If thus guarded, your principle is the best; and I trust that you will put a guard upon it beyond what you have threatened."

"I have been reading your Review; and, as I made some *a priori* remarks on it the other day, I feel bound to add a few *a posteriori*. I hardly know which you will like best.

"If the thing must be done, I am quite satisfied that (with one exception, of which anon,) it could not be better done. You have taken up the thing right and thoroughly,—have laid bare, with great clearness and strength, the book and its pretensions, and have given an air of completeness to your work. Consequently you will hear the article well spoken of; but, when *you do not hear*, people will talk of the thing I allude to above as an *exception*. I will talk of it to you, and not behind your back; and I am sure you will take the criticism as kindly as it is meant.

"There is a certain *tone* about it, an *air*, which will be to most serious readers offensive; it will be felt to be unsuited to the character of the subjects connected with the discussion, as adapted less to convince and amend, than to wound, vex, and irritate; something too much of the manner of petty squabbles in politics and newspapers, and therefore below the dignity, and foreign to the solemnity, of religious discussion. You will say that I am severe. I do state the thing in strong terms, though the specimen you have given of this manner does not come up to the strength of my description. I mean to point out the full grown appearance of a style, on the borders of which you tread, (excuse confusion of figures,) and which all opponents will ascribe to your piece in its full enormity, while many of your best friends will be wounded to witness it in any degree. Read over the article, and imagine it written for 'The Spirit of the Pilgrims,' in review of a book of yours or mine, and you will perceive what I mean.

"Now, I think that it is of great importance to good feeling, as well as moral duty, to avoid, in controversy, all that tends, unnecessarily, to irritate and offend. I think that a writer's *real influence* depends on his doing so. He that gets the reputation of saying things *tartly*, soon comes to be distrusted by his own party, and to lose all possibility of benefiting the other. Now, I should be extremely grieved to have you inadvertently fall into this error. You have the power to become a person of influence in the religious community, and to take a leading part in the direction of the religious mind. God has so gifted you, that this becomes your lot and your duty;—a nobler lot, a more exalted, yet fearful duty, cannot pertain to man. I look with the greatest interest to the part which you shall act; it cannot be, it must not be, a second one, it ought not to be a mistaken one; and I feel at this moment thankful, that my connexion warrants me in giving you a caution against a certain way of expressing yourself, which, if it should become habitual or characteristic, would infallibly injure your influence and detract from your usefulness. If you will govern your powerful and acute pen by the rules of dignity and suavity, and, even when duty demands severity, will qualify it with kindness, ('rebuking the elder as *fathers*, and the younger as *brothers*,' as Paul says,) and studiously avoid all expressions of contempt, you may do great service without any drawback, and be one of the *trusted*, as well as *praised*.

"I almost fear I have used too many words, but you will excuse me for my motive's sake."

The most noticeable characteristic of his intellect seems to have been that general equality of the different faculties,—that just proportion and balance of power among them,—which constitutes the most useful and available mind. It was the intellect of this description, sanctified, as it were, by the moral elements of his character, which gave him his strong hold on the love and confidence of men. Perhaps the most important of these elements was a perfect and entire sympathy with, and love of, mankind, under all circumstances and conditions, with all degrees of cultivation, and with every variety of moral character. This had much to do with his general acceptance, and his power of exercising influence over all classes of men. With most persons, even many who would little suspect it, this sympathy is limited. It relates to people of a certain sort, of their own condition, or the good and virtuous of all conditions. But with him there was no such limitation. He always practically recognized the perfect equality of his fellow men as the subjects of religion. Looking at them in this way, he felt a like interest in all, and adventitious distinctions became comparatively as nothing. He enjoyed highly the society of his worldly equals, the cultivated portion of the community; but he could also enjoy the society of those who would be reputed his inferiors. He sympathized with both alike: for he knew, that in their essential features, as the subjects of religion, different classes differed much less, than their external condition and cultivation, and even their external observances of religion, would seem to imply.

The predominating element in his religious character, from which others flowed as a necessary consequence, was the entireness of his *faith*. I do not mean, merely, entireness of *belief* in the reality of religion; but that total surrender of his whole moral and intellectual being to it, which is indicated by a constant and complete *perception* of its universal relations to the world without us and the world within us. So much had this become the prevailing tenor of his mind, that it seemed almost like the result of instinct. Doubtless he had to go through with that struggle against tendencies to evil, which is essential to the formation of a moral character; but, to aid him in this struggle, he had, from the earliest period of life, established convictions and feelings on religion, such as most men attain to only after long and painful efforts. He seems never to have suffered that unsettled condition of mind, in which men are passing from aversion, or indifference, to interest in religion, and from doubt, or, at best, hesitancy, to conviction; and never to have undergone that terrible trial, to which many persons of the best understandings have been subjected, in which our virtue is assaulted through our faith, and the temptations of life derive half their force from our doubts. He had of course gone through an examination into the evidences of religion; and, to a mind like his, fully aware of the painful state of uncertainty into which so many fall, it must have been a high enjoyment to survey the impregnable array, by which the truth of Christianity is fortified. But I doubt whether his own feeling of security was ever made stronger by such studies. He engaged in them as a part of professional preparation, and delighted to dwell on them as a preacher, and to analyze and display them as an instructor, because he knew well how necessary they are to many minds; but he did not require them in order to increase his own assurance of the truth.

Another of his characteristics was the just estimate he formed of his own capacity. He knew well where his strength lay; in what he should succeed, and in what he should fail. He had measured himself, better than most others had measured him; and he well knew that he was not suited to certain offices and enterprises, for which many regarded him as being fit. As a consequence of this, he had great courage, self-dependence, and assurance of success, when engaged in that to which he felt himself adequate; but these qualities would have failed him entirely, had he ever sought to distinguish himself by efforts which he knew to be out of his proper sphere; and he would have shrunk back under the paralyzing influence of his natural diffidence.

In one respect this remark may not seem to hold perfectly true. He did not always duly estimate the *amount* he had the ability to accomplish, though he judged rightly as to the *kind*. It was characteristic of him through life to be full of schemes and projects. If one occurred to him which struck him favorably, he seized upon it with avidity, laid it out in his mind, methodized it, saw of what it was capable, devised means for its accomplishment, and dashed into it at once with great ardor, but without duly considering whether he would have time to go on, or how many other plans he had on hand, which he had entertained with a like zeal, but which absolute necessity had compelled him to suspend or lay aside. This was especially true of his literary projects. To a certain extent, this practice was an improving process; it produced a facility of invention and arrangement, which was of great service, particularly in the composition of sermons; since he thus had always many laid out in his mind, or sketched on paper, which it required only the time of composition to complete.

He could scarcely be said to have *habits* of study. During his ministry, his whole aim was to perform well the duties of his office, and to promote, incidentally, such other objects as are properly within the province of a Christian minister. Distinct from this, he had no literary or professional purpose to answer, and no reputation to seek. His pursuits, therefore, did not require that systematic and continued study, which is necessary to those whose object is high professional learning. Generally, he had some practical purpose directly in view, to which his reading and thoughts were particularly directed; when this was not the case, they were apt to be guided very much by accident, and were therefore desultory. But it will be seen, by referring to the list of his writings,* that he must have had some of them almost constantly in contemplation or in preparation, with a view to their being speedily published;

*See Appendix B.

and that most of them, also, were intended to answer some immediate end. Thus his course of study and thinking was always directed by a regard to the purpose which interested him at the time. But, as his purposes varied indefinitely, so he had no fixed course of study. His whole soul was given to the object before him; when this was accomplished, his attention to it remitted, and, in a certain sense, his interest in it was lost, or at least his mind ceased to dwell upon it. Hence, although there are not many men who have been more constantly active, have read more books, or have written more, yet there was perhaps no one branch of professional study, of which he had made himself thoroughly master.

So, too, when a teacher in the Divinity School; his department required rather personal acquaintance with the duties and difficulties of the ministerial office, than the thorough discipline of an accomplished theologian. Fitness for this place would be more the result of a faithful and successful devotion to the actual labors of a pastor, than of extensive acquaintance with books. It required wisdom rather than learning, and a practical man more than a scholar.

He could not therefore be called, in the common sense of the words, a hard student or an accomplished scholar, though he studied a great deal and read a great many books, and read them, so far as his objects in life were concerned, to great advantage. We see in certain men, whose ruling passion in life is the love of wealth or of reputation, that their great purpose is ever before them; everything is made subservient to it, and they touch nothing which does not seem to turn, under their hands, to gold or to fame. It was so with our subject. He never lost sight of the purpose of his life; not only his studies, but his lighter reading, his recreations and amusements, his intercourse with man and with nature, were all turned to its service, and made to furnish materials for its accomplishment. It was a steady earnestness in his regard to the end, which supplied in him the place of a methodical and systematic arrangement of means. His aims were perfectly single and definite; and yet he might seem, as indeed he was, exceedingly desultory and miscellaneous in the manner in which he occupied himself in seeking to effect them.

He was very happy, during all the earlier portion of his life, in the possession of a certain tranquillity of spirit, which prevented him from being disturbed in his occupations by the little, common interruptions, which are so annoying to most students. He had, to a great degree, the power of abstracting himself from the things about him. He preferred to read and write in the same room with his family. The conversation of others, the sports of his children, did not perplex him. He could at intervals listen to, and take a part in, whatever was going on, and yet, in the main, keep close to the train of his own thoughts. He often wrote with one of his children in his arms, and some of his letters and sermons bear marks of other hands than his own.

He was naturally disposed to indolence, and it required an effort to *begin* any occupation requiring much exertion either of body or mind; consequently he was very unequal in his devotion to study. It was only when he had committed himself to the accomplishment of some object, or felt the actual pressure of his regular engagements, that he could set himself resolutely to work. But, when actually at work and warm in the harness, he became excited; and it was rather a pleasure to keep on at the top of his speed, till his task was done. In this mood, he often indulged himself in protracted periods of labor, and continued writing to a very late hour at night.

This disposition led to a habit of procrastination and of irresolution in undertaking many things, to which he felt that he ought to attend. It was often the source of self-reproach and sometimes of mortification. It caused him to defer attention to persons and things in which he really felt a deep interest, while it would very naturally seem to others that its omission was intentional. There was some excuse for this, undoubtedly, in his very frequent indisposition, and the interruptions, almost innumerable, to which he was subject. But *he* never felt this to be a sufficient apology; and his journal, when he kept one, contained frequent expressions of self-reproach for such neglects,—for waste of time and opportunity,—and many plans for a more methodical and persevering devotion of himself to his duties. "As for myself," he says in a letter, "I am such an irresolute, inconstant, inconsistent being, that I have no plan. I talk instead of reading, sleep instead of studying, and make resolutions instead of keeping them."

If he had properly a worldly ambition for anything, it was for the fame of a poet. He had constantly in view great objects to accomplish, and he therefore derived the greatest satisfaction from those employments which promoted them. But, apart from this source of interest, he took more pleasure in poetical composition, than in any other occupation; and, although he indulged himself in it but little, it was an occupation more to his original taste than any other. When his mind was entirely unbent, when he had no immediate purpose to accomplish, as in travelling or in sickness, he almost instinctively turned to poetry for rest and refreshment. But, with this strong love for it, it was after all only an accident in his life. He has only left enough to show of what he was capable, had he not been so exclusively occupied with what, in his view, had higher claims on his attention. His friend Dr. Gannett, in a notice already quoted, says: "There was in the exercise of his intellectual powers a peculiarity, which can be explained only by reference to the purpose for which he was resolved to live. I do not remember, in all the prose compositions which came from his pen, numerous as they were, one which indicates the possession of uncommon talent; while two or three poetical pieces, which he produced in moments of leisure, are marked with the attributes of genius. I apprehend, that, so stern was his fidelity to the purpose of usefulness which he cherished, it deterred him from infusing into his sermons and religious essays the qualities, which might have raised them in some measure above the common mind, and have therefore limited their beneficial influence. By a reference to this ruling passion of his mind, as we might be justified in styling it, we know may be explained another circumstance, connected with his writings, which many may have lamented. He undertook no work that should elevate him by the side of those theologians, or instructors of their age, whose volumes are studied by subsequent generations."

His wife one day said to him, when he had been giving a good deal of time to the revision of sermons, and articles for periodicals, newspapers, &c., that "she wished instead of frittering away his time and thoughts in this way, upon ephemeral productions, he would concentrate the same amount upon some single work, which would be of substantial value." He looked up with a smile and replied: "Now that is your ambition for me; for my part, I am glad to do the little good I can in any way that presents itself; no matter if all is forgotten to-morrow, provided a seed is sown to-day; it will germinate some time or other."

He was, as far as any man can be, devoid of the natural desire of worldly possessions. The love of property, for its own sake, was a feeling that seemed never to have a place in his mind. He had indeed, considering his feeble hold on life, too little prospective regard for his condition in this respect; and the idea of accumulation, even for future necessity, was one to which he was brought only with much difficulty. His emoluments were never great, even for his profession; whilst, from frequent sickness in his family, and from the great number of friends and strangers whom he was called upon to entertain, his means were at no time more than sufficient for his expenses, and, during most of his life, would not have been sufficient for them, without other resources than the income of his office. He was therefore generally somewhat straitened in his circumstances, especially as there was, combined with this, a natural indifference to money, and a want of regard to the due proportion between different branches of expenditure. He often wished for wealth, but it was usually when he saw some good cause languishing for want of that sort of aid which wealth alone can give; and, in such a case, he was always ready to contribute far more than his share, without any forethought of his own wants.

He was frequently made the medium of pecuniary

donations by the rich for benevolent purposes; he was also in the habit of applying freely to them for aid; and, while a teacher in the Theological School, he sought and received contributions to a large amount for the purpose of assisting indigent students of divinity. He stated, as a very gratifying fact in its connexion with the character of men of wealth in this community, that, of all his applications of this description, he recollected but a single instance which was not successful, whilst, on the other hand, most of those to whom he applied, were not only willing, but seemed grateful for an opportunity of promoting such a purpose.

I have only to add to these records of my own recollections, a few of those for which I am obliged to others. To some reminiscences furnished me by one of his valued parishioners, Mr. Peter Mackintosh, Jr., I have been already much indebted in the account given of his ministerial life. The following passages, also, are extracted from them. Speaking of the Hancock Sunday School, Mr. Mackintosh says:

"I had often the pleasure of witnessing the deep interest taken by Mr. Ware in this Sunday school. He seemed to view it with a prophetic eye, as the nucleus of a great religious instrumentality; one calculated to give a new impulse to the cause of Christ. Hence his influence, his advice, his labor, so far as he could bestow them, were never withheld. I well know his heart was ever full of love for all children; but to poor, ignorant, and neglected children, whose religious education had never been cared for, whose only church was a wharf or a blind court,—to those his heart yearned with a love like the Saviour's. At this time (1823) there was no Sunday school connected with the Second Church. This circumstance afforded him more opportunities and greater facilities for advancing the best interests of this school. The children of the poor, and those of parents in more favored circumstances, met together; and in their midst he was to be found, who, in the spirit of his Master, 'went about doing good.' . . . . .

"Mr. Ware was ever kind to the poor members of his flock. Being Treasurer of the church, I had abundant opportunity to know this fact. Formerly, it was the custom of the deacons to act as almoners to the parish. But, finding that Mr. Ware was in the habit of disposing freely of his own funds, a plan was adopted of placing a portion of the money at his disposal for private distribution. This plan enabled him to relieve many persons, who would have shrunk from receiving charity at any other hands than those of their beloved pastor."

In the early part of this Memoir were inserted some notices of his college life and character, by his early friend and classmate, Mr. Loring. The letter containing them has also some other remarks, which are here inserted.

"As I have listened with intense interest to his discourses from the pulpit, and none ever went deeper to my heart, I have often wondered how he could produce such astonishing results upon the minds of his audience, with the apparently simple materials he had collected. His exordium and the early portions of his address would seem almost trite and common-place, but for the beautiful transparency of the style, and the apostolic simplicity of his manner: ere long, however, these seemingly quiet, inert elements were, by some sudden yet perfectly natural and almost unperceived combination, collected like scattered rays into a focus, shedding the brightest light upon some topic of moral duty, or exhibiting in a broad glare the hideous deformity of some common sin, or kindling the flame of earnest devotion, throughout the whole assembly. And I delight to trace the beautiful analogy of his life and writings; his widely extended fame and beneficial influence on society,—a light shining far and wide,—the beaming combination of all those quiet and unpretending yet most earnest Christian graces and virtues, which marked him from the cradle to the grave.

"His rank in his class was constantly progressive, as it ever after continued to be among men. And he was one, and to me the most striking, of the examples of the superiority of that class of intellects over the precocious and brilliant, which was first deeply impressed upon my mind, and which the observation of all subsequent life has confirmed."

Of that very important part of his relation to the Theological School, his personal connexion with the pupils, I have in the course of the above narrative said nothing. I have preferred to leave it to this place, and to trust, for the illustration of his character in this respect, to the following passages, derived from various sources. The Rev. Chandler Robbins, a student in the School at the time of his accession, writes thus:

"I well remember the joy which was awakened in the School, at the announcement of his election. No instructor was ever more warmly welcomed by his pupils, at the commencement of his relation to them. This ardor of our interest, however gratifying to him, and on many accounts advantageous, was, of course, not without its dangers and discouragements. Should he fail to fulfil our high expectations, our disappointment would be the greater, and his regrets the more distressing. Besides, it would require unusual richness of ability and steadiness of exertion to sustain so exalted a regard in the continuance and details of a difficult and responsible office. But it is not probable that Mr. Ware fully realized the strength of our attachment, or the greatness of our anticipations; and, therefore, it is unlikely that he had an adequate idea either of its dangers or its advantages. He certainly seemed to us to enter upon his duties with entire simplicity and composure of spirit; neither elated nor depressed; neither promising much on his own part, nor exacting, nor deprecating, anything on the part of the Students;—with mingled humility and confidence.

"This deportment would have been *prudent* under such circumstances; but with him it was evidently less the result of premeditation, than the inartificial manifestation of his ordinary character. We saw at once, that there was nothing factitious about him. We perceived, that he was not influenced by any selfish motives. We felt, that the quiet and patient performance of his present duties to us, and not our appreciation of him, was the great matter that occupied his thoughts.

"This absence of personal ambition and of the anxiety of selfishness,—one of the most beautiful and truly Christian characteristics of Mr. Ware,—was the first quality, that, distinctly and from experience, impressed itself upon me in the School;—an impression which my long and intimate subsequent acquaintance only deepened. I think that others, if they will analyze their feelings as they remember him, will agree with me in selecting the conviction of this virtue, as one of the earliest and strongest which they formed in regard to his character. And I believe, that, with all of us, this was at the basis of our singular confidence, and esteem for him. After this discovery was made, we never entertained a doubt of his perfect sincerity. We never so much as thought to question the purity of his motives, or the honesty of all he said and did. We had a perpetual and sufficient pledge, that we might rely upon him. Henceforth, his kindness became doubly precious. We were sure that its smile did not shine the sake of the reflection. His dignity, the more commanding and impressive. We saw that it was not assumed for effect.

"I here speak particularly of *kindness* and *dignity*, because these two words, taken together, are descriptive of Mr. Ware's demeanor towards the Students. All felt the one, and none ever forgot the other. He was easy of access to all, yet no one ever ventured upon familiarity. We were not denied his sympathy,—we could not withhold from him our respect.

"As a Teacher, Mr. Ware's principal aim seemed to be, not so much to impart knowledge, as to provoke and elicit thought. He did not present truth in direct statements, embodying the result of his own study and reflection, to be received into the mind of his pupil; but, by means of sagacious questions, led along the intellect, by a gradual process, towards the result at which he wished it to arrive; so that the thought or principle appeared to be rather drawn out from the reason or judgment of the scholar, than imparted from his own. The conversational method of instruction was his usual and most successful one. For this, he was in a rare degree qualified. To clearness of thought and simplicity of diction, he united patience and condescension, a quick perception of the meaning of others, and a habit of kindling in the contact of mind with mind. I have often wondered, in his recitation-room, at his long-suffering towards the slow-minded; at the facility with which he adapted himself to the humblest capacity; and; at the amount of good and valuable thoughts, which he was sometimes enabled in this way to draw out of those, from whom a teacher of less forbearance and wisdom would have expected and obtained comparatively little. The debt, which minds of this class owe to him, is beyond all estimate.

"Mr. Ware was accustomed to visit the Students occasionally in their rooms, that he might converse with them, in private and confidentially, upon matters relating to their theological studies and their moral culture. If it appeared to him that any one particularly needed his advice, I believe he never neglected to seek an opportunity to give it; though there was nothing approaching to obtrusiveness or officiousness in his manner of rendering this valuable service. He manifested remarkable skilfulness and wisdom in selecting both the time and the mode of friendly counsel. He used great plainness of speech, softened by kindness, in indicating to individuals their defects, for which he was always furnished with remedial suggestions. This quickness of discernment in detecting our faults, whether of character, or of intellectual habits, or of style in the composition or delivery of sermons, was equalled by his happy faculty of making them evident to us without giving offence, and his rare capacity of pointing out the exact method of their correction. So useful were his critical hints, that I am sure the only desire of every pupil was, that they might be more frequently applied.

"For the special branches of Theological study in which he was appointed to give instruction, Mr. Ware was eminently qualified, both by experience and taste. His own style of eloquence was peculiarly adapted to the pulpit and its sacred themes. Its characteristics were simplicity, gravity, impressiveness, and earnestness. His idea of preaching was the truest and highest. He communicated it clearly and forcibly. He illustrated it well in his own practice. We felt, that in this great art we had in him a master. And the same is true of the other department of his Professorship. It was the universal conviction of the Students, that no more competent guide to the thorough understanding and successful discharge of the important offices of the Pastoral Care could have been found. If any, who have enjoyed the benefit of his ample and minute directions, have failed in this sphere of the duties of their calling, the deficiency can never be attributed in any degree to their instruction in the School; whilst those who have succeeded, will gratefully acknowledge their many obligations to him, who so well knew what the secrets of pastoral influence are, and how to teach them.

"Mr. Ware's moral and religious influence upon the School was very great. Perhaps the most valuable effect of his connexion with the Students was here. He raised the standard of ministerial character, the tone of religious sentiment. His own had been formed and imbibed in the school of Christ; and, as from his Master, a Christian virtue went out of him to his disciples, as he went about doing good before and among them, or sat down to teach. He not only imparted the instructions of sacred wisdom and truth, but communicated, even involuntarily, the inspiration of the true life. His best pupils may show the effect of his discipline in the manner and matter of their pulpit discourses, and exhibit the benefit of his lessons in their plans of pastoral usefulness; but it is in the deep places of their moral and spiritual energy, that they feel his most salutary influence; it is upon the character of their own souls, that he has left the deepest impression."

The following paragraphs are contained in a letter, which I have already quoted, from the Rev. John H. Morison.

"In the autumn of 1831, I occupied a room in his house, and was his son John's instructor. While I was in this situation, his little son Robert died. Soon after the death of his child, that same evening, he came into my room, and, with feelings deeply touched, but perfectly calm, talked of his child and of death in so sweet a spirit, that it gave to the whole subject a new meaning, clothing the gauntness of death with the beauty of an angel. At the close of the evening the family were called as usual to prayers; and as the words, at first of broken, humble supplication, rose into strains of sublime devotion, the world and its trials were left behind, and it seemed as if the tears and sobs, with which the service began, had been changed into a song of triumph.

"Indeed, your brother's devotional powers always appeared to me his peculiar gift, the spontaneous outpouring of his soul, when all his faculties were most alive. The language was so simple, the spirit so humble, and yet borne up as by a march so majestic and sublime! I remember him particularly in the exercises at the College Chapel once, on the morning of the 22d of February. The sound of the distant guns told us of the day; and the prayer, more than any eulogy that I ever heard, filled the heart with gratitude and praise. So once at Divinity Hall, at the time of prayer, there was a sudden and severe shower with heavy peals of thunder; and the voice of devotion, harmonizing with the solemn grandeur of the scene, seemed mightier far, in its quiet, inspiring tones, than the voice and darkness of the storm. Prayer was not a regular part of the service when he gave his lectures on the Pastoral Office. The lectures themselves were miscellaneous in their character, the same discourse treating, perhaps, of unwise marriages, of economy in the use of money, and of the highest duties of the profession. And usually the progress of feeling was such, that at the close of the lecture, without a word, but as by an involuntary motion, we all rose in prayer, and went away, I believe, most of us, to meditate and pray.

"I was connected with the Divinity School less than a year, being struck down by violent sickness before I had entered upon the year (the last) when I should have been most in your brother's department. My impression is, that his instructions were not at all systematic, but rather desultory, embracing, as they must have done, a wide variety of topics, and often deranged by his feeble health. They were of great value, both on account of their sound practical wisdom, and of the information they conveyed. But beyond any direct instruction possible, he was useful in the School as a sort of better genius, to whom we might have access at all times, and from whom, without any intentional action on his part, a purer influence came. We could go to him in perfect confidence;

and the amount of labor thus brought upon him must have been exceedingly exhausting. We were sure to find the greatest kindness and the most perfect truthfulness. However he might feel for us, he could not spare our faults."

APPENDIX.

(A.)

The body was examined the day after his death, by Dr. Whitney, his attending physician, and my friend, Dr. J. B. S. Jackson. There were evidences of long-continued and various disease. The lungs, contrary to expectation, were comparatively healthy, and seemed to have recovered almost perfectly from the attacks under which he had suffered. There were only the slight remains of tubercular disease in one of them. There was some enlargement of the heart. The immediate occasion of death was in the brain; and the sufferings of the last two years had probably been chiefly caused by a disease of this organ, known under the name of "Softening," or "*Ramollissement*," accompanied by a change in the texture of the arteries. This had terminated, as it usually does, in successive effusions of blood into the substance of the part, the last of which had destroyed life. There was also a diseased structure of the kidneys, known to physicians by the name of "Bright's Disease," or "Granulated Kidney," which had probably preceded even the affection of the brain.

(B.)

CATALOGUE OF PUBLISHED WRITINGS.

1811.

An Essay in "The Weekly Messenger," instituting a comparison between *Homer and Walter Scott*. (Signed Charles.)

1812.

A few fragments of Poetry in "The Constitutionalist," a newspaper, at Exeter, N. H.

1815.

A Poem on occasion of the Peace.

1817.

Sermon on the Death of the Rev. Thomas Prentiss.

1819.

Christian Disciple. Vol. I. New Series.

1820.

Christian Disciple. Vol. II.

Sermon before the Evangelical Missionary Society in Mass., June 7.
Two Letters to Dr. McLeod, on 1 John v. 7.—(Two Editions.)

1821.

Christian Disciple. Vol. III.

	Page
Dr. Mayhew's Works, ...	45
Dedication at New York, and N. Y. Collection of Hymns,	76
Various Notices, ... 158, 159,	160
Dr. Watts, ...	190
Review of W. J. Fox's Sermon on Deism, ...	202
Notices of New Publications, ...	235
Notice of Spurious Editions of Griesbach, ...	321
Use of Solitude to the Christian, ...	329
Review of Moore's Ordination Sermon, ...	377
Notices of New Publications, ...	399
On Discontent, ...	407

Two Historical Discourses, on completing a Century.

Christian Register.

Mr. Wayland's Ordination. Aug. 31.	(Signed ARTINIUS.)
Foster's Sermons. Sept. 7	"
Percival's Poems. Sept. 14.	"
Mr. Woodbridge's Defamation. Sept. 14.	"
Mr. Lowell's Historical Discourse. Sept. 21.	"
Ordination at Wareham. Oct. 12.	"
Newspaper Criticisms of Pulpit Services. Oct. 19.	"
Same subject. Nov. 9.	"

1822.

Three Important Questions Answered. January.
Sermon at Amherst, N. H. August.

Christian Disciple. Vol. IV.

Review of Gilman's Sermon, ...	33
" Clerical Discipline, ...	103
" Flint's Historical Discourses, ...	121
Domestic Missions, ...	169
Review of A New England Tale, ...	205
Unitarian Defendant, ...	219

Christian Register.

Mr. Torrey's Forefathers Sermon. April 5.

1823.

Address before the Massachusetts Society for the Suppression of Intemperance. May.
Letters to McLeod. 3d Edition.
Three Important Questions Answered. 3d Edition.
Report of the Massachusetts Bible Society.

Christian Disciple. Vol. V.

1824.

Hints on Extemporaneous Preaching. Jan. 5.
Recollections of Jotham Anderson—Collected and published.
S. T. B. T., in the Newspapers, &c. &c. February.
The Vision of Liberty; a Poem recited before the Society of *Φ Β Κ*. August 26.

North American Review.

Notice of Cowper's Private Correspondence.

Christian Examiner.

1825.

Sermon at the Ordination of W. H. Furness, at **Philadelphia.** Jan. 12.
Recollections of Jotham Anderson. xix. xxi.
Robert Fowle. March.
Sermons on the Offices and Character of Jesus Christ. May 25.
The Faith once delivered to the Saints.—A Tract for the American Unitarian Association. September.
Sermon at the Dedication, Northampton. Dec. 7.

Christian Examiner.

Thanksgiving Hymn.
Review of Hadad, in the *Literary Gazette.*

1826.

January.—Review of Greenwood's and Wayland's Sermons, in the *Journal of Education.*
" Milton's Christian Doctrine, in the *Literary Gazette.*
" Percival's Φ Β Κ Poem, in the *N. A. Review.*
" Poems from the Literary Gazette, in the *Christian Register.*
Four Notices of Milton, in the *Christian Register.* (Signed Limnot.)
Editorial Article on Family Prayer, and on Modern Degeneracy.
February.—The Faith once delivered to the Saints. 2d Edition.

1827.

Sermon on Small Sins.

1828.

Notice of Judge Howe, in the *Christian Visitant.*
Letter to a Sister, " "
Note to the Editor of the (N. Y.) *Unitarian.* (Signed H.)
Brief Letter on Pollok's Course of Time, in the *Christian Register.*
Review of Remains of N. A. Haven, in the *Christian Examiner.*
Sermon on the Duty of Usefulness, in the *Liberal Preacher.*
Reply to a Gentleman's Letter. (Four Editions.)
Address before the Kennebunk Unitarian Association.
Recollections of Jotham Anderson. 2d Edition.

1829. 1830. 1831.

The Formation of the Christian Character. May, 1831.
Sermon on the Duty of Improvement, in the *Liberal Preacher.*
Farewell Address to the Second Church. Oct. 4, 1830.
Introductory Address at Cambridge. Oct. 1830.
Sermon, in Beard's "*Family Sermons,*" on Religious Principles and Affections.
Account of R. Hall, in the *Unitarian Advocate.* 1831.
Preface to an Album, in the *Unitarian Advocate.* May.

1832.

Introduction to the Memoirs of Oberlin.
Address before the Cambridge Temperance Society. March.
Outline of Scripture Testimony of the Trinity.

1833.

Life of the Saviour. January.
Sermon at the Ordination of C. Robbins. December.
Preface to Mrs. Farrar's Life of Howard.

1834.

Sermon on the Promise of Universal Peace.
Life and Character of Dr. Priestley.
Sermon on Faith, in the *Western Messenger.*

1835.

Memoir of Dr. Parker.
Annual Address delivered before the Berry-Street Conference, in the *Christian Examiner*. September.
Sober Thoughts on the State of the Times.
A Hint from Mrs. H. More, in the *Boston Observer*, No. 2.
A Great Scheme, " No. 4.
A Word about a Hint, " No. 13.

1837.

Sermon at the Ordination of C. A. Bartol. March 1.
The Feast of Tabernacles. March.
Review of Muzzey's Young Man's Friend, in the *Christian Examiner*. May.
Notice of Mr. Norton's "Evidences," in the *Christian Register*. April.
Two Discourses at the Close of the Academic Year.
Tract for the American Unitarian Association. On Faith. No. 125.
Review of Miriam, in the *N. A. Review*.

1838.

Review of Beard's Collection of Hymns, in the *Christian Examiner*.
" Stephens's Incidents of Travel, "
" Todd and Muzzey on Sunday Schools, "
Sermon on the Duel in which Cilley was killed.
" before the Book and Pamphlet Society.
" on the Personality of the Deity.
Notice of Mrs. Sanford and of Winslow, on Woman; in the *N. A. Review*.
Review of the Christian Preacher, in the *Christian Examiner*.

1839.

How to spend a Day. *Monthly Miscellany*.
Art of Hearing. "
David Ellington's Subscription. "
Review of Southey's Poems, in the *N. A. Review*.
" Milnes's Poems, "
Notice of Lamson's Centennial Discourses, in the *N. A. Review*.
" The Huguenots, "
Sermon at Ordination of R. C. Waterston.
Notice of Buckminster, in the *Monthly Miscellany*.

1840.

Sermon at Ordination of E. H. Sears, Lancaster.

Tract for the American Unitarian Association. The New. Year. No. 150.

How are the great Evils in the World to be removed? *Monthly Miscellany.*

Saturday Evening at David Ellington's. *Monthly Miscellany.*

A Sunday's Walk with David Ellington. "

1841.

Sermon on the Moral Principle of the Temperance Movements, in the *Christian Examiner.*

1843.

Progress of Peace Principles, in the *Christian Examiner.*

Review of Dr. Greenwood's Sermons of Consolation, in the *Christian Examiner.*

1844.

Memoirs of the Rev. Noah Worcester, D. D., with a Preface, Notes, and a concluding Chapter, by Samuel Worcester.

THE END.

www.ingramcontent.com/pod-product-compliance
Lightning Source LLC
LaVergne TN
LVHW021234110826
845150LV00002B/333

9781425561956